WOVEN INTO THE URBAN FABRIC

SEUH
STUDIES IN EUROPEAN URBAN HISTORY
(1100-1800)

VOLUME 54

Series Editors
Marc Boone
Anne-Laure Van Bruaene
Ghent University

Woven into the Urban Fabric

Cloth Manufacture and Economic Development in the Flemish West-Quarter (1300-1600)

JIM VAN DER MEULEN

BREPOLS

Cover illustration: Nieuwkerke in Flandria Illustrata

D/2021/0095/300
ISBN 978-2-503-59455-2
eISBN 978-2-503-59456-9
DOI 10.1484/M.SEUH-EB.5.123359

ISSN 1780-3241
eISSN 2294-8368

Printed in the EU on acid-free paper.

Contents

Acknowledgements

This is a history of ordinary people. And yet, this book would not have seen the light of day if it were not for a number of *extraordinary* people that helped along the way. If the past few years have taught me one thing, it is that proper academic research, and especially writing, is always a joint effort. The quality of this book, such as it is, has accordingly been uplifted by my fertile interactions with excellent colleagues, some of whom have become friends in the process.

And so, I would like to begin by thanking Tim Soens and Peter Stabel, my former supervisors at the University of Antwerp. It is in their minds that the idea for this research first germinated, and I am grateful that they entrusted me with the care, and eventually the harvest, of the fruits that sprouted from this idea. Special thanks go out to Frederik Buylaert, who allowed me (and indeed, encouraged me) to keep working on the book while I had to turn to new avenues of research as well. I much appreciate Frederik's management style, which can best be described as 'big brotherly' – without the Orwellian overtones, that is. I also want to thank Julie Marfany, Peter Hoppenbrouwers, and Reinoud Vermoesen for their insightful criticisms on the PhD-thesis that was to be the blueprint for this book. On the same note, I am grateful to the anonymous reviewers of the manuscript for their detailed scrutiny. Their helpful and constructive feedback have much elevated the end result. Other esteemed colleagues that deserve my gratitude for their thoughtful input along the way are Mathieu Arnoux, Bruno Blondé, Mario Damen, Maïka De Keyzer, Bert De Munck, Luc Duerloo, Jan Dumolyn, Justine Firnhaber-Baker, Hilde Greefs, Jean-Pierre Jessenne, Iason Jongepier, Michael Limberger, Guido Marnef, Kim Overlaet, Ulrich Pfister, Jeroen Puttevils, Erik Thoen, Arie van Steensel, and Jaco Zuijderduijn. I also thank Dominiek Dendooven and all the people at the *In Flanders Fields Museum* in Ypres for hosting a most enjoyable workshop in the city's awe-inspiring Cloth Hall in September of 2017.

My fellow researchers at the University of Antwerp were a big help while I was coming to grips with the complex themes and materials that are the basis of this study. I am especially grateful to Pieter De Graef, Janna Everaert, Sam Geens, Hadewijch Masure, Steven Thiry, Filip Van Roosbroeck, Eline Van Onacker, Lies Vervaet, and last but never least Tineke Van de Walle. This book has further benefited from the fruitful work environment that is Ghent University; in particular, I thank Erika Graham-Goering, Thijs Lambrecht, Micol Long, and Steven Vanderputten for the stimulating interactions. I am also grateful to Ludo Vandamme for his useful comments, and for sending me some crucial publications in the nick of time that would otherwise have been unavailable to me.

The original research for this study was funded by the Research Foundation Flanders (FWO) and carried out at the University of Antwerp; and the reworking and writing of the book were completed under the auspices of the European Research Council (ERC) while I worked as a postdoctoral researcher at Ghent University. It almost goes without saying, but I am grateful to these government organizations for giving aspirant academics the financial backing to engage in historical research in a professional capacity. I would also like to thank the editors of the Studies in European Urban History Series (1100-1800), Marc Boone and Anne-Laure Van Bruaene, for their willingness to incorporate this book into their series. Chris VandenBorre, my publisher at Brepols, deserves a special mention for his pleasant communication style, not to mention his patience.

My family and friends, of course, were invaluable 'spotters' while I was making my way down along the deep descent into early modern and late medieval Flanders. I am particularly grateful to my parents, Karen Verheggen and Louis van der Meulen – who would be the rope in this undeserving analogy. Trude, lastly, has been of such support as I could never hope to put into words properly.

Illustrations

Figures

Tables

Abbreviations

ADN	Archives Départementales du Nord, Lille
BAB	Bishopric's Archives Bruges (Bisschoppelijk Archief Brugge)
CAA	City Archives Antwerp (Stadsarchief Antwerpen / Felixarchief)
CAB	City Archives Bruges (Stadsarchief Brugge)
CABZ	City Archives Bergen op Zoom (Stadsarchief Bergen op Zoom)
CAY	City Archives Ypres (Stadsarchief Ieper)
CA	Chamber of Accounts, Brussels (Rekenkamer / Chambre des Comptes)
GSAB	General State Archives Brussels (Algemeen Rijksarchief / Archives Générales du Royaume).
NAP	National Archives Paris (Archives Nationales, Paris)
RDHIDF-1	*Recueil de documents relatifs à l'histoire de l'industrie drapière en Flandre: des origines à l'époque bourguignonne*, ed. by Georges Espinas and Henri Pirenne, 4 vols (Brussels: Kiessling et Imbreghts, 1906-24).
RDHIDF-2	*Recueil de documents relatifs à l'histoire de l'industrie drapière en Flandre. Deuxième partie: le sud-ouest de la Flandre depuis l'époque bourguignonne*, ed. by Henri De Sagher and others, 3 vols (Brussels: Kiessling et Imbreghts, 1951-66).
RLB	Royal Library Brussels (Koninklijke Bibliotheek Brussel / Bibliothèque Royale de Belgique)
SAB	State Archives Bruges (Rijksarchief Brugge)
SAG	State Archives Ghent (Rijksarchief Gent)

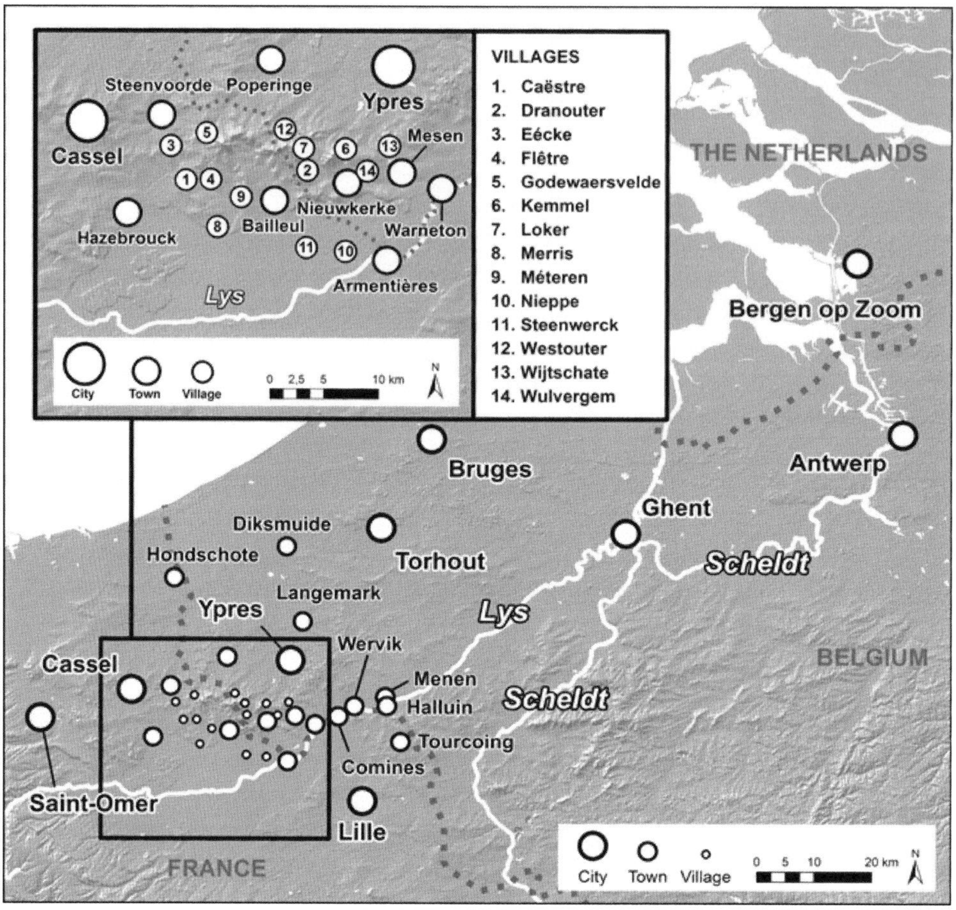

Figure I. Map of the cloth centres in the Flemish West-Quarter, 14th-16th century

Source: Iason Jongepier, GIStorical Antwerp II (UAntwerpen/Hercules Foundation).

Introduction

Ever since the second half of the twentieth century, companies in the Western world have been strategically outsourcing industrial production and manufacture to countries where cheap labour is in abundance. This replacement of local labour with foreign workers is sometimes called 'offshoring'. Globalization and liberalization of trade, as well as improved modes of communication have opened up these economic alleyways. Offshoring allows organizations to cut back on their production costs, their fiscal duties, and the social and humanitarian insulation of their workers.[1] The global trade in textiles and clothing today is one of the prime examples of this phenomenon. In the first quarter of the 21st century, a minimum wage in the Netherlands, where I live, theoretically buys me at least two jumpers (€19.99 each) per day at the local store of an international clothing-retail corporation. Meanwhile, the fabric of my smart new attire only contains 5 per cent natural fibres, the remaining 95 per cent consisting of cheap, synthetic alternatives.[2]

Leaving aside the global stage, the textile economy of the early 21st century has gone through a development that is similar to that of its antecedents of the pre-industrial period. Starting in the late thirteenth century, entrepreneurs in urbanized European regions like the Italian Peninsula and the Low Countries also began to 'offshore' the labour-intensive stages of textile manufacture to other locations.[3] The key difference with the present day is that these entrepreneurs did not have to look overseas, as alternative sources of labour were readily available to them in the countryside that surrounded the towns where they lived. These pre-industrial town dwellers acted out of the same considerations as major retailers that relocate their factories to countries such as Bangladesh in our own day: namely, the desire to cut back on costs for wages and to enjoy the benefits of the foreign jurisdiction's looser regulations.[4] The benefits to consumers with a smaller purse today are also roughly similar to those of their predecessors of the late medieval and Early Modern Period: the option to pick inexpensive fabrics – often woven from cheaper fibres – over costlier, locally

1 Peter Ørberg Jensen and Torben Pedersen, 'Offshoring and International Competitiveness: Antecedents of Offshoring Advanced Tasks', *Journal of the Academy of Marketing Science*, 40 (2012), 313-328 (pp. 313-14).

2 60 % polyester, 35 % polyamide, and 5 % wool.

3 Bertrand Haquette, 'Les précurseurs de la délocalisation: entre commerce triangulaire et économie *offshore*: le rôle des financiers italiens dans les villages drapiers de la vallée de la Lys', *Publications du Centre Européen d'Etudes Bourguignonnes*, 49 (2009), 131-58.

4 See, for example: Sarah Butler, 'Bangladesh Fashion Factory Safety Work Severely behind Schedule', *The Guardian*, 28 January 2016.

sourced products. In doing so, consumers boost the demand for these products and perpetuate the system.[5]

But of course, the similarities have to run out at some point. Enterprises on the scale of modern multinationals could not have existed in the late medieval and Early Modern Period. To begin with, pre-industrial textile entrepreneurs lacked the machine-power that drives the productivity levels of modern economies – both directly and indirectly, as the mechanization of modern agriculture freed up more people to work in other sectors.[6] But the difference was also one of organization; first, in how much 'the market' predominated as 'a *system* of organizing production and exchange'; second, in the power relations between the employers and the actual manufacturers; and third, in the specific social, political and economic interconnections between premodern town and countryside.[7]

It is these organizational aspects of the pre-industrial textile economy that will, above all, be central in this book. This applies as much to the organization of social relations within the rural production centres that are our key focus, as to the organization of commercial relations between the entrepreneurs from these villages and urban merchants in the market cities. Thus, the main goal of the book is to assess how ordinary people in the countryside kept their textile enterprises afloat amidst the slings and arrows of external competition and extra-economic pressure from urban rivals, internal conflicts, and evolving political circumstances at the wider regional level. Yet through this focus, the textile sector in a relatively small sub-region – in this case in the Netherlandish county of Flanders – can serve as a vehicle to investigate overarching aspects of the interactions between (political) economy and society in premodern Europe more broadly.

This question remains highly relevant. While scholars have consistently tried to reconstruct the 'grand narratives' of economic and social history, often through the question why certain regions get rich while others remain poor, their sweeping studies tend to favour a single explanation or theoretical model for the long-term development of vast geographic regions.[8] The present book's focus on a discrete region in the Low Countries and a single economic sector facilitates an integrated approach that allows us to combine the insights of several

5 John Munro, 'Hanseatic Commerce in Textiles from the Low Countries and England during the Late Middle Ages: Changing Trends in Textiles, Markets, Prices, and Values, 1290-1579', in *Von Nowgorod bis London. Studien zu Handel, Wirtschaft und Gesellschaft im mittelalterlichen Europa*, ed. by Marie-Luise Heckmann and Jens Rörhrkasten (Göttingen: V&R Unipress, 2008), pp. 97-181 (pp. 110-11).

6 A discussion of medieval antecedents to mechanization falls outside the scope of this study, but for an introduction, see: Jean Gimpel, *The Medieval Machine: The Industrial Revolution of the Middle Ages* (New York: Penguin Books, 1976). On the medieval textile industry in particular, see the somewhat controversial: Eleanora Carus-Wilson, 'An Industrial Revolution of the Thirteenth Century', *The Economic History Review*, 11 (1941), 39-60.

7 Peer Vries, *Escaping Poverty: The Origins of Modern Economic Growth* (Vienna: Vienna University Press, 2013), p. 429.

8 At this moment in time, in the early 21st century, the dominant theoretical model is that of the 'New Institutional Economics' (see below). A prominent example is: Daron Acemoglu and James Robinson, *Why Nations Fail: The Origins of Power, Prosperity, and Poverty* (New York: Crown Business, 2012).

theoretical frameworks to arrive at more nuanced conclusions. Perhaps most importantly, I will approach the region in question both as an urban and as a rural historian. As we shall see, this is useful to understand the developments in this particular textile economy, which showed increasing signs of a hybrid rural-urban character over the course of the late Middle Ages.

Woven into the Urban Fabric centres on the region known as the Flemish 'West-Quarter' (*Westkwartier*), a sub-district of the historic county of Flanders – in turn, one of the principalities that made up the wider area referred to as the Low Countries, which more or less corresponded to the present-day countries of Belgium, the Netherlands, and Luxembourg but also included parts of northern France and the German Rhineland. The Flemish West-Quarter roughly covered the region northwest of the river Lys (or *Leie*, in Dutch) and south of the city of Ypres, which acted as regional capital to this quarter of the county of Flanders (see **Map I**). And this area witnessed the rise of several vibrant rural cloth centres in the 1300s and 1400s. Their economic success steadily grew in the second half of the fifteenth century; so much so that, by the middle of the sixteenth century, 27 per cent of all of Flanders's woollens were manufactured in this region (see **Table I**).[9]

What makes these cloth villages of further interest is that they produced relatively high-grade fabrics. Partly manufactured from expensive, imported wool from Spain and Scotland, these cloths belonged to the middle segment of the international cloth market in their time (see **Table II**). This is a contrast with most pre-industrial textile centres in the countryside. As with the aforementioned offshoring in the present day, the relocation of late medieval cloth production to the countryside is usually associated with cheap textiles. After all, the low labour costs of the workforce are what makes for the competitive edge. In late medieval Flanders, a clear example of this phenomenon was the light-textile centre of Hondschoote.[10] However, the mid-priced fabrics of West-Quarter villages such as Kemmel, Dranouter, and especially the booming industrial centre of Nieuwkerke, required relatively large inputs of capital. And so, paradox

9 This figure is based on: Hugo Soly and Alfons Thijs, 'Nijverheid in de Zuidelijke Nederlanden, 1490-1580', in *Algemene Geschiedenis der Nederlanden*, 15 vols, ed. by J. A. Van Houtte, J. F. Niermeyer, J. Presser (Haarlem: Fibula-Van Dishoeck, 1977-1983), VI (1979), pp. 38-41. See also: Tim Soens, Peter Stabel, and Tineke Van de Walle, 'An Urbanised Countryside? A Regional Perspective on Rural Textile Production in the Flemish West-Quarter', in *Economies, Public Finances, and the Impact of Institutional Changes in Interregional Perspective: The Low Countries and Neighbouring German Territories (14th-17th Centuries)*, Studies in European Urban History 36, ed. by Remi van Schaïk, (Turnhout: Brepols, 2015), pp. 35-60 (pp. 35-36).

10 John Munro, 'The Origins of the English "New Draperies": The Resurrection of an Old Flemish Industry, 1250-1570', in *The New Draperies in the Low Countries and England, 1300-1800*, Pasold Studies in Textile Industry 10, ed. by N. B. Harte (New York: Oxford University Press, 1997), pp. 35-128 (esp. pp. 71-74); Peter Stabel, '"Dmeeste, oirboirlixste en proffitelixste let ende neringhe": een kwantitatieve benadering van de lakenproductie in het laatmiddeleeuwse en vroegmoderne Vlaanderen', *Handelingen van de Maatschappij voor Geschiedenis en Oudheidkunde te Gent*, 51 (1997), 113-53.

Table I. Pieces of woollen cloth produced in Flanders (without Walloon-Flanders)

	1400	1450	1500	1550
Urban drapery	88,000	61,000	55,000	21,000
Rural drapery		3000	6000	15,000
Total	88,000	64,000	61,000	36,000
Hondschoote says	1000	4000	7000	>26,000

Source: Stabel, '"Dmeeste, oirboirlixste ende proffitelixste let ende neringhe"', p. 147.

Table II. Prices of Flemish cloth on the Antwerp market, 1575 (d./ell)

	Name of cloth	Lowest price	Highest price
Ypres	*metten Andries*	112	122
Ypres	*met Ons Lieff Vrouwe*	82	104
Armentières	*oultrefin*	60	85
Nieuwkerke	*kepers*	46	48
Hondschoote	*saai*	10	25

Source: Thijs, 'Les textiles au marchés anversois', pp. 82-84.

rears its attractive head. Quite apart from the need for capital concentration, the West-Quarter's upscale products called for a high level of skill among the workers, along with a well-developed commercial infrastructure. All elements, in short, that one would sooner expect to find within urban societies, and not in the countryside.[11] Nevertheless, none of these cloth villages ever acquired an actual urban franchise via an official charter. But then, as I will argue, the so-called rural entrepreneurs of these production centres were essentially part of urban society already. And so, this paradoxical case study challenges the idea that the rise of textile production in the pre-industrial countryside was a clear case of a one-sided economic relation whereby mighty urban employers dipped into a cheap and unregulated rural labour pool.

The specific contribution of this study is threefold. The first contribution is essentially methodological: by combining different analytical models and methodologies of urban and rural history, this book offers a perspective on how these scholarly subdisciplines can (and, on occasion, should) be integrated. While the historiography has moved away from framing premodern town-country relations as purely antagonistic, most authors still take one of these spheres and its associated analytical frameworks as their point-of-departure.[12] In contrast,

11 Stabel, Soens and Van de Walle, pp. 39-40.

12 Peter Stabel, 'Town and Countryside in Medieval Europe: Beyond the Divide', in *Town and Country in Medieval North Western Europe: Dynamic Interactions*, The Medieval Countryside 11, ed. by Alexis Wilkin, John Naylor, Derek Keene, and A.J.A. Bijsterveld (Brepols: Turnhout, 2015), pp. 313-23.

I will at times treat the cloth centres of the Flemish West-Quarter as if they were rural settlements, addressing such things as their agricultural sector (Chapter 1); and alternately as if they were towns, for instance by examining local cultural associations (Chapter 4). This relatively innovative approach has the advantage that it exposes interconnections that might otherwise go unnoticed, such as the relationship between sheep-rearing, the trade in woollen cloth, and the attendance of theatrical events at fairs. Needless to say, this integrative approach carries through into the treatment of the sources. This helps to counter the problem that there is a definite dearth of remaining records for this region of Flanders. The main culprit for this shortage of historic evidence is the First World War; specifically, the artillery fire that hit the belfry of the city of Ypres on 22 November 1914 while it was serving as a depository for the city's archives. Few sources of the West-Quarter draperies have survived for the fifteenth, and virtually nothing for the fourteenth century. Therefore, this book builds upon a wide range of fragmented materials of differing natures. The majority of these available records consist of duplicates that were kept elsewhere.[13] Yet there is little 'hard' data to work from. Nevertheless, to quote Christine Carpenter, 'as a general principle, the evidence has been pushed as far as it will reasonably go, on the grounds that it is better to be wrong asking the right questions than not to ask the questions at all'.[14] To be specific, this means that we will often have to rely on approximation and estimates when it comes to quantitative analysis. I will consistently address the shortcomings of the materials as and when I use them for these estimations.

The second contribution of this book is closely connected to the first: namely, to examine an important regional case study that has been relatively ignored for a long time. The scarcity of surviving source material certainly has not helped here. But another reason for this lacuna is a kind of law of diminishing returns. Well-known economic historians, most notably Henri Pirenne, had already devoted cursory attention to the West-Quarter's cloth industry during the first half of the twentieth century. And perhaps this subsequently led to the misconception that everything useful has already been said on the topic.[15] As I intend to demonstrate, however, this is far from true. There are, in fact, several aspects of the rural textile economy of pre-industrial Flanders to which this

---

13 Attentive readers may notice that the 'Acquits' (receipts) of the Chamber of Accounts in Lille feature prominently among the sources cited throughout this study. This is because this princely institution was charged with the official oversight of the cloth industry of Nieuwkerke (the most productive village in the region) from the second half of the fifteenth century onwards. Thus, while the original records of the village were lost in the destruction of the Ypres archives, those kept in Lille (and later partly relocated to Brussels) were fortunately spared the same fate. This is also why so little evidence survives for the fourteenth century, as the Chamber of Accounts had not yet taken its role of official overseer at that time.

14 Christine Carpenter, *Locality and Polity: A Study of Warwickshire Landed Society, 1401-1499* (Cambridge: Cambridge University Press, 1992), p. 12.

15 Henri Pirenne, *Histoire de Belgique*, 7 vols (Brussels: H. Lamertin, 1900-1932), II (1903), pp. 182-83; Émile Coornaert, *Un centre industriel d'autrefois: la draperie-sayetterie d'Hondschoote (XIVe-XVIIIe siècles)* (Paris: Presses universitaires de France, 1930), Appendix IVbis.

book offers new insights. Among other things, it provides novel insights into the relationship between this region's artisanal labour force and its agricultural economy; the social relations between these workers and the entrepreneurs who employed them; and the commercial dimension of their trade in textiles. The choice for a regional study is partly inspired by the current emphasis on regional approaches among rural historians of the Low Countries. Following on from the works of Erik Thoen and Bas van Bavel, various authors have begun to progressively 'map' the socio-economic development of the entire Netherlandish countryside in the pre-industrial period.[16] These historians often focus on the relationship between such economic evolutions and the normative (social and political) frameworks of their research regions. This means that the field of rural history of the Low Countries is currently heavily influenced by *New Institutional Economics* (NIE). NIE focuses on how norms and values affect the economy through their impact upon transaction costs.[17] Many urban historians that study commercialization, including those specialized in the Low Countries, also follow this analytical perspective.[18] This facilitates the integrative approach of the present book.

Which brings us to the third contribution of this study, as well as its broader significance for the fields of social and economic history. The book's final objective is to offer a fresh perspective on the factors that drove economic development in pre-industrial European societies. It does so through the already mentioned in-depth examination of the long-term economic trajectory of the textile sector within the relatively modest-sized region that was the West-Quarter of Flanders. In fact, the emphasis will often be on one production centre in particular: the village of Nieuwkerke. This discrete geographic focus allows us to descend to the level of the ordinary men and women involved in the manufacture and sale of cloth. By doing so, the present study can provide a detailed picture of a society as it was becoming more and more market-oriented. In that sense, it is perhaps no coincidence that the West-Quarter's industrial expansion occurred between the early fourteenth and the later sixteenth century. This was a period when trading via 'the market' – as opposed to, say, exchange within familial networks – was becoming more and more common, and ordinary people increasingly engaged in everyday transactions. That 'Commercial Revolution'

---

16 For an introduction, see: Daniel Curtis, 'Trends in Rural Social and Economic History of the Pre-Industrial Low Countries: Recent Themes and Ideas in Journals and Books of the Past Five Years (2007-2013)', *BMGN – Low Countries Historical Review*, 128 (2013), 60-95.

17 The classic study is Douglass North, *Institutions, Institutional Change and Economic Performance* (Cambridge: Cambridge University Press, 1990); Douglass North, 'Institutions', *Journal of Economic Perspectives*, 5 (1991), 97-112. Note that a similar approach was already to be found in the works of Michael Postan: John Munro, 'The "New Institutional Economics" and the Changing Fortunes of Fairs in Medieval and Early Modern Europe: The Textile Trades, Warfare, and Transaction Costs', *Vierteljahrschrift für Sozial- und Wirtschaftsgeschichte*, 138 (2001), 1-47 (pp. 2-3).

18 For example: Oscar Gelderblom, 'The Governance of Early Modern trade: The Case of Hans Thijs, 1556-1611', *Enterprise and Society*, 4 (2003), 606-39 (esp. pp. 606-07, 612-14); Oscar Gelderblom, *Cities of Commerce: The Institutional Foundations of International Trade in the Low Countries, 1250-1650* (Princeton: Princeton University Press, 2013).

may have started from around the year 1000 onwards, but certainly took off between 1300 and 1600. And this commercialization was interlinked with the wave of urbanization that swept through Europe at the same time. This period, of urbanization, commercialization, nascent consumerism and the 'rise of the West-Quarter', establishes the chronological boundaries of this study.[19]

Of course, the question what drove pre-industrial economic development is an old one. And it is closely connected to the issue of the rise of modern market economies, or the issue of a 'transition from feudalism to capitalism' as the dominant economic system. Unsurprisingly, there is still much disagreement over if and when there was such a thing as a watershed moment that marked the start or critical mass of these economic transformations (let alone what caused them).[20] The matter becomes more complicated because scholars have adopted different definitions for, and focus on different versions of, capitalism and commercialization.

Thus, some have contended that 'commercial capitalism' (now more often called 'merchant capitalism') was born during the Commercial Revolution of the high Middle Ages, in the towns of the Low Countries among other places. Many have agreed that such an economic system, 'characterized by the divorce of capital and labour, by the dependence of legally free wage labourers on employers, and by the realization of profit', indeed had its origins in the Middle Ages.[21] But even supporters have noted that it was not until the sixteenth century that 'market exchange became dominant' as a platform of economic exchange.[22] Others hold that while capitalist relations of production already existed during the Middle Ages, one of the true signs of a (modern) market economy is a certain 'continuity' of commercialization and productivity within a given region, and therefore the first modern economy only emerged in the course of the seventeenth century.[23] Still others have argued that market-orientation was altogether limited in the

---

19 Robert Lopez, *The Commercial Revolution of the Middle Ages, 950-1350* (New York: Cambridge University Press, 1976). See also: Katherine Anne Wilson, 'Commerce and Consumers: The Ubiquitous Chest of the Late Middle Ages', *Journal of Interdisciplinary History*, 51 (2021), 377-404; Elizabeth Gemmill, 'Debt, Distraint, Display and Dead Men's Treasure: Material Culture in Late Medieval Aberdeen, *Journal of Medieval History*, 46 (2020), 350-72.

20 Notable examples are: Bas van Bavel, *The Invisible Hand? How Market Economies Have Emerged and Declined since AD 500* (Oxford: Oxford University Press, 2016), pp. 1-11; S.R. Epstein, *Freedom and Growth: The Rise of States and Markets in Europe, 1300-1750* (London: Routledge, 2000), pp. 170-74; Jan Luiten van Zanden, *The Rise and Decline of Holland's Economy: Merchant Capitalism and the Labour Market* (Manchester: Manchester University Press, 1993), pp. 11-16.

21 Catharina Lis and Hugo Soly, *Poverty and Capitalism in Pre-Industrial Europe* (Brighton: The Harvester Press, 1979), pp. 9-10; Fernand Braudel, *Civilization and Capitalism, 15th-18th Century*, 3 vols (New York: Harper & Row, 1982-1984), II (1983), *The Wheels of Commerce*, pp. 227-230. See also: Jan Luiten van Zanden, 'Do We Need a Theory of Merchant Capitalism?', *Review (Fernand Braudel Center)*, 20 (1997), 255-67.

22 Bas van Bavel, 'The Medieval Origins of Capitalism in the Low Countries', *BMGN – Low Countries Historical Review*, 125 (2010), 45-79.

23 Jan de Vries and Ad van der Woude, *The First Modern Economy: Success, Failure, and Perseverance of the Dutch Economy, 1500-1815* (Cambridge: Cambridge University Press, 1997; 2010 ed.), pp. 693-694.

pre-industrial period through ideological factors, as people did not place their trust in the 'self-regulating mechanism' of the market.[24] Historians like Fernand Braudel, then, have downplayed the idea that societies are pervaded by a single economic system. Braudel posited instead that certain sectors can be capitalist while others do not (yet) support the same kind of capital formation.[25]

Needless to say, it would be futile to review all these perspectives here.[26] What is principally relevant to this study, is the related question in what degree the driving forces of pre-industrial economic change should be located in the countryside, or rather in the urban sphere. This essentially comes down to an assessment of the relative importance of rural proletarianization and urban commercialization and entrepreneurship. The history of textiles has gone in and out of fashion as a means to trace these transformations. In Belgium, the already-mentioned Henri Pirenne, as well as his successors George Espinas and Émile Coornaert, tested their mettle on this subject during the first half of the twentieth century. In fact, the historiographical emphasis on the Netherlandish textile economy led the historian Léopold Génicot to remark in 1946 that 'Les médiévistes belges sont été pour ainsi dire hypnotisés par la draperie'.[27] So Espinas demonstrated how the emergence of capitalist relations of production may be traced through a focus on a single entrepreneur: the 'embryonic capitalist' Jehan Boinebroke of thirteenth-century Douai.[28] Coornaert did something similar, but he departed from a single textile centre: namely, the Flemish boom town of Hondschoote. Hondschoote's light textiles (*sayetterie*) rose to prominence in unison with the more expensive fabrics of the West-Quarter; but in contrast to the villages of the latter region, Hondschoote actually became an enfranchised town, and its industry survived the adverse effects of the Dutch Revolt (1566-1648).[29]

Based on the Flemish textile economy in general, then, Henri Pirenne posited that the roots of modern capitalist enterprise lay in the shift from traditional manufacture by medieval craft corporations in towns towards the 'grand' industry that developed in the countryside in the fifteenth and sixteenth centuries – which he labelled as 'caractéristique de l'époque moderne'.[30] Two features were central in these rural industries: first, the progressive separation

---

24 Martha Howell, *Commerce before Capitalism in Europe, 1300-1600* (New York: Cambridge University Press, 2010), pp. 5-13.

25 Braudel, *Civilization and Capitalism*, II, pp. 247-49.

26 For a general discussion about the changing views and discussions on the transition from the medieval to the modern economy: Maarten Prak, 'Early Modern Capitalism: An Introduction', in *Early Modern Capitalism: Economic and Social Change in Europe, 1400-1800*, ed. by Maarten Prak (London: Routledge, 2001), 1-20 (esp. pp. 1-14).

27 Léopold Genicot, 'L'industrie dans le comté de Namur à la fin du moyen âge (1350-1430)', *Namurcum*, 21 (1946), 49-57 (p. 49).

28 Georges Espinas, *Les origines du capitalisme*, 2 vols (Lille: Raoust, 1933-49), I, *Sire Jehan Boinebroke: patricien et drapier douasien* (1933), esp. P. 216.

29 Coornaert, *Un centre industriel d'autrefois*, Part I, Chapter 4.

30 Henri Pirenne, 'Une crise industrielle au XVIe siècle: la draperie urbaine et la "nouvelle draperie" en Flandre', *Bulletin de l'Académie royale de Belgique, Classe des Lettres*, 5 (1905), 489-521 (pp. 504-14); Henri Pirenne, 'Note sur la fabrication des tapisseries en Flandre au XVIe siècle : contribution à

of the labour force from alternative sources of income in the form of land; and second, a *laissez-faire* entrepreneurial climate devoid of guild regulations, where the success of an enterprise was only determined by market competition (again, there are clear similarities with present-day offshoring).

Of course, the ideas of Pirenne and his successors have been qualified over the course of more than a century of scholarship. Primarily, the strict separation between town and countryside, which has been called the 'dichotomie pirennienne', is no longer accepted.[31] That said, social and economic historians specializing in the late medieval textile economy still largely depart from Pirenne's commercial and entrepreneurial perspective; wherein they have been further influenced by the supply-oriented approach of Herman Van der Wee.[32] In recent decades, the most notable contributions on the Low Countries in this regard have arguably come from Peter Stabel and John Munro. Their studies, which emphasize the synergies between textile production and the urban sphere, have chiefly expanded upon the works of Pirenne and Van der Wee by providing solid empirical quantifications of the (evolving) textile outputs of different Netherlandish cloth centres.[33] Of course, it is not just the Low Countries that have been the subject of this kind of analysis. The textile economies of late medieval England, France, and Italy have been researched along similar lines; with renewed vigour in recent years, in fact.[34]

Standing opposite these commercial, urban approaches are rural historians who posit that the crucial preconditions for commercialization were changes in the social property relations in the pre-industrial countryside. A key proponent of this position was the English historian Robert Brenner, who wrote an influential article on the subject in 1976.[35] Brenner claimed that the agrarian economy of late

l'histoire de l'industrie capitaliste', *Vierteljahrschrift für Sozial- und Wirtschafsgeschichte*, 4 (1906), 325-39 (pp. 334-36); Henri Pirenne, *Histoire de Belgique*, II, p. 390; Henri Pirenne, *Histoire de Belgique*, III, pp. 228-39.

31 Yoshio Fuji, 'Draperie urbaine et draperie rurale dans les Pays Bas meridionaux au bas moyen âge: une mise ou point des recherches après H. Pirenne', *Journal of Medieval History*, 16 (1990), 77-98 (p. 86).

32 Herman Van der Wee, 'Structural Changes and Specialization in the Industry of the Southern Netherlands, 1100-1600', *The Economic History Review*, 28 (1975), 203-21.

33 See especially: Stabel, 'Een kwantitatieve benadering'; and Peter Stabel, *Dwarfs among Giants: The Flemish Urban Network in the Late Middle Ages* (Leuven: Garant, 1997), pp. 148-50; John Munro, 'Three Centuries of Luxury Textile Consumption in the Low Countries and England, 1330-1570: Trends and Comparisons of Real Values of Woollen Broadcloths (Then and Now)', in *The Medieval Broadcloth: Changing Trends in Fashions, Manufacturing and Consumption*, ed. by Kathrine Vestergård Pedersen and Marie-Louise Nosch (Oxford: Oxbow Books, 2009), 1-73; John Munro, 'Medieval Woollens: Textiles, Textile Technology and Industrial Organisation', in *The Cambridge History of Western Textiles*, 2 vols, ed. by David Jenkins (Cambridge: Cambridge University Press, 2003), I, pp. 181-227.

34 John S. Lee, *The Medieval Clothier* (Woodbridge: Boydell, 2018), esp. pp. 22-26; Jean-Louis Roch, *Un autre monde du travail: la draperie en Nordmandie au Moyen Âge* (Rouen: Presses Universitaires du Rouen et du Havre, 2013); *At the Centre of the Old World: Trade and Manufacturing in Venice and the Venetian Mainland, 1400-1800*, ed. by Paola Lanaro (Toronto: CRRS Publications, 2006).

35 For an introduction: *The Brenner Debate: Agrarian Class Structure and Economic Development in Pre-Industrial Europe*, ed. by T.H. Aston and C.H.E. Philpin (Cambridge: Cambridge University Press, 1985). The original article: Robert Brenner, 'Agrarian Class Structure and Economic Development

medieval England was the first to develop markets for the key commodities of land, labour, and capital (also called the 'factors of production'). This enabled the rise of 'agrarian capitalism': the formation of larger farms that were extensively cultivated by wage labourers, and through relatively large capital investments. Brenner's position was taken up and adapted by historians such as Jane Whittle, who further highlighted the significance of this change as regards access to the means of production. The key organizational innovation under agrarian capitalism was that workers were freed from constraints on their capacity to sell their labour power via the market, but they were also 'freed' from ownership of the means of production (in this case, land). Those means of production were concentrated in the hands of owners who were able – or indeed forced – to employ 'free' labourers via the market.[36]

The hybrid rural-urban textile industries of the late medieval West-Quarter make for an ideal test case to show that these alternative explanatory models are, in fact, complementary. To that end, this study considers the organizational aspects of these production centres from a variety of analytical angles, which also means that we will adopt subtly different definitions of what constitutes a 'capitalist' or 'market-oriented' economy. So Chapters 1 and 2 assess how convincing it is that rural proletarianization (or the 'freeing' of peasants from ownership of the productive commodities, not just of land but of craft instruments as well) led to capitalist relations of production in the textile centres of the West-Quarter; in other words, whether we can establish a skewed economic relationship between (land-) poor textile workers, who were unable to acquire their own tools and raw materials, and the well-to-do entrepreneurs for whom they were forced to work, who had sole access to these productive means. But then, in Chapter 3, we will also entertain the notion that the commercial organization of the West-Quarter industries qualifies as 'merchant capitalist' because these textile entrepreneurs combined their interference in the production process with a monopolization of the trade in finished fabrics. By combining these and other outlooks, I will ultimately demonstrate that the economic trajectory of the cloth-producing villages in this part of pre-industrial Flanders can be explained through a combination of factors, which partly derived from region-specific social relations in the agricultural economy, and partly from the initiatives of entrepreneurs with close ties to the cities and commercial institutions of the Low Countries. Indeed, I contend that the relationship between town and countryside was a two-way street in this region and period.

At the same time, it is easy to avoid the temptation of interpreting the economic evolution of the Flemish West-Quarter along the lines of a grand narrative towards modernity, because the region's buzzing with industry fell virtually silent after

in Pre-Industrial Europe', *Past & Present*, 70 (1976), 30-75. See also: Robert Brenner, 'The Low Countries in the Transition to Capitalism', *Journal of Agrarian Change*, 1 (2001), 169-241.

36 Jane Whittle, *The Development of Agrarian Capitalism: Land and Labour in Norfolk, 1440-1580* (Oxford: Oxford University Press 2000), p. 9.

the second half of the sixteenth century.[37] In fact, a 21st-century visitor to these parts would hardly guess that it was once a hotbed of cloth manufacture with villages numbering several thousands of workers. Today, Nieuwkerke and its neighbouring villages are purely agricultural settlements once more. Population numbers have, accordingly, reverted back to their medieval levels from before the textile boom.[38] In some respects, then, the region has come full circle since the year 1300. But this does not mean that we should dismiss its trajectory as irrelevant to current discussions about what drives economic growth. Quite the contrary: the historic case can serve as a 'laboratory' to test the underlying forces that shape economic upturns and downturns – as long as we also bear in mind the historical particularism.[39]

This book deals with these questions over the course of five chapters. Chapter 1 begins by sketching out demographic evolutions in the late medieval West-Quarter in relation to the textile boom. It subsequently deals with the question how the region's rural textile industries can be connected to the structure of the regional agrarian economy. Specifically, we will examine in what degree a lack of land drove peasant families to engage in part time cloth manufacture for the export market (a phenomenon known as 'proto-industry'; see Chapters 1 and 2). Chapter 2 focuses on the organizational aspect of the cloth industries themselves; that is, on the relative importance of an unrestricted labour market and the profit-minded actions of local entrepreneurs. These aspects of the textile economy are placed within a broader discussion about the role of different forms of entrepreneurship in this period, and the extent to which these were market-oriented or capitalist. In Chapter 3, the actual marketing and trade of fabrics take central stage, with a focus on the question whether the cloth entrepreneurs of the West-Quarter can be seen as aspiring 'merchant-capitalists'. This chapter also addresses the tension between the evolution of formal commercial institutions and the informal, personal aspects of trade. Chapter 4 constitutes something of a reckoning concerning the urban characteristics of these textile centres, and of Nieuwkerke in particular. The final chapter, Chapter 5, is a sort of micro-analysis: an attempt to explain the cyclical development of the woollen sector in Nieuwkerke between 1300 and 1600 in light of the internal interactions within the village's cloth corporation. The conclusion provides a synthesis of the principal findings in the main text but finishes by offering more general hypotheses about the driving forces of economic development in pre-industrial Europe.

---

37 For a prominent example of this idea of a linear path to modernity: Francis Fukuyama, *The End of History and the Last Man* (New York: Free Press, 1992; 2006 ed.), pp. xi-xxiii.

38 The present-day municipality of 'Heuvelland' in the country of Belgium – where most of the cloth villages are located – currently numbers 240 farms, and agricultural land encompasses 85 out of a total 94 km²: *Lokaal sociaal beleidsplan Heuvelland 2008-2013*, on: www.economischekaart.be/heuvelland [accessed 11 March 2021]. In 2007, the entire municipality of Heuvelland only counted 8179 inhabitants, while Nieuwkerke, Dranouter, Westouter and Wijtschate together already counted some 3695 inhabitants in 1469 (see Chapter 1).

39 Bas van Bavel, 'History as a Laboratory to Better Understand the Formation of Institutions', *Journal of Institutional Economics*, 11 (2015), 69-91.

CHAPTER 1

The ties between agriculture and industry

On 25 March 1574, the aldermen of Ypres gave a certain Willem Van den Walle of Nieuwkerke permission to come live within the city's jurisdiction. When asked about his occupation, he professed to be both farmer (*landsman*) and cloth entrepreneur (*drapier*).[1] Thereby Van de Walle embodied the split nature of the late medieval rural economy of the Flemish West-Quarter: on the one hand, the region featured prominent rural textile centres, but on the other hand, the local population had not abandoned agriculture altogether. This raises the question to what extent the spectacular rise of cloth manufacture between the fourteenth and late sixteenth century was ingrained in the structure of the regional agrarian economy. This type of enquiry has some pedigree in economic history. In her 1961 study of seventeenth-century England, Joan Thirsk posited that 'the location of handicraft industries is not altogether haphazard, but is associated with certain types of farming community and certain kinds of social organisation'.[2] Over the last few decades, historians of the late medieval Low Countries have begun to advocate for a similar approach to the rural economy. Most notable in this regard are the works of Erik Thoen and Bas van Bavel, whose regional focuses and analyses of economic development in terms of social structure have in turn spawned studies covering several principalities of the pre-industrial Low Countries.[3]

This chapter takes its cue from these works, addressing the relationship between the agricultural and industrial branches of the regional economy in the Flemish West-Quarter. The purpose is to assess how long-term developments in the regional landholding structure were tied to surpluses of labour and capital

1 In Middle Dutch: 'landsman ende drapier'. *Landsman* could also simply mean 'man from the countryside' or 'fellow countryman', but within this context it clearly meant a farmer because the Ypres aldermen were enquiring after new residents' occupations: Kristof Papin and Arnold Preneel, '*Ne peuis adveniat*: sociale politiek en bevolkingsmigraties in de stad Ieper (1571-1575)', *Westhoek. Tijdschrift voor Geschiedenis & Familiekunde in de Vlaamse & Franse Westhoek*, 15 (1999), 4-52 (p. 45).

2 Joan Thirsk, 'Industries in the Countryside', in *Essays in the Economic and Social History of Tudor and Stuart England: In Honour of R.H. Tawney*, ed. by F.J. Fisher (Cambridge: Cambridge University Press, 1961), pp. 70-88 (p. 88).

3 Bas van Bavel, *Manors and Markets: Economy and Society in the Low Countries AD 500-1600* (Oxford: Oxford University Press, 2010); Erik Thoen, '"Social Agrosystems" as an Economic Concept to Explain Regional Differences: An Essay Taking the Former County of Flanders as an Example (Middle Ages – 19th Century)', in *Landholding and Land Transfer in the North Sea Area (Late Middle Ages – 19th century)*, ed. by Bas van Bavel and Peter Hoppenbrouwers (Turnhout: Brepols, 2004), pp. 47-66; Maïka De Keyzer, *Inclusive Commons and the Sustainability of Peasant Communities in the Medieval Low Countries* (New York: Routledge, 2018); Tim Soens, *De spade in de dijk? Waterbeheer en rurale samenleving in de Vlaamse kustvlakte (1280-1580)* (Ghent: Academia Press, 2009); Eline Van Onacker, *Village Elites and Social Structures in the Fifteenth- and Sixteenth-Century Campine Region* (Turnhout: Brepols, 2015).

that may have facilitated the efflorescence of cloth production. Akin to most modern industries, capital and labour were fundamental factors in medieval textile production, and those of the West-Quarter were no exception.[4] For one thing, to produce more than a thousand pieces of fabric each year – a level reached by several of these villages in the late-fifteenth and sixteenth centuries – required the input of many workers. For another, the medium-quality fabrics produced by the likes of Nieuwkerke, Dranouter and Kemmel also required relatively large capital inputs compared to other rural regions. After all, these industries relied on expensive Spanish and Scottish wool to supplement locally sourced materials, not to mention the costly dyestuffs.[5] This means that the textile entrepreneurs of these villages had to enjoy a certain level of wealth, or at least creditworthiness, which in turn suggests that they may have had recourse to relatively large stretches of land – the most reliable commodity in the eyes of pre-industrial countryfolk and town dwellers alike.

The focus on these key elements (or 'factors of production') of land, labour, and capital also means that the present analysis touches upon the debate about 'proto-industrialization' – a debate which Joan Thirsk's 1961 article foreshadowed by more than a decade.[6] The concept of proto-industrialization was originally conceived of as a prior phase to the factory industrialization of the eighteenth and nineteenth centuries, but that thesis has been largely rejected.[7] The surviving core of the theory still considers proto-industrialization as a stage in economic development, however, and historians are looking further and further back in time to trace its dynamics at work. It now appears that many parts of Europe already showed signs of proto-industry from the sixteenth century onwards.[8] Proto-industrialization was characterized by the spread of domestic manufacture in the countryside, concentrated in small geographical areas, and offering by-employment to the peasant population. What distinguished proto-industry from

4 John Munro, 'Spanish Merino Wools and the *Nouvelles Draperies*: An Industrial Transformation in the Late Medieval Low Countries', *Economic History Review*, 58 (2005), 431-84 (pp. 450-51).

5 *Les arrets et jugés du Parlement de Paris sur appels flamands conservés dans les registres du Parlement*, ed. by Serge Dauchy and others, 3 vols (Brussels: Ministère de la justice, 1966-2002), I (1966), pp. 576-78.

6 Michael Zell, *Industry in the Countryside: Wealden Society in the Sixteenth Century* (Cambridge: Cambridge University Press, 2004), pp. 2-5. Thirsk herself was influenced by the work of Eleanora Carus-Wilson, who underlined the importance of waterpower for the growth of rural cloth industry: Eleanora Carus-Wilson, 'An Industrial Revolution of the thirteenth Century', *The Economic History Review*, 11 (1941), 39-60 (pp. 55-60).

7 Franklin Mendels, 'Proto-Industrialization: The First Phase of the Industrialization Process', *The Journal of Economic History*, 32 (1972), 241-61; Sheilagh Ogilvie and Markus Cerman, 'The Theories of Proto-Industrialization', in *European Proto-Industrialization: An Introductory Handbook*, ed. by Markus Cerman and Sheilagh Ogilvie (Cambridge NY: Cambridge University Press, 1996), pp. 1-11 (pp. 1-3, 7-11); Julie Marfany, 'Is It Still Helpful to Speak of Proto-Industrialization? Some Suggestions from a Catalan Case-Study', *Economic History Review*, 63 (2010), 942-73.

8 Bas van Bavel, 'Early Proto-Industrialization in the Low Countries? The Importance and Nature of Market-Oriented Non-Agricultural Activities on the Countryside in Flanders and Holland, *c.* 1250-1570', *Revue belge de philologie et d'histoire*, 81 (2003), 1109-65 (pp. 1110-11); Marci Sortor, 'Saint-Omer and its Textile Trades in the Late Middle Ages: A Contribution to the Proto-Industrialisation Debate', *The American Historical Review*, 99 (1993), 1475-99 (pp. 1495-99).

other forms of domestic manufacture is that the output was sold and consumed beyond the region of production. The idea is that proto-industrialization had the potential to raise the overall economic productivity of a society, thereby supporting demographic growth while ultimately precipitating the rise of distinct economic zones, of rural industry on the one hand, and commercial agriculture on the other.[9]

From the perspective of peasant families, part-time employment in manufacture was one of the available strategies to supplement the food or minor income they generated through producing crops or rearing livestock on their own farms. Alternative options were to specialize in certain commercial crops or to work for wages on somebody else's farm. Depending on the regional economy, pre-industrial peasant families often used a combination of these different strategies to maintain subsistence.[10] The development that created the need for these varied income strategies was the progressive fragmentation of landholdings that occurred throughout the medieval countryside of Europe, with a notable peak at the end of the thirteenth century. Landholdings were split up into increasingly smaller units through a combination of rising demographic pressure and the practice of partible inheritance. Due to the latter, family holdings were divided between the different heirs instead of keeping their integrity by resting with the eldest son.[11] Although this phenomenon showed regional variation, wherever rural households were able to keep effective ownership of their farms, the ever-shrinking size of their holdings increasingly drove them towards 'the market'.[12] This included by-employment in domestic textile manufacture. Thus, developments in demography and landholding may have led to the success of cloth manufacture in the countryside of the Flemish West-Quarter by begetting the labour reserve that was essential for the growth of these rural industries.[13]

9 Ogilvie and Cerman, pp. 1-6; Marfany, pp. 968-69.

10 Jan de Vries, *The Industrious Revolution: Consumer Behavior and the Household Economy, 1650 to the Present* (Cambridge: Cambridge University Press, 2008), pp. 71-72, 81-82.

11 Emmanuel Le Roy Ladurie, *The French peasantry, 1450-1660* (Berkeley CA: University of California Press, 1987), pp. 56-8; Erik Thoen, 'A "Commercial Survival Economy" in Evolution: The Flemish Countryside and the Transition to Capitalism (Middle Ages – 19th century)', in *Peasants into Farmers: The Transformation of Rural Economy and Society in the Low Countries (Middle Ages – 19th century) in light of the Brenner Debate*, ed. by Peter Hoppenbrouwers and Jan Luiten van Zanden (Turnhout: Brepols, 2001), pp. 102-57 (p. 113).

12 Peter Hoppenbrouwers, 'Town and Country in Holland, 1350-1550', in *Town and Country in Europe, 1300-1800*, ed. by S.R. Epstein (Cambridge: Cambridge University Press, 2001), pp. 54-79 (pp. 59-60); Govind Sreenivasan, *The Peasants of Ottobeuren, 1487-1726: A Rural Society in Early Modern Europe* (Cambridge: Cambridge University Press, 2004), pp. 149-50, 152-53; Lawrence Poos, *A Rural Society after the Black Death: Essex, 1350-1525*, Cambridge Studies in Population, Economy and Society in Past Time (Cambridge: Cambridge University Press, 1991), pp. 71-72; Zell, pp. 22-26.

13 Erik Thoen and Tim Soens, 'The Family or the Farm: A Sophie's Choice? The Late Medieval Crisis in Flanders', in *Crisis in the Later Middle Ages: Beyond the Postan-Duby Paradigm*, ed. by John Drendel (Turnhout: Brepols, 2015), pp. 195-224 (p. 211); Bas van Bavel, 'Rural Wage Labour in the Sixteenth-Century Low Countries: An Assessment of the Importance and Nature of Wage Labour in the Countryside of Holland, Guelders and Flanders', *Continuity and Change*, 21 (2006), 37-72.

This chapter therefore proceeds by examining demographic developments in the late medieval West-Quarter of Flanders. We will subsequently take a closer look at the long-term development of landholding in the region; that is, reconstructing the evolution of farm sizes over the late Middle Ages and determining whether this evolution can be linked to specific geographic and political characteristics of the West-Quarter. The next section explores how this long-term trajectory in the agrarian economy impacted upon the availability of labour, and to what extent proto-industrial by-employment may have buttressed the rise of the rural textile industries in this part of Flanders. In the same vein, the latter part of this chapter assesses in what degree the landholding structure of the research region may have contributed to the industrial entrepreneurs' access to capital.

A note on demographic developments

As Alain Derville once wrote: 'la démographie est comme la géographie: si elle commande rien, elle conditionne tout'.[14] Indeed, a basic awareness of evolving population levels in the West-Quarter towards the end of the Middle Ages is helpful to understand developments in the region's landholding pattern, since the increasing subdivision of farmland was predicated upon demographic pressure. Population estimates are further relevant because they help contextualize the relative weight of the cloth industry in providing employment opportunities to the regional inhabitants. Note that population estimates are not unproblematic for this period, so all figures have to be taken with a grain of salt. In fact, before the year 1469, very little is known about population numbers in the West-Quarter, with the exception of the city of Ypres. The largest and most powerful town in this part of Flanders, Ypres was marked by a swift population decline after the thirteenth century, from around 40,000 inhabitants circa 1300 to a mere 10,000 at the beginning of the fifteenth century (and still dropping). Although there are no specific estimates of the impact of the Black Death on the population of Ypres, it is likely that the outbreak of several epidemics took their toll in the course of the fourteenth century.[15] Another important cause of the demographic decline in Ypres was hardship to the city's leading economic sector: the cloth industry. Responding to shifts in market conditions in the late 1200s, Ypres' cloth entrepreneurs reoriented towards the production of luxury fabrics, which resulted

14 Alain Derville, 'La population du Nord au Moyen Âge, II: de 1384 à 1549', *Revue du Nord*, 81 (1999), 65-82 (p. 82).

15 For instance, between 25 April and 9 October 1316, 2573 people died of some kind of epidemic in Ypres: Henri Pirenne, 'Les dénombrements de la population d'Ypres au XVe siècle (1412-1506)', *Vierteljahrschrift für Sozial- und Wirtschaftsgeschichte*, 1 (1903), 1-32 (p. 3). See also: Martine Aubry, 'Les mortalités lilloises (1328-1369)', *Revue du Nord*, 65 (1983), 327-42; Wim Blockmans, 'The Social and Economic Effects of Plague in the Low Countries, 1349-1500', *Revue belge de philologie et d'histoire*, 58 (1980), 833-63.

in a less labour-intensive industry.[16] There were fewer jobs for the resident cloth workers, who were either driven towards other occupations, or saw no other option than to migrate elsewhere. There is evidence to suggest that this migration wave of skilled workers from Ypres stimulated the industrial development of secondary cloth centres in its vicinity (see Chapter 5). Strikingly, this is the exact opposite of what happened in England in the same period. There, a significant proportion of the textile labour force – specifically, the fullers – were drawn to the towns in the fourteenth century, following a general shift in production, away from lighter worsteds and towards heavy broadcloth.[17]

The foundation of an extra chapel in Nieuwkerke in 1272 suggests that the West-Quarter had gone along with the general demographic growth in Europe in the thirteenth century.[18] Other than that, the thirteenth and fourteenth centuries are marked by a dearth of relevant source material on this point. What is clear is that, along with industrial output, the population levels of the rural cloth centres in the region rose to their highest pre-industrial levels around the middle of the sixteenth century. Without question, the village of Nieuwkerke was most impressive in its industrial development, dwarfing the other settlements and industries. When the West-Quarter's cloth output peaked around the year 1550, it produced 27 per cent of Flanders's traditional woollens, and Nieuwkerke was responsible for more than half of this.[19] The question is in what degree this impressive industrial output was tied to rising population levels. P. J. Vandendorpe, a parson of Nieuwkerke who wrote an extensive log during his time in office in the late eighteenth century, postulated that Nieuwkerke 'has always been highly populated, harbouring (…) sometimes five-, six-, yes, even eleven-thousand communicants'.[20] It is impossible to disprove or verify Vandendorpe's figures because the church accounts of the parish he had access to are now lost. Yet, although he probably had the demographic peak of the mid-1500s in mind when he wrote these words, the numbers nonetheless seem exaggerated, especially because they would not even include those parishioners too young to receive communion.

16 Peter Stabel, *Dwarfs among Giants: The Flemish Urban Network in the Late Middle Ages* (Leuven: Garant, 1997), pp. 28-29; Pirenne, 'Les dénombrements de la population d'Ypres', pp. 2-5.

17 Milan Pajic, 'The Fortunes of Urban Fullers in Fourteenth-Century England', *Historical Research*, 93 (2020), 227-51.

18 Ferdinand Van de Putte, 'Notes et analectes devant servir à une histoire complète de Neuve-Église', *Annales de la société d'émulation pour l'étude de l'histoire et des antiquités de la Flandre*, 8 (1850), 254-90 (pp. 261-65).

19 Tim Soens, Peter Stabel, and Tineke Van de Walle, 'An Urbanised Countryside? A Regional Perspective on Rural Textile Production in the Flemish West-Quarter', in *Economies, Public Finances, and the Impact of Institutional Changes in Interregional Perspective: The Low Countries and Neighbouring German Territories (14th-17th Centuries)*, Studies in European Urban History 36, ed. by Remi van Schaïk (Turnhout: Brepols, 2015), pp. 35-60 (p. 36).

20 'Dese plaetse (…) is altyd veel bevolkt geweest, besluytende (…) somtyds vijf, zes, jae ook elf duysent communicanten': P. J. Vandendorpe, *Het handboek van P. J. Vandendorpe, pastoor van Nieuwkerke (1730-1806)*, ed. by Jozef Geldhof (Bruges: Genootschap voor Geschiedenis, 1974), p. 21.

Different methods of calculation, however, indicate that Nieuwkerke did indeed witness a swift demographic upsurge from the late fifteenth century. Population estimates for the year 1469 are most reliable here, because they stem from a hearth tax instituted by Duke Charles 'the Bold' of Burgundy in several principalities of the Low Countries in that year.[21] Each hearth can be equated to a household and family, allowing an approximate calculation of how many indwelling individuals a settlement had. Without recourse to hard data about specific family composition and size in the research region, I have opted for the usual 'urban' multiplier of 4.5, notwithstanding the higher and lower coefficients other historians sometimes apply.[22] Of course, the results still constitute an isolated snapshot, but there is no direct reason to assume that these figures are far off the mark (**Table 1.1**).[23] Not coincidentally, Nieuwkerke and Eécke, the largest industrial centres at that time, also counted the most inhabitants, both rising above the 1000 mark.[24] To be sure, this means that they were already sizable villages at the time, but it certainly did not make them spectacular boomtowns (yet).

No hearth taxes of the research region are extant for the sixteenth century – an unfortunate contrast with other areas in the Low Countries which are better-documented in this regard, such as the duchy of Brabant, the county

21 Walter Prevenier, 'La démographie des villes du comté de Flandre aux XIIIe et XVe siècles; état de la question: essai d'interprétation', *Revue du Nord*, 65 (1983), 255-75 (p. 262). These figures probably include the poor households. While there is no explicit mention of this, the poor households were included in the total amount in the neighbouring castellany of Cassel: M. Le Glay, 'Tableaux de la population des châtellenies de Cassel, Bergues et Bailleul, en 1469', *Bulletin du Comité Flamand de France*, 1 (1857), 344-47. Both Walter Prevenier and Peter Stabel (see next note) presume the same thing.

22 Peter Stabel was able to arrive at a more refined (on average, lower) coefficient based on a classification of the primary householders through an in-depth study of family compositions in his particular case-study: Peter Stabel, 'Bevolking en sociale gelaagdheid: Eeklo en Kaprijke gedurende de late middeleeuwen', *Appeltjes van het Meetjesland*, 38 (1987), 161-84 (pp. 162-64). Both Stabel and Alain Derville apply a higher multiplier of 5 for rural households: Alain Derville, 'L'urbanisation de la Flandre Wallonne d'après les enquêtes fiscales (1449-1549)', *Revue du Nord*, 79 (1997), 295-302 (p. 297). But in order to boost the comparison with urban demography, I deem the standard urban coefficient of 4.5 preferable to the rural multiplier of 5.

23 The West-Quarter figures do not deviate strongly from the other Flemish settlements: Prevenier, p. 263 That said, in the better-documented region of Walloon Flanders, the hearth counts of 1469 are unusually low compared to household taxes in 1448-49 and 1485: Alain Derville, *Enquêtes fiscales de la Flandre wallonne, 1449-1549*, 3 vols (Lille: Commission historique du Nord, 1983-2003), II, pp. 19-20. A notable omission from the 1469 survey is the village of Kemmel. The hearth tax of Western Ypres does include 4 hearths for Kemmel, but the parish itself belonged to the castellany of Warneton, for which no records survive: Pieter Donche, 'De haardentelling van Westieperambacht, 1469', *Vlaamse Stam*, 24 (1988), 517-39 (p. 517).

24 This margin of error is because both places may have counted hearths that belonged to a jurisdiction outside the castellany of Bailleul. The 124 hearths of Nieuwkerke taxed in the castellany of Ypres could have belonged to villagers who had acquired external citizenship (*buitenpoorterij*) of the city of Ypres (see Chapter 4). However, it is more likely that the Nieuwkerke included in that taxation was an entirely different settlement, known today as Oostnieuwkerke and located 5 kilometres off Roeselare. In this period, however, it was still known as 'Nieuwkerke' or sometimes 'the fifth part of Nieuwkerke': General State Archives Brussels (subsequently GSAB), Chamber of Accounts (subsequently CA), Acquits en portefeuilles 802, (non foliated) loose quires referring to "*t vijftendeel van Nieukerke*".

of Holland, or even parts of Walloon-Flanders.[25] Still, it is possible to arrive at some estimates about population growth in the West-Quarter based on fiscal information for the region. For starters, we can compare the 1469 hearth counts of parishes in the comital district or 'castellany' (*kasselrij*) of Bailleul, which covered the larger part of the West-Quarter, with those same parishes' contributions to a general taxation in 1517, to infer demographic developments in between these moments. The tax in question was the so-called *Transport* of Flanders, a punitive burden imposed upon the people of Flanders as stipulated in the treaty of Athis-sur-Orge in 1305, following military defeat against France. The amount each Flemish locality had to contribute to this general tax was readjusted in 1517, and that readjustment was partially based on demographic shifts in the county since the late fifteenth century.[26]

While the parish of Nieuwkerke constituted 11.0 per cent of the total number of 2041 rural hearths in the castellany of Bailleul in 1469, in 1517, the village came to bear no less than 18.1 per cent of the burden of the Transport in that same district (**Table 1.2**). This means that, had the total number of residents in the castellany remained stable, Nieuwkerke's population would have grown by about 64 per cent in the interim. Actually, there is good reason to believe that the district of Bailleul saw an all-out population increase between the early fifteenth and early sixteenth century, as the 1517 readjustment of the Transport of Flanders raised the entire castellany's contribution.[27] In absolute terms, Nieuwkerke's share in the Transport of 1517 was already on par with that of several small Flemish towns, while it was still modest compared to the cities. For example, Nieuwkerke contributed more than towns such as Veurne and Oostende, but still only about half the amount of a small urban textile centre like Poperinge, and a mere fraction of the city of Ypres, even though the latter two's share in the Transport had shrunk considerably since the fifteenth century.[28]

---

25 For Brabant: *Les dénombrements de foyers en Brabant (XIVe-XVIe siècle)*, ed. by Joseph Cuvelier, 2 vols (Brussels: Kiessling et Imbreghts, 1912). For Holland: *Enqueste ende informatie upt stuck van der reductie ende reformatie van den schiltaelen, voertijts getaxeert ende gestelt geweest over de landen van Hollant ende Vrieslant. Gedaen in den jaere MCCCCXCIIII*, ed. by Robert Fruin (Leiden: Brill, 1876); *Informacie up den staet, faculteyt ende gelegentheyt van de steden ende dorpen van Hollant ende Vrieslant, om daernae te reguleren de nyeuwe schiltaele, gedaen in den jaere MCXIV*, ed. by Robert Fruin (Leiden: Brill, 1866). For French-Flanders: Derville, *Enquêtes fiscales de la Flandre wallonne.*

26 Willy Buntinx, 'Het Transport van Vlaanderen (1305-1517): bijdrage tot de geschiedenis van de financiële instellingen van het Graafschap Vlaanderen' (unpublished Masters-thesis, Ghent University, 1965), pp. 174-76, 187-91. Prevenier does something similar to calculate populations in 1469 for those parishes that have left no sources, but in those cases, he was able to use the figures of 1408 as well: Prevenier, pp. 263-64. The Transport of 1517 also gives an accurate depiction of the economic divisions (with the exception of the large cities): Peter Stabel, 'Demography and Hierarchy: The Small Towns and the Urban Network in Sixteenth-Century Flanders', in *Small Towns in Early Modern Europe*, ed. by Peter Clark (Cambridge: Cambridge University Press, 1995), pp. 206-28 (p. 214).

27 Buntinx, pp. 192, 198, 210-12.

28 Nieuwkerke: £3 7s.; Veurne: £2 10s.; Oostende: £3; Poperinge: £6 10s.; Ypres: £70: Buntinx, pp. 367-69; *Documents inedits relatifs à la ville de Bailleul*, ed. by Ignace De Coussemaker, 3 vols (Lille: Quarré du coulombier, 1877-78), I (1877), CCXVI.

Table 1.1. Populations in West-Quarter cloth centres, 1469

	N° of hearths	N° of inhabitants
Caëstres	177	797
Dranouter	126	567
Eécke	129 (354[a])	581 (1593[a])
Flêtre	132	594
Godewaersvelde	166	747
Merris	184	828
Météren	207	932
Nieppe	204	918
Nieuwkerke	225 (349[b])	1013 (1571[b])
Steenwerck	204	918
Westouter	117	527

Source: Le Glay, 'Tableaux de la population', pp. 344-347; Donche, p. 517.

[a] Combination of numbers for the castellanies of Bailleul and Cassel.
[b] Combination of numbers for the castellanies of Bailleul and Ypres (but the figures for Ypres probably refer to another settlement).

Table 1.2. Demographic developments in the castellany of Bailleul

	1469 Hearth count (% of castellany total[a])	1517 Transport of Flanders (% of castellany total[a])	1565-1566 (May-April) Excise or *imposten*[b] (% of castellany total[a])
Caëstres	8.7	7.2	6.3
Dranouter	6.2	6.5	4.1
Eécke	6.3	4.1	3.9
Merris	9.0	7.0	2.7
Méteren	10.1	12.7	5.5
Nieppe	10.0	7.1	8.9
Nieuwkerke	11.0	18.1	34.4
Steenwerck	10.0	3.7	4.4
Westouter	5.7	1.6	0.4

Source: Le Glay, 'Tableaux de la population', pp. 344-7; De Coussemaker, CXXVI; GSAB, CA, Acquits de Lille 809 – 814bis.

[a] Excluding Bailleul, the capital and only town proper in the castellany.
[b] Based on sums paid for the right to levy these taxes (the *imposten*); a right leased out every half year per locality.

Nieuwkerke's presumed population growth between 1469 and 1517 would fit into the pattern visible for other rural textile centres that are better documented on this point, specifically those in Walloon Flanders. The village of Tourcoing in the castellany of Lille even rose from 264 taxable householders in 1449 (circa 1188 inhabitants), to 607 hearths in 1505 (circa 2732 inhabitants): a whacking population growth of 230 per cent.[29]

But the true population boom of Nieuwkerke occurred between around 1500 and the middle of the sixteenth century. Not coincidentally, this was also the period when the production output of the village's woollen industry skyrocketed. Once again, the fiscal records allow for some estimate of relative population increase, in this case between the Transport of Flanders of 1517 and comital excises (*imposten*) on beer, meat and everyday commercial transactions (*coopmanscepe*) that were instituted by Emperor Charles V in the 1540s.[30] The latter provide a decent proxy for demographic size because the consumer demand they represent will have roughly reflected population numbers. That said, the right to levy these excises was auctioned off beforehand, so the figures do not indicate the actual level of consumption so much as they reveal contemporary expectations about the minimum sums to be gained from collecting these taxes.[31] Comparing the contributions of the different settlements of the castellany of Bailleul to the excise duties of 1565-66, however, there is little doubt that Nieuwkerke underwent an explosive population growth in a matter of only fifty years. The village's relative share in this tax was almost twice as high as its contribution to the Transport of Flanders in 1517, and three times higher than its population level relative to the rest of the castellany in 1469 (**Table 1.2**)!

So how many people lived in this boomtown by that time, approximately? Some estimates are possible, and they are based on what we know of Nieuwkerke's textile industry. From the number of active cloth entrepreneurs in the village in 1564-65, we can infer that the parish counted at least 4000 residents at the time, and probably as many as 6500 (**Table 1.3**). In that accounting year, 346 drapers were active in Nieuwkerke's cloth industry.[32] For the sake of calculation, these individuals can be equated to 346 master-weavers.[33] According to Walter Prevenier, each master-weaver required two assistants (*cnapen*) per loom. But, strictly speaking, only one extra worker was necessary if a child was given the task of passing the shuttle between the weavers. So that would give another 346 adult assistants. Further following Prevenier's ratio of two fullers for every three weavers, we arrive at a number of 923 households led by people involved in the textile industry, or 4154 people.[34]

29 Derville, *Enquêtes fiscales*, I, pp. 101-03; III, pp. 192-93.
30 Klaas Maddens, 'De invoering van de "nieuwe middelen" in het graafschap Vlaanderen tijdens de regering van Keizer Karel V', *Revue belge de philologie et d'histoire*, 57 (1979), 342-63, 861-98.
31 GSAB, CA, Acquits de Lille 809-814bis.
32 GSAB, CA, Acquits en portefeuilles 1367/34 (non foliated quires).
33 Stabel, 'Bevolking en sociale gelijkheid', p. 167.
34 Prevenier, pp. 260-62. Henri Pirenne already noted that textile workers in medieval Ypres did not habitually live within the household of their masters: Pirenne, 'Les dénombrements de la population', p. 19.

Table 1.3. Population estimates for Nieuwkerke, 1469-1874

Year	1469	1517	1564-65	1769	1874
N° of inhabitants	1013	1662	4000-6500	2000	2600
Population density (n° of inhabitants per km²)*	57	93	223-363	112	145

Source: De Coussemaker, CXXVI; Van de Putte, 'Notes et analectes', p. 267; Le Glay, 'Tableaux de la population', pp. 344-347; Verhelst, pp. 183-85; GSAB, CA, Acquits en portefeuilles 1367/34.

* The population density is based on a total surface area of 1791 hectares or 17.9 km² (the parish size in 1874).

Yet this would be an absolute minimum, since it departs from the assumption that there was only one loom for each draper, and because it does not include other textile crafts like shearing or dyeing. When we calculate Nieuwkerke's population of resident cloth workers based on the labour requirement of the village's annual woollen output, however, the figure drops somewhat. Following Walter Endrei's labour estimate of 29.5 working hours per m² of cloth, which departs from a fictitious piece of fabric that is remarkably similar to Nieuwkerke's chief product, the village would have required between 2811 and 3514 manufacturers to reach the mid-century peak of 12,398.5 whole pieces.[35] Note that these are all rough estimates, but also note that these figures do not even account for people working outside the textile industry. In fact, if we apply Bas van Bavel's approximation that 57 per cent of Flemish countryfolk were still working in agriculture around 1550, Nieuwkerke may have numbered as many as 8000 people at this time.[36] This is unlikely, though, because all anecdotal evidence indicates that the village population was predominantly involved in manufacture. Still, as a final validation that an estimated 4000 inhabitants is at the low end of the spectrum: the evidence for Tourcoing in Walloon Flanders reveals that this rural cloth centre counted 120 drapers and between 400 and 500 hearths in 1498, so that families led by drapers composed about a third or a fourth of the total number of residents.[37] Extrapolating this number to Nieuwkerke's 346

35 This estimate is based on a piece of 26.899 m² (see Chapter 3, Table 3.2). That gives 333,513.30 m² in the village's peak production year (1548-49); which, when multiplied by 29.5 working hours/m² makes 9,838,642.41 working hours. Based on Anthony J. Veal's estimate of 'male manual workers in Britain' in 1550 (low estimate: 2800 working hours/year/ male; high estimate: 3500 working hours), that would give 2811 or 3513.80 working 'men': Walter Endrei, 'Manufacturing a Piece of Woollen Cloth in Medieval Flanders: How Many Work Hours?', in *Textiles of the Low Countries in European Economic History: Proceedings of the Tenth International Economic History Congress, Leuven August 1990*, Studies in Social and Economic History, ed. by Erik Aerts and John Munro (Leuven: Leuven University Press, 1990), pp. 14-23 (pp. 16, 21); Anthony J. Veal, 'A Brief History of Work and its Relationship to Leisure', in *Work and Leasure*, ed. by John T. Haworth and Anthony J. Veal (London and New York: Routledge, 2004), pp. 15-33 (pp. 28-29; Figure 1.1).

36 Van Bavel, 'Rural Wage Labour', p. 44.

37 Derville, *Enquêtes fiscales*, III, p. 43.

drapers in 1564-65 would suggest that the village's population sooner ran in the 5000s and 6000s than in the low 4000s.[38]

This places Nieuwkerke among a select number of Flemish settlements whose populations more or less doubled between the start and middle of the sixteenth century; slightly outranked by more famous boomtowns like Oudenaarde (*c.* 9000 inhabitants) and Hondschoote (*c.* 15,000) but in the same league of small urban cloth centres such as Eeklo (*c.* 4800).[39] Just how exceptional this demographic development was for a late medieval 'rural' settlement becomes apparent when looking at Nieuwkerke's population density at its sixteenth-century peak. The average population density of Flanders in 1469 – not distinguishing between cities and countryside – had been 77.9 inhabitants per km², with the highest concentrations of people to be found in the area around the city of Bruges (> 84 inhabitants per km²).[40] In 1469, Nieuwkerke, which was not a small parish (17.9 km²), still fell below this mark, with around 57 inhabitants/km², but the village rose well above the fifteenth-century average in the course of the sixteenth century, peaking at well over 200 people (probably as many as 350) per km² around the middle of the century (**Table 1.3**).

Whether through immigration or because the thriving economy boosted birth rates and induced people to stay behind, Nieuwkerke's population growth between the late fifteenth and mid-sixteenth century was probably a consequence of its successful cloth industry. Of course, lacking sufficient records to give an impression of population levels in the other rural settlements of the West-Quarter, the possibility remains that Nieuwkerke simply absorbed a proportion of their populations in the course of the late 1400s and early 1500s. This is unlikely, however, as several other settlements in the region had vigorous textile industries of their own in this period: Eécke and Dranouter consistently produced around 2500 pieces of cloth per annum, the village of Météren around 1000 pieces, in this same period.[41]

Returning to the rationale for these calculations: it appears that a considerable proportion of the rural population in the Flemish West-Quarter was not solely involved in agriculture in the sixteenth century.[42] This was perhaps to be expected, as the amount of land was a more or less constant variable while the population had steadily grown. Even if the agricultural economy had become increasingly

38 Tourcoing's 400-500 hearths and 120 drapers correspond to a multiplier of 3.33-4.17 to arrive at the total number of hearths, which in turn has to be multiplied by 4.5 to beget the number of people. For Nieuwkerke, this means somewhere between 1153 and 1443 hearths, or 5190 and 6493 people.

39 Stabel, 'Demography and hierarchy', p. 215.

40 Prevenier, pp. 272-73; Peter Stabel, 'Patronen van verstedelijking in het laatmiddeleeuwse en vroegmoderne Vlaanderen: demografische ontwikkelingen en economische functies van de kleine en secundaire steden in het Gentse kwartier (14-16de eeuw)' (unpublished doctoral thesis, Ghent University, 1995), p. 19.

41 Peter Stabel, '"Dmeeste, oirboirlixste en proffitelixste let ende neringhe": een kwantitatieve benadering van de lakenproductie in het laatmiddeleeuwse en vroegmoderne Vlaanderen', *Handelingen van de Maatschappij voor Geschiedenis en Oudheidkunde te Gent*, 51 (1997), 113-53 (pp. 138-39).

42 Marfany, pp. 959-68.

specialized, farm work alone probably could not provide enough employment opportunities to support the many new mouths to feed. Anecdotal evidence reinforces that conclusion: in 1545, two former inhabitants of the cloth centre of Dranouter testified before the magistrates of Bailleul that their parish lacked sufficient land for everybody and that 'the inhabitants of Dranouter would not be able to support themselves in the manner they are presently accustomed to doing without practising the craft and trade of drapery'.[43] Although a certain scepticism is in order with regards to the motivations of these witnesses (who clearly sought to preserve Dranouter's textile privileges), their testimonies seem more or less reliable on this point. One of them, for example, supported his claim by providing intimate knowledge of the division of farmland in the parish, a third of which apparently consisted of tenancies under the authority of the Lord of Dranouter.

In Nieuwkerke, moreover, a proportion of the population was at least partially dependent upon the market for their provision of foodstuffs. This is suggested by the discrepancy between the already-mentioned excise duties instituted in the 1540s, and real estate taxes from the same period. Much like the Transport of Flanders of 1517, these 'penny taxes', which were raised by the princely government between 1569-72, were first and foremost levies on real estate, more specifically on land use.[44] Not counting the town of Bailleul, Nieuwkerke's relative contribution to these taxes was only 11.4 per cent of the castellany total in 1569-72.[45] This contrasted sharply with the village's relative contribution in the excise duties on beer, meat, and other consumer commodities from the 1540s onwards. Throughout the 1550s and 1560s, Nieuwkerke's share in these duties was consistently around 30 per cent of the castellany total (see also **Table 1.2**).[46] As we have seen, this consumption tax is indicative of the village's relatively large population at the time. Focusing on the details of these excises, however, they also hint at a widespread market-orientation or even partial market-dependence of the villagers. In 1545, the brewers and innkeepers of Nieuwkerke sold around 75,000 litres of beer; enough to quench the daily thirst of several hundred people.[47] Clearly, as more and more workers got involved

43 'Ende naer zynen dyncken de inwonende van Dranoultre hemlieden niet goedelycx zouden connen ontdraghen zo zy hemlieden nu ontdraghende zyn zonder den styl ende negotiatie van de draprie te doene': RDHIDF-2, III, pp. 605-08.

44 Buntinx, pp. 191-205; Peter Stabel and Filips Vermeylen, *Het fiscale vermogen in Brabant, Vlaanderen en in de heerlijkheid Mechelen: de Honderdste Penning van de hertog van Alva (1569-1572)* (Brussels: Koninklijke academie van België, Koninklijke commissie voor geschiedenis, 1997), pp. 22-26, 235-38.

45 De Coussemaker, I, No. CCXVI.

46 GSAB, CA, Acquits en portefeuilles 809-14.

47 The beer was enough to provide in the daily needs of 203-480 people for a year. A more exact calculation is problematic. Generally speaking, in the Low Countries in the period 1411-1650, yearly consumption varied from 156 litres to 369 litres per person. Between December 1544 and November 1545, the total beer tax of Nieuwkerke amounted to £216 19s. par. Where mentioned, the source makes clear that each *ton* beer was taxed 8s. par., which makes a total of 542.4 *tonnen*. Maddens posits that each *ton* consisted of 60 *stopen* of 2.3 liters each, or 138 liter per *ton*, resulting in 74,847.75 liters: GSAB, CA, Acquits en portefeuilles 802bis (loose, non foliated quires). See also: Richard Unger, *Beer in the Middle Ages and the Renaissaince* (Philadelphia, 2004), pp. 126-33; Maddens, II,

in cloth production and the local population grew, the need for a substantial tertiary sector had grown with it. Indeed, already in 1533-34, Nieuwkerke had harboured no fewer than twelve active beer sellers.[48]

There are several other indications that, in the course of the fifteenth century, a substantial part of the West-Quarter's inhabitants' involvement in agriculture had become more and more negligible. As early as 1428, the duke of Burgundy – who was also the count of Flanders – had endorsed a complaint of cloth workers in Ypres that the local population of the West-Quarter were abandoning the fields on a massive scale in order to manufacture cloth.[49] In the 1460s, the industrial officers of Nieppe and Dranouter also claimed that the greater part of their population's livelihood wholly depended upon textile production.[50] Likewise, in 1532, a draper from Nieuwkerke complained to the Flemish Chamber of Accounts that some of his colleagues were enlisting workers from outside the parish, which was to the detriment of those locals 'who cannot make a living other than by weaving, fulling, or shearing'.[51] Of course, these may all have been exaggerated claims aimed at pushing economic or political interests, but they recur too frequently on both sides not to have had some basis in reality.

Furthermore, in Nieuwkerke, there are traces of purely industrial workers who relied on nothing but their salaries to buy food supplies. In 1465, during a court case over marketing rights in the village, three wealthy landowners testified that they sold the 'poor people of Nieuwkerke [...] corn, beans, oats, peas, butter and other dairy on a daily basis', stressing that a central outlet for these victuals was necessary as their customers would otherwise have to 'neglect their craft and trade' to go and buy their food in far-off places.[52] Another clue to the same effect occurred almost exactly a century later, in a register of certified transactions (*certificatieboeken*) of the city Antwerp. On October 31st, 1565, two drapers from Nieuwkerke bought more than 38,000 litres of wheat in Antwerp

pp. 874-75. On Early Modern beer consumption, see also: Jan Luiten van Zanden, 'Early Modern Economic Growth: A Survey of the European Economy, 1500-1800', in *Early Modern Capitalism: Economic and Social Change in Europe, 1400-1800*, ed. by Maarten Prak (London: Routledge, 2001), pp. 67-84 (p. 82); de Vries, p. 165 (n. 128).

48 A case-in-point were the employment opportunities in Ypres while it was a hotbed of textile production: Pirenne, 'Les dénombrements de la population', pp. 23-28. Nieuwkerke's beer sellers of 1533-34 were a mixture of brewers (7) and innkeepers (4), as well as 1 brewer/innkeeper. Yet some, if not all, innkeepers produced their own brew. Jacob Hughebaert, for example, was alternatively identified as an innkeeper in 1533-34 and as a brewer in 1545: State Archives Bruges (subsequently SAB), Aanwinsten 504, fol. 10r; GSAB, CA, Acquits en portefeuilles 802bis (quires of December 1544 – February 1545, and June–July 1545).

49 RDHDF-2, I, pp. 3-7.

50 RDHDF-2, II, pp. 253-56 (the village of Dranouter); III, pp. 233-35 (the village of Nieppe).

51 'Lesquelz n'ont autrement de quoy vivre sinon [...] tiltre, fouler et tondre." RDHDF-2, III, p. 132.

52 'De zelve drie personen zijn rijke lantslieden wonende te Nieukerke, die daghelicx an t'aerme volc binnen Nieukerke ende daerontrent groote wunninghe doen in 't vercoopen van [...] coorne, boonen, evene, haerweten, botere ende andere zuvele [...] dat den aermen volke te lastich wezen zoude om zulke cleene provanche te gane te Belle of eldere ontrent Nieukerke, want zij daermede huerlieder ambacht ende neeringhe verletten zouden': State Archives Ghent (subsequently SAG), Raad van Vlaanderen, Enkwesten 8606, quire of 20 November 1465, fol. 2.

with the intention of selling it in and around their village.[53] Admittedly, this transaction probably occurred because of exceptional circumstances, namely a very serious harvest failure that would lead to the 'hunger year' of 1566.[54] Nevertheless, it would be a peculiar action to take if the larger part of the village population still lived off farming. Instead, it has more of an 'urban' ring to it, a necessity shared with virtually all towns, where the bulk of the population also worked in industry and trade.

'Very confusing and obscure': the social agrosystem of the West-Quarter

As we shall see, by the second half of the sixteenth century, the Flemish West-Quarter had in fact developed a landholding pattern concurrent with an emphasis on subsistence-agriculture. In that sense, the rural economy in the region bore a close resemblance to that of inland Flanders, where the bulk of the population consisted of peasants who combined work on their small farms with additional forms of income, including textile production (albeit predominantly linen). Or rather, the rural economy may have been more akin to that of the county of Holland in this same period, where farm plots had become too small to maintain a household, thereby forcing peasant families to engage in various (proto-) industrial by-employments – a situation that may have also applied to the Flemish boomtown of Hondschoote.[55] In either scenario, the implication is that the cloth industries in the Flemish West-Quarter were able to thrive because of large labour reserves, as a by-product of the agricultural regime; or what is sometimes called the 'social agrosystem'. This concept was coined by Erik Thoen, who defines a social agrosystem as a 'rural production system based on region-specific social relations involved in the economic reproduction of a given geographical area'.[56] Thoen distinguishes between two social agrosystems for the late medieval county of Flanders: on the one hand, the subsistence-oriented system of 'Interior Flanders', where peasant households were able to keep a small farm through a combination of strong property rights

53 City Archives Antwerp (subsequently CAA), Certificatieboeken 24, fol. 366. They bought 480 *viertel*, with one *viertel* amounting to 79.627 litres. That makes 38,221 litres of wheat: Herman Van der Wee, *The Growth of the Antwerp Market and the European Economy*, 3 vols (The Hague: Nijhoff, 1963), I, p. 173.

54 Erich Kuttner and J. M. Romein, *Het Hongerjaar 1566* (Amsterdam: Amsterdamsche boek- en courantmaatschappij, 1949), pp. 218-20; Van der Wee, I, pp. 178, 187.

55 Thoen and Soens, p. 208; Jan Luiten van Zanden, 'A Third Road to Capitalism? Proto-Industrialisation and the Moderate Nature of the Late Medieval Crisis in Flanders and Holland, 1350-1550', in *Peasants into Farmers? The Transformation of Rural Economy and Society in the Low Countries (Middle Ages – 19th century) in light of the Brenner Debate*, ed. by Peter Hoppenbrouwes and Jan Luiten van Zanden (Turnhout: Brepols, 2001), pp. 85-101 (pp. 88-89, 97).

56 Thoen defines a social agrosystem as a 'rural production system based on region-specific social relations involved in the economic reproduction of a given geographical area': Thoen, '"Social agrosystems" as an economic concept', p. 47.

and opportunities of by-employment; on the other hand, a contrasting system in 'Coastal Flanders', where rural families gradually lost their holdings and were forced to work on large commercial farms held by a fortunate few. Underlying these divergent developments were the different social, political and physical make-ups of the respective regions.[57] Following that same framework, the current section explores the influence of these structural elements on developments in the rural economy of the West-Quarter. The goal is twofold: first, to provide a contribution to the general discussion about regional patterns in the agricultural economy of Flanders; second, and more important for the general purpose of this book, to assess how these developments in the regional landholding pattern stimulated the formation of the textile industries that were so characteristic of this part of the county.

Although there were more fertile grounds with higher loam concentrations and stretches of alluvial plains in the south (towards the Lys river), the predominant soil type of the West-Quarter resembled Interior Flanders in its emphasis on sand-loam.[58] As opposed to Coastal Flanders, the physical environment of the region had not prevented settlement in the early Middle Ages. Already in Roman times, two roads led from Cassel to Wervik, one of them via the later textile village of Flêtre, in what was then called the *Civitas Menapiorum*.[59] It is striking that most of the cloth centres in the West-Quarter were located within a few kilometres of (the remnants of) these ancient links of transportation. Even though the region had many streams, there were no large waterways to speak of, therefore the roads would have retained their value as lines of physical communication during the textile boom.[60] In fact, in the early fifteenth century, the cloth entrepreneurs of Nieuwkerke apparently transported their fabrics to Wervik by road, so as to ship them to commercial outlets from there.[61]

In spite of these Roman antecedents, however, it is unclear when farming became widespread during the Middle Ages in what would later come to be known as the 'West-Quarter' of Flanders, nor when the first medieval villages appeared. The earliest reference to the churches of Wijtschate (*Widisgatis*) and

57 Thoen, '"Social agrosystems" as an economic concept', pp. 52-62.

58 See: *Bodemkaart België*, reproduced on: http://aardrijkskunde.dbz.be/ [accessed 28 July 2017].

59 Frank Vermeulen, 'The Basic Roman Road Network in the *Civitas Menapiorum*', in *Ancient Lines in the Landscape: A Geo-Archeological Study of Protohistoric and Roman Roads and Field Systems in Northwestern Gaul*, ed. by Frank Vermeulen and Marc Antrop (Leuven: Peeters, 2001), pp. 77-81 (p. 78).

60 The Roman roads would have required significant upkeep and it is unknown to what extent they deteriorated during the early Middle Ages: Frances Gies and Joseph Gies, *Cathedral, Forge, and Waterwheel: Technology and Invention in the Middle Ages* (London: Harper Perennial, 1994; 1995 ed.), pp. 57-58. See also: Umberto Moscatelli, 'Le briciole di Pollicino: vita nascosta delle strade tra età romana e Medioevo', *Il Capitale Culturale – Studies on the Value of Cultural Heritage*, 7 (2013), 211-25 (pp. 221-22). Contemporaries of the region also understood the importance of road maintenance for a prosperous industry: Émile Coornaert, *Un centre industriel d'autrefois: la draperie-sayetterie d'Hondschoote (XIVe-XVIIIe siècles)* (Paris: Presses universitaires de France, 1930), p. 257.

61 GSAB, Acquits de Lille 192-93; GSAB, Rekeningen Zaal Ieper, years 1445-58 (non foliated document of 1428; no month mentioned).

Kemmel (*Kenilis*) occurs in a comital charter dated 961.[62] Although the document has been exposed as a forgery from the thirteenth century, a tenth-century origin for these churches is probably accurate.[63] Fortunately, the records on regional farming practices get slightly richer from the 1100s onwards. In this period, the budding cities of Lille and Ypres and their hinterlands, developed into complementary foci of food production; the first mainly concentrating on grain cultivation, and the second more on cattle-breeding and dairy farming.[64] That said, a contemporary record of comital levies on agricultural products indicates that farming in the region around Bailleul was actually more diversified, partly centred on the production of wheat and oats, but also on the rearing of sheep.[65] Contrary to the predominantly pastoral focus Joan Thirsk identified for the manufacturing regions of pre-industrial England, then, the West-Quarter's physical environment clearly allowed for a range of different farming activities in spite of its undulating landscape and sometimes marshy soil.[66] The natural conditions of the landscape were certainly not unfavourable for textile production, however: the abundance of flowing water helped with the washing of wool and dyeing of cloth, while ready access to 'fuller's earth' (bentonite) in the soil helped the fulling process.[67]

Probably of equal importance was the relative distribution of power in the area, because it influenced the direction in which property rights developed. In that regard, the West-Quarter showed parallels with both Inland and Coastal Flanders. As in the Flemish inlands, the medieval counts of Flanders had to contend with the pre-existence of local lordships.[68] Then again, the counts themselves owned much of the territory in this region, and their approach

62 Aubertus Miraeus, *Opera diplomatica et historica, in quibus continentur chartæ fundationum ac donationum piarum, testamenta, privilegia, fœdera principum, & alia tum sacræ tum profanæ antiquitatis monumenta, à pontificibus, imperatoribus, regibus, principibusque Belgii edita*, 2 vols (Leuven: typis Ægidii Denique, 1723), I, pp. 43-45.

63 Albert Derolez, 'De valse oorkonde van graaf Arnulf I van Vlaanderen voor het Sint-Donatiaanskapittel te Brugge (961, juli 31)', *Handelingen van de Koninklijke Commissie voor Geschiedenis / Bulletin de la Commission Royale d'Histoire*, 140 (1974), 431-99.

64 Adriaan Verhulst, *The Rise of Cities in North-West Europe* (Cambridge: Cambridge University Press, 1999), pp. 107-08.

65 From his *officium* in Bailleul, the count received 368.25 *havot* of wheat (*tritici*), or *c.* 67,000 litres, and 713 '*h*' oats (*evene*) (it is unclear which unit of measurement was used here), but also 195 lambs (*caput lamprorum*). The *officia* in nearby Hazebrouck, Saint-Omer, Koudeschure, and Watou show similar patterns: Adriaan Verhulst and Maurits Gysseling, *Le compte général de 1187, connu sous le nom de "gros brief", et les institutions financières du comté de Flandre au XIIe siècle* (Brussels Palais des Académies, 1962), pp. 153, 160, 162, 178.

66 Thirsk, pp. 83-87.

67 For references to streams, see: SAG, Schenking de Breyne 106, fols 29^r-30^v. On fuller's earth: RDHDF-2, III, pp. 605-08; A.H. Ruffel and others., 'Fuller's Earth (Bentonite) in the Lower Cretaceous (Upper Aptian) of Shanklin (Isle of Wight, Southern England)', *Proceedings of the Geologists' Association*, 113 (2002), 281-90 (p. 281).

68 Jean-Marie Duvosquel, 'La villa de Dêulémont partagée par Baudoin V de Flandre entre le chapitre de Lille et l'abbaye de Messines en 1066: cartographie d'un domaine comtal', *Peasants and Townsmen in Medieval Europe: Studia in Honorem Adriaan Verhulsti*, ed. by Jean-Marie Duvosquel and Erik Thoen (Ghent Snoeck-Ducaju & Zoon, 1995), pp. 397-427 (p. 415).

towards these lands therefore resembled the policy they pursued in the coastal heartland of their power.[69] By the twelfth century at the latest, the counts already possessed large tracts of land in the West-Quarter. This is borne out by the earliest surviving account of the comital domain, the *Grote Brief* (*Brevia Magna*) of 1187, in which Bailleul occurs as a centre (*officium*) established to collect the dues from the surrounding princely territory.[70] That Bailleul contained an independent *officium*, despite the fact that the town and its hinterland were still officially part of the castellany of Saint-Omer at this point, could be a testament to the counts' early possession of it.[71] Indeed, Bailleul probably contained a comital residence, much like the *villa* of nearby Hazebrouck, which also served as an *officium*.[72]

As with their 'old domain' in Coastal Flanders, the counts primarily portioned out larger estates in the West-Quarter to ecclesiastical institutions, rather than to lay magnates, presumably to prevent the development of powerful lordships that might detract from comital authority.[73] In fact, some estates had originally belonged to lay lords, but were acquired by the princes and redistributed to religious houses. A good example of this was a lordship in Nieuwkerke, formerly in the hands of one Walter de Fladersloo, but which Count Philip of Alsace donated to the abbey of Mesen in 1180 in exchange for perpetual masses for his soul and those of his predecessors.[74] The abbey of Mesen was one of the main beneficiaries in the region, along with the abbey of Saint-Peter in Lille, the abbey of Voormezele, and the deanery (*proosdij*) of Saint-Donatian of Bruges.[75] These grants have been interpreted as a way to establish a firmer, more orderly hold on the region, since the counts of Flanders appear to have deliberately yielded territorial blocks in such a way that each religious institution only held lands within one of the county's new administrative units, the castellanies (*kasselrijen*).[76] As in Coastal Flanders, the counts relied on their highest officer, the castellan, to represent comital authority within each of these territorial units. That said, initially, the castellan of Saint-Omer held full jurisdiction in the greater part of the West-Quarter. The separate castellanies of Cassel and Bailleul – where the majority of the textile centres were located in the late Middle Ages – were not founded until the end of the thirteenth century.[77]

---

69 Thoen, '"Social agrosystems" as an economic concept', pp. 56-57.

70 Verhulst and Gysseling, pp. 96, 178.

71 Verhulst and Gysseling, pp., 96; A. Koch, 'L'origine et la formation territoriale des châtellenies de Cassel et de Bailleul', *Revue du Nord*, 29 (1947), 5-25 (pp. 13, 19-20).

72 The comital residence is implied by references to consumption *in domo comitis*: Verhulst and Gysseling, pp. 95-96, 100.

73 Dries Tys, 'Domeinvorming in de "wildernis" en de ontwikkeling van vorstelijke macht: het voorbeeld van het bezit van de graven van Vlaanderen in het IJzerestuarium tussen 900 en 1200', *Jaarboek voor Middeleeuwse Geschiedenis*, 7 (2004), 31-83 (pp. 31, 37-38); Thoen, 'A "Commercial Survival Economy" in Evolution', pp. 124-25.

74 Isidore Diegerick, *Inventaire analytique & chronologique des chartes et documents appartenant aux archives de l'ancienne abbaye de Messines* (Bruges: De Zuttere, 1876), XXIII-XXIV.

75 Duvosquel, pp. 397-99.

76 Duvosquel, pp. 404-07.

77 Thoen, '"Social Agrosystems" as an Economic Concept', p. 56; Koch, pp. 20-21.

At the same time, these comital endowments in the West-Quarter differed from those in Coastal Flanders, as the former often came with more extensive juridical authority. This happened in the case recounted above: Count Philip of Alsace gave the abbess of Mesen 'lands in Nieuwkerke and Bailleul with all appurtenances', including 'full jurisdiction'.[78] The same applied to the village seigneurie of the later textile centre of Nieppe (Niepkerke), which Margaret of Constantinople, countess of Flanders, passed over to the local provost with all its revenues as well as 'high justice, middle, and low' in 1245.[79] In a similar vein, by his own saying, the provost of Saint-Donatian still held 'all justice: high, middle, and low' in his lordship of the 'Deanery of Bailleul' (*Proosdij van Belle*) in 1495.[80] This marks a contrast with comital policy in Coastal Flanders, where even this powerful provost merely enjoyed rights to the *foncier*: that is, a seigneurial estate, not a seigneurial court of justice. Grants of the latter kind only included the right to collect fines below 3*s* par., and no authority over physical punishments.[81]

As a consequence, in Coastal Flanders, the beneficiaries were incentivized to keep these domains intact and exploit them as large commercial farms. The example of Interior Flanders, on the other hand, teaches us that where fiefs included more extensive legal purviews, lords tended to focus instead on collecting seigneurial levies. There is a double significance to this. First, the fact that lords increasingly converted these duties into fixed money rents meant that as time wore on, the sums depreciated to an almost symbolic level. Second, it was the taxation of the local population that was central in this system, not the land, and so a veritable tug-of-war ensued between neighbouring lords in order to expand their tax base. To keep their residents on the land, these lords had to dole out extensive privileges. Even more so, because, in an attempt to break independent seigneurial power, the counts of Flanders had started offering far-reaching liberties to town dwellers as early as the eleventh century. Fearing depopulation, Flemish lords had no other choice than to grant similar privileges

78 'Totam terram in Niwekerke et Balliolo cum pertinentiis omnibus': Diegerick, *Inventaire analytique*, XXIII-XXIV. The Archbishop of Reims later ratified the transaction, referring to the 'terram in Nova Ecclesia et in Balliolo *cum omni jure* et pertinentiis suis' (my emphasis): Diegerick, *Inventaire analytique*, XXXII.

79 The countess gave out 'le manoir, mayson, lieu et pourpris là où elle demeuroit et faysoit sa résidence aud[t] lieu de Niepes, ensemble toutes appartenances et appendances, terres, rentes, possessions et aultres revenus, la haulte justice, moyenne et basse, et aultres prééminences et prérogatives, et générallement toutte aultre mesme revenu, émoluments à elle appartenant aud[t] lieu de Niepes': Isidore Diegerick, 'Le prieuré de Nieppe', *Société des Antiquaires de la Morinie – Bulletin Historique Trimestriel*, 1 (Saint-Omer, 1852), 61-73 (p. 64).

80 'Der heerlicheede van den voorseit Proostye van St. Donaes in Brugghe die hier bestreckt binnen diversche pletsen in Vlaendren, ende onder anderen in diversche prochien binnen Bellambocht, aldaer hy hadde ende heeft alle justicie, hooghe, middele ende nedere': SAB, Proosdij van Sint-Donaas 1658, fol. 1[r].

81 Tys, pp. 45-46; Filips Wielant, *Tractaet van den leenrechten na de hoven van Vlaenderen, metgaders de diensten daertoe staende* (Antwerp, 1557), pp. 19-20.

to their own inhabitants, who subsequently gained a more secure hold on their farms.[82]

By that token, one might expect that the West-Quarter developed a social agrosystem that was a hybrid of the two dominant agrosystems identified by Erik Thoen and others, as property relations in some areas corresponded to those prevailing in Interior Flanders whereas others showed more similarities to the Coastal system. The village Lord of Nieuwkerke, for instance, abolished certain seigneurial duties on his residents in 1232, which seems like an enticement to get people to stay on the land or to have others come in and settle.[83] Also, in the lordship of Oosthove ('Eastern Court'), which was divided between the parishes of Nieuwkerke and Nieppe, the low level of rent paid for seigneurial tenancies in the early 1500s suggests that these rents had been fixed from an early date.[84] In other cases, however, rents were still specified in kind as late as the sixteenth century, and converted according to the current market price. These pronounced differences are exemplified on a local level by an account of the abbess of Mesen from 1522, which features an entry that lists a rather small cash sum from annual rents in Nieuwkerke, while several other entries related to the same parish stipulate much more lucrative levies in kind. Perhaps it is significant that the latter all applied to lands that had originally belonged to comital *officia*.[85] Quite possibly, these rents were part of a subsection of the abbey's former demesne land (*Fronland*) that the abbess of Mesen had given out as land tenures to 21 colonists (*hospites*) for an annual payment in kind in 1185.[86] Note

82 Thoen, 'A "Commercial Survival Economy" in Evolution', pp. 124-25; Thoen and Soens, pp. 203-06; Erik Thoen, 'Rechten en plichten van plattelanders als instrumenten van machtspolitieke strijd tussen adel, stedelijke burgerij en grafelijk gezag in het laat-middeleeuwse Vlaanderen: buitenpoorterij en mortemain-rechten ten persoonlijken titel in de kasselrijen van Aalst en Oudenaarde vooral toegepast op de periode rond 1400', *Machtsstructuren in de plattelandsgemeenschappen in België en aangrenzende gebieden: Handelingen van het 13de Internationaal Colloquium Spa, 3-5 sept. 1986*, Gemeentekrediet, Historische Reeks in-8°, 77 (Brussels: Gemeentekrediet van België, 1986) pp. 469-90 (pp. 480-81).

83 *Inventaire sommaire des archives départementales antérieures à 1790: Nord, Archives civiles, série B: Chambre des Comptes de Lille, art. 653 à 1560*, ed. by Chrétien Dehaisnes and Jules Finot, 8 vols (Lille: Danel, 1877-1906), I (1877), p. 121.

84 Often, the annual rent amounted to a mere 2s. par. per *bunder* (3.19 ha): SAG, Schenking de Breyne 106, fols 16v-17v.

85 The rents in kind refer to the 'Spycker' and to 'Camercoorne'. This suggests a connection with a *spicarium*, a type of comital *officium* specifically devoted to the collection of grain. The reference to *Camer* implies a connection to the *Brevia Camere*: accounts of the old chamberlains of the count. Meanwhile, the money rents follow an entry of the 'Groote Briefven van Brugghe', and refer to 'hooftmanscepe in Nieukercke'. The *hooftman* was a person charged with collecting the dues from the *spicarium*: SAB, Aanwinsten 4186, fols 1v, 15v-16r; Verhulst and Gysseling, pp. 78-79; *Coutumes des pays et comté de Flandre. Quartier de Bruges: Coutumes des petites villes et seigneuries enclavées*, ed. by Louis Gilliodts-Van Severen, 6 vols (Brussels: Gobbaerts, 1890-93) IV (1892), pp. 344-45; Tys, 'Domeinvorming in de "wildernis"', 44.

86 'Terram nostram que Fronland dicebatur XXX-ta uidelicet bonaria et unum ita quod deinceps de singulis bonariis persoluent nobis unam raeriam frumenti et duas raserias auene sicut soliti sunt et amplius IIII-or capones salua omni consuetudine quam hucusque debebant tam ipsi quam alii hospites nostri': Diegerick, *Inventaire analytique et chronologique*, XLI-XLII. The name *Fronland* implies that this had been part of a demesne. On the word *hospites*, see: Richard Koebner, 'The

that when rent tenures were expressed as bundles of grain, the tenants were a lot more vulnerable than when their rent rate was fixed, as bad harvests raised the real value (and, accordingly, the cost) of their dues. They were therefore more prone to lose control over their farms, while their counterparts beholden to a negligible flat rate enjoyed increasingly secure property rights.

In the long term, however, the West-Quarter did not develop this hybridized version of the Interior and Coastal agrosystems. One reason for this may have been the sheer splintering of legal authority in the region. By the fourteenth century, the seigneurial landscape had gradually become fragmented, first because of the counts of Flanders's various grants to ecclesiastical lords (see above). Second, the lay lords of the West-Quarter, in their turn, continuously traded pieces of their seigneurial jurisdictions back and forth. In 1215, for example, one of the vassals of Lord Hendrik of Nieuwkerke endowed the abbey of Mesen with a fief-rent (*redditus*) in the parish of Dranouter (*Drounoutra*), and in 1236 and 1237 the Lord of Nieuwkerke himself donated lands and feudal estates to the abbess.[87] Third, the fracturing of juridical authority was exacerbated by the fact that Nieuwkerke, like most other parishes in the West-Quarter, had already consisted of several different seigneuries from an early period. So, a charter of 1225 mentions one Lord Thomas of Nieuwkerke 'alias of Westhove' (*sive de Westhove vocatur*), implying he was the lord of this 'Western Court'.[88] Shortly afterwards, we also encounter the first reference to a seigneurie called 'Eastern Court' (*Oosthove*).[89] The counts of Flanders, meanwhile, controlled a number of additional seigneuries in the parish, such as Spiere and Oudeneem.[90] To further add to this juridical fragmentation: as the parishes usually consisted of several seigneuries, so the jurisdictions of most lordships also covered parts of different parishes. Flash forward to the sixteenth century, and the seigneurial landscape of the cloth villages in this region has become riddled with very small feudal estates (**Tables 1.4 and 1.5**).

While not all these fiefs formed legal units with degrees of juridical independence, the feudal fragmentation nonetheless resulted in much uncertainty and controversy about who held sway in a given area. Indeed, in the later fourteenth century, Louis of Namur, lord of Bailleul, complained how the juridical status

---

Settlement and Colonization of Europe', in *The Cambridge Economic History of Europe*, ed. by Michael Postan and others, 8 vols (Cambridge: Cambridge University Press, 1966-1989), I (1966), pp. 1-91 (pp. 49-50).

87 Jan Dhondt, 'Bijdrage tot het cartularium van Meesen (1065-1334)', *Handelingen van de Koninklijke Commissie voor Geschiedenis / Bulletin de la Commission Royale d'Histoire*, 106 (1941), 95-234 (pp. 181-82); Diegerick, *Inventaire analytique et chronologique*, XCVI, XCVII.

88 *Cronica et cartularium Monasterii de Dunis*, ed. by Ferdinand Van de Putte and Désiré Van de Casteele (Bruges: Vandecasteele-Werbrouck, 1864), CCCLII; Archives Départementales du Nord (subsequently ADN), B 3898/7 (loose *dénombrement* of 28 June 1546).

89 Fabrice De Meulenaere, 'Le château d'Oosthove à Nieppe, Neuve-Église et Ploegsteert du XIIIe au début du XXe siècle', *Mémoires de la Société d'Histoire de Comines-Warneton et de la Région*, 19 (1989), 43-72 (pp. 48-49).

90 GSAB, CA, Oorkonden van Vlaanderen 776; GSAB, CA, Inventaire des comptes en rouleaux : Oudeneem 150-151.

Table 1.4. Customary tenants in the seigneurie of Westhove (Nieuwkerke), 1331

Holding size	Tenants	% of tenants	Area (ha)*	% of area
< 1 ha	13	35.1	7.0	5.5
1-2 ha	7	18.9	12.8	10.0
2-3 ha	7	18.9	18.8	14.7
3-4 ha	0	-	-	-
4-5 ha	1	2.7	4.6	3.6
5-10 ha	4	10.8	23.5	18.3
10-20 ha	5	13.5	61.5	48.0
> 20 ha	0	-	-	-
Total	37	100	128.2	100

Source: GSAB, CA 100, fol. 42.

* These are approximate calculations based upon a correlation of the rent price in 1331 with the most recurrent ratio of rent : area in the nearby lordship of Oosthove in 1505 (2s./*bunder*).

of Nieuwkerke was 'very confusing and obscure' because of the actions of a previous Lord Hendrik II of Nieuwkerke. Presumably a descendant of his already-mentioned namesake, this Lord Hendrik had granted the monks of St. John in Thérouanne (or Terwaan) 'total jurisdiction [...] without exception', during the reign of Count Guy of Dampierre (1278-1305).[91] But Louis of Namur maintained that it had never been Hendrik's right to do so, since the lords of Bailleul had final authority over Nieuwkerke. In the legal dispute that ensued, the monks of St. John retorted that it was in fact the lord of Koolskamp and the abbess of Mesen who held high jurisdiction in Nieuwkerke. Louis of Namur did not dispute this altogether, but he claimed that the physical range of this high jurisdiction did not extend to 'the lordship that belonged to Lord Hendrik'.[92]

And so, even contemporaries could hardly keep track of whose authority should be honoured where, because lordships had become so strongly fractured before 1300. As these seigneurial jurisdictions ended up in the hands of new lords over the next few centuries, confusions over juridical authority continued to abound, sometimes leading to differing interpretations of (customary) law. For instance, in 1505, the lord of Oosthove held a seigneurie with 'viscount' (*vicontier*) jurisdiction from the lord of Nieuwkerke. According to Filips Wielant, a contemporary scholar of Flemish feudal law, this 'middle' grade of jurisdiction

91 'Dat so seere confuus ende obscuur es [...] Dat myn heere Henric van Nieukerke den vorscreven religieusen [van St-Jans] gaf alle juredictien in de vorscreve plecke [van Nieukerke] sonder eenighe exeptie': De Coussemaker, LXXVII.

92 'Daer de religieusen segghen, dat de heer van Coelscamp ende de abdesse van Mesene hoghe justicie hebben in Nieukerke, etc. Andword mynheere Lodewyc, ende seght, dat mueghelic es dat sy ofte handeren te enichgher stede hoghe justicie binnen der prochien van Nieukerke moghen hebben, *maer niet int heerscap dat mynheer Henrike van Nieukerke toebehoorde*, of sine vorders ende naercommers' (my emphasis): De Coussemaker, LXXVII.

Table 1.5. Feudal fragmentation in the Flemish West-Quarter, 16th century

	N° of fief-holders			% of fief-holders		
Holding size	Oosthove (Nieuwkerke & Nieppe) 1505	Westhove (Nieuwkerke) 1546	Dranouter 1501	Oosthove (Nieuwkerke & Nieppe) 1505	Westhove (Nieuwkerke) 1546	Dranouter 1501
< 1 ha	9	4	32	22.0	30.8	56.1
1-2 ha	11	1	11	26.8	7.7	19.3
2-3 ha	1	-	4	2.4	-	7.0
3-4 ha	6	1	2	14.6	7.7	3.5
4-5 ha	-	-	2	-	-	3.5
5-10 ha	6	3	4	14.6	23.1	7.0
10-20 ha	4	3	1	9.8	23.1	1.8
> 20 ha	4	1	1	9.8	7.7	1.8
Total	41	13	57	100	100	100

Source: SAG, *Schenking de Breyne* 106; ADN, B 3898/7; ADN, J 431/5.

would not have included the right to inflict corporal punishments, but the lord of Oosthove was under the impression that 'all those holding viscount jurisdiction may hang a thief if he deserves it […] according to the customs and laws of the Court of Lille'.[93]

This juridical fragmentation mainly shaped the regional agrarian economy because institutional ambiguity frustrated the formation of large farm estates. Purely in terms of landscape, certain stretches of the West-Quarter provided favourable opportunities for the formation of sizeable landholdings. The fact that these potential estates were interrupted by many small pockets of conflicting jurisdictions, however, may have obstructed their physical integration into larger units. Certainly by the second half of the sixteenth century, the landholding pattern in the West-Quarter had become hard to distinguish from the one that predominated in Interior Flanders. But in fact, the lordship of Westhove in Nieuwkerke had already showed an emphasis on small acreages among its customary tenants in 1331 – a trend we can still see in the neighbouring jurisdiction of Oosthove and in the seigneurie of Dranouter a few kilometres away, around the year 1500 (**Tables 1.4 and 1.5**).

Not until the second half of the sixteenth century do we get a more thorough insight into the West-Quarter's agricultural economy, through the first comprehensive overviews of land use in the research region that have been passed down in the form of the so-called 'penny tax' registers (*penningkohieren*), which we have already encountered.[94] As mentioned, these records were drafted between 1569 and 1572 for the purpose of levies on real estate, proceeding from estimated values. These registers record the names of all the people who used farmland in a given parish, distinguishing between owners and leaseholders. The penny tax registers provide an ideal point of comparison with other social agrosystems, not just in Flanders but in the rest of the Low Countries as well, because the Habsburg government imposed these penny taxes throughout their Netherlandish territories. Consequently, most researchers working on the Netherlandish rural economy use the very same sources.[95] Unfortunately, however, no complete penny tax registers are extant for Nieuwkerke or any of the other important cloth centres of the Flemish West-Quarter.[96] Therefore, we have to turn to settlements for which these registers have survived, but which lacked a noteworthy textile industry. While this is not unproblematic, the expectation

---

93 'Dat es te verstaene dat alle de ghunne die justicie viscontiere heift zoude wel moghen doen hanghen eenen dief indien hy 't verdient hadde. Aldus was 't my ghezeit te Rysele, van eeneghe costumenen, ja, naer de wetten van der Zale van Ryssele': SAG, Schenking de Breyne 106, fol. 66^{v}. Compare: Wielant, pp. 19-20.

94 Stabel and Vermeylen, pp. 18, 22-24, 27. See also: Maddens, pp. 342-63.

95 Thoen, 'A "Commercial Survival Economy" in Evolution', p. 132; Soens, *De spade in de dijk*, pp. 85-86; Thijs Lambrecht, *Een grote hoeve in een klein dorp: relaties van arbeid en pacht op het Vlaamse platteland tijdens de 18de eeuw*, Reeks Historische Economie en Ecologie, 8 (Ghent: Academia Press, 2002), pp. 27-29.

96 There are partial records of later augmentations or amendments to the general accounts, but these are insufficient for our purpose: GSAB, Audiëntie van de Rekenkamer 618/20 (Nieuwkerke), 618/31-32 (Dranouter), 618/34 (Godewaersvelde).

is that characteristics on the local level generally reflect the pattern of the wider region. The best candidates for this pragmatic, *pars pro toto* approach are the parishes of Bailleul-Westhoek and Wijtschate, both located in the heart of the West-Quarter's textile region and within only ten kilometres of Nieuwkerke.

The penny tax registers of these parishes suggest that by far the majority of farms in the West-Quarter fell below subsistence-level in the second half of the sixteenth century. Almost 80 per cent of the holdings in both parishes were smaller than 5 hectares, which is usually considered the minimum surface area for subsistence farming in the late Middle Ages. Anything above 20 or 25 hectares, by contrast, would signify a large estate, while the ones in between 5 and 20 hectares are considered medium-sized holdings.[97] Comparing the data for Wijtschate and Bailleul-Westhoek to the village of Meigem, it therefore appears that the social agrosystem of the West-Quarter closely resembled that of Interior Flanders (**Tables 1.6a and 1.6b**). By contrast, the landholding pattern in these parishes was decidedly different from the trend in Coastal Flanders, as demonstrated by the distribution of farmland in the seigneurie of Watervliet in 1544.[98] It is worth noting that this seigneurie – which had been recently (1501) created by the count of Flanders to reward one of his loyal followers – received a formal license to manufacture woollen cloth (*draps*) in 1502. However, in this coastal locality, almost 20 per cent of the farms were larger than 20 hectares, comprising nearly 60 per cent of the arable land. In the West-Quarter, estates like these were very rare, even though they still covered *c.* 20-25 per cent of the available farmland. It is safe to say, therefore, that the social agrosystem of the late medieval Flemish West-Quarter was more akin to that of Interior Flanders.

That said, the penny taxes for the West-Quarter indicate an even greater fragmentation of land in this region than in Interior Flanders, with a greater emphasis on micro-holdings and fewer farms larger than 20 hectares.[99] In the same vein, these parishes show a more pronounced emphasis on peasant proprietors, as opposed to small leaseholders. Whereas in Interior Flanders – and Coastal Flanders, for that matter – holdings larger than 5 hectares were generally leased out, in the West-Quarter, a sizeable proportion of the estates measuring between 5 and 20 hectares were (partly) used by the owners. Also, the traces of former comital domains had become few and far between in the region. To be sure, in both Wijtschate and Bailleul-Westhoek at least one such estate was left more or less intact. In Wijtschate, the provost of Voormezele owned a stretch of land of 105 hectares – although he only used 28 hectares and leased out the rest to various farmers. In Bailleul-Westhoek, meanwhile, the single most impressive estate (measuring no fewer than 184 hectares) belonged to the abbess of Brayelle in Artois – who leased it out all at once to a man called

---

97 Herbert Hallam, 'The Life of the People', in *The Agrarian History of England and Wales*, ed. by Joan Thirsk and others (Cambridge: Cambridge University Press, 1981-91), II (1983), 818-53 (p. 824); Thoen, 'A "Commercial Survival Economy" in Evolution', p. 111. Soens, *De spade in de dijk*, pp. 73-74.

98 Gilliodts-Van Severen, *Coutumes des petites villes et seigneuries enclavées*, V, 298-300.

99 Thoen and Soens, pp. 196-97.

Table 1.6a. Land distributions in the Flemish West-Quarter

	Wijtschate, 1569						Bailleul-Westhoek, 1569					
Holding size	Property	Lease	Mixed	Total	% of landholders	% of surface area	Property	Lease	Mixed	Total	% of landholders	% of surface area
< 1 ha	79	52	3	134	34.3	3.1	67	48	4	119	37.0	5.3
1-2 ha	44	18	21	83	21.2	6.4	26	16	12	54	16.8	6.9
2-3 ha	25	14	11	50	12.8	7.0	14	18	12	44	13.7	9.1
3-4 ha	10	11	6	27	6.9	5.1	8	8	6	22	6.8	6.5
4-5 ha	6	7	5	18	4.6	4.8	2	9	4	15	4.7	5.7
5-10 ha	15	13	15	43	11.0	20.8	4	12	31	47	14.6	27.8
10-20 ha	6	19	2	27	6.9	28.2	0	3	15	18	5.6	19.6
> 20 ha	3	5	1	9	2.3	24.5	0	2	1	3	0.9	19.1
Total	188	139	64	391	100	100	121	116	85	322	100	100

Source: GSAB, CA, Audiëntie van de Rekenkamer 618/30, 618/34.

Table 1.6b. Land distributions in Interior Flanders and Coastal Flanders

	Meigem, 1971 (Interior Flanders)					Watervliet, 1544 (Coastal Flanders)					
Holding size	Property	Lease	Mixed	Total	% of landholders	Property	Lease	Mixed	Total	% of landholders	% of surface area
< 1 ha	9	9	2	20	26.7	11	3	0	14	10.1	0.7
1-2 ha	1	1	2	4	5.3	11	6	1	18	13.0	2.0
2-3 ha	1	3	7	11	14.7	10	13	3	26	18.8	4.4
3-4 ha	2	4	5	11	14.7	0	2	2	4	2.9	1.0
4-5 ha	0	2	2	4	5.3	4	9	4	17	12.3	5.3
5-10 ha	0	3	5	8	10.7	1	11	6	18	13.0	9.1
10-20 ha	0	2	5	7	9.3	0	8	8	16	11.6	19.4
> 20 ha	0	3	7	10	13.3	0	14	14	25	18.1	58.1
Total	13	27	35	75	100	121	38	38	138	100.0	100.0

Source: Thoen, 'A "Commercial Survival Economy" in Evolution', *p.*132; Soens, *De spade in de dijk*, p. 86.

Claude Berthout. These are exceptions, however. Overall, the West-Quarter agrosystem was clearly characterized by peasants who practised subsistence agriculture, or rather, a kind of micro-farming that, on its own, could hardly ensure the survival of their families.

This meant that the lion's share of countryfolk in the West-Quarter had to supplement their small incomes through extra work outside their own (or leased) farms. Now, in certain regions, and especially those focused on animal husbandry, peasant-smallholders like these could nonetheless sustain themselves through an inclusive, communal system, in which the entire village community had access to common fields.[100] But it appears that, insofar as we can find traces of them, the commons in textile villages such as Nieuwkerke did not fulfil this function, at least not in the sixteenth century. In 1533, a few private individuals did rent a total of 9 hectares of land called 'the Wasteland of Eggerloo' (*la Garenne d'Egherlo*) from the lord of this village, but it is just as likely that these were hunting grounds as that they were commons.[101] This lack of common land is reminiscent of the rural textile centres in Walloon-Flanders (Bondues, Houplines, Bousbecque, Halluin, Tourcoing), where an inquest conducted at the behest of the princely government in 1505 reported that only in the village of Houplines were certain meadows temporarily allocated as commons each year following the feast day of St. John the Baptist on 28 August (in other words: after the main harvest).[102]

The implication of all this is that the peasant smallholders of the West-Quarter could not survive without seeking additional sources of revenue. And, under these circumstances, the opportunity costs to switch to (part time) textile manufacture were low.[103] Nevertheless, we should not automatically assume that the rural populace engaged in proto-industrial by-employment just because the textile industry was a prominent employer in this region. It would still have been more logical for these people to supplement their incomes by performing agricultural work on some of the larger agricultural estates. Presumably, this would have been less of a risk than seeking employment in cloth manufacture. Also, although relatively small in number, the medium to large farms still covered a considerable proportion of the available land in the West-Quarter: farms larger than 10 hectares made up 38 per cent of the arable soil in Bailleul-Westhoek, and even as much as 53 per cent in Wijtschate.

100 Note, however, that the level of access local peasants had to the commons varied from region to region: Maïka De Keyzer, 'The Impact of Different Distributions of Power on Access Rights to the Common Wastelands: The Campine, Brecklands and Geest Compared', *Journal of Institutional Economics*, 9 (2013), 517-42 (pp. 537-38).

101 SAB, Aanwinsten 504, 8^{v}-9^{r}.

102 Derville, *Enquêtes fiscales*, III, pp. 176, 186-89, 192-93.

103 See also: Marfany, pp. 948-49.

A dual economy or a split economy?

Theoretically, the predominance of smallholding in the Flemish West-Quarter was a fruitful breeding ground for labour surpluses and, by extension, for industrial side-activities in rural households. Evidence from the Flemish linen industry in the eighteenth century demonstrates that manufacturing stages like spinning and weaving were often carried out in addition to agricultural activities by subsistence-farmers.[104] The penny tax registers suggest that something similar may have occurred in the woollen industry of the sixteenth-century West-Quarter, as these documents reveal that only a small proportion of the parish populations had no land whatsoever (either leased or owned). While the tax registers do not explicitly list the 'landless' inhabitants, their numbers can still be inferred from those entries that solely feature local residents in reference to (parts of) a house they owned or rented. And these people without any land were few and far between. In Bailleul-Westhoek, only 19 householders out of a total number of 343 people listed by name (5.5 per cent) went entirely without land. In Wijtschate, that proportion was even smaller: only 6 heads of a household (1.5 per cent) are listed without any land.

That said, these are very low percentages of landless inhabitants even for proto-industrial regions.[105] We have to be careful, therefore, not to read too much into this lack of 'landlessness'. After all, Wijtschate and Bailleul-Westhoek did not have cloth industries of their own. In other words, while we can be fairly sure that the general pattern of land distribution in these parishes also reflected that of Nieuwkerke and the other cloth centres, the same does not automatically apply to landlessness. In fact, different sources of information hint at an all-out separation of the agricultural and industrial economies in the West-Quarter – in Nieuwkerke, at least. As recounted above, contemporaries alluded to the existence of a workforce of landless artisans and industrial labourers. So, rather than a 'dual' economy where industry was a means to cushion the blow of unemployment – whether seasonal or structural – on the farm, in the West-Quarter the two sectors may have been quite disconnected.[106] Another possibility, which is more in line with the evidence for Wijtschate and Bailleul-Westhoek, is that a large proportion of the rural population in the West-Quarter were not so much

104 Chris Vandenbroeke, 'Sociale en konjunkturele facetten van de linnennijverheid in Vlaanderen (late 14e – midden 19e eeuw)', *Handelingen der Maatschappij voor Geschiedenis en Oudheidkunde*, 33 (1979), 117-74 (p. 117).

105 In Olesa in Catalonia, for example, 11.3 per cent of the population were landless (and 74.2 per cent held less than 5 ha) in the eighteenth century: Marfany, p. 948.

106 On dual economies: Daniel Curtis, 'A North Sea Coastal Area under Pressure of Land Consolidation: Transition from a Farmer's Republic to an Unequal Polder Society in the Oldambt of Groningen, 1700-1900', in *Coping with Crisis: The Resilience and Vulnerability of Pre-Industrial Settlements*, ed. by Daniel Curtis (Burlington: Ashgate, 2014), pp. 181-222 (pp. 184, 195-97); Sebastian Keibek and Leigh Shaw-Taylor, 'Early Modern Rural By-Employments: A Re-examination of the Probate Inventory Evidence', *Agricultural History Society*, 111 (2013), 244-81 (p. 245).

landless as they were extremely 'land-poor', which made them highly dependent upon other forms of income (and therefore virtually landless in practical terms).

Now, it is possible that the rural households of this region were professionally diversified, with some family members sticking to farming while, for instance, the mother spun, and a younger son wove. That the family was the unit of production in these textile industries is certainly suggested by anecdotal evidence of 1572, when a widow of Nieuwkerke specified the different occupations of the members of her household. She herself engaged in spinning yarn for light fabrics (*baijwevele*), assisted by her sixteen-year-old daughter who combed the raw wool, while a seventeen-year-old son wove the cloth.[107] Note, however, that in this example, the whole family worked in manufacture. Nevertheless, a proportion of peasant women and younger men were probably involved in combing, carding, and, most importantly, the labour-intensive spinning process.[108] Delegating yarn preparation to rural women was an established strategy in the neighbouring cloth industries of the Lys valley in this period, as well as in the rural hinterland of the city of Lille.[109] While no direct traces of similar practices survive for the textile centres of the West-Quarter, as we shall see in Chapter 2, this form of rural side-employment was almost certainly practised in this region as well.

After the wool preparation phase, however, it would seem that a purely industrial workforce carried out the remainder of the production stages. This is suggested by the monthly production rhythm in the village of Nieuwkerke, which can be reconstructed for 1516-17 and 1564-65 by using records of how many pieces of cloth received an official quality hallmark (**Figure 1.1**). Admittedly, these inspections did not necessarily coincide with the exact moment when the cloth was finished, so the graph of Figure 1.1 is not a perfect representation of the output tempo. The inspectors or 'wardens' charged with examining the fabrics and recording who had produced them certainly had a busy time of it, as attested by the large number of fabrics that passed through their hands. This notwithstanding, at the end of each month, their records should roughly represent the output over that same period, because the documents reveal that they made their inspections every few days or so.[110] The graphs of these sixteenth-century accounting years also follow a similar trajectory, albeit one slightly out of sync.

Yet the records for both of these years expose discrepancies between the monthly cloth production rhythm and the labour requirements of the agricultural year. On the one hand, the harvest season (July, August) corresponded with a

107 Papin and Preneel, pp. 13-14.

108 Endrei, pp. 16-17, 21.

109 Bertrand Haquette, 'Des lices et des joncs: rivière et draperies de la vallée de la Lys à la fin du Moyen Age', *Revue du Nord*, 79 (1997), 859-82 (pp. 871-72); Michel Baelde, 'Un conflit économique entre Lille et Roubaix, 1553', *Revue du Nord*, 66 (1984), 1071-74 (p. 1071).

110 For instance, the ledger mentions inspections on 2 May, then 4 May, then 5, 6, 7, then 9, 10, 11, 12, 13, 14, then 19, 20, 21 and 25, then 27, 28, and finally 31. Often, the wardens' activities of the morning were separated from the rest of the day by reference to rounds conducted 'in the afternoon' (*s'achternoens*). This was a departure from the original regulations of 1358, which specified that inspections had to be concluded before noon: RDHIDF-1, III, pp. 59-60.

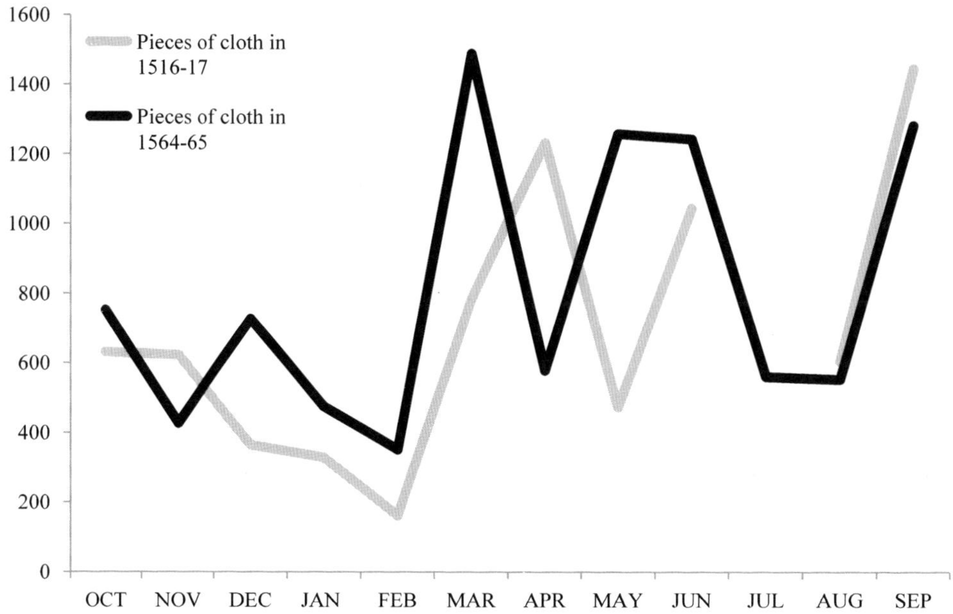

Figure 1.1. Monthly rhythm of cloth production in Nieuwkerke, 16th century

Source: RDHIDF-2, III, p. 209; GSAB, CA, Acquits en portefeuilles 1367/34.

slight slump in woollen outputs, which might suggest that the textile industry was partly dependent upon seasonal labour. In that scenario, labourers would work the land in the agricultural high seasons and contribute to cloth production during the quiet months on the farm. On the other hand, June was the shearing season, and September the season to 'put the rams to the ewes', and textile production peaked in these months.[111] In other words, it is entirely possible that some of the handicraft workers also lent a hand during the summer harvest (which did not require a lot of skill, after all). But it is unlikely that the reverse phenomenon – peasants seeking seasonal work or by-employment in woollen manufacture – occurred on a notable scale. Had that been the case, the inactive winter months on the farm should be inversely proportional to a spike of production in the workshops, yet no such pattern can be observed. Some historians have even raised the question whether it was feasible to combine farming and manufacture, since the high seasons of both occupations often overlapped.[112] The annual production rhythms of Nieuwkerke confirm this suspicion. These figures suggest that cloth production operated largely independently from the agricultural economy and was more likely structured along the occurrence of marketing opportunities (see Chapter 3).

111 'Put thy rammes to thy ewes': Master Fitzherbert, *The Book of Husbandry by Master Fitzherbert: Reprinted from the Edition of 1534*, ed. by Walter Skeat (London: Trübner & Co., Ludgate Hill, 1882), pp. 17-42.

112 Keibek and Shaw-Taylor, p. 246.

Whether or not the peasant families of the Flemish West-Quarter jumped at the chance of part time employment in the woollen industry was therefore as much a question of opportunity as it was a question of feasibility. While unskilled farm work by its very nature offered temporary job opportunities to pretty much everybody, the same did not apply to the textile industries of the rural West-Quarter. The level of skill involved dictated that at least part of the workers were fully educated artisans, rather than opportunistic workers with only superficial training. The production process involved costly raw materials that, if ruined by an inexperienced hand, could bring an unwelcome debt unto the owner. Consider that, around 1500, the average price of the Spanish wool used by the artisans of Nieuwkerke was 10.5d. Flemish groats per kilogram, then also consider that one piece of cloth weighed several kilograms and that the piece-rate earned by a master-weaver probably amounted to only 24d. Fl. gr. – the risks were simply too high.[113] Equally important to the present discussion, there was a technological determinism at work here that precluded peasant households from performing certain craft stages in their own homes. Now, the industrial side-activities of peasants in Interior Flanders mainly revolved around the weaving of linen, on handlooms that were operable by a single weaver.[114] This meant that anybody with some technical know-how, equipped with a loom, could produce linen cloth on an individual basis. But the woollen fabrics of Nieuwkerke and its neighbours consisted of broad pieces nearly two metres in width.[115] Three people were needed per loom, namely two weavers and one person to pass the shuttle between them (although a child could perform the latter task).[116] Then, the production of the woollen cloths required additional processes, such as shearing and, in particular, fulling. The latter usually required the labour of a master and two workers at the same time, and it was usually prohibited to enlist the help of women and children.[117] These technical requirements would have seriously inhibited small landowners from weaving at home or lending oneself to a workshop, as it was unlikely that the farm could spare so many hands all at once.

Finally, on the rare occasions that complete overviews of specific artisan's properties have survived, they indicate that most of these craftsmen possessed no land whatsoever. Out of the ten cloth manufacturers of Nieuwkerke whose goods were confiscated for their evangelical leanings in 1566-68 (seven fullers, two weavers and one shearer), only two owned any land. Moreover, their plots were no larger than 1 hectare, and one of them was simply half a homestead

113 The piece-rate is based on the charter of Kemmel in 1479: RDHDF-2, III, pp. 614-17.

114 Vandenbroeke, p. 130.

115 The width on the loom was 11.5 *vierendeel*, with a *vierendeel* comprising 1/4 of an ell, so the width of the fabric was 2.875 ells. In the castellany of Bailleul, the ell measured 0.693 metres, so 2.875 ells was 1.992 metres: RDHDF-2, III, pp. 112-20.

116 Prevenier, p. 19.

117 Hanno Brand and Peter Stabel, 'De ontwikkeling van vollerslonen in enkele laat-middeleeuwse textielcentra in de Nederlanden: een poging tot reconstructie', in: *Peasants and Townsmen in Medieval Europe: Studia in Honorem Adriaan Verhulst*, ed. by Jean-Marie Duvosquel and Erik Thoen (Ghent: Snoeck-Ducaju & Zoon, 1995), pp. 203-222 (p. 207); RDHDF-2, III, pp. 191-93.

(*hofstee*).[118] Of course, this is a very small sample. Also, these confiscations do not rule out that the artisans in question rented or leased additional holdings. But that would still not really fit the image of an economic system wherein peasant proprietors had to engage in industry to supplement the income from their own farms. It is possible that subsistence-farmers initially combined agriculture with some spinning or other ancillary task in the textile industry, but as revenues from the former dwindled through the subdivision of their inherited plots and the projected income from the latter kept rising, abandoning the farm was a smart choice. Alternatively, these smallholder-artisans may have chosen a safer option, and merely leased out their farmland for a fixed period while they themselves devoted their time to manufacturing woollens. Indeed, many people in Wijtschate leased out very small parcels of their land: some 75 per cent of all lessors leased out fewer than 3 hectares, and as much as 45 per cent even leased out holdings smaller than 1 hectare (**Table 1.6a**). Quite possibly, these small parcels were the patrimonies of countryfolk who were no longer engaged in agriculture, but who were reluctant to sell their inheritance altogether. There is even evidence to tentatively suggest that some cloth entrepreneurs from Nieuwkerke leased out parcels in Wijtschate.[119] Such an entanglement of the two parishes is not unlikely, as the village-seigneurie of Nieuwkerke alo included an arrière-fief of around 40 hectares in that nearby parish.[120] But these connections between the agricultural and industrial sectors remain sketchy. Combining the various sources of landholding and cloth production, the impression that remains is that the two were largely – if not entirely – separated (see also Chapter 2).

Land, capital, and enterprises

Yet, while the West-Quarter apparently had a split economy in terms of the provision of labour, this does not rule out the possibility that agricultural capital buttressed the regional woollen industry. It is still possible, after all, that the rural draperies of the West-Quarter were (partly) financed by capital insertions from relatively wealthy farmers. Accepted: the general landholding pattern was characterized by a predominance of smallholding. But this does not mean that a small number of larger farmers could not have provided the drapers with the capital needed for their enterprises, or that these farmers could not run cloth

118 ADN, B 7050, fols 57^{r}-63^{r}; B 7045, fols 30^{v}-37^{r}.

119 There is much uncertainty on this point, however, since it only rests on the names of certain individuals, and it may therefore concern entirely different people. Examples are Jan Blanckaert, who leased out 0.66 ha; Willem De Brouckere, 0.35 ha; Jacob De Coninck, 3.5 ha; Frans Godeschalck, 2.06 ha; Jacob Godeschalck, 25.36 ha; Jan Godeschalck, 2.20 ha; Cornelis Liebaert, 10.91 ha; Jacob Liebaert, 1.32 ha; Frans Mahieu, 25.89 ha; Jan Trioen, 0.71 ha; Jacob Wicke, 6.39 ha. The Poor Table of Nieuwkerke (or 'Dis') also leased out 1.59 ha in Wijtschate: GSAB, CA, Audiëntie van de Rekenkamer 618/30. The connection with clothiers from Nieuwkerke is based on: GSAB, CA, Acquits en portefeuilles 1367/34 (non foliated register of 1564-65).

120 SAB, Aanwinsten 504, fol. 3^{r}.

workshops of their own. After all, this is what happened in the Weald of Kent in England during this same period. Kentish cloth entrepreneurs were often the sons of prosperous farmers, while the weavers usually held small farms to see them through periods when work was sparse.[121] In fact, there is still a possibility that the distribution of farmland within the West-Quarter was subject to sub-regional variation, and that the actual cloth centres conformed to a different pattern than those of Wijtschate and Bailleul-Westhoek. Certainly, the region north-east of the city Ypres, at around 25 kilometres from Nieuwkerke, showed an emphasis on medium-sized farms of 5-20 hectares around the middle of the sixteenth century.[122]

In keeping with this notion that there were such draper-farmers, anecdotal evidence does indeed suggest that some of the cloth entrepreneurs in the West-Quarter had quite extensive landholdings, which could have provided the capital inputs to fund their craft operations. One such individual was Christiaan De Schilder, who owned no less than 42 hectares of land in the parishes of Nieuwkerke and Nieppe in the early sixteenth century.[123] De Schilder was clearly a prominent draper, as he had 24 woollens under production in Nieppe at a given moment in 1481 (assuming that this was the same individual, of course).[124] As a cloth entrepreneur, a Christiaan De Schilder also bought seven bales of Spanish wool (*c.* 585 kilograms) through a broker in Bruges, in 1506.[125] However, it is unclear whether he had inherited the greater part of his landed wealth or whether he used his cloth enterprise to buy land – a safe financial strategy followed by drapers in other semi-rural textile centres as well.[126] Uncertainty abounds, therefore, about De Schilder's professional origins: was he a draper who solidified his revenues by investing in land or was he a wealthy landowner who branched out to industry (while his name suggests that he came from a family of house painters)?

There are scattered traces of other drapers who almost certainly combined their textile enterprise with farming. In 1469, Jan De Raedt, one of the '*marchans drappiers*' of Nieuwkerke, leased 11 hectares in that village from the convent of Voormezele.[127] The fact that he leased it is significant, because this implies that he intended to cultivate it himself, or hire agricultural labourers to do the work for him, making him a farmer. Another more curious example is Klaas Hessele, who was treasurer (*ontvanger*) of the drapery in Nieuwkerke from

121 Zell, pp. 190-93, 176-78.

122 Tim Soens and I are preparing an article about this 'third' (or fourth) agrosystem of late medieval Flanders.

123 SAG, Schenking de Breyne 106.

124 RDHDF-2, I, p. 28.

125 City Archives Bruges (subsequently CAB), Reeks 305, Wouter Ameyde, Journaal B.

126 Coornaert, p. 365. The land register was composed over a longer period, so that former owners occur next to the current possessor. De Schilder occurs both in the old 'layer' and the new one, which implies that he built up an increasingly larger estate: SAG, Schenking de Breyne 106.

127 His name was listed among a group of *marchans drappiers* in 1459: RDHDF-2, III, pp. 103-07; Bishopric's Archives Bruges (subsequently BAB), Klooster Voormezele, C 167/4, non foliated register.

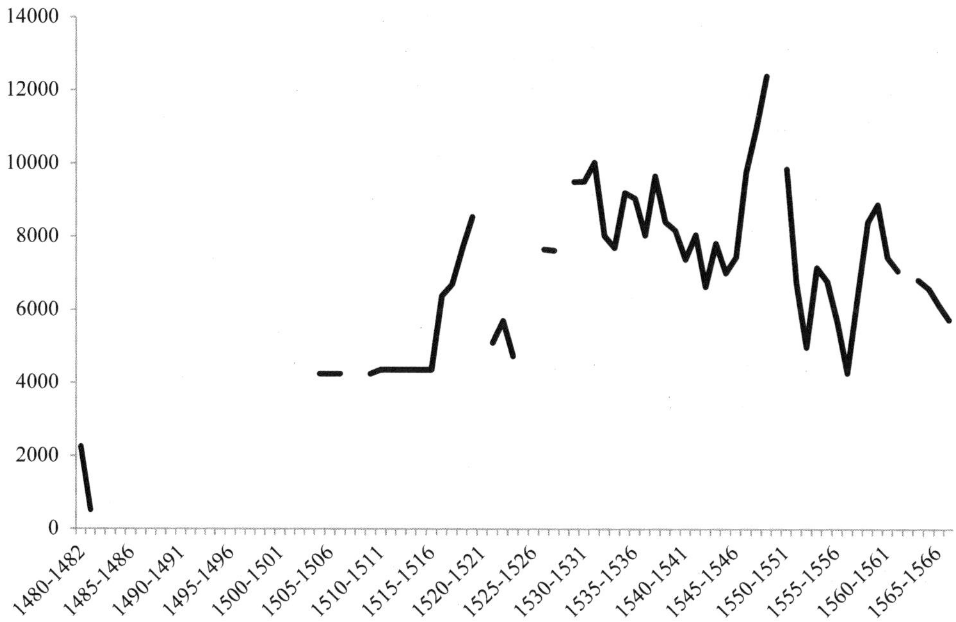

Figure 1.2. Cloth output in Nieuwkerke, 15th-16th century

Source: RDHIDF-2, III, pp. 210-11; ADN, B 4821, B 4829.

1516 until 1549, right during the village's textile boom (**Figure 1.2**).[128] Hessele was deeply embedded in the industry. In 1532, for instance, a draper from the village of Dranouter requisitioned him to collect debts at the fairs of Bergen op Zoom in the duchy of Brabant. Hessele also bought the tavern called *'t Schaeck*, which was possibly a former comital *officium* but now functioned as a locale for the ratification of industrial regulations.[129] Next to these ventures, he leased an additional 12 hectares from the lord of Nieuwkerke from 1521 onwards.[130] Given his extensive industrial and commercial engagements, it seems unlikely that Hessele literally tilled the soil himself, but the sheer size of this leasehold indicates that he should probably be considered a farmer.

Meanwhile, the mid-sixteenth-century consumption taxes or *imposten*, mentioned at the start of this chapter, offer proof that a number of cloth

128 RDHDF-2, III, pp. 129-30; GSAB, CA 44562/1-16.

129 The name *'t Schaeck* is the Middle-Dutch version of the word 'chess', but also of the word 'exchequer' (*scaccarium*), the term used for an *officium* devoted to collecting monetary dues. It was a popular name for taverns in this region and period, possibly because of a chess-board pattern on their floors, but just as likely because these were central buildings originally functioning as *scaccaria*: Corneel Slootmans, *Paas- en koudemarkten te Bergen op Zoom, 1365-1565*, Bijdragen tot de geschiedenis van het Zuiden van Nederland, 64-66, 3 vols (Tilburg: Stichting Zuidelijk historisch contact, 1985), III, p. 1399; J. Th. De Smidt and others, *Chronologische lijsten van de geëxtendeerde sententiën (dossiers) berustende in het archief van de Grote Raad van Mechelen*, 6 vols (Brussels: Koninklijke Commissie voor de Uitgave der Oude Wetten en Werordeningen van België, 1966-88), III (1979), p. 227; RDHDF-2, III, pp. 199-200.

130 SAB, Aanwinsten 504, fol. 8r.

entrepreneurs in the West-Quarter were also involved in the local trade in meat and beer. In 1545, no fewer than 17 drapers of Dranouter featured among those dealing in livestock within the parish, although none of them sold more than 5 animals in total. Between December 1544 and July 1545, 7 of their fellow textile entrepreneurs in Nieuwkerke were also involved in meat transactions. This is a small number by comparison, yet even within that shorter time period, one of these drapers traded 9, another even as many as 25 animals.[131] It is worth noting that in the cloth village of Dranouter, meat sales consisted exclusively of heads of beef, veal, and pork, whereas in Nieuwkerke, 93 out of the 172 individually recorded animal sales concerned sheep. Only eight of these were lambs, the majority were ewes (*beiten*), and only 23 were castrated rams or 'wethers' (*weiren*). This balance supports the idea that Nieuwkerke's sheep were primarily reared for their wool. Wethers produced more wool than ewes and their fleeces were of a superior quality, so that they would have been kept alive longer (which, in turn, made them less suitable for consumption), while the ewes were slaughtered with greater frequency.[132] Presumably, lambs offered the most delectable meat, but lambswool was banned from the industry altogether, which could explain the low volume of trade in these animals.[133] On the whole, these meat transactions make it likely that at least some of the drapers in Nieuwkerke had their own flocks of sheep, probably to supplement the pricey foreign wool with their own. This signals their eagerness to control different stages in the production chain; in this case, the supply of raw materials (see Chapter 2). Another notable difference between Dranouter and Nieuwkerke is that in the latter village, three of the local drapers also sold beer in 1545. Perhaps these individuals were brewers first and got involved in the textile industry because of their ready access to 'liquid' capital? Such was probably the case with Frans Baelde. His connection to the cloth trade can be inferred from his purchase of five sacks of Spanish wool in 1538. But he only featured as one of the partners in this transaction, making it more likely that he was merely a financial sponsor.[134]

The recounted examples raise the question whether we are dealing with farmers that also operated a cloth business, or whether these were drapers who invested part of their revenues in agriculture. For starters, we should be aware that although 'draping' as a craft or trade technically only referred to ownership of the fabric as it was being processed, in practice, it required a great degree of know-how about the various production stages. This would make sporadic bouts of cloth entrepreneurship inconvenient. Yet farmers with larger holdings could still make powerful contributions to the expansion of the industry, namely

131 GSAB, CA, Acquits en portefeuilles 802bis (loose, non foliated quires, covering the period December 1544-November 1545).

132 Frances Gies and Joseph Gies, *Life in a Medieval Village* (New York: Harper and Row, 1990), p. 53; Christopher Dyer, *A Country Merchant, 1495-1520: Trading and Farming at the End of the Middle Ages* (Oxford: Oxford University Press, 2014), pp. 155-56.

133 RDHDF-2, III, 112-20, 137-39.

134 CAB, Reeks 304, Archief van het Spaanse Consulaat, Juan Castro de Muxica, Journaal (*libros diarios*), 1535-1538.

by lending money, or granting credit, to aspiring drapers and artisans to allow them to set up an enterprise. A possible example of such a creditor was Frans Hacke, a draper from Nieuwkerke who was exiled for sympathizing with the 'new faith' in 1568. From his conviction record, we learn that Hacke owned 10 hectares, including three homesteads (*lieu manoir*) in the parish, which either suggests that these buildings were his cloth workshops (see also Chapter 2), or that he invested in real estate to rent it out to others – possibly even to other cloth entrepreneurs or master-artisans.[135] This Frans Hacke also invested in annuities: Jan Rijckewaert, a weaver from Nieuwkerke, paid him £3 par. in rent each year, which may have been a debt related to the cloth industry, or it was the relict of a lump sum Rijckewaert had needed to purchase his own plot of 1 hectare.[136] Other cases show that some cloth entrepreneurs pursued similar strategies to enlarge their income. For instance, in 1562, the draper Jan De Hane lent his colleague Jan De Brune £8 6s. 8d. Flemish groats in return for an annuity of £10 par., for which De Brune put up his property of 2 hectares as collateral.[137]

Perhaps these examples are too limited to attribute much weight to. They nonetheless highlight how the considerable landed estates of certain textile entrepreneurs may have helped them to play a dominant role on the local credit market. Investments in annuities are of further interest in that regard. Not many references to the sale of annuities have survived. But the only remaining seigneurial account for Nieuwkerke, of 1533-34, lists eleven people selling annuities that were ratified by the lord's court in that year.[138] In no fewer than five of these cases, the buyers were drapers.[139] It therefore seems that, rather than investing directly in land, these entrepreneurs opted for a less complicated strategy and settled for a yearly pension. Of course, these would have been useful to finance their enterprises, but by buying annuities the clothiers were also effectively acting as moneylenders.

The problem is that once we attempt a more extensive examination of an entire generation of cloth entrepreneurs, this connection between agricultural capital and the rural drapery becomes less apparent. This is approximately possible for the mid-sixteenth century, by cross-referencing a comprehensive list of drapers from Nieuwkerke in 1564-65 with various contemporary registers of land sales and leases. From these sources, it appears that at least 51 out of the 346 drapers had some property in that parish, but none of them had more than 5 hectares and more than 90 per cent even had fewer than 3 hectares (**Figure 1.3**). Also, only 9 cloth entrepreneurs can be connected to lease-holdings, and these

135 Ludo Vandamme, 'Calvinisme, textielindustrie en drapeniers te Nieuwkerke in de 16e eeuw', in: *Westhoek – Jaarboek*, 1 (Ypres: Westhoek, 1984), 114-30 (p. 126).

136 ADN, B 7050, fols 58, 69^{v}.

137 City Archives Ypres (subsequently CAY), Kasselrijarchief Eerste Reeks 2665, fol. 34^{r}.

138 It concerned *rentes à rachat* (*losrenten*, in Dutch), which could be redeemed by producing a large enough sum. SAB, Aanwinsten 504, fols 11^{v}-16^{v}.

139 These were: Jan Baelde, Hendrik Godeschalck, Jacob Van der Schaghe, and Joost De Raedt (who bought two). Some of the others also belonged to families of textile entrepreneurs (De Beuf, Godeschalck, Zwynghedau).

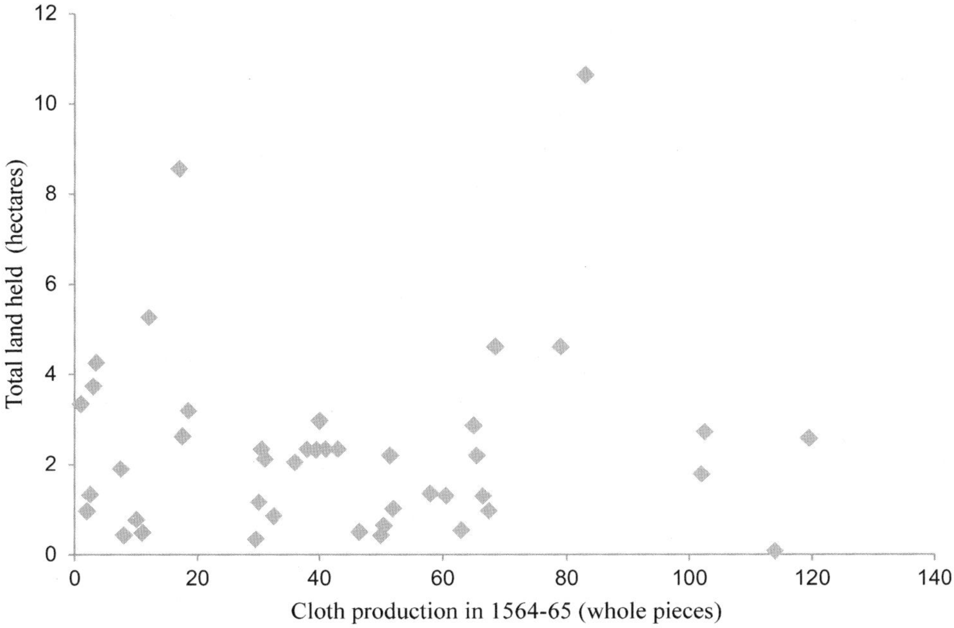

Figure 1.3. Correlation cloth-output and landholding in Nieuwkerke, mid-16th century

Source: GSAB, CA, Acquits en portefeuilles 1367/34; CAY, Kasselrijarchief, Eerste reeks 2665; SAB, Gemeentearchief Nieuwkerke 8, 27; BAB, C 126/10, C 126/11, C126/15; CAA, Certificatieboeken 19 (1563) (*Correlation-coefficient: -0.019*).

were smaller than 1 hectare half the time. These figures would hardly hint at commercial agriculture beyond subsistence-level. Of course, the numbers are absolute minimums, since the sources do not form a closed series. However, if large landownership was common among the cloth entrepreneurs of Nieuwkerke, we should at least find a small number of them with properties of note. But even such notable merchant-drapers as Gillis Tayspil, who mainly resided in Antwerp, only owned a modest property. In the case of Tayspil, an overview of all his parcels in Nieuwkerke has survived, and these only amounted to 5 hectares, mainly consisting of sowing land (*saylant*).[140] The single known exception to this rule is the already mentioned Frans Hacke, who owned around 10 hectares. In the majority of cases, these cloth entrepreneurs only possessed small stretches of farmland. This could mean that we are dealing with a kind of 'residual patrimony': inherited lands of ancestors who had been (partly) engaged in agriculture. But if this was a recurring phenomenon, we would expect to see more traces of drapers with medium-sized properties in the fifteenth century.

In sum, it seems that by the time of the textile boom in the mid-1500s, the rural draperies of the Flemish West-Quarter were full-fledged industries that were largely independent from the agricultural economy. Or at least, this is the

140 A total of 4.1 ha was sowing land, the rest was meadowland (*meersch*): CAA, Certificatieboeken 19 (1563), fol. 213r.

Table 1.7. Customary tenants in the village seigneurie of Nieuwkerke, 1601-20

Holding size	Tenants	% of tenants	Area (ha)	% of area
< 1 ha	30	15.5	19.0	2.2
1-2 ha	43	22.2	63.5	7.5
2-3 ha	29	14.9	71.9	8.5
3-4 ha	27	13.9	95.4	11.3
4-5 ha	14	7.2	62.6	7.4
5-10 ha	34	17.5	242.6	28.7
10-20 ha	14	7.2	204.0	24.1
> 20 ha	3	1.5	87.5	10.3
Total	194	100	846.6	100

Source: SAB, Aanwinsten 121.

impression we get from the evidence for the largest cloth centre, Nieuwkerke. Indeed, in 1506 a draper from that village purchased half a tun (*c.* 74 litres) of butter via the city of Bruges that was presumably destined for fulling cloth.[141] Clearly, this entrepreneur preferred to rely on the urban market rather than on dairy farming and he did not source his agricultural requirements locally. By the early seventeenth century, moreover, Nieuwkerke's customary tenants were still predominantly smallholders. Looking at the sizes of customary tenures in 1620, the pre-eminence of properties in the 1-5 hectares range is unquestionable, making up 74 per cent in the village (**Table 1.7**). While these figures relate to the distribution of land several generations after the textile boom, they further suggest that the drapers of the village had not lastingly invested industrial revenues in land. Out of the 51 tenants with more than 5 hectares in the early seventeenth century, only three had identifiable connections to the textile industry. One of them was a man called Jacob Baelde, who, with four looms to call his own, was apparently the largest textile operator in 1593, and even he owned less than 7 hectares.[142]

Conclusion

Throughout late medieval and early modern Europe, spells of industrial efflorescence in the countryside were often tied to developments in the agricultural economy. Rural historians of the Low Countries, meanwhile, have partly linked long-term evolutions in regional rural economies to the influence of environment and geography, but mainly to the direction in which social property relations developed. The county of Flanders is an interesting case on both fronts, first because

141 CAB, Reeks 305, Wouter Ameyde, Journaal B, fol. 216r. A tun consisted of 256 pints, and one pint was 0.5766 litre, which gives 147.610 litres per tun, or 73.805 litres in this case.

142 RDHDF-2, III, pp. 216-19.

it evolved into such divergent directions in sub-regions that were characterized by distinctive 'social agrosystems'. Second, as we have seen, the research region of the Flemish West-Quarter, where woollen cloth manufacture became an important branch of the late medieval economy, shared similarities with both of the previously recognized agrosystems of Interior Flanders and Coastal Flanders. It is not inconceivable, therefore, that the industrial efflorescence of this region was tied to developments in the agricultural economy. But this connection turns out to have been less pronounced than one might initially expect.

By the second half of the sixteenth century, the structural characteristics of the agrarian economy in the Flemish West-Quarter no longer resembled those of Flanders's Coastal area. Instead, the regional agrosystem was largely indistinguishable from that of the county's Interior region. Between the second half of the fifteenth century and the mid-1500s, a vast demographic expansion put pressure on the availability of farmland, stimulating subdivision and ultimately resulting in a predominance of smallholding – without a pronounced rise of large commercial farm estates. As opposed to what happened in the agrosystem of the Flemish inlands, however, it was probably not the proto-industrial by-employment of subsistence farmers that provided the main supply of labour needed for the West-Quarters vibrant woollen industries. This is why the connection between the social agrosystem and the woollen cloth industry of places like Nieuwkerke, Kemmel, and Dranouter is problematic. The technical nature, as well as the sheer scope and level of specialization of these textile industries, probably required a labour force of full-time cloth workers. And there are several traces in the sources to suggest that such a labour force existed in Nieuwkerke from the early fifteenth century onwards. So, smallholding and the continued subdivision of family-holdings may have stimulated the formation of a mass of landless families, and it certainly resulted in many land-poor workers. But the sources suggest that, in the long run, by-employment of the peasant population cannot have formed the mainstay of the labour supply. As to the possible role of larger farms in the availability of capital-inputs: there are fragmentary references to drapers with larger estates, but these were probably exceptions. When closely examining one generation of cloth entrepreneurs from the mid-sixteenth century, no structural connection between industry and landownership can be inferred. It remains possible that certain wealthy drapers-*cum*-landowners supplied other aspiring traders and artisans with loans to build up a business. But this is getting a little speculative. The textile entrepreneurs of Nieuwkerke, for one, do not appear to have reinvested much of their revenues in land either – although we should be aware of the impact of emigration during the wave of religious persecutions of the second half of the sixteenth century (see Chapter 5).

In other words, while the influence of developments in the agricultural economy should certainly not be discounted, this cannot be hailed as the essential factor in the success of the West-Quarter's woollen industry. The fact that, from an early moment, there were traces of purely industrial workers, coupled with the lack of an obvious connection between cloth manufacture and agricultural capital, points in other directions. It supports the idea that the region was not marked by a dual economy, but that the industries of Nieuwkerke and, to a lesser extent, those of the other villages as well, were largely split off from agriculture. Possibly, the capital deployed in these draperies was increasingly a product of revenues from the trade in fabrics itself. The successful expansion of these cloth industries may also have served as a pull-factor attracting migrant labour, while prompting the reorientation of local people towards an occupation in manufacture. That said, the presented evidence is still insufficient to affirm that the phenomenon we encounter in this region shared no characteristics whatsoever with proto-industries elsewhere. For that, we have to look closer at the actual organization of the West-Quarter cloth industries, which is the subject of the next chapter.

CHAPTER 2

Entrepreneurship and industrial organization

In the first decade of the twentieth century, Henri Pirenne wrote two articles in quick succession about the industrial development of Flanders between the fourteenth and the sixteenth century. The central thesis underlying both studies was that the first traces of capitalist enterprise in the historic county were either located in, or had close connections to, the countryside. The reasons for this, so Pirenne affirmed, were twofold: first, these enterprises had access to a cheaper rural labour force; and second, the rural production centres lacked the prohibitive regulations so characteristic of urban industries in this period.[1] Oudenaarde was the prime example of a town where urban merchants – in that case investing in the tapestry trade – successfully established skewed, capitalist relations of production with a proletariat in the countryside. But Pirenne also hailed Hondschoote, Armentières, and indeed Nieuwkerke, as examples of rural cloth centres whose industrial organizations showed patterns that were clearly headed in the same direction. As he noted, however, these rural textile centres contained an inherent tension between the interests of the individual 'capitalist' and those of the collective trade association. The aim of the present chapter is to pull at this analytical thread first picked loose by Pirenne, in an attempt to qualify his original claim that entrepreneurship in Nieuwkerke 'was on a clear course towards the factory'.[2]

In doing so, this chapter essentially returns to the debate about proto-industrialization. As discussed in Chapter 1, proto-industrial by-employment of rural weavers (or artisans devoted to other specialized production stages) cannot have been the foundation of the Flemish West-Quarter's textile economy, as the production outputs of Nieuwkerke peaked during the spring and summer months, when demand for labour would have been high on the local farms. But this raises the question how the labour force was organized in general: were all the production stages carried out by specialized craftsmen, then? The overarching issue, derived from Henri Pirenne but with more than a small nod to Karl Marx, is to what extent the relationship between capital and labour became skewed in these rural textile industries. If the majority of rural manufacturers were

1 Henri Pirenne, 'Une crise industrielle au XVIe siècle: la draperie urbaine et la "nouvelle draperie" en Flandre', *Bulletin de l'Académie royale de Belgique, Classe des Lettres*, 5 (1905), 489-521 (pp. 504-14); Henri Pirenne, 'Note sur la fabrication des tapisseries en Flandre au XVIe siècle : contribution à l'histoire de l'industrie capitaliste', *Vierteljahrschrift für Sozial- und Wirtschafsgeschichte*, 4 (1906), 325-39 (pp. 334-36).

2 'C'est là un acheminement évident vers la fabrique': Pirenne, 'Une crise industrielle au XVIe siècle', p. 513; Pirenne, 'Note sur la fabrication des tapisseries', pp. 331-32.

increasingly unable to purchase their own raw materials and market their own products – in other words, if they were only in a position to sell their labour power – this would be a tell-tale sign of market-dependent or 'capitalist' relations of production in the pre-industrial Flemish countryside.

Late medieval textile industries have been primarily associated with early or prior stages to modern market economies because cloth entrepreneurs organized the labour force through the so-called 'putting-out system' or *Verlag*. Putting-out has been defined in various ways, but the core concept Rudolf Holbach distilled from many different studies is the 'decentralized preparation (or production) of specific products by legally more or less independent producers – as a rule without direct contact with consumers – for one or more buyers and resellers who provide at least a proportion of the financing or the equipment'.[3] The 'putter-out' or *Verleger* was therefore an entrepreneur who more or less monopolized access to the markets for raw materials and finished goods. If the artisans themselves had access to the raw materials and effectively owned the work-in-progress, this phenomenon is sometimes defined as *Kauf* instead of *Verlag*. The difference lies mainly in the level of bargaining power, respectively of traders and craftsmen.[4] The classic Flemish example of such a *Verleger* is Jean Boinebroke, a thirteenth-century draper-*cum*-wool-merchant from the city of Douai. Boinebroke employed artisans spanning several craft stages to produce cloth from raw wool that he provided, while these artisans worked from their own homes.[5] Francesco di Marco Datini, another famous cloth merchant who was active in the Florentine town of Prato in the fourteenth century, also utilized the labour of a large number of decentralized workers, especially for spinning.[6] Note, however, that both of these men were merchant-entrepreneurs based in towns, and both operated in a slightly earlier period than the one that is central in this study.

As with the debate on proto-industry, it is unclear to what extent the putting-out system laid the foundation for subsequent forms of increasingly market-oriented labour organization in the pre-industrial economy, culminating in factory industrialization. Scholars working in the nineteenth- and early twentieth centuries, Karl Marx chief amongst them, still considered *Verlag* as an interim

3 'Die dezentrale Fertigung (oder Gewinnung) von bestimmten Produkten durch in der Regel ohne direkte Beziehung zum Konsumenten arbeitende, rechtlich mehr oder weniger selbständige Produzenten für einen oder mehrere, zumindest Teile der Finanzierung oder Ausstattung übernehmende Abnehmer und Weiterverkäufer': Rudolf Holbach, *Frühformen von Verlag und Grossbetrieb in der gewerblichen Produktion (13.-16. Jahrhundert)* (Stuttgart: Steiner, 1994), p. 33.

4 Holbach, *Frühformen von Verlag*, p. 38.

5 See, in general: Georges Espinas, *Les origines du capitalisme*, 2 vols (Lille: Raoust, 1933-49), I, *Sire Jehan Boinebroke: patricien et drapier douasien* (1933), pp. 215-25; Hans Van Werveke, 'De koopman-ondernemer en de ondernemer in de Vlaamsche lakennijverheid van de middeleeuwen', *Mededeelingen van de Koninklijke Vlaamsche Academie voor Wetenschappen, Letteren en Schoone Kunsten van België*, 8 (1946), 5-26 (pp. 20-22). For a discussion of Boinebroke's representativity, as well as the accuracy of Espinas's depiction, see: Holbach, *Frühformen von Verlag*, pp. 51-57.

6 Francesco Ammanniti, 'Francesco di Marco Datini's Wool Workshops', in *Francesco di Marco Datini: The Man, the Merchant*, ed. by Giampiero Nigro (Florence: Firenze University Press, 2010), pp. 489-514 (pp. 492-93).

stage in the European economy's linear trajectory towards industrial capitalism. According to that interpretation, after putting-out came the 'manufactory' system (*Manufaktur*), which was characterized by large groups of workers clustered within the same workhouse, but without recourse to extensive mechanization. This would subsequently evolve into factory industrialization.[7] Historians have increasingly challenged this notion of a straight trajectory between premodern forms of labour organization such as putting-out and *Manufaktur*, and the factory industrialization of modern market economies. They hold that, in the pre-industrial cloth trade, different forms of industrial organization often existed side by side. For example, Jean-Louis Roch has recently shown that the woollen entrepreneurs of late medieval Normandy adopted a range of different strategies of labour organization – some more akin to *Verlag*, others to *Kauf* – while their industry also shared characteristics with the 'small commodity production' that predominated in certain Netherlandish cities, and perhaps even resembled 'bazar economies' such as exist in present-day North-Africa and East-Asia.[8]

But this does not mean that *Verlag* and its variations are no longer of interest to economic historians. After all, these were pre-industrial forms of entrepreneurial organization which displayed signs of market-orientation, some of which may have carried through into subsequent centuries, even though others disappeared. Also, as mentioned in the introduction, Fernand Braudel already warned against the idea that societies have to conform to a single economic system. Certain sectors can, in fact, be more capitalist and market-dependent than others.[9] So it may have been, too, within one and the same pre-industrial sector: some entrepreneurs were probably ahead of others in their level of market-orientation. According to Joseph Schumpeter's theory of economic development, these would have been the true entrepreneurs that brought innovations and growth to the economy. Indeed, John Oldland has recently suggested that in the rural textile centres of late medieval England, it was the entrepreneurs that triggered the progressive market-orientation of the textile economy: 'clothiers' growing market power, capital, and ability to divert production to dependent clothworkers put great pressure on the independent artisan who was often forced to work for clothiers to make a living'.[10]

---

7 Holbach, *Frühformen von Verlag*, pp. 17-20. Examples of *Manufaktur* can already be found in the early fifteenth century, for instance in the silk industry in Vicenza: Edoardo Demo, 'Mercati e manifatture nel Veneto tardomedievale', *Reti Medievali Rivista*, 2 (2001), online publication (https://doi.org/10.6092/1593-2214/225).

8 Jean-Louis Roch, 'Artisans ou marchands: la draperie médiévale de l'Italie à la Normandie', *Revue historique*, 695 (2020), 39-58; Jean-Louis Roch, 'De la nature du drapier medieval: l'exemple rouennais', *Revue Historique*, 613 (2000), 3-31 (p. 5). On early manufactories: Eduardo Demo, 'Wool and Silk: The Textile Urban Industry of the Venetian Mainland (15th-17th Centuries)', in *At the Centre of the Old World: Trade and Manufacturing in Venice and the Venetian Mainland, 1400-1800*, ed. by Paola Lanaro (Toronto: CRRS Publications, 2006), 217-44 (p. 225).

9 Fernand Braudel, *Civilization and Capitalism, 15th-18th Century*, 3 vols (New York: Harper & Row, 1982-1984), II (1983), *The Wheels of Commerce*, pp. 247-49.

10 John Oldland, 'The Clothiers' Century, 1450-1550', *Rural History*, 29 (2018), 1-22 (p. 8). On Schumpeter and entrepreneurship: Cor Trompetter, 'On Entrepreneurship and Capitalism: Joseph Schumpeter and Max Weber on the Role of the Entrepreneur in Capitalist Development', *Economisch- en Sociaal-Historisch Jaarboek*, 52 (1989), 270-87 (pp. 277-79).

To examine how the draperies of the Flemish West-Quarter fit into these wider economic patterns, this chapter focuses on professional interactions between the cloth entrepreneurs and the manual labour force of the Flemish West-Quarter. The first aim is to examine to what extent these interactions were centred around an actual market for labour, how that market was regulated, and how this may have affected the success of the rural textile industries. To answer these questions, the chapter begins by examining the normative regulations of the West-Quarter draperies and how these draperies were embedded in a broader institutional framework (sections one and two). The second aim is to determine the role of the cloth entrepreneurs, or drapers, in the organization of this regional textile economy. And so, the chapter goes on to provide an insight into how the power relations between these drapers and their employees played out, both in theory an in practice. This partly comes down to how (de) centralized the different manufacturing stages were (sections three and four). In the final two parts, we begin by examining the relative importance of industrial entrepreneurship in the West-Quarter. Lastly, we will assess how profitable these enterprises were (sections five and six).

Formal licenses for licentious cloth production

In pre-industrial cloth industries such as those in the county of Flanders, the professional relationship between workers and employers was monitored to varying degrees, both from the top down and from the bottom up. But then, even in modern and present-day market economies, there is no such thing as an entirely unregulated or free-functioning market. In practice, markets are always subject to formal rules and informal social mechanisms that shape the quality and efficiency of exchange. These 'unfree' elements of the market should not be mistaken for defects, however. In fact, they are foundational to any economy, be it that of a twentieth-century industrialized nation or of a cloth-manufacturing town in the late medieval Low Countries.[11] That said, persistent over-regulation or alternative forms of exchange (such as forced labour service) may prevent a market from functioning properly. As regards pre-industrial economies, the question is to what degree the collection of informal and formal rules that affected exchange (or their 'institutional frameworks') allowed for the actual commodification of the key factors of economic production (land, labour, and capital), resulting in a form of market economy or 'capitalism'. The present section addresses this question by examining the distinctive *formal* rules of the textile industries of the Flemish West-Quarter, as apparent from the surviving written regulations that guided the production process in these places.

---

11 Bas van Bavel, *The Invisible Hand? How Market Economies Have Emerged and Declined since AD 500* (Oxford: Oxford University Press, 2016), pp. 8-11.

Within the context of the late medieval European cloth trade, an important wellspring of these formal (and informal) rules for market exchange were the guilds.[12] One of the main benefits of these regulatory bodies was that they solved 'information asymmetries', which is to say that they assured a potential buyer that the product he or she considered buying conformed to a uniform and reliable level of quality.[13] The villages of the Flemish West-Quarter, however, had no craft guilds as such. Instead, the '*draperies*' – as the formal associations were called in these places – were governed by, and primarily served the interests of, the eponymous drapers: the cloth entrepreneurs. Although these *draperies* were therefore more like trading associations than craft guilds, they essentially fulfilled the same function to the outside world. For the consumer, quality control was embodied by the cloth seal, a leaden hallmark attached to each piece of chartered cloth, identifying at least the place of origin, and sometimes additional details such as measurements.[14] Essentially, these cloth seals were like a late medieval mixture between brands and Protected Designations of Origin on foodstuffs in the present day. Strictly speaking, they were not brands, because they could not be held on the level of the individual. They differed from PDOs, because the latter are regulated and administered by independent agencies like the European Union, whereas in the medieval industries members of the drapery itself conducted the day-to-day regulation.[15] That being said, it was usually the princely government or the highest local authority that provided this legitimization of cloth industries. To that effect, these governments granted towns and villages a charter, or *keure*, which came with the official sanction of a cloth seal. Charters like these were granted from the late-thirteenth century onwards as a way to protect the producers of 'good' cloth from those of inferior products (who hurt the general reputation of Flemish textiles).

Without a doubt, having such an official sign of approval was good for business. Possession of a *keure* put the locality or corporation that held it in the position to outstrip competitors who lacked the same license.[16] By the second half of the fifteenth century, the charters had become an absolute prerequisite to

12 The most comprehensive economic study is: Sheilagh Ogilvie, *The European Guilds: An Economic Analysis* (Princeton: Princeton University Press, 2019). On the socio-political and cultural aspects of guilds, see: Jelle Haemers and Jan Dumolyn, '"Let Each Man Carry on with his Trade and Remain Silent": Middle-Class Ideology in the Urban Literature of the Late Medieval Low Countries', *Cultural and Social History*, 10 (2013), 169-89; Jan Dumolyn, 'Guild Politics and Political Guilds in Fourteenth-Century Flanders', in *The Voices of the People in Late Medieval Europe: Communication and Popular Politics*, ed. by Jan Dumolyn and others (Turnhout: Brepols, 2014), pp. 15-48.

13 Sheilagh Ogilvie, 'The Economics of guilds', *Journal of Economic Perspectives*, 28 (2014), 169-92 (pp. 179-80).

14 Walter Endrei and Geoffrey Egan, 'The Sealing of Cloth in Europe, with Special Reference to the English Evidence', *Textile history*, 13 (1982), 47-75 (p. 75).

15 Bert De Munck, 'The Agency of Branding and the Location of Value: Hallmarks and Monograms in Early Modern Tableware Industries', *Business History*, 54 (2012), 1-22 (pp. 13-14).

16 David Nicholas, *Town and Countryside: Social, Economic, and Political Tensions in Fourteenth-Century Flanders* (Bruges: De Tempel, 1971), pp. 76-116; Coornaert, *Un centre industriel d'autrefois*, p. 73.

participate on the export-oriented textile market. This is illustrated by a request that the drapers of the villages Kemmel and Wulvergem in the Flemish West-Quarter sent to their local lord in 1468, in which they pleaded for a cloth seal. The entrepreneurs claimed they needed this official license because their fabrics were currently being dismissed at fairs, as well as refused by urban dyeing centres for lack of it. Indeed, Nieuwkerke had been the only village in the castellany of Bailleul to acquire a cloth seal before 1400, and this probably contributed to its continued exalted position around these parts (see also Chapter 5).[17] Similar to what happens in modern economies, however, a potential downside to this kind of official protection was that it could frustrate innovation, or even lead to monopolization.[18]

This brings us to a paradox of late medieval and early modern textile industries: on the one hand, regulation was good for maintaining quality and thereby protecting the reputation of the product. On the other hand, fewer rules meant more room for improvisation, which offered entrepreneurs and manufacturers opportunities to cut costs. The problem was how to strike an optimal balance between the two. This balancing act occurred by default rather than by design: it was the result of a tug-of-war between interested parties rather than of straightforward top-down implementation. Rural drapers had the advantage over their urban colleagues here, because they did not have to deal with a labour force that was organized into craft guilds. One of the reasons why textile entrepreneurs moved production to the countryside in the first place was to escape the fixed wages instituted by craft guilds at the behest of artisanal interests.[19] So, although there was nothing intrinsically 'urban' about craft guilds, they were virtually non-existent in the countryside – in the Southern Low Countries, that is. Perhaps '*laissez-faire* reigned supreme' in the villages and seigneuries of the West-Quarter as much as it apparently did in certain cloth-producing manors in medieval England, then?[20]

To a degree, this was indeed the case. The cloth-producing villages of the late medieval West-Quarter were characterized by relatively loose industrial regulations when compared to most urban, or even semi-urban settlements. This is partly apparent from the limited number of formal rules expressed in the cloth-charters of these rural production centres. As indicated by their small

---

17 RDHDF-2, III, p. 611. It appears not even Bailleul had a *keure* before the sixteenth century. The town had been a prominent export centre in the thirteenth century, but dwindled after 1300: RDHDF-2, I, pp. 497-98.

18 Calestous Juma, *Innovation and its Enemies: Why People Resist New Technologies* (Oxford: Oxford University Press, 2016), pp. 111-13; Van Bavel, *The Invisible Hand*, pp. 235-37.

19 Pirenne, 'Note sur la fabrication des tapisseries', pp. 334-36. See also: Émile Coornaert, 'Draperies rurales, draperies urbaines: l'évolution de l'industrie flamande au moyen âge et au XVIe siècle', *Revue Belge de Philologie et d'Histoire*, 28 (1950), 59-96 (p. 84); Jim van der Meulen, 'Get Rich and Try Dyeing: Cloth Production and Social Inequality in Town and Countryside (Sixteenth Century)', in *Inequality and the city in the Low Countries (1200-2020)*, Studies in European Urban History (1100-1800), 50, ed. by Bruno Blondé and others (Turnhout: Brepols, 2020), 45-62, (pp. 51-55).

20 Ogilvie, *The European Guilds*, p. 548. Eleanora Carus-Wilson, 'Evidences of Industrial Growth on Some Fifteenth-Century Manors', *The Economic History Review*, 12 (1959), 190-205 (p. 203).

number of bylaws, the surviving *keures* only gave some rudimentary guidelines and restrictions (Dranouter, 1473: 15 bylaws; Flêtre, 1524: 15 bylaws; Kemmel and Wulvergem, 1468: 9 bylaws; Nieppe, 1460: 6 bylaws). However, the most successful cloth centre of the region, Nieuwkerke, somewhat broke this pattern. The village's earliest *keure* of 1358 only counted 4 bylaws, but it was substantially expanded to 47 separate regulations during the 1460s. Including all the additions and redactions up until the 1550s, Nieuwkerke's cloth charter would peak at 82 bylaws.[21] On the one hand, these were still low numbers compared to those of other Flemish textile industries – even those of small towns and semi-urban centres. The cloth charter of the *sayetterie* boomtown of Hondschoote, for example, counted 126 bylaws in 1576, and the *keure* of the small urban woollen centre of Armentiéres had no fewer than 227 separate statutes in 1538.[22] On the other hand, these comparisons expose an important flaw in the argument that 'liberal' regulation was the crux of industrial flourishing in the West-Quarter: given the economic successes of Hondschoote, Armentières, and indeed Nieuwkerke, one could hardly contend that they suffered from overregulation.

The pertinent question, then, should not be whether the West-Quarter draperies had relatively few regulations or not, but whether their bylaws shared certain characteristics that were markedly different from those of urban centres whose woollen industries apparently fell on hard times from the fourteenth century onwards. Specifically, did the rural cloth centres share typical regulations that may have resulted in a competitive or organizational advantage compared to the urban, guild-dominated industries?

The short answer is 'yes', and it concerns the formal rules relating to the use of raw wool and spun yarn in these rural centres. Or rather, the lack of such rules, as the crucial difference between the West-Quarter draperies and textile centres elsewhere lies in what the regulations of the former did *not* specify. We are venturing, in other words, into the dangerous territory of arguing from silence. That said, such an approach is not uncommon in the historiography: in his classic study on Hondschoote, Émile Coornaert argued that, as the earliest charter of that textile centre (1374) did not specify that manufacturers were forbidden to work after dark – while this was already explicitly prohibited in Nieuwkerke's charter of 1358, for example – the artisans of Hondschoote probably continued working after sundown.[23] More importantly, considering that the lack of bylaws concerning wool and yarn was so commonplace amongst the West-Quarter industries, we can be fairly confident that it played some role in their economic success.

This relaxed attitude towards wool set the West-Quarter draperies apart from the rest of Flanders. Traditional Flemish cloth industries in urban production centres such as Ypres usually had extensive standards and guidelines when it

21 It remains difficult to count the bylaws, however. And, technically, redactions of specific statutes replaced preexisting ones: RDHDF-2, III, pp. 144-45, 145-56, 152-56, 189-91.

22 RDHDF-2, I, pp. 181-91; II, 346-60.

23 Coornaert, *Un centre industriel d'autrefois*, pp. 73-74; RDHDF-1, III, p. 59.

came to wool and yarn, both in terms of where and how these essential materials could be sourced and in terms of overseeing the spinning itself. One such rule was that weavers of woollen cloth were not allowed to work with raw fibres or yarns which had been sourced from outside the city bounds. This regulation occurs in the drapery charter of Ypres from around 1300, but it also crops up in the *keures* of smaller urban centres, such as Langemark in 1444, and Poperinge in 1567. Incidentally, in each of these examples, the bans on using outside wool either heralded, or coincided with, a relative industrial downturn.[24] The charters of the rural West-Quarter draperies, by contrast, rarely even mention wool or yarn. Apart from prohibiting the use of certain inferior kinds of fleece (such as lambswool) or 'leftover' fibres (*schoorlinc, drommen, vlocken*), for the most part, a variety of wool types were tolerated. The charters simply relied on the judgment and expertise of the craftsmen and entrepreneurs, leaving it up to them to restrict cloth production to 'traditional' types of wool, 'which we have long been accustomed to use for drapery'.[25]

This seemingly blasé attitude towards raw materials may have worked because the West-Quarter cloth manufacturers focused on the production of fabrics that belonged to the middle market segment. So, other successful cloth centres of this period that were of a similar size to Nieuwkerke but focused on higher-quality woollens, like Armentières and Menen in the Lys valley, had far stricter regulations. The bylaws of Armentières, for instance, stipulated the exact types and proportions of English and Spanish wool that were to be used for the manufacture of 'ultrafine' fabrics (*oultrefins*) – the town's staple product – as well as how many finished pieces could and should be fabricated per parcel (*sarpillier*).[26] Careful orchestrations like these made more sense within industries that aimed for a medium-high market segment, because the raw materials were costly and it was consequently more important to monitor them. That said, the fabrics from rural cloth centres like Nieuwkerke, Éecke, and Dranouter were certainly not cheap either, so the quality argument does not hold entirely. It seems that most other cloth charters simply had detailed bylaws devoted to licensed wool as a matter of course. After all, this was an easy way of ensuring the quality of the finished woollens, if only through specifying their minimum required weight.[27]

The main asset of the flexible attitude towards raw wool that reigned in the West-Quarter, however, was that it left entrepreneurs and manufacturers room for improvisation. As long as it did not show in the finished product, using cheaper wool was a legitimate way to raise profit margins. Consider also that,

24 RDHDF-1, III, DCCLIII (Ypres, *c.* 1300), bylaw 30; RDHDF-2, II, CCCLXXVII (Langemark, 1444), bylaws 39, 52; RDHDF-2, III, DIV (Poperinge, 1576), bylaws 5, 6.

25 Nieuwkerke, 1462: 'alle manieren van wullen alzoo men van ouden tyden gecostumeert heift, uuytghedaen lamwulle, schoorlinghen ende dieregelyck': RDHDF-2, III, p. 113; Dranouter, 1473: 'toutes manieres de laines, ainsi comme l'on a d'ancienneté acoustumé drapper': RDHDF-2, II, p. 254.

26 RDHDF-2, I, pp. 102-03.

27 For example: RDHDF-2, II, CCCLXXVII, bylaws 63, 64 (Langemark, 1444); RDHDF-2, III, DIV, bylaw 6 (Poperinge, 1567).

as we have seen in the previous chapter, certain drapers of Nieuwkerke were active in the local sheep trade and probably tended flocks of their own. In no way did the village's bylaws prevent these drapers from becoming their own wool suppliers – for a proportion of the fleeces, that is, because the lower-middle grade fabrics they produced still required the addition of expensive fibres that came from Spain or Scotland.[28]

No less importantly, the West-Quarter draperies further stood apart from most other (urban) production centres in Flanders, in that their *keures* hardly regulated the different acts of preparing the wool for weaving either (spinning, washing, carding). This was a clear departure from the norm as well. The purchase and sale of processed yarns, for one, was a closely choreographed affair in most Flemish cloth towns. So, the separate charter that the magistrate of Ypres devoted entirely to the spinning stage around the end of the thirteenth century stipulated that yarn sales were to be regulated by tolling a bell, and could only be conducted on certain designated streets.[29] In a similar vein, most Flemish cloth centres kept tabs on the spinsters and spinners as they were processing raw fibres into the durable threads that were so essential to the industry. The cloth inspectors or 'wardens' (*wardeinen, eswardeurs*) of Menen, for example, monitored the spinning of yarn for the town's high-quality woollens by way of a separate set of regulations. These wardens were supposed to make impromptu inspections of the spinning process in drapers' workshops (although, to be fair, we learn of this precisely because they had been neglecting their duties in this regard, only making the rounds as and when the drapers declared their workshops ready for inspection). In Poperinge, meanwhile, even the wool used for the lower-quality baizes (*baaien*), which the town began producing around the middle of the sixteenth century, was subject to close scrutiny: drapers and weavers had to make a formal statement about the provenance of the wool and yarns they had used to manufacture each piece.[30]

Just as the cloth charters of the Flemish West-Quarter barely mentioned the wool itself, so, too, were they virtually silent on how the raw fleeces should be prepared for weaving. The bylaws of Nieuwkerke only specified that the wardens of the looms were responsible for inspecting the yarns used by weavers, but otherwise there was absolutely no institutional regulation of spinning.[31] This has major implications for the potential marshalling of a proto-industrial labour force in these rural localities. As the wool preparation stages were usually carried out by women, and as these constituted around 60 per cent of the workload in terms of 'man' hours, this could mean that the by-employment of rural women was the cornerstone of these industries in terms of labour input. Even more so, because

---

28 *Les arrets et jugés du Parlement de Paris sur appels flamands conservés dans les registres du Parlement*, ed. by Serge Dauchy and others, 3 vols (Brussels: Ministère de la justice, 1966-2002), I (1966), p. 578.

29 RDHDF-1, III, DCCLVIII (Ypres, late thirteenth century), bylaws 7, 8, 12, 13, 14, 21, 22.

30 RDHDF-1, III, DCXVI (Menen – dated 1501, but referring to an earlier *keure* that was clearly more than a century old); RDHDF-2, III, CDXCV (Poperinge, 1558), bylaws 5, 6.

31 RDHDF-2, III, p. 114.

the Spanish wool mixed into the fabrics of Nieuwkerke and some other villages was especially hard and time-consuming to process.[32] A backbone of female labour power is therefore a likely scenario. This would explain how the majority of peasant families in the West-Quarter were able to sustain themselves with only very small plots of land, as well as why proto-industrial activities seemingly had no impact on the monthly cloth production rhythm in sixteenth-century Nieuwkerke (see Chapter 1). Tasks such as spinning and carding could be carried out almost anywhere and at any time, perhaps compensating for the fact that they only fetched minor sums to supplement the family income. Coupled with the lower costs for the raw materials themselves, this part-time, informal usage of female labour power goes some way towards explaining the successes of the West-Quarter draperies.

Yet the question is whether these interrelated phenomena would constitute market-oriented, or even market-dependant, forms of allocating labour and capital goods. The fact that wool preparation in the Flemish West-Quarter took place entirely off the record could very well mean that it belonged to the 'informal sector' of the regional economy. This would not detract from its economic significance but would essentially make it antithetical to the development of a market economy, where formal, waged labour is the norm.[33]

We know from other cases, however, that even the extremely decentralized labour activities of rural spinsters could be scrupulously organized from central market outlets. This is how the urban entrepreneurs of pre-industrial Bruges organized the linen industry between their city and the surrounding countryside. It is also how the tapestry entrepreneurs of Oudenaarde – the proto-capitalists *par excellence*, according to Pirenne – contracted labour from the town's suburbs.[34] Within the medieval Flemish woollen industry, the best examples of similar practices were the 'yarn market' instituted by the urban draperies of Menen and Kortrijk, and the competing '*fillerie*' set up by the city of Wervik in the fourteenth century. These markets served as central platforms for a system wherein urban entrepreneurs could contract rural spinsters from a radius of *c.* 20 kilometres to process the raw wool that they supplied, to be returned to them as spun yarn on a later occasion in return for payment.[35] Traces of a similar system do not survive for the West-Quarter. Yet, as we shall see, while the industrial organization of the cloth centres in this region remained

32 Walter Endrei, 'Manufacturing a Piece of Woollen Cloth in Medieval Flanders: How Many Work Hours?', in *Textiles of the Low Countries in European Economic History: Proceedings of the Tenth International Economic History Congress, Leuven August 1990*, Studies in Social and Economic History, ed. by Erik Aerts and John Munro (Leuven: Leuven University Press, 1990), pp. 14-23, pp. 16-17, 21; Jos Vermaut, 'De textielnijverheid in Brugge en op het platteland, Westelijk Vlaanderen voor 1800: konjunktuurverloop, organisatie en sociale verhoudingen' (unpublished doctoral thesis, Ghent University, 1977), pp. 77-78.

33 For a critical reflection: Martha Chen and Françoise Carré, 'Introduction', in *The Informal Economy Revisited: Examining the Past, Envisioning the Future*, ed. by Martha Chen and Françoise Carré (London and New York: Routledge, 2020), pp. 1-28 (pp. 4-9).

34 Vermaut, p. 512.

35 Haquette, 'Des lices et des joncs', pp. 871-72.

largely 'informal', the rural draperies nevertheless showed clear signs of market orientation, especially as regarded the role of the cloth entrepreneurs. Let us turn to this tension between formal and informal, and between central and decentralized aspects, of the West-Quarter cloth trade.

The benefits of juridical fragmentation

First, however, it is worth to pause for a moment and to consider how the rural textile industries of the West-Quarter were embedded within the overarching power structure(s) of the region. This is essentially a continuation of the discussion on the region's social agrosystem as begun in the previous chapter. Yet in what follows, the principal focus is on 'region-specific social relations' as they impacted upon the manufacturing sector, rather than on the agricultural economy. As with the social agrosystem proper, the picture that emerges from this examination is far from unambiguous. For one thing, the draperies of these textile villages differed from one to the next in their industrial organization. For another, even within the same village, entrepreneurs and artisans pursued various strategies to make a living.

We have already seen how a lack of formal oversight could be beneficial to the rural cloth industries because the women and men involved in them were relatively free to improvise and could therefore cut down on certain production costs. Presumably also desirable, both on the individual level and on that of the drapery corporation as a whole, was a high level of autonomy with regards to external political authorities. However, there were quite some differences from one cloth centre to the next in this regard. Strictly speaking, none of these village draperies were entirely autonomous, as they did not derive their legitimacy – in the form of the cloth charter – from themselves but from the count of Flanders or another lord. But the more relevant question is to what extent they were free from outside control in conducting the day-to-day operations within their industries.[36]

The claims of political authority that the counts of Flanders and the lords of local seigneuries enjoyed over their textile centres determined their financial stakes in these industries. Lordship over a cloth-producing village in Flanders generally came with the right, first to claim a fixed duty on each piece of fabric that received the official industrial hallmark, the cloth seal; and second, to collect fines for infringements on the bylaws. We are best informed about the workings of this financial oversight for the village of Nieuwkerke. Here, the village lord obtained all industrial fines under 5s. par. as laid down in the cloth charter of 1462. Because the lord did not hold high jurisdiction in his seigneurie, however, the spoils from harsher penalties fell to the count of Flanders, who

36 Max Weber distinguished between *autocephaly* (acting by the autonomous order of the corporate group itself), and *heterocephaly* (being under the authority of outsiders): Max Weber, *The Theory of Social and Economic Organization* (New York: Oxford University Press, 1964), p. 148,

also retained the right to prosecute residents charged with capital offenses.[37] The shared basis of authority in this case meant that both the lord and the count also received 12d. par. for each cloth seal that was hammered onto a piece of cloth.[38] The lords of Kemmel and Wulvergem, by contrast, held high jurisdiction in their seigneuries. This meant that they collected all fines within these rural industries, and that the entire proceeds of the cloth seal reverted to their seigneurial treasury.[39] Then again, the lords of Hondschoote also had high jurisdiction over their cloth centre, and still their involvement in the daily affairs of the *sayetterie* was highly limited. In this semi-urban borough, the power to interfere in the textile industry effectively rested with the aldermen. Officially, it was the lord or lady who hand-picked them. But they could only select from a list provided by the current bench of aldermen, which resulted in a *de facto* system of co-optation.[40]

A similar situation prevailed in the cloth industry of Nieuwkerke. Officially, comital agents had a prominent say in the village's industrial affairs, certainly after 1462. In that year, Charles 'the Bold' of Burgundy – son of the count of Flanders, and lord of Bailleul – decreed that the village's cloth industry was henceforth subject to annual audits from the Chamber of Accounts in Lille. He also instituted the office of 'bailiff of the drapery' (*baljuw van de draperie*) to operate alongside the village's juridical bailiff. This new agent's tasks included fine collection and the election of the wardens, the officials charged with inspecting the cloth.[41] After Charles of Burgundy had become count of Flanders in 1467, high jurisdiction over Bailleul and its appurtenant jurisdictions – including Nieuwkerke – would remain with the comital dynasty until the end of the research period. However, the bailiff of the drapery was not as powerful as his official purviews would suggest. Although he was technically in charge of selecting the new wardens, he could only do so after consulting with the local council of elders, which was elected from within the ranks of the drapers themselves.[42]

Once we examine who filled the various offices in fifteenth- and sixteenth-century Nieuwkerke, moreover, it turns out that drapers and former drapers not only dominated in the textile industry, but that they pervaded the entire power structure. The judicial bailiffs and aldermen of the different seigneuries of the parish mainly belonged to a select number of families with ties to the drapery,

---

37 ADN, B 5669, fol. 6^{v}; RDHDF-2, III, p. 119. On the juridical rights of seigneuries in Flanders, see: Frederik Buylaert, *Eeuwen van ambitie: de adel in laat-middeleeuws Vlaanderen* (Brussels: KVAB, 2010), pp. 63-67.

38 The lord's right was not laid down in the charter itself, yet in the archives of the lords of Egmont there is mention of a 'confirmation du don d'un gros sur la drapperie a Neuffeglise, joinct la Seigneurie dudit lieu par le Ducq Philippe en l'an 1433': National Archives Paris (subsequently NAP), Papiers de comte d'Egmont-Pignatelli, émigré, T 159/05, fol. 19^{v}. The accounts of the lordship reveal that the lords did indeed collect it: SAB, Aanwinsten 504, fol. 9^{v}.

39 RDHDF-2, III, pp. 611-14.

40 Coornaert, *Un centre industriel d'autrefois*, pp. 76-97.

41 RDHDF-2, III, pp. 109-11.

42 RDHDF-2, III, p. 118.

and usually these men were cloth entrepreneurs themselves.[43] Of course, the wardens had to be drapers or master-artisans in order to qualify for their job, which required hands-on technical expertise. But even the so-called 'receivers' (*ontvangers*) of the count and the local lord, insofar as they can be identified, apparently engaged in cloth enterprises themselves.[44] The same applied to another pivotal financial agent, the sworn clerk of the drapery, who divvied up the various proceeds from fines and taxes amongst the industrial officials. For instance, after his term in office had ended in 1540, the former clerk Jacob Wils continued as a draper, producing 44 pieces of fabric in 1564-65.[45]

Little wonder, then, that issues over fraudulent activities are a recurring theme in the sources relating to Nieuwkerke's cloth corporation. As late as 1577, the receiver of Western-Flanders noted that, but for the bailiff of the drapery, the village's industry was open to monopoly (*monipole*), and 'great fraud and disorder'.[46] The potential conflicts of interest borne of entanglements between industrial officials and local entrepreneurs were well-recognized at the time. At times, these problems were successfully averted internally. And so, when a man called Frans Wicke took over as clerk of the drapery of Nieuwkerke in 1564, his brother and children temporarily managed his cloth enterprise, which meant that they continued to produce fabrics in his name. It is probable that Wicke was pressured by his fellow drapers in the cloth corporation to take a leave of absence while he was clerk, as it was also prohibited for wardens to seal their own cloth.[47] At other times, though, the downside of the industry's practical independence from outside control became readily apparent. In 1546, for example, the lady of Nieuwkerke had to resort to a lawsuit before the Great Council of Mechelen – the supreme court of the Habsburg Low Countries – to get her local receiver to relinquish the seigneurial revenues and financial records of the village.[48]

This independence in all but name was facilitated by the West-Quarter's juridical fragmentation (see Chapter 1). While the official nucleus of each rural cloth centre was the village square, which usually hosted the cloth hall and seal house, it was the parish that was the official administrative unit according to the cloth charter. And as we have seen, the parishes of the West-Quarter usually encompassed more than one, often several lordships. Since drapers and artisans could reside in any one of these lordships as long as it belonged to the proper parish, they could sometimes ignore the bylaws of the *keure* with impunity. The

43 Hubert Masquelin and Ludo Vandamme, 'De familie Tayspil als spiegel van de geschiedenis van Nieuwkerke tijdens de 16de eeuw', in *Histories van Heuvelland: bijdragen ter herinnering aan Hubert Masquelin*, ed. by Koen Baert and others (Heuvelland: VVV Heuvelland, 2011), pp. 157-68 (pp. 162-66). In 1553, five of the village aldermen of Nieuwkerke were drapers: RDHDF-2, III, pp. 160-62.

44 For instance: RDHDF-2, III, pp. 199-200.

45 GSAB, CA 44562/6-7; CA, Acquits en portefeuilles 1367.

46 'Grande fraulde et desordre': ADN, B 18118, document of 23 February 1577. Cases of fraud were usually related to counterfeit cloth seals, SAB, Aanwinsten 504, fol. 9^{v}; GSAB, CA 44562/15.

47 In 1564-65, he himself produced 10.5 pieces; his children produced 4, and his brother 43.5 (but all in his name): GSAB, CA, Acquits en portefeuilles 1367; RDHDF-2, III, pp. 134-36.

48 Smidt, *Chronologische lijsten van de geëxtendeerde sententiën*, IV, DCCLXXVI (17 July 1546).

1460 cloth charter of Nieppe tried to address this problem by stipulating that any incurred industrial fines would fall to the lordship where the transgressor lived.[49] However, Flemish seigneuries often cut across two or more different parishes as well. This meant that resident cloth entrepreneurs were free to choose in which parish they wanted to receive their hallmarks. One such example was the seigneurie of Inghelant ('England'), on the borders between the parishes of Nieppe and Nieuwkerke.[50] Theoretically, Inghelant's inhabitants could seal their cloth in either one or both of these parishes, according to their wishes at a given moment. Perhaps it is no coincidence that the seigneurie of Inghelant was held in fief by the Tayspil family, which counted several generations of prominent cloth entrepreneurs. Nor would it come as a surprise that a great number of weavers apparently lived along the *Lange Horsmolenstraat*, a street that extended from the village of Nieuwkerke into this seigneurie.[51]

Seigneurial lords, for their part, could profit from the rural cloth industries by collecting the fiscal duties on the cloth seals. Towards the end of the fifteenth century, such textile taxes were among the few seigneurial rights that remained lucrative in Flanders (with the obvious exception of rights to land).[52] For one thing, this meant that lords had a vested interest in the production output of their local industries (see Chapter 5). For another, it meant that it was not uncommon for lords to engage in a tug-of-war over these cloth taxes. So, the lady abbess of Mesen filed a complaint with the highest financial officer of Flanders in 1515, stating that the lord of Nieuwkerke had allowed, and even encouraged, the drapers from one of her seigneuries to seal their fabrics in his village. She was fighting a losing battle, however, as the seigneurie in question was partly located within the parish of Nieuwkerke, and Nieuwkerke's cloth charter clearly specified that all fabrics manufactured within that parish were entitled to a seal in the village.[53] In other cases, the competition over textiles was subsumed into a wider struggle over seigneurial rights. Thus, in 1539, one Pieter Martin, bailiff of the drapery of Nieuwkerke, confiscated a piece of woollen cloth from the home of a certain draper living in the lordship of Spiere, on the charge that it had been woven from non-regulation wool. The lord of Spiere consequently sued Martin before the Council of Flanders for depriving him of the spoils of his seigneurial jurisdiction. The Council ruled in favour of the plaintiff, and the bailiff had to return the piece of cloth to the lord of Spiere.[54]

---

49 RDHDF-2, III, pp. 233-35.

50 SAG, Schenking de Breyne 106, fol. 1^{v}.

51 Masquelin and Vandamme, 'De familie Tayspil als spiegel', pp. 162-165. In an overview of the year 1564, six members of the Tayspil family are listed as drapers: GSAB, CA, Acquits en portefeuilles 1367. During the 1580s, several drapers still lived in the seigneurie of Inghelant, such as Frans De Kersghieter, who was an alderman in 1586-98 and possessed three looms in 1593. CAY, Kasselrijarchief, Eerste Reeks 2655, fols 44^{v}, 46^{r}, 52^{r}, 54^{v}, 56^{v}-57^{r}, 60^{r}, 63^{v}; RDHDF-2, III, pp. 216-19. See also: Robert Passchier, *Memorieboek Nieuwkerke* (Nieuwkerke, 1943), manuscript.

52 Erik Thoen, *Landbouwekonomie en bevolking in Vlaanderen gedurende de late Middeleeuwen en het begin van de Moderne Tijden. Testregio: de kasselrijen en van Oudenaarde en Aalst (eind 13de – eerste helft 16de eeuw)* (Leuven: Belgisch centrum voor landelijke geschiedenis, 1988), pp. 605-12.

53 RDHDF-2, III, pp. 112-20, 250-51.

54 RDHDF-2, III, 137-39.

Traces of decentralized cloth production

The rural cloth entrepreneurs of the Flemish West-Quarter may have benefited from the region's juridical fragmentation because it led to a high degree of practical independence. And the absence of craft guilds technically enabled these entrepreneurs to engage professionally with local artisans without the 'interference' of the latter's extra-economic bargaining power. However, it is still not clear to what extent this translated into a manufacturing sector where labour power was predominantly exchanged via the market, nor whether the West-Quarter drapers were able to accumulate large amounts of capital in the process. These questions can best be answered by examining the ways in which the rural cloth enterprises were set up, among other things by focusing on how the drapers solicited artisanal labour, where these artisans worked, how high the production volumes were, and how skewed the power relations between workers and employers were. The historiography on textile production in the pre-industrial countryside mainly emphasizes these issues relating to labour organization and the internal power balance. Rudolf Holbach, for example, has noted that there were many potential economic boons to decentralized forms of industrial organization. However, he adds that the important question to ask is who was able to exploit these advantages and how.[55]

The answer to this question is not self-evident for the pre-industrial Flemish West-Quarter, primarily because the normative sources are not always in agreement with what can be deduced from other records. As we have seen, labour relations within these textile centres were officially laid down in the bylaws of the cloth charters. It appears that these regulations were chiefly meant to ensure that the different production stages were carried out by separate craft groups. This probably derived from the ideological context of the Flemish towns, where the different stages of woollen cloth production were the exclusive prerogative of members of the craft guilds. From the fourteenth century onwards, the urban governments and craft guilds in the Low Countries further consolidated this division of labour by prohibiting (partnerships of) entrepreneurs from controlling several production stages.[56] After 1462, similar regulations were imposed upon the drapers of Nieuwkerke, who were explicitly banned from combining their enterprises with more than one craft stage and were precluded from dyeing their own cloth altogether.[57] Because of this, entrepreneurs were forced to continuously buy the labour power of more or less independent artisans. But these restrictions were also intended to prevent drapers from achieving the 'vertical integration'

55 Rudolf Holbach, 'Some Remarks on the Role of "Putting-Out" in Flemish and Northwest European Cloth Production', in *La draperie ancienne des Pays-Bas: débouchés et stratégies de survie*, ed. by Marc Boone and Walter Prevenier (Leuven: Garant, 1993), pp. 207-49 (pp. 248-49).

56 Holbach, 'Some remarks', pp. 223-25. See also: Tine De Moor, 'The Silent Revolution: A New Perspective on the Emergence of Commons, Guilds, and Other Forms of Corporate Collective Action in Western Europe', *International Review of Social History*, 53, Supplement 16: The Return of the Guilds (2008), 179-212.

57 RDHDF-2, III, pp. 103-07. See also: Van der Meulen, 'Get Rich and Try Dyeing', pp. 53-54.

of their cloth operations, which is to say that they were unable to control the entire production process. In a similar vein, Flemish cloth charters of this period often imposed a maximum number of tools or limits on production outputs per operation, thereby stimulating decentralized production. This, too, went into effect in Nieuwkerke after 1462.[58] As a consequence, large workshops with on-site production chains were essentially banned from the village.

If the intention of government regulations against centralized cloth production and vertical integration was to protect the artisans, putting-out was the entrepreneurs' response to these restrictions on their operations. Ironically, these attempts to curb the formation of larger enterprises could indirectly contribute to the superior economic position of wealthy entrepreneurs. As a response to increasing regulations, entrepreneurs enlisted artisans from outside the urban community. The cloth charters did not apply to these rural workers, and so contracting them served to undercut members of the urban craft guilds. This decentralized form of textile production was a potential threat to town governments and craft associations in various parts of pre-industrial Europe. Some urban corporations were able to channel the decentralization to their benefit, but others had a harder time of it. The city of Rouen in Normandy, for instance, created a new institution called the 'foreign drapery' (*draperie foraine*) in the fifteenth century, which enabled the urban government to levy taxes on extra-mural industrial activities and exert control over it in general. In Flanders, the aforementioned rural yarn market created at the initiative of the draperies of Menen and Kortrijk fulfilled a similar function, as it ensured that urban entrepreneurs could dip into the cheap labour pool of rural spinsters.[59]

The urban craft associations of the Flemish city of Ypres were less successful, however, which had important consequences for the rural cloth centres in the West-Quarter. In fact, putting-out by urban drapers from Ypres may have been instrumental in the initial expansion of textile industries in the West-Quarter villages. Such is at least suggested by a series of complaints and strikes against rural cloth production, most notably in 1428. These protests stemmed from within the ranks of the craftsmen and -women of Ypres, and *not* from the urban drapers or cloth merchants.[60] Presumably, the discontentment among these workers was a consequence of direct competition with rural weavers, fullers and others. In other words, the urban protesters were vying for a chance of employment with the same group of entrepreneurs. These entrepreneurs, by

58 RDHDF-2, III, pp. 103-07; I, pp. 102-17.

59 Jean-Louis Roch, 'Entre draperie rurale et draperie urbaine? La draperie foraine de Rouen à la fin du Moyen Âge', *Annales de Normandie*, 48 (1998), 211-30 (pp. 225-26); Haquette, 'Des lices et des joncs', p. 871; Holbach, *Frühformen von Verlag*, p. 61.

60 Olivier van Dixmude (?), *Merkwaerdige gebeurtenissen, vooral in Vlaenderen en Brabant, en ook aengrenzende landstreken, van 1377 tot 1443: letterlyk gevolgd naer het oorspronkelyk onuitgegeven en titelloos handschrift van Olivier van Dixmude*, ed. by Jean-Jacques Lambin (Ypres: Lambin, 1835), pp. 119-22. See also the explicit reference to the consequences of rural drapery for Ypres' inhabitants: those mentioned were the 'tisserans, foulons et leurs femmes et enfants'. So, again, not the drapers: RDHDF-2, I, p. 4.

contrast, were spoilt for choice when it came to hiring labour. This suggests that the textile industries of the rural West-Quarter partly took off through a kind of medieval 'offshoring' initiated by the urban entrepreneurs of Ypres: an industrial reorientation towards the unconstrained and cheaper labour pool of the countryside. As a reaction, and building on the political influence of the craft guilds, the urban corporations of Ypres acquired privileges in 1357 and 1428 which forbade all activities related to export-oriented drapery within three miles of the city.[61] If these charters were not entirely successful in banning the city drapers from putting-out in the countryside, they failed dismally at weeding out entrepreneurial activities among the local populations.[62] Indeed, it hardly seems a coincidence that the drapers of Nieuwkerke acquired their first cloth charter in 1359, shortly after Ypres' 1357 privilege. These rural entrepreneurs were unhindered by politically empowered craft associations. For a long time, they were not limited by regulations that prevented the accumulation of different craft stages either. The fact that this changed in the second half of the fifteenth century, not only in Nieuwkerke but also in Dranouter, and that nearly all the village industries simultaneously adopted bylaws that forbade entrepreneurs from contracting labour from outside the parish, is a sure sign that these rural cloth centres were becoming ever more 'urban' in the course of their success.[63]

So the village industries of the West-Quarter did not immediately gravitate towards *Verlag* as a key form of labour organization in the same way that their urban counterparts did. But decentralized production became more and more frequent after the village industries were officially enfranchised in the second half of the fifteenth century. In Nieuwkerke, for example, a certain Franse Coene 'was allowed to finish weaving a woollen cloth in his possession which belonged to Joris Godeschalck' in 1481.[64] The specification 'in his possession' suggests that he was currently working on it in his own home. Other evidence of putting-out can be found in a report drafted by agents of the count of Flanders in 1502 after they had seized illegal fabrics in the village of Kemmel. They referred to several woollens – some still on the loom – found in the homes (*ostel*) of such and such, but belonging to other people, including to one fuller (*follain*).[65] This clearly indicates decentralized production. Note that in these examples, the cloth did not belong to the workers themselves, which indicates that we are dealing with *Verlag* rather than *Kauf*. Indeed, a passage in Dranouter's cloth charter of 1473 refers to weavers 'weaving for wages' (*loyer de son tissaige*) rather than operating

61 RDHDF-2, I, pp. 3-7; RDHDF-1, III, pp. 777-81.

62 The drapers that were convicted for acting against the charter, insofar as they can be identified, appear to largely belong to families who had a history of residing in Nieuwkerke. Examples are the De Bac, Van der Donck, Haghebaert, De Hooghe, De Raedt, Tayspil: RDHDF-2, I, pp. 7-15, 24-28, 32-54. Connections with Nieuwkerke are based upon a register of tenants of the seigneurie of Westhove in 1331: GSAB, CA 100, fol. 42.

63 RDHDF-1, III, 59-60; RDHDF-2, II, pp. 253-56

64 'Franse Coene es gheconsenteirt te moghen afweven een laken dat hy heift, toebehorende Joris Godscalc': RDHDF-2, I, p. 26.

65 RDHDF-2, I, p. 87.

as the independent owners of the raw materials, as one would expect with *Kauf*. Then again, the 1479 cloth charter of Kemmel established piece rates for weaving and fulling. This suggests that the nature of labour organization may have differed from one West-Quarter village to the next.[66]

From the perspective of the cloth entrepreneurs, an important prerequisite to reap the full benefit of putting-out was that they – and they alone – had sole access to the markets for raw materials and finished products. This would make the late medieval West-Quarter textile sector more market-oriented or 'capitalist', since it would mean that workers were separated from the means of production and only had their labour power to bargain with. As we have already seen, however, a common denominator between the West-Quarter draperies was that the procurement of wool was hardly regulated at all; a characteristic that continued to define the region's cloth industry until the very end of the research period. Technically, therefore, not only drapers but also weavers, fullers and other artisans could possess and process their own wool. This may hint at a different form of industrial organization, one less sloped towards the primacy of the drapers.

Still, while the evidence is inconclusive on this point, it is skewed in favour of a market for raw materials and finished products that was relatively inaccessible to the artisans. The competitive advantage to produce better cloth clearly resided with those who could tap into the better fleeces, and these had to be imported. In theory, these commodities were available to all, as some international merchants plied their trade in the hinterland of Ypres, including in villages like Kemmel.[67] However, the Spanish and Scottish wool used for the better fabrics of Nieuwkerke, Dranouter and Eécke were expensive materials. Around the year 1500, drapers from these villages bought fleeces from Spanish merchants in Bruges that cost a minimum of 20d. Flemish groats per *naghel*.[68] These fleeces were sold by the bale, each weighing around 30 *naghel*, which amounts to a minimum of £2 10s. Flemish groats per transaction. Based on the piece rates earned by artisans of Kemmel in 1479, a master-fuller would have had to save up his entire earnings for 17 pieces of cloth to get hold of such a sum, while a master-weaver even had to

66 RDHDF-2, II, p. 255. De Sagher put forward that this indicated an organization 'au base capitaliste'. However, there is the possibility that *loyer* refers to applying a seal indicating poor quality, as a form of punishment: 'Item, seront tenus les tisserans de bien et loyaulment tistre les draps sans les fourmanier, sur l'amende du loyer de son tissaige ou aultrement a la correction des eswardeurs': RDHDF-2, II, pp. 252, 255. For Kemmel's charter, see: RDHDF-2, III, pp. 614-17.

67 Diego de Miranda, a Spanish merchant, sold Spanish wool in Ypres and 'Yperambacht, Waestene ende Waestenambacht'. In 1533, some drapers from Kemmel testified that he was known as such in Kemmel and in the countryside surrounding the city of Ypres: State Archives Ghent (subsequently SAG), Raad van Vlaanderen, Enkwesten 3756.

68 According to a sixteenth-century trading manual, 1 *nagel* in Bruges weighed 6 pounds, or 2.7834 kg: Anonymous, *Handel Buch, darin angezeigt wird, welcher Gestalt inn den den fürnembsten Hendelstetten Europa, allerley Wahren anfencklich kaufft, dieselvig wider mit nutz verkaufft, wie die Wechsel gemacht, ßfund, Ellen, unnd Muntz uberal verglichen, und zu welcher Zeit die Merckten gewonlich gehalten werden* (Nuremberg, 1558), fol. 13.

finish 25 cloths to earn this much – the equivalent of 3250 work hours![69] Clearly then, in practice, the better wool was only available to wealthy merchants and entrepreneurs, who may have subsequently 'put it out' to craftsmen.

Of course, inland varieties of wool were more readily available, and cheaper as well. Because of this, some artisans may have owned the raw materials to produce lower-grade fabrics. We know that the rural cloth centres in the West-Quarter also produced such cheaper textiles, in which the proportion of locally sourced wool would have been higher.[70] Unfortunately, the sources do not provide an insight into the sale and use of these local fleeces. As recounted in Chapter 1, some drapers probably did own their own flocks of sheep, though. Also, there are scattered references to 'sheep yards' (*schaephovekes*) in the seigneurie of Inghelant, and to shepherds in the seigneurie of Oosthove.[71] In the latter case, the flocks did not belong to the shepherds themselves but to employers whose last names hint at a connection with known drapers, but the records offer no more specific details on this point.[72]

Nor is it entirely clear to what extent artisans would have been able to market their products in the West-Quarter. Some of the evidence implies that they were essentially incapable of selling finished cloth, whereas other findings suggest that they should have been able to do so. In any case, there is no definitive proof that manufacturers sold fabrics on the marketplace. Once again, there was no rule that forbade artisans like weavers and fullers to sell cloth. But they faced practical obstacles that were less of a concern for the more opulent drapers. One such hindrance was that the main platforms for the (interregional) trade in textiles were remote cities that were costly to reach. While the costs of the journey itself may have been negligible, the undertaking would have required a considerable investment of time during which the artisan in question was absent from his workshop.[73] This was particularly the case with regards to the fairs in

69 In 1479, master-fullers in Kemmel earned a piece rate of 36d. Fl. gr., and master-weavers 24d. Fl. gr. The £2 10s. per transaction gives (600: 36 =) 16.667 pieces for the fuller, and (600: 24 =) 25 for the weaver. Meanwhile, one piece of cloth in Nieuwkerke took approximately 130 weaving hours, so that makes (25 × 130 =) 3250 hours: RDHDF-2, III, pp. 614-17; Endrei, 'Manufacturing a Piece of Woollen Cloth', pp. 17-18. For a discussion of piece rates versus hourly wages in fulling in medieval Flanders: Brand and Stabel, 'De ontwikkeling van vollerslonen'.

70 Like the *doycke* of Eécke: Peter Stabel, '"Dmeeste, oirboirlixste en proffitelixste let ende neringhe": een kwantitatieve benadering van de lakenproductie in het laatmiddeleeuwse en vroegmoderne Vlaanderen', *Handelingen van de Maatschappij voor Geschiedenis en Oudheidkunde te Gent*, 51 (1997), 113-53 (pp. 137, 139).

71 CAY, Kasselrijarchief, Eerste Reeks 2655, fol. 47^{r}; SAB, Gemeentearchief Nieuwkerke 8, fol. 2^{v}.

72 The document mentions 'den scaepherder Clais De Roode ghenaempt Collijn de la Baye of Collijn du Heem ende [...] den scaepherder van Heinderyc Ureel': SAB, Gemeentearchief Nieuwkerke 8, fol. 2^{v}. In 1553, one Frans Oreel was listed as a draper: RDHDF-2, III, pp. 157-58. In 1564-65, two of the De Roo(de) family were also drapers in Nieuwkerke: GSAB, CA, Acquits en portefeuilles 1367.

73 Peter Stabel, 'Marketing Cloth in the Low Countries: Manufacturers, Brokers and Merchants (14th-16th Centuries)', in *International Trade in the Low Countries (14th-16th Centuries): Merchants, Organization, Infrastructure. Proceedings of the International Conference Ghent-Antwerp, 12th-13th January 1997*, ed. by Peter Stabel, Bruno Blondé and Anke Greve (Leuven: Garant, 2000), pp. 15-36 (pp. 34-35).

the duchy of Brabant, which became the main gateways for cloth exports from the end of the fifteenth century onwards. These outlets were at some 130-60 kilometres distance from the Flemish West-Quarter.[74] The Flemish fairs of Torhout, Kortrijk and Bruges, which the drapers of Nieuwkerke also attended, were closer. But at 35-70 kilometres removed, these towns were still two to three days march from the village.[75] People could sell their fabrics in the village cloth hall, of course, but taxes on merchandise for the year 1544-45 suggest that the overall scope of these local transactions was insignificant.[76]

What of the smaller market towns in the vicinity of Nieuwkerke? Potentially, these offered a better outlet for artisans who wished to sell their own products. The fairs of the small town of Mesen, for instance, would have been well-suited for this purpose. The Mesen fair was only a couple of hours walk from most of the textile villages in the West-Quarter and it was mainly devoted to the cloth trade.[77] But this fair was purportedly little frequented during the fifteenth and early sixteenth centuries.[78] A more likely trade platform would have been the marketplace of the castellany-capital of Bailleul, certainly from the early sixteenth century onwards. In 1501, the town of Bailleul acquired the privilege to organize a fair devoted to textiles each September.[79] It must have been reasonably well-attended, too, because in 1517 the right to farm the stalls was leased out for £37 10s. par.[80] This was quite a large amount, considering that covered stands cost 15d. par. to rent, and uncovered ones even as little as 6d. par.[81] Likewise, the fairs of the city of Ypres would have been accessible enough. Even in a bad year like 1476, the rural cloth centres still sold plenty of pieces there. During a single market, Eécke sold 120 woollens, Kemmel

---

74 Stabel, '"Dmeeste, oirboirlixste ende proffitelixste let ende neringhe"', pp. 137-40.

75 Attendance of these fairs is attested by the transactions between the firm of the Spanish wool merchant Juan Castro de Muxica and several drapers of Nieuwkerke (and Dranouter): SAB, Archief van het Spaanse Consulaat, Grootboek van Juan Castro (de Muxica), 1534-1535, pp. 20 (*feria de Bergas*), 204 (*feria de Coutray*; *feria de Brujas*), 227 (*feria de Turote*), 324 (*feria de Ypre de Ascenzion*).

76 In that year, Nieuwkerke produced over 10,000 pieces. Meanwhile, commercial transactions in Nieuwkerke (excluding beer and livestock sales) amounted to £ 9 7s. 2d. par. Even if all of these were cloth transactions, which were subjected to a tax of 1d. for every 30d., that would give a total of £ 280 15s. par. of sold cloth within the village. Since Nieuwkerke's chartered cloths went for £ 54 par. on the Bruges market in 1552, that means the entire amount of commercial goods sold within Nieuwkerke corresponded with only about 5 whole pieces. For the production figures: RDHDF-2, III, pp. 210-11. For the taxation of 1545: GSAB, CA, Acquits en portefeuilles 802bis (separate, unnumbered, and non foliated installments covering December 1544 – November 1545). For the price of Nieuwkerke cloth in 1552, see: GSAB, CA 23482, e.g. on fol. 10^{r}.

77 Victor Gaillard, 'Études sur le commerce de la Flandre au Moyen-Âge: les foires', *Messager des Sciences Historiques, des Arts et de la Bibliographie de Belgique* (Ghent: Hebbelynck, 1851), pp. 193-220 (pp. 193-96, 213).

78 RDHDF-2, III, pp. 77-82.

79 Gaillard, p. 200; *Documents inedits relatifs à la ville de Bailleul*, ed. by Ignace De Coussemaker, 3 vols (Lille: Quarré du coulombier, 1877-78), I (1877), CXIX.

80 ADN, J 766, fol. 1^{v}.

81 *Documents inedits relatifs à la ville de Bailleul*, I, CXXX. This suggests that the person farming the lease would only make a profit if they rented out more than 600 covered, or 1500 uncovered stalls in the course of the entire event.

138, Godewaersvelde 180, Nieppe 284, and Nieuwkerke 396.[82] Of course, rich entrepreneurs still had a competitive advantage over the rural manufacturers because they could conduct larger transactions, thereby out-competing small artisans on their prices. However, what little information we have on sales of Nieuwkerke's woollens suggests that dealers bought very diverse volumes, ranging from small parcels of 4 'mixed Nieuwkerke's', via 48 'half-cloths', to 20 pieces of *kepers* (the village's most expensive woollens).[83] Moreover, in the sixteenth century, Nieuwkerke's prices were rather uniform, which discounts the notion of hypothetical price-advantages through sales in bulk.

Based on these observations, the West-Quarter cloth entrepreneurs did not have exclusive access to markets for raw materials and finished goods. But neither are there any records that conclusively prove that weavers or other manufacturers purchased wool or sold their own cloth. By contrast, there are plenty of recorded transactions conducted by drapers. Therefore, it seems that in practice, the drapers were more or less able to monopolize access to markets. This meant that the manufacturers were at least partly separated from the means of economic production. That said, after the fifteenth-century enfranchisement of most of these rural cloth centres, there is increasing evidence that different forms of decentralized production were in use, and that artisans depended upon entrepreneurs to varying degrees. Thus, the expansion of commercial textile production in the pre-industrial countryside may have gone hand in glove with an expansion of official regulations. And so, these village industries gradually came to resemble urban cloth corporations. As we are about to see, however, some of the West-Quarter entrepreneurs evaded these formal constraints and built larger enterprises, defying the general trend towards decentralization that is usually associated with proto-industrialization.

Beyond putting-out: centralized production

The late thirteenth century had marked a general shift in power relations within the cloth trade of most cities of the southern Low Countries. In response to changes in the international market, many cloth centres adapted their textile sector to secure its economic viability. Cities such as Ypres and Mechelen began to specialize in expensive, luxury woollens, carving out their own market niche in the process. As a side-effect, the textile artisans in these cities attained a greater political bargaining power. Using their essential skills and technical expertise (or 'human capital') as leverage, formal associations of these artisans – the oft-mentioned craft guilds – were able to take charge of labour organization

82 Octaaf Mus, 'Pieter Lansaem, promotor van de nieuwe draperie te Ieper in de tweede helft van de 15e eeuw', *Handelingen van het Genootschap voor Geschiedenis, gesticht onder de benaming 'Société d'Émulation' te Brugge*, 130 (1993), 61-88 (p. 87).

83 *Nieukerkes melees, demy draps de Nieukerke,* and *draps kepers* (the most expensive fabrics): GSAB, CA 23482, fols 14^{r}, 15^{r}; CA 23484, fol. 5^{r}.

within their economic sector. This included most weavers' guilds.[84] In the city of Ypres, the upper layer of these textile guilds initially consisted of a new group of industrial entrepreneurs: the aforementioned drapers. If they started off as champions of the craftsmen, however, the drapers of Ypres soon started to cuddle up to the city's merchant elite. Already in 1303, the drapers had supported the merchants during a riot of the weavers and fullers. And, over the course of the fourteenth century, they gradually attained commercial privileges alongside their industrial role. This culminated in the drapers' licence to trade both wool and cloth, although this was only effectively allowed between 1375 and 1387.[85]

It is within this context that we have come to understand the economic attraction of the countryside as outlined by Pirenne. Prior to the second half of the fifteenth century, none of the village industries in the West-Quarter were subjected to formal regulations that prohibited the combination of selling wool and cloth, nor did they have restrictions on concentrating manufacture into large workshops. Where guilds regulated the urban industry of Ypres, the rural draperies were wide open for entrepreneurial activity because similar institutions simply did not exist there. Nor are there any signs that craft associations arose at any time during the West-Quarter's relatively long-lived economic success.[86] This explains the initial lure of the countryside to urban cloth entrepreneurs from Ypres. But the lack of regulations also had a lasting influence upon the subsequent industrial development *in situ*. Crucially, the rural drapers, who stood at the helm of the cloth industries of Nieuwkerke and the other villages from the early 1400s onwards, retained their combined commercial and industrial role. And, while there is little concrete evidence to suggest that these rural drapers became very wealthy (see below), some of them did succeed in concentrating certain stages of cloth manufacture in centralized establishments.

Given that the various stages of wool preparation were particularly unregulated in the West-Quarter's rural draperies, it is not altogether surprising that local entrepreneurs tried to set up centralized operations devoted to these activities. Wool warehouses where yarn preparation was clustered under the supervision of cloth entrepreneurs were also a common feature of the rural cloth industry in England in this same period – sometimes employing as many as 100 (part time) women.[87] The remaining sources for the West-Quarter industries do not explicitly refer to this phenomenon. But in a register that lists the tenants of the lordship of Berthove around the year 1500, for example, the seigneurial clerk

---

84 Peter Stabel, 'Labour Time, Guild time? Working Hours in the Cloth Industry of Medieval Flanders and Artois (Thirteenth-Fourteenth Centuries)', *TSEG – The Low Countries Journal of Social and Economic History*, 11 (2014), 27-54 (pp. 33-34); Dumolyn, 'Guild Politics and Political Guilds', pp. 19-20.

85 Jules Demey, 'De Vlaamse ondernemer in de middeleeuwse nijverheid: de Ieperse drapiers en "upsetters" op het einde der XIIIe en in de XIVe eeuw', *BMGN – Low Countries Historical Review*, 4 (1949), 1-15, reprinted in *Prisma van de geschiedenis van Ieper: een bundel historische opstellen*, ed. by Octaaf Mus and J. A. Van Houtte (Ypres: Stadsbestuur, 1974), 143-56 (pp. 146, 149).

86 Stabel, 'Labour time, guild time?', p. 34; van der Meulen, 'Get Rich and Try Dyeing'.

87 Oldland, pp. 6-7.

does at one point refer to the 'carding yard' belonging to Christiaan Baelde, on an estate called 'The Castle'.[88] Carding was one of the preparatory stages of wool manufacture, with the purpose of aligning the fibres before they could be spun into yarn. Now, a Christiaan Baelde was definitely a cloth entrepreneur in Nieuwkerke in the final decades of the fifteenth century. Indeed, he had been bailiff of the drapery in 1481.[89] As the scribe explicitly connected this patch of land to carding, he was probably not referring to an occasional pastime of Baelde's wife and children either. This is attested by the rarity of such a reference to an artisanal landmark, which was not usually part of the 'spatial grammar' of local officials.[90] If its economic function was common knowledge among the local populace, this suggests that we are dealing with an actual workshop where the carding stage was clustered, to a degree at least. Local sheep husbandry also took place in close proximity to Baelde's carding yard, perhaps directly provisioning fleeces to be processed into yarn.[91]

Even though large-scale wool warehouses are also known to have existed in England in this period, Baelde's carding workshop still seems peculiar within a rural context. After all, the preparatory stages of cloth production were the easiest to carry out in workers' own homes, as a side-activity to, say, farming. Concentration of this kind would have been relatively capital-intensive, and rather the opposite of what one would expect from a proto-industrial textile centre. However, with a consistently high demand, it could have been a feasible commercial venture. In that sense, it is telling that the bylaws of Ypres' *estainfort* industry of around 1300 already mention that yarn sales for the production of these fabrics were to take place in between the Hondstraat and the nearby hospital, and that certain types of yarn could only be sold 'behind those of Nieuwkerke'. Adding the fact that a Christiaan Baelde listed a house in the Hondstraat as his official domicile when he registered as 'external citizen' (*buitenpoorter*) of Ypres in 1490, there is even the possibility that his rural carding yard supplied wool to a customer base well beyond the drapers of Nieuwkerke alone.[92] We may be dealing with a certain specialization among Nieuwkerke's rural enterprises, as a Gillis Baelde (who was probably Christiaan's brother) is recorded as having bought over 1000 kilograms of wool from a Castilian merchant firm in 1506 for

88 'Lands ghenaempt den Casteel', and 'Christiaen Baels caerdehovekin': SAG, Schenking de Breyne 106, fol. 56v. Possibly, *caerde* referred to thistles in this context. But even if this were the case, the exceptional mention would denote that thistles were purposefully grown here. And the only conceivable reason for this would be to serve as carding tools.

89 RDHDF-2, I, pp. 120-21.

90 Daniel Lord Smail, *Imaginary Cartographies: Possession and Identity in Late Medieval Marseille* (Ithaca NY: Cornell University Press, 1999), pp. 161-64, 179-84.

91 At least, a parcel close by was referred to as the 'courtyard where the shepherd(s) lived' ('der stede daer de scapere woonde'): SAG, Schenking de Breyne 106, fol. 59v.

92 The *estainfort* charter mentions yarn sales 'derrière cheaus de Nueveglise': RDHDF-1, III, DCCLIV, bylaw 22. On the domicile in the Hondstraat: Royal Library Brussels (subsequently RLB), Fonds Merghelynck, M 23, p. 3. See also: Simon Deschodt, 'De Ieperse buitenpoorterij in de 15de tot begin 16de eeuw: studie naar de conflictueuze relatie tussen de stad Ieper en haar hinterland', (unpublished Masters-thesis, Ghent University, 2019).

a total cost of £49 5.5d.![93] Perhaps the Baelde family mainly focused on the early production stages and sold on their yarns to other entrepreneurs, both in the West-Quarter villages and beyond.

As mentioned before, the spinning stage – which was so pivotal in terms of the amount of labour it required – could also be carried out in spinsters' own homes. However, there is evidence to suggest that it, too, took place in clustered production sites and as a waged activity in the cloth villages of the West-Quarter. The cloth charter of Nieppe drafted in 1460, for example, refers to *filleresses* that were entirely the responsibility of the drapers. The same passage states that the drapers were liable for infractions committed by '*their* labourers, weavers, fullers, dyers, shearers, and others' (my emphasis).[94] This could suggest that Nieppe's cloth entrepreneurs employed spinsters and other workers in actual workshops, and paid them in wages. As with spinning in general, however, the sources offer little hard proof.

In other cases, there is no doubt that the rural textile entrepreneurs of the West-Quarter used workshops with on-site production chains. At the same time, these attempts at centralization were clearly controversial within the industry. In fact, it was the concentration of various production stages in single workshops in the 1450s that directly led to the vast expansion of the bylaws in Charles of Burgundy's 1462 redaction of Nieuwkerke's cloth charter.[95] Leading up to this new charter, a number of wealthy entrepreneurs were vilified by their fellows within the corporation, first for not hiring independent craftsmen and -women from the village, instead contracting external workers and employing them in their own (that is, the drapers') workshops (*leurz hostelz*). Second, they were accused of meddling in several production stages all at once. This does not necessarily mean that these activities were clustered within veritable manufactories, but a reference to 'setting [people] to work in their workshops' is highly suggestive of this.[96] Towards the middle of the sixteenth century, the same conflict resurfaced within Nieuwkerke's drapery. There were again several attempts to uphold what had by then become official limits on the number of different craft stages that drapers were allowed to perform, or have others carry out, in their own shops.[97] These repetitions indicate that there was a certain persistence or periodic recurrence of attempts to centralize and vertically integrate cloth enterprises.

In the same vein, in 1534 the lady of Nieuwkerke rented out a specific section of meadowland in the village to various people, a number of whom were drapers. This implies a degree of spatial concentration of cloth production, much like the clustering of weavers along the 'Horsmolen' street that ran from

93 Both a Gillis and a Christiaan are at one point referred to as 'son of Michiel' (*filius Michiel*): RDHDF-2, I, p. 37; CAB, Reeks 305, Wouter Ameyde, Journaal B, fols 206^{v}-207^{r}, 213^{v}, 217^{v}.

94 'Et, s'il advient que aucun drappier face plainte par devant les dis seelleurs a l'encontre de ses ouvriers, filleresses, tisserans, foulons, tainturiers, tondeurs, ou d'autres': RDHDF-2, III, p. 235.

95 RDHDF-2, III, pp. 112-20.

96 'Les dis deffendeurs ne font point drapper, tistre, fouller ne trondre leur draps aus dictes povres gens, mais les font faire en leurz hostelz': RDHDF-2, III, p. 104.

97 RDHDF-2, III, pp. 131-33, 134-36, 136-37, 151-52.

Nieuwkerke to the seigneurie of Inghelant (see above). Although not the same thing as centralization, the fact that several drapers rented plots of this meadow from the lady of Nieuwkerke could suggest that manufacture was centralized in larger workshops there.[98] As for fulling: in 1564, the drapers of Nieuwkerke got permission to full their lower-quality cloths using a fulling mill, something which several other places (Ypres, Bailleul, Nieppe, Météren, Flêtre, Eécke, Godewaersvelde) were apparently already doing at the time.[99] Fulling mills were perhaps the best candidates of the period to qualify as proto-factories, since labour was not only centralized but also partly mechanized, and the mill's construction required a considerable input of capital. In contrast to other rural textile areas in pre-industrial Europe, however, mechanized fulling was not the foundation of the countryside's competitive advantage in late medieval Flanders.[100]

The construction of this fulling mill in Nieuwkerke in 1564 is nevertheless significant for two reasons. First, it is indicative of power relations within the industry, which were clearly tilted in favour of the drapers, and not the fullers or other artisans. The proposal to erect this industrial mill owed its momentum to the 'assiduous desire of the drapers', and was initiated 'notwithstanding possible opposition by the fullers, as had previously occurred in Ypres in particular'.[101] The suggestion that the fullers' guild in the city of Ypres may have been able to fight off such innovations that were inimical to their position on the labour market is remarkable, since fullers generally had the least political leverage of all the urban craft corporations.[102] For the fullers, a partial switch to fulling by mill meant the replacement of much manpower with machine power, with the loss of livelihood for many as a result. However, apparently sensitive to the drapers' assurances that everybody stood to gain more by accepting the proposition, all but one of the forty-seven master-fullers of Nieuwkerke lent their support. As a compromise, they were given the option to wash, card and 'beat' the woollens in question, for a fixed salary of 24s. par. per cloth.[103] Considering that the fullers of Kemmel received 36s. par. per cloth as early as 1479, this must have been a

98 Two of the renters on this meadow were Pieter De Raedt and Joris De Hane; they (or their namesakes) were drapers in 1564-65. Several other names also suggest connections with drapers (De Beuf, De Corte, Liebaert, Tayspil): SAB, Aanwinsten 504, fols 3^{v}-6^{r}; GSAB, CA, Acquits en portefeuilles 1367.

99 They filed this request in 1562, and the Chamber of Accounts granted them the privilege in 1564: RDHDF-2, III, pp. 189-91, 205-06. See also: Vermaut, p. 699.

100 Oldland, p. 11. The classic (though controversial) study on fulling mills is still: Eleanora Carus-Wilson, 'An Industrial Revolution of the thirteenth Century', *The Economic History Review*, 11 (1941), 39-60 (see esp. p. 50). On Flemish fulling mills: Raymond Van Uytven, 'The Fulling Mill: Dynamic of the Revolution in Industrial Attitudes', *Acta Historiae Neerlandicae*, 5 (1971), 1-14.

101 'Ter nerstigher begherte van de voors. drapiers': RDHDF-2, III, p. 203. And 'nietjeghestaende datter mach oppositie ghevallen zyn van den vulders, alzoo't gheschiet es zonderlinghe t'Ypre': RDHDF-2, III, p. 192.

102 John Munro, 'The Symbiosis between Towns and Textiles: Urban Institutions and the Changing Fortunes of Cloth Manufacturing in the Low Countries and England, 1270-1570', *Journal of Early Modern History*, 3 (1999), 1-74 (p. 51).

103 'Behoudens dat de vullers van de voors. prochie sullen hebben over heurl. salaris van de voors. laekenen te wasschen, caerden ende inslaen de somme van vierentwyntich scelle par. van elcken laekene': RDHDF-2, III, pp. 191-93.

meagre peace offering. Moreover, the power to oversee mill fulling resided with Nieuwkerke's wardens of the 'high perch' – controlled by the drapers – rather than with those of the fuller's perch.[104]

Second, the use of the fulling mill may have opened up additional benefits to one draper, or a small group of them, in particular. Nieuwkerke's drapers got permission to full by mill in February 1564, and it seems the only other fulling mill within the castellany of Bailleul (location unknown) was running on overdrive by April. Soon afterwards, one Mathieu De Brune received licence from the Chamber of Accounts in Lille to construct two new mills on parcels he owned or leased in the parishes of Steenwerck and Sint-Jans-Cappel.[105] Now, it may be a coincidence, but a Mathieu De Brune was also active as a draper in Nieuwkerke, and one of the wardens of the high perch who first suggested the idea of fulling certain fabrics by mill.[106] If this was the same person, he had succeeded in putting himself in a near-monopolistic position, since his only responsibility was paying an annual sum of 13s. 4d. Flemish groats to the count of Flanders, while he was free to determine his own operating fee.[107] Indeed, the monopolies provided by fulling mills were highly coveted and much contested in the Middle Ages, and contemporaries deemed millers notorious opponents of honest conduct.[108] By contrast, in the Occitan city of Toulouse in the twelfth century, a group of citizens had pooled their resources to buy a watermill, and proceeded to trade the shares – which were subject to fluctuations in value – in their joint stock enterprise *avant la lettre*.[109] De Brune may have equally had co-investors, but there is little doubt that he and his potential partners were primarily out for their own interests in this case.

Getting things done? The drapers of Nieuwkerke

It would not be an exaggeration to say that the drapers were the pivotal agents in late medieval cloth industries, certainly in the Flemish West-Quarter. Among

104 RDHDF-2, III, pp. 614-17, 193.

105 RDHDF-2, III, pp. 409-11. He is referred to as living in Bailleul: 'Maillieu De Brune [...] demourant en la ville de Bailleul'.

106 He was banished in 1569 by the Council of Troubles: ADN, B 7050, fols 60^{v}-61^{r}; RDHDF-2, III, p. 192 ('Mahieu De Brune, de 35 ans [...] esgardz de la haulte perche ou loye de la dicte draperye'). The fact that he was a warden in 1564 could explain why he does not feature in the overviews of sealed cloth in that year. However, a 'Jan De Brune' was identified as a *notable* draper in 1563, and in 1564-65 he ('Jan De Bruyne') produced 17.5 pieces. A Jan De Brune from Nieuwkerke was also connected to the town of Bailleul in this period, where he was married in 1537: GSAB, CA, Acquits en portefeuilles 1367; RLB, Fonds Merghelynck, M 18/15, p. 43.

107 RDHDF-2, III, p. 411 (£4 *Carolusgulden*).

108 This is evidenced most eloquently by Geoffrey Chaucer's portrayal of the Miller in the *Canterbury Tales*,. For an accessible prose translation: Geoffrey Chaucer, *The Canterbury Tales: A Retelling*, ed. and trans. by Peter Ackroyd (New York: Viking, 2009), pp. 79-81, 99-110. See also: Carus-Wilson, 'An Industrial Revolution', pp. 51-54.

109 Jean Gimpel, *The Medieval Machine: The Industrial Revolution of the Middle Ages* (New York: Penguin Books, 1976), pp. 12-13.

the drapers, those that were the first to set up large-scale cloth enterprises in the countryside in the fourteenth century forced competitors from cities like Ypres to either follow suit or see themselves outcompeted, thereby pushing economic development. In other words, this group of drapers came remarkably close to the definition of 'entrepreneurs' as innovators, as envisioned by the economist Joseph Schumpeter.[110] Somewhere in the early fifteenth century, the drapers of Nieuwkerke and the neighbouring cloth villages innovated the regional textile sector, first by reintroducing fabrics with a warp consisting of worsted-yarns while the weft was actual wool.[111] Their use of a combination of Spanish, Scottish, and local wool was also innovative. In doing these things, they did not only cut costs, but also conquered the underrepresented market segment of medium-quality cloths. Moreover, they did so at a time when this segment was expanding as the customers for it were a growing demographic.[112] In addition, these entrepreneurs had to deal with a cheaper, less politically assertive labour force, which they could employ at their own initiative at reduced cost. Finally, their product may have been of exceptional quality for the price. This is evidenced by a court case of 1561, when an Italian merchant was prosecuted for selling a batch of fabrics from Nieuwkerke, passing them off as the much more expensive *oultrefins* from the town of Armentières – an act of counterfeiting which went unnoticed for some time.[113] These factors combined come close to an empirically borne out historic example of 'creative destruction', because most urban textile centres – Ypres again being the prime example – were unable to compete on the middle-segment for their failure to adopt the same approaches as Nieuwkerke.[114]

That the rural drapers were the group responsible for 'getting things done' (to borrow a phrase from Schumpeter), is chiefly attested by the eagerness with which urban governments sought to attract their enterprises.[115] During each batch of persecutions following on from a reinstatement of Ypres' prohibitive privilege of 1428, the city's government opened the gates to all rural drapers, bidding them to set up shop in the city. Some of them did indeed move there,

110 Trompetter, pp. 276-78.

111 In this, they followed a procedure that was already practised in the draperies of the Lys valley, chiefly in Wervik: Bertrand Haquette, 'Les précurseurs de la délocalisation: entre commerce triangulaire et économie *offshore*: le rôle des financiers italiens dans les villages drapiers de la vallée de la Lys', *Publications du Centre Européen d'Etudes Bourguignonnes*, 49 (2009), 131-58 (pp. 136-37).

112 Herman Van der Wee, 'Industrial Dynamics and the Process of Urbanization and De-urbanization in the Low Countries from the Late Middle Ages to the Eighteenth Century: A Synthesis', in *The Rise and Decline of Urban Industries in Italy and the Low Countries (Late Middle Ages – Early Modern Times)*, ed. by Herman Van der Wee (Leuven: Leuven University Press, 1988), p. 322; Herman Van der Wee, 'Structural Changes and Specialization in the Industry of the Southern Netherlands, 1100-1600', *The Economic History Review*, 28 (1975), 203-21 (pp. 209-10, 212, 215); Stabel, '"Dmeeste, oirboirlixste encd proffitelixste let dnde neringhe"', pp. 124-25.

113 RDHDF-2, I, pp. 326-32; Alfons Thijs, 'Les textiles au marché anversois au XVIe siècle', in *Textiles of the Low Countries*, ed. by Aerts and Munro, pp. 76-86 (pp. 82-83).

114 Stabel,'"Dmeeste, oirboirlixste ende proffitelixste let ende neringhe"', pp. 124-30; Mus, 'Pieter Lansaem', p. 73.

115 Joseph Schumpeter, *Capitalism, Socialism and Democracy* (New York: Harper & Brothers, 1942; 2008 ed.), p. 132.

and they may have been partly responsible for the brief spikes in Ypres' cloth output during these periods.[116] In similar fashion, after the city proclaimed its privilege once again in 1501, the magistrates of the Flemish city of Veurne also attempted to reinvigorate their cloth industry by attracting drapers from Nieuwkerke, inviting envoys from the village to discuss opportunities in their town.[117] These negotiations ran to ground, however. More success was awarded to the government of Bruges, which also jumped at the opportunity to divert part of the migration wave after 1501 to their own doorstep, all 'in light of the great prosperity and profit that this city and its inhabitants would gain by [their] coming'.[118] In that case, sixteen drapers and their families actually made the transition. They would be awarded a premium for each piece of cloth they produced, were granted all privileges of citizens, and were allowed to perform all manufacturing stages within their workshops. Some of them were given loans of £20 Fl. gr. each, a debt that would automatically expire if they kept up their residence in Bruges for more than three years. This is significant, because it confirms the idea that the cloth entrepreneurs of Nieuwkerke were not simply investors, but played a crucial part in the production process itself (or were believed to do so, anyway). It was their skill, their human capital, and not their economic capital, that opened doors for them.

This primacy of the West-Quarter drapers' human capital is further underpinned by well-documented attempts to headhunt them by the government of Diksmuide. Already in 1428, this Flemish town sent an emissary to the villages of Nieuwkerke, Nieppe, Eécke, and Godewaersvelde in order to entice entrepreneurs to immigrate, in pursuit of 'the common profit of the town'.[119] It is unclear whether any of them came at that time. But, following Ypres' mass convictions of the West-Quarter's entrepreneurs in the 1480s, Diksmuide

116 Octaaf Mus calculated the outputs of Ypres' cloth for the period around the turn of the sixteenth century, using a certain tax on cloth. Outputs (three-quarters of which he estimated to be 'new drapery', i.e. the lighter kind also produced in Nieuwkerke):
1498: 10,000 pieces
1500: 10,600 pieces
1501: 10,600 pieces
1502: 15,370 pieces
1503: 16,000 pieces
1504: 16,400 pieces
1505: 12,900 pieces
See: Mus, 'Pieter Lansaem', p. 72. Witness the brief production increase after Ypres' reinstated privilege of 1501, and the subsequent fallback in 1505 (when Nieuwkerke started to contest the city's restrictions): Isidore Diegerick, *Inventaire analytique et chronologique des chartes et documents appartenant aux archives de la ville d'Ypres*, 6 vols (Bruges, 1853-1868), MCCCXCII-MCCCXCVI, MCCCC; RDHDF-2, III, pp. 93-97.

117 D. Dalle, 'Pogingen tot heropbeuring van de wolnijverheid te Veurne (15e-17e eeuw)', *Handelingen van de Maatschappij voor Geschiedenis en Oudheidkunde te Gent*, 13 (1959), 103-12 (p. 106). The envoys were Augustijn Boddaert and Michiel Van der Meersch.

118 'Considererende den grooten oirboir ende proffyt dat dese stede ende inzetene van diere apparent was te ghebuerne metter comste ende woenste van den voornoemde van Nieukerke': RDHDF-2, III, pp. 126-28.

119 'Omme 't ghemeene prouffyt deser stede': RDHDF-2, II, p. 202.

was successful in setting up a small group of drapers from Kemmel. As in the case of Bruges, the urban treasury provided loans for start-up capital, in this case £90 Fl. gr. in total.[120] These ventures must not have been lastingly fruitful in the longer term, however, because the magistrates of Diksmuide were still looking to install drapers from the West-Quarter in 1545, when Ypres' privilege was reinstated a final time. In that instance, they succeeded in attracting several drapers from Nieuwkerke, not only granting them massive loans of up to £50 Fl. gr. per person, but also gifting them with £5 each.[121]

Clearly, the rural cloth entrepreneurs possessed something other than money that made them good entrepreneurs. It may have been a question of technical proficiency in the form of a special production technique, but this was probably not the whole story. For one thing, if there had simply been a secret technique – which was not unheard of in this period – there were easier ways of transferring this knowledge, and, once given up, the secret would have been out.[122] For another, if it came down to a production technique, or even a certain 'recipe' of specific proportions of different types of wool, then why did the drapery in the Nieuwkerke style fail to gain a firmer foothold in these various cities? The evidence points to a short-lived experiment in each instance. Incidentally, the same applies to ephemeral implementations of drapery in the style of the town of Poperinge, or the failed attempts to install light drapery of the kind produced in Hondschoote.[123]

Most likely, the 'secret' of drapers from Nieuwkerke and the other villages was twofold. First, apart from economic capital and human capital, they also possessed much 'social capital', that is to say well-developed trade networks.[124] These will be further examined in the next chapter, but suffice it to say for now that the drapers' contacts in the market cities of the Low Countries gave them access to better and cheaper raw materials on the one hand, and provided them with a steady outlet for their products on the other (see Chapter 3). Second, the secret to these drapers' success within rural society lay in their ability to almost completely dominate the industrial process, notwithstanding the increasing barriers to vertical integration after the 1460s that we saw in Nieuwkerke. While this worked within the rural, un-guilded context that these entrepreneurs

---

120 RDHDF-2, II, pp. 214-16.

121 RDHDF-2, II, pp. 166-67, 174-78, 182, 184-85. A fuller was also given £1 Fl. gr.

122 For example: the rural drapery of Oisterwijk in the duchy of Brabant possessed a secret technique for preparing and spinning the yarn. This secret came in the possession of a citizen of Antwerp, who sold it to the industries of Hasselt, Sint-Truiden and Turnhout in 1561: Leo Adriaenssen, 'De plaats van Oisterwijk in het Kempense lakenlandschap', *Textielhistorische Bijdragen*, 41 (2001), 27-48 (p. 36). See also the reference to a special technique of spinning used in the region of Bailleul: 'twisting' the thread (*tordre le fil*). Coornaert interpreted this as a partial substitution of linen for wool: Émile Coornaert, *L'industrie de la laine à Bergues-Saint-Winoc: une industrie urbaine du XIVe au XVIIe siècle* (Paris: Presses universitaires de France, 1930), p. 96.

123 RDHDF-2, II, pp. 97, 196, 198, 200, 201; Coornaert, *Un centre industriel d'autrefois*, p. 20; Dalle, pp. 105-06.

124 Pierre Bourdieu, 'The Forms of Capital', in *Handbook of Theory and Research for the Sociology of Education*, ed. by John Richardson (New York: Greenwood, 1986), pp. 246-58 (pp. 251-53).

were used to, in the cities of the Low Countries regulations were often much more extensive, and artisans were a privileged group carrying political weight. Presumably, this greater institutionalization was reflected in higher, less flexible wages, as well as tighter controls on production methods. As a point of reference: consider (not so) hypothetical attempts of present-day governments in the Western World to compete with countries where low wages and few regulations abound in economic sectors where labour inputs have a significant impact on production costs.[125] For one thing, it is hardly feasible for these societies to reverse the institutional arrangements in place to lower wage levels and the costs of regulation. For another, they cannot defeat their competitors on prices, since these competitors are free of the same formal constraints. A similar lot befell the drapers of the pre-industrial West-Quarter once they were transported to a more tightly regulated context. Suddenly, they had to rival their former rural colleagues on price level. This must have been impossible, if only because they lost their connections to the local female labour force that was vital to reduce the costs of wool preparation.[126] Furthermore, due to their contracts with the town to which they had moved, they were now obliged to produce a certain number of cloths per year. Some of them were unable to achieve this, with the result that they reneged on their contract and had to repay their loan to the urban treasury.[127]

Of course, it is slightly misleading to treat the Nieuwkerke drapers as one uniform group. From a Schumpeterian perspective, not all of them would qualify as 'entrepreneurs', only the true innovators would merit this label.[128] According to that standard, only certain groups would have counted as proper entrepreneurs: first, the generation of urban drapers from around 1400 who were the first to 'offshore' to the countryside; second, those who founded a commercial collective around the end of the fifteenth century (see Chapters 3 and 5); and third, perhaps also those drapers who proposed a shift to lighter textiles fulled by mill in the 1560s (although their initiative did not prove successful for long). However, given the continuous struggle for the legitimacy of Nieuwkerke's industry, one could also argue that each generation between 1400 and 1570 knew a number of Schumpeterian entrepreneurs who ensured the survival of the local textile economy through less noticeable economic decisions on the individual level. The important thing is that, in Nieuwkerke at least, it was always the drapers that pulled the strings. And so, they formed the core of this rural industrial development, even though the various village industries obviously counted numerous unsung 'working-class' heroes as well.

---

125 I am thinking of President Donald J. Trump's failed attempts to revive the American coal mining industry during his time in office as president of the United States (2016-2020).

126 Mus, 'Pieter Lansaem', p. 73.

127 RDHDF-2, II, pp. 182-83, 188-89, 192.

128 Trompetter, pp. 276-77.

Stratification within the drapery

In order to better understand how the rural drapers of the Flemish West-Quarter operated their enterprises, it is important to be aware of the internal stratification within their ranks. The drapers of Nieuwkerke – the most successful, and best-documented cloth village – formed a remarkably heterogeneous group. As mentioned previously, the drapers were a type of cloth entrepreneur that only emerged in Flanders around the end of the thirteenth century.[129] According to the basic definition, drapers were simply entrepreneurs who invested capital to purchase raw materials and manufacture cloth, after which they sold the finished product. But prior to 1300, it had been urban merchants who dominated the industrial process. Thereafter, these merchants remained involved in the commercial aspect of the urban industries, while the drapers became the industrial entrepreneurs with hands-on control over the textile crafts. This coincided with an increase in the involvement of foreign merchants in the Flemish cloth industries, who mainly came from the Italian Peninsula and the northern German Empire.[130] Indeed, in the fifteenth and sixteenth centuries, the important *sayetterie* of Hondschoote was largely controlled by external merchants, mainly trading firms from Antwerp. While Hondschoote did contain a group of local cloth merchants who were in close collusion with the 'notable' drapers, those drapers continued to fulfil a purely industrial role.[131]

Nieuwkerke's industry confounds this picture of a strict separation between merchants and drapers. In fact, a charter of 1459 explicitly refers to the village's *marchans drappiers*. And all of the listed individuals belonged to local families.[132] There is not a single document referring to external merchants' direct involvement in the industry. This is all the more surprising given Nieuwkerke's very limited regulations on draping activity, and its virtual lack of regulations concerning the marketing of cloth. One might expect the village to be crowded by opportunistic merchants from outside the community. Instead, the industry was primarily driven by the local drapers themselves.

There were certain basic similarities between all the drapers of Nieuwkerke. First, just like all those aspiring to become master-craftsmen in the parish, they had to reside and be taxable (*taillable*) there.[133] This bylaw was not mentioned in the cloth charters of urban centres such as Armentières, and was probably a means to exclude outsiders within a rural context, similar to how urban corporations could require drapers to be citizens.[134] Within the West-Quarter,

129 Henri Pirenne, *Histoire de Belgique*, 7 vols (Brussels: H. Lamertin, 1900-1932), II (1903), pp. 63-68; Van Werveke, pp. 20-22.

130 Van Werveke, p. 8.

131 Florence Edler, 'Le commerce d'exportation des sayes d'Hondschoote vers l'Italie d'après la correspondance d'une firme anversoise entre 1538 et 1544', *Revue du Nord*, 22 (1936), 249-66 (pp. 251-52); Coornaert, *Un centre industriel d'autrefois*, pp. 374-79.

132 RDHDF-2, III, p. 103.

133 RDHDF-2, III, p. 113.

134 RDHDF-2, I, pp. 102-17; Coornaert, *Une industrie urbaine*, p. 47.

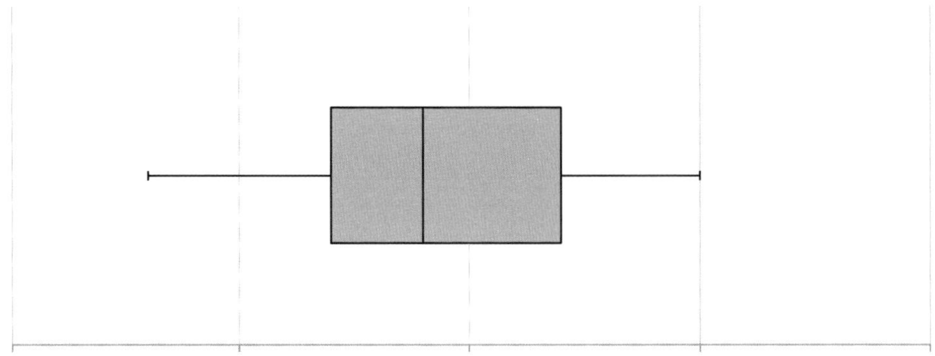

Figure 2.1. Boxplot of drapers' starting ages (n = 39)

Source: RDHIDF-2, III, pp. 169-76.

this is one area wherein Nieuwkerke distinguished itself from the other villages, as the other centres apparently lacked a similar rule. In fact, the 1479 charter of Kemmel and Wulvergem explicitly referred to members of the drapery, 'whether they live inside (these parishes) or outside', even though the cloth could only be produced within the bounds of these seigneuries.[135] An overview of drapers in Nieuwkerke for the year 1564-65 reveals that its law for the protection of local interests was successful. The only aberration was one Frans Mathieu, whose name is consistently followed by the note 'Lille' (*Rijsel*) in the record.[136] Another characteristic shared among all drapers since 1462, was that each had to be identifiable and accountable through his or her draper's mark, which had to be woven into every piece of cloth manufactured under their auspices.[137] Finally, there was probably some form of shared education prior to becoming a draper. The regulations remain silent on this point, nor are there references to apprentices or journeymen anywhere. But a source of 1553 makes it possible to infer that a kind of training program was required to become a draper in Nieuwkerke. In that document, several drapers mentioned at what age they first became drapers, probably as a way of affirming their experience and seniority.[138] Barring a few exceptions, most of them started between the ages of 22 and 27, averaging at 24.5 (**Figure 2.1**). Of course, this figure might simply indicate the ages around which people attained enough capital to start their own enterprises, or the moment when they inherited a family business. But in that case, one would expect less uniformity. The slightness of variation between the different ages suggests that, in order to become a draper in Nieuwkerke, one probably had to complete some form of education.

135 'Tous ceulx qui ce mesleront de la dicte drapperie es dictes paroiches, soient demourans en icelles ou dehors': RDHDF-2, III, p. 616.
136 GSAB, CA, Acquits en portefeuilles 1367/34.
137 RDHDF-2, III, p. 114. See also: Oldland, p. 9.
138 RDHDF-2, III, pp. 175-76.

Yet there were also many differences between the cloth entrepreneurs. For starters, among this predominantly male profession, there were a number of women, too. As opposed to the Flemish craft guilds, which had begun to exclude female artisans between 1300 and 1400, the gender roles were not so fixed within commercial enterprises.[139] In fact, Nieuwkerke's industrial regulation of 1462 explicitly referred to drapers 'or draperesses' (*drapiers ofte drapiereghen*).[140] Nevertheless, only 15 out of the 346 drapers active in 1564 were female. And these women were usually referred to as 'the widow of' such and such, from which we may deduce that women were primarily allowed to carry on the business of their departed husbands.[141] Some single women did run a cloth enterprise under their own name, like Christiana De Hane, 'draperess since the age of twenty-four',[142] and the 'Lady De Corte',[143] but these were exceptions. It is interesting to see that, while the Flemish countryside escaped the 'guild revolution' that 'was in many ways also a revolution of gender roles', textile entrepreneurship was still a predominantly male occupation. If the household was the unit of economic production in the West-Quarter villages, the husband stood at the helm of this unit (even though female labour power was in many ways the linchpin of this patriarchal system).[144]

There was also much variation between drapers, be they male or female, in terms of their production outputs. This was not unusual for the period: the town of Leiden in the county of Holland, for example, was also marked by a division between wealthy drapers (who straddled the imposed upper limit of 240 cloths per year) and 'poor' drapers (who produced no more than 30 pieces).[145] In the city of Bruges as well, there were distinct socio-economic positions within the draper's community, ranging from opulent entrepreneurs with close contacts to merchants to impoverished drapers who were virtually indistinguishable from master-artisans.[146] For Nieuwkerke, an overview of the cloth tax for the accounting year of 1564 (which ran from 1 October 1564 until 31 September 1565) reveals a similar level of stratification. This document consists of a register kept by the wardens, listing periodic checks of completed pieces of cloth. Once kept together by small nails, it is currently in disarray and

139 Peter Stabel, 'Working Alone? Single Women in the Urban Economy of Late Medieval Flanders (Thirteenth-Early Fifteenth Centuries)', in *Single Life and the City, 1200-1900*, ed. by Julie De Groot, Isabelle Devos and Ariadne Schmidt (Houndmills: Palgrave, 2015), pp. 27-49 (p. 39).

140 RDHDF-2, III, p. 115.

141 GSAB, CA, Acquits en portefeuilles 1367/34; Marianne Danneel, *Weduwen en wezen in het laat-middeleeuwse Gent* (Leuven: Garant, 1996), pp. 349-62, 377-82.

142 'Drapière pendant 24 ans': RDHDF-2, III, p. 175.

143 'De vrouwe Corten': GSAB, CA, Acquits en portefeuilles 1367/34. Possibly, this was Lady Marie De Corte, wife of Master Claude de Conrouble, fief-holder of Westhove in 1585: ADN, B 3898/11.a.

144 Peter Stabel and Anke De Meyer, 'Craft guilds as Vectors of Middle-Class Values', in *Inequality and the City*, ed. by Blondé, pp. 271-87 (p. 273). Consider that in 1431, 43.6 per cent of working women in Ypres were engaged in textile production, and 90.1 per cent of them were spinsters: Stabel, 'Working alone?', pp. 38-39, 43.

145 N. W. Posthumus, *De geschiedenis van de Leidsche lakenindustrie*, 3 vols (The Hague: M. Nijhoff, 1908-1939), I (1908), pp. 274-75.

146 Vermaut, pp. 480-89.

Table 2.1. Stratification of drapers in Nieuwkerke, based on production output, 1564-65

Pieces of cloth	N° of drapers	Percent of drapers	Percent of total production
≤5	100	28.90	2.72
>5 ≤25	98	28.32	14.20
>25 ≤50	84	24.28	32.31
>50 ≤100	53	15.32	36.59
>100	11	3.18	14.19
Total	346	100	100

Source: GSAB, CA, Acquits en portefeuilles 1367/34.

had to be puzzled back together, but it is probably still complete, or otherwise nearly so. The wardens' accounts reveal no fewer than 346 different drapers, with tremendous differences in output (**Table 2.1**). Of course, this is only a momentary glimpse, and from a time when the industry was just past its peak. Also, there were signs of discord over inequality within the drapery during this period (see Chapter 5). It is therefore possible that the boom years between 1530 and 1550 had seen a more balanced distribution within the village's cloth corporation. Yet this would mainly translate to fewer outliers in the upper layer during. Furthermore, although decline had set in at this point, it is obvious that the industry still persevered during the 1560s. While one should bear this context in mind, it therefore remains a representative sample to examine the stratification within Nieuwkerke's entrepreneurial class.

Perhaps most notable is that the majority of drapers produced only 25 pieces or fewer per year. This group probably consisted of craftsmen and -women who worked for themselves and featured in the register as occasional drapers. This was possible in Nieuwkerke, because it had always been allowed to combine a draping enterprise with at least one craft, except fulling (until 1535) and dyeing.[147] During conflicts within the drapery, the main contentious issue usually related to this accumulation of different manufacturing stages by one entrepreneur or partnership of entrepreneurs.[148] A small group of wealthy drapers were continuously in favour of concentration and vertical integration, and they managed to acquire increasing licence to combine the manufacturing stages to that effect, especially towards the middle of the sixteenth century. One encounters a similar phenomenon in Hondschoote during this same period.[149] As a side effect, the permission to combine draping with, say, fulling, also meant that fullers could now become entrepreneurs and commission their own fabrics. Indeed, out of the 47 master-fullers active in Nieuwkerke in 1564, six occurred

147 RDHDF-2, III, pp. 112-20, 136-37.

148 RDHDF-2, III, pp. 102-03, 134-36, 151-52.

149 This culminated in 1551-53: from then on, people were allowed to combine draping with three craft stages, except dyeing: RDHDF-2, III, pp. 151-52; Van der Meulen, 'Get Rich and Try Dyeing', pp. 52-55.

as drapers in the register of the wardens – albeit as minor operators.[150] This was not so much a problem for the wealthy upper layer of the drapery, but it did mean extra competition for the mid-level entrepreneurs.

This competition from below may have been exacerbated by the fact that Nieuwkerke had a relatively 'open' drapery corporation. That said, it is not easy to establish how closed the ranks were in practice. There was certainly no written law against occasional engagement in cloth entrepreneurship, as long as one lived in the parish and paid taxes there. The only other thing required in order to 'drape' was the ability to bear the financial responsibility for the product, although as we shall see later on, some form of monitoring entrance to the drapery can also be inferred (see Chapter 5). At first glance, though, it was easy to invest in the local cloth industry. Take the example of Klaas Tayspil, one of the largest brewers of the parish in 1545, who appears to have produced (or commissioned) three pieces of cloth in 1564-65.[151] In fact, this openness may have been one of the industry's assets, because it stimulated an easy flow of capital from one branch of the local economy to the next.

At the same time, inequality between the local drapers was more pronounced in Nieuwkerke than in other Flemish industrial centres in this period. In order to provide a suitable comparative framework, we will put Nieuwkerke's individual production outputs in 1564-65 next to those of the town of Armentières on the one hand, and of the village of Flêtre on the other. Extant output figures for Armentières in 1575 offer a useful perspective because, much like Nieuwkerke, this urban production centre was just beyond its boom period in that year.[152] Meanwhile, Flêtre was one of the smaller cloth villages of the West-Quarter, and it had also just passed its apogee in the years for which records have survived (*c.* 1550).[153] Conventional ways to measure (in)equality are the so-called Gini-coefficient and Lorenz-curve. The former is a number between 0 and 1, where 0 indicates complete equality (i.e. everybody produced exactly the same number of cloths), and 1 marks utter inequality (i.e. production is monopolized by a single draper). The Lorenz-curve is the graph corresponding to the same principle: the more closely it resembles a 45°-degree angle, the more equally distributed the production outputs (**Figures 2.2a-c**). Based on these methods, cloth outputs were much more equally distributed between the drapers in Armentières and Flêtre, with Gini-coefficients of 0.272 and 0.357 respectively, than they were in Nieuwkerke with its coefficient of 0.532. The difference with Armentières is

150 RDHDF-2, III, pp. 202-03.

151 He brewed 11.5 *smalle tonnen* and 10 *buusen* in 1544-45: GSAB, CA, Acquits en portefeuilles 802bis; 1367/34.

152 Around the middle of the sixteenth century, Armentières had still been responsible for 42 per cent of Flanders's total woollen output: Tim Soens, Peter Stabel, and Tineke Van de Walle, 'An Urbanised Countryside? A Regional Perspective on Rural Textile Production in the Flemish West-Quarter', in *Economies, Public Finances, and the Impact of Institutional Changes in Interregional Perspective: The Low Countries and Neighbouring German Territories (14th-17th Centuries)*, Studies in European Urban History 36, ed. by Remi van Schaïk (Turnhout: Brepols, 2015), pp. 35-60 (p. 36).

153 RDHDF-2, II, pp. 283-85.

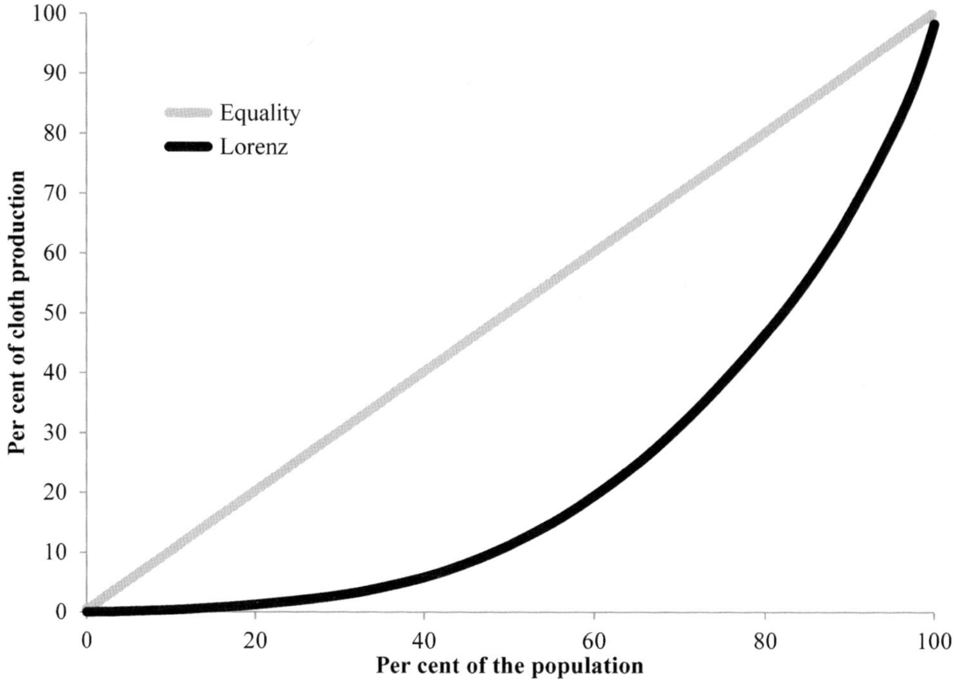

Figure 2.2a. Lorenz curve (of cloth output), Nieuwkerke, 1564-65

Source: GSAB, CA, Acquits en portefeuilles 1367/34.

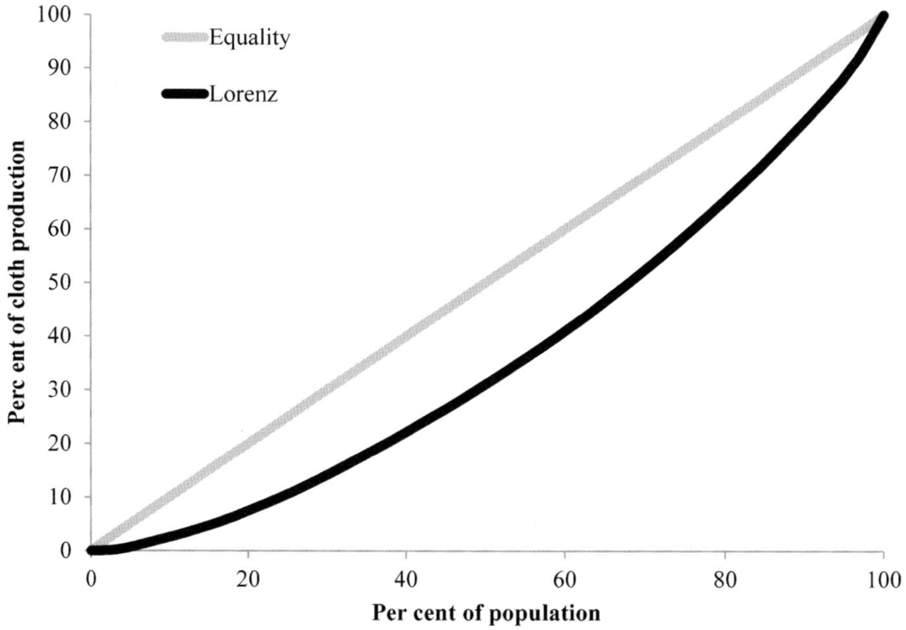

Figure 2.2b. Lorenz curve (of cloth output), Armentières, February – May 1575

Source: RDHIDF-2, I, pp. 459-62.

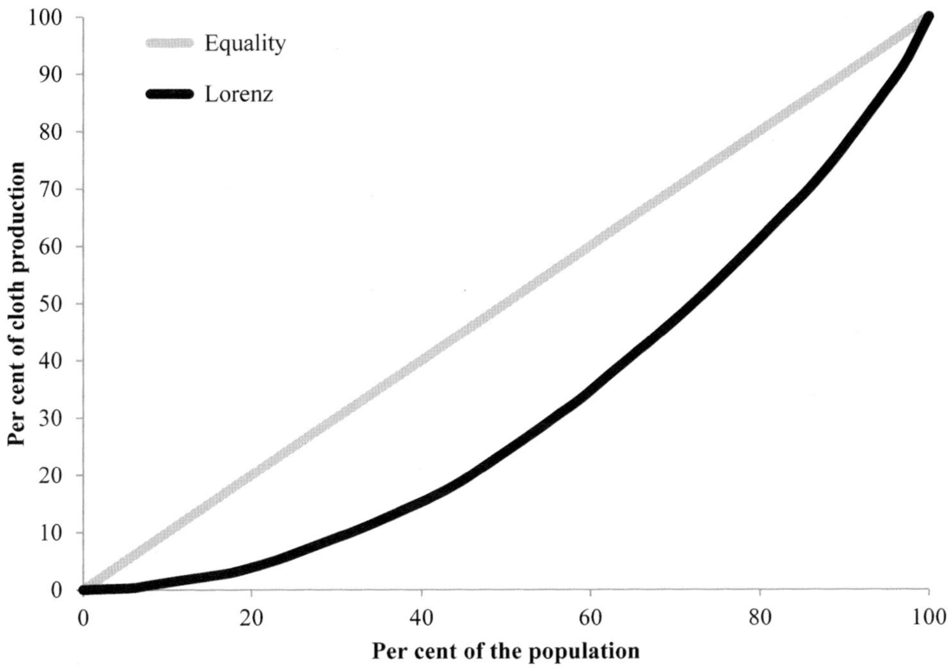

Figure 2.2c. Lorenz curve (of cloth output), Flêtre, 1551-52

Source: GSAB, CA, Acquits en portefeuilles 1367/34.

perhaps less surprising, given that this town's industry was more regulated and had specific bylaws devoted to monitoring equality. Flêtre's drapery, by contrast, knew only a few formal rules. And yet individual cloth outputs were also more homogenous in this village than in its larger neighbour.[154] Of course, Flêtre's industry was smaller and, as such, possibly less competitive than the other two, with a total of 34 drapers producing a mere 610 pieces of cloth in 1551-52. Also, Flêtre was a secondary production centre, manufacturing undyed fabrics that were finished elsewhere, probably in Lille.[155] Coupled with an industrial bylaw that stated the merchant (*coopman*) could determine the length of the cloth, it must have been external merchants who sold Flêtre's fabrics.[156] In other words, the drapers here were less autonomous than those of Nieuwkerke, relying upon outside capital to manufacture their (relatively expensive) products.[157]

Despite these pronounced differences in production levels between the drapers of Nieuwkerke, the wealthiest among them were still of relatively modest

154 RDHDF-2, II, pp. 285-90.

155 RDHDF-2, II, p. 283 (n. 2).

156 'Waerby die coopman mach weten hoe hooghe dat 't zelve laken gecammet sal werden': RDHDF-2, II, p. 286.

157 In 1563, the most expensive cloth of Flêtre sold for 36d. Fl. gr. per ell in Bruges, i.e. around the same price as Nieuwkerke's: *Précis analytique des documents, que renferme le dépot des archives de la Flandre-occidentale à Bruges*, ed. by Octave-Joseph Delepierre and Frédéric-Pierre Priem, 12 vols (Bruges, 1840-1858), III (1842), p. 243.

means compared to the rich upper layers of most Flemish towns. To be sure, there is only a small sample to go on to offer such assessments of individual wealth, namely registers of confiscated property of people persecuted for their Protestant leanings in the period 1566-72. But a direct comparison with other settlements, based on the same type of source, suggests that even in successful and unequal Nieuwkerke, the entrepreneurs were not very wealthy. Nobody in the village belonged to the upper financial layer of people with over 5000 *Carolus* guilders (£833 6s. 8d. Fl. gr.) in estimated capital, for instance. By contrast, the records show 14.75 per cent in this category in the city of Bruges, 10.74 per cent in Ghent, and still 2.00 per cent in a small cloth town such as Eeklo. In fact, the assets of the richest person in Nieuwkerke only amounted to £357 7d. Fl. gr., while 68 per cent of the village had less than £5 Fl. gr. to their name.[158] This is important, because it implies that in spite of Nieuwkerke's industrial success, entrepreneurial capital was mainly tied down in business ventures. Perhaps the wealth of the entrepreneurs mainly consisted of outstanding credit and debts with merchants in the market cities. The wool transactions conducted between drapers from Nieuwkerke and the Castilian trading company of Juan Castro de Muxica in the 1530s support this idea of a continuous flow of purchases (partly) based on credit. De Muxica's ledgers reveal that debts were to be redeemed within a set period, at which point the credit was extended (see Chapter 3). Such a system is indicative of a relatively advanced economy – not to mention a relentless one, since it demanded an unbroken chain of production and trade in order to finance the next shipment of raw materials.

While it is debatable whether we should call this system with constant reinvestment of proceeds 'capitalist' in the sense that early twentieth-century historians like Henri Pirenne understood the term, it certainly betrays a distinct market-orientation, even market-dependence.

Indeed, notwithstanding their apparently modest wealth, some of the entrepreneurs in the rural West-Quarter pursued several policies at once to amass wealth, in addition to the proceeds of their cloth sales. A good example is Cornelis Liebaert, who had the second-largest drapery output of Nieuwkerke in 1564-65, with 131.5 cloths to his name. That this entrepreneur did not shy away from dubious practices to increase his fortune can be gleaned from the fact that he was convicted by the bailiff of the drapery for selling cloths without seals during one Ypres fair.[159] He also held a stake in other ventures aside from the cloth trade. In 1530, for instance, Liebaert acquired the right to lease out the stalls at the fair of Mesen for twelve consecutive years.[160] Another example of a draper hedging his bets by investing in multiple ventures was Gillis De Coninck, who

158 Vandamme, 'Calvinisme, textielindustrie en drapeniers', pp. 124-25. A total of 53 people from Nieuwkerke are included in this assessment.

159 GSAB, Dozen van de Rekenkamer 261. Cited in: Vandamme, 'Calvinisme, textielindustrie en drapeniers', p. 127 (n. 2).

160 SAB, Aanwinsten 3640, fol. 13^{v}. The annual cost was £30 par.

in 1508-09 leased the right to the seal of the drapery in the seigneurie of 'Little Mesen', which was partially located in the parish of Nieuwkerke.[161]

These entrepreneurs were the closest thing to industrial capitalists within this period and region. They certainly had the edge over most of their fellows in 1564-65, whose enterprises still fell within the bounds of what one might call 'small commodity production'. On the whole, though, the relative productive contribution of this draper elite was not pronounced enough to have constituted the foundation of the industry.[162] In fact, the top producers of more than 100 pieces per annum were only responsible for 14 per cent of the total output (**Table 2.1**). Should we include the runners-up (with 50-100 cloths) in this elite, then its relative contribution would become 51 per cent; or, looking at the Lorenz-curve, the top 10 per cent of entrepreneurs was responsible for 33 per cent of total production. This is certainly more than the 25 per cent of sales by the top 10 per cent of entrepreneurs in the small town of Menen in the early sixteenth century. But in the latter case, the absolute sales volumes per draper were presumably a lot higher.[163] Indeed, Nieuwkerke's most productive drapers would constitute a very modest elite compared to the opulent top layer of society in other places. In Hondschoote, for instance, around one hundred traders all commissioned at least 1000 fabrics each year between 1528 and 1578.[164] This suggests that in absolute terms as well, the economic power of the top layer of the West-Quarter drapery was limited, even for this time and place.

Conclusion

The purpose of this chapter has been to pull at a thread first picked loose by Henri Pirenne around the turn of the twentieth century, and to assess in what degree the draperies in the rural West-Quarter showed signs of 'capitalist' enterprise between the fourteenth and sixteenth centuries. Having reviewed the available material about these cloth centres' industrial organization, and specifically the relationship between entrepreneur-employers and artisan-workers, a certain ambivalence still remains as to how market-oriented these textile-producing villages were. One thing that has emerged is that Pirenne was correct when he affirmed that the rural draperies of the West-Quarter were generally characterized by limited official regulations. In practice, these rural industries were allowed to

---

161 SAB, Aanwinsten 3682, fol. 18^{v}. That he was a draper is apparent from his purchase of wool in Bruges in 1506: CAB, Reeks 305, Wouter Ameyde, Journaal B, fol. 215^{v}.

162 Robert Duplessis and Martha Howell, 'Reconsidering the Early Modern Urban Economy: The Cases of Leiden and Lille', *Past & Present*, 94 (1982), 49-84. See also: Roch, 'Artisans ou marchands', pp. 49-51.

163 Peter Stabel, 'Guilds in Late Medieval Flanders: Myths and Realities of Guild Life in an Export-Oriented Environment', *Journal of Medieval History*, 30 (2004), 187-212 (p. 209).

164 Coornaert, *Un centre industriel d'autrefois*, p. 360.

operate with only minor intervention from outside (by comital and seigneurial officials, for example). Even in Nieuwkerke, where both the count of Flanders and the village lord had claims upon the industry, the drapers could conduct their businesses relatively autonomously. This was partly a consequence of the election process of the cloth officials, and partly because these positions were filled by members of local families.

The advantage of this 'liberal' climate was that it left the entrepreneurs with options to improvise. This was the case with regards to the types of wool that were allowed within the industry, and equally in terms of how this raw wool was processed into yarn. The most striking common denominator between the West-Quarter cloth industries was their sheer lack of regulations concerning these preparatory stages of woollen production. Spinning, in particular, was left almost entirely to the care of the cloth entrepreneurs themselves. This is significant, as spinning, and wool preparation more broadly, accounted for the vast majority of working hours in late medieval cloth manufacture. As these tasks were virtually monopolized by women, female labour power was of the utmost importance to the industrial successes of this rural region. But the lack of written evidence about these activities makes it hard to determine to what extent this predominantly female labour power was exchanged via the market. The dearth of evidence and the likelihood that wool preparation was a side-activity rather than a full-time occupation suggest that the initial production stages were predominantly part of the informal economy. This remains the most puzzling aspect of the West-Quarter's industrial organization, however, as there is also evidence of centralized wool warehouses (or 'carding yards').

Looking at the other production stages, it turns out that the rural entrepreneurs of the West-Quarter had multiple ways of organizing labour power, with varying degrees of market-orientation. On the one hand, decentralized manufacture certainly occurred, with the entrepreneurs providing the wool to local artisans while retaining ownership of the works-in-progress ('putting-out'). On the other hand, in addition to variations on putting-out, there were also enterprises with centralized workshops. Some of these enterprises may even have employed various artisans covering the greater part of the production process, from yarn to dyed cloth. Technically, the official licences and regulations which governed cloth production, the *keures*, did not prevent the artisans from participating on the markets for raw materials and finished woollens. In theory, they could own and sell the cloths they manufactured. This is unrecorded, however. It appears that the artisans principally relied on selling their labour power to the drapers, sometimes working for wages and sometimes for piece-rates. Both in theory and in practice, it was these drapers that were in the best position to buy wool and sell fabrics on the market. In that sense, the pre-industrial draperies of the West-Quarter were predominantly market-oriented as regards the different economic positions of entrepreneur-employers and artisan-workers.

The lack of politically active craft guilds such as existed in most urban cloth centres of this period may have contributed to this market-orientation. By that same token, the apparent stratification within the drapery of Nieuwkerke in

1564-65 could signal that a group of budding capitalists primarily served their own interests rather than those of the general entrepreneurial community. Indeed, production outputs within the urban industry of Armentières, and even within a smaller village like Flêtre, were much more equally distributed than in Nieuwkerke. Then again, it is debatable whether it was the initiatives and innovations of a small top layer that propelled the rural industries forwards, since the wealthiest drapers were still not that rich compared to the economic elites of most Flemish towns.

Taking this evidence together, Pirenne certainly had a point when he stated that the cloth industry of Nieuwkerke was 'on a clear course towards the factory'. However, the present chapter makes clear that this course was not that 'clear' after all, nor was it linear. Periodic attempts to combine the various production stages (what is called vertical integration) consistently met with resistance from within the drapery corporation. In other words, much as in the late medieval cities, the industrial organization in these Flemish cloth villages was marked by a continuous tension between the individual and the collective.[165] As we shall see in later chapters, this tension had an impact upon the long-term trajectory of Nieuwkerke's textile economy, and was interconnected with the commercial sphere and even with the villagers' contemporary rhetoric and ideology of community.

165 Pirenne, 'Note sur la fabrication des tapisseries', p. 332.

CHAPTER 3

The commercial aspect

In 1513, Cornelis Everaert wrote a play entitled *Farce of the Merchant who Kissed Goodbye to Five Pound Groats.*[1] In this piece, the Flemish playwright-*cum*-master-fuller introduces the audience to a merchant from Bruges who travels to the small town of Roeselare to collect a £5 debt from an innkeeper residing in that town.[2] However, during the confrontation with his debtor in the latter's tavern, he has a few cups too many and, sodden with drink, agrees to negate the deficit if the innkeeper's wife will consent to kiss him. The town's burgomaster, also present at the inn and sharing a few drinks besides, officially ratifies the transaction and even has it notarized by a clerk. So it transpires, and the following morning the merchant awakens to more than just a hangover, having squandered his money in this peculiar fashion.[3] Everaert's comic piece was primarily a warning against the excesses of inebriation, as well as a gentle ridicule of merchants. But underneath the surface lies a strong awareness of the social and institutional mechanisms governing commercial life in his time. The informal setting and atmosphere of the inn, as well as the role of alcohol: these things contrast sharply with the binding nature of the contract drawn up by the town clerk. Indeed, despite the merchant's complaints that the proceedings are unlawful, the burgomaster is implacable: 'assent makes legality', he says.[4] This institutional aspect of trade will later be echoed, and criticized, in William Shakespeare's far more famous *The Merchant of Venice.* An aspect of that story, similar to Everaert's. is the contract between Shylock and Antonio according to which the latter has to pay one pound of flesh if he is unable to pay his outstanding debt within a set time limit.[5]

Both the kisses of Everaert's play and the pound of flesh in Shakespeare's are intended to be perceived by the audience as ludicrous, even scandalous, modes of payment. The English play is more critical than the Flemish, breathing concern about commercial laws that supersede social and cultural norms, whereas Everaert

---

1 'Esbatement van den coopman die vyf pondt grooten vercuste': Cornelis Everaert, *Cornelis Everaert: Spelen*, ed. by Jacob Muller and Lodewijk Scharpé (Leiden: Brill, 1920), pp. 103-16. For a more recent version: Cornelis Everaert, *De spelen van Cornelis Everaert*, ed. by Wim Hüsken, 2 vols (Hilversum: Verloren, 2005), I, pp. 250-73.

2 On Everaert's profession: Jan Dumolyn and Jelle Haemers, '"Let Each Man Carry on with his Trade and Remain Silent": Middle-Class Ideology in the Urban Literature of the Late Medieval Low Countries', *Cultural and Social History*, 10 (2013), 169-89 (pp. 173-74).

3 On the role of the burgomaster: Muller and Scharpé, *Spelen*, pp. 111-14.

4 'Consent maect wet': Muller and Scharpé, *Spelen*, p. 116.

5 The works of Shakespeare are all available online in open access. I used Victoria University's Quarto 1 version (1600): *The Merchant of Venice (Quarto 1, 1600)*, ed. by J. Jenstad. See: http://internetshakespeare.uvic.ca [accessed 23 March 2021].

primarily exploits such legal institutions towards achieving a comical effect.[6] In doing so, these cultural expressions underline the advanced institutionalization of commerce in the sixteenth-century market place, while also betraying a certain resistance to this institutionalization within contemporary society: a tension between the rigidity of formal laws on the one hand, and the more informal and personal aspects of trade on the other. Economic historians identify both of these aspects of trade as potential key factors to lower transaction costs in late medieval and early modern mercantile activity. One part of this has to do with successful contract enforcement, the other with countering so-called 'information asymmetries'. Through a lack of enforced international standards and procedures in pre-industrial Europe, there was no guarantee that traded products would live up to standards, nor that prices were just, nor that goods would be delivered on time – or at all, in fact. To combat these and other problems, traders founded institutions such as merchant associations in the later Middle Ages.[7] The public-order institutions of cities or entire principalities increasingly contributed to solving these issues as well.[8] At the same time, trust remained very important as well, and studies about various parts of European trade keep confirming the significance of networks based on personal relationships.[9]

These two aspects, commercial institutions and personal networks, form the main focus of the present chapter, which addresses the commercial dimension of the rural cloth industries of the Flemish West-Quarter. I will argue that the drapers of the textile villages could bring their businesses to fruition by using an array of available commercial institutions, which they coupled with their personal connections to fellow traders. But one factor in particular contributed to the successes of these draperies, namely the vertical integration of manufacture and trade (see also Chapter 2).[10] As will become clear, the rural fabrics of the West-Quarter were brought to market by some of the same people who were at least partially involved in the manufacturing process, if only in a supervisory capacity. Thus, the present chapter is connected to yet another debate in economic history, namely that on 'merchant capitalism'. Merchant

---

6 Walter Lim, 'Surety and Spiritual Commercialism in The Merchant of Venice', *Studies in English literature, 1500-1900*, 50 (2010), 355-81 (pp. 370-72, 374-75).

7 Wim Blockmans, 'Constructing a Sense of Community in Rapidly Growing European Cities in the Eleventh to Thirteenth Centuries', *Historical Research*, 83 (2010), 575-87 (pp. 586-87); Regina Grafe and Oscar Gelderblom, 'The Rise and Fall of the Merchant Guilds: Re-thinking the Comparative Study of Commercial Institutions in Premodern Europe', *The Journal of Interdisciplinary History*, 40 (2010), 477-511 (p. 487); Sheilagh Ogilvie, 'The Economics of guilds', *Journal of Economic Perspectives*, 28 (2014), 169-92 (pp. 170-73).

8 Ogilvie, 'The economics of guilds', pp. 177-79.

9 Oscar Gelderblom, 'The Governance of Early Modern Trade: The Case of Hans Thijs, 1556-1611', *Enterprise and Society*, 4 (2003), 606-39 (pp. 606-07, 612-14); Guido Alfani and Vincent Gourdon, 'Entrepreneurs, Formalization of Social Ties, and Trust Building in Europe (Fourteenth to Twentieth Centuries)', *The Economic History Review*, 45 (2012), 1005-28 (pp. 1009, 1012-13, 1025-26). See also the contributions in: *Entrepreneurs and Entrepreneurship in Early Modern Times: Merchants and Industrialists within the Orbit of the Dutch Staple Market*, ed. by Clé Lesger and Leo Noordegraaf (The Hague: Stichting Hollandsche Historische Reeks, 1995).

10 Grafe and Gelderblom, pp. 486-87.

capitalism is sometimes considered a phase in Europe's premodern economic development: a commercial system dominated by merchant-entrepreneurs who interfered in industrial processes and traded the manufactured products on the international market. As with proto-industrialization, the significance of this organizational aspect of the textile economy lies in its market-orientation. And indeed, merchant capitalism and proto-industry often went hand in hand in pre-industrial Europe.[11]

Not surprisingly, Everaert considered the figure of the merchant-entrepreneur as the main culprit behind, or at least an important accessory in, the morally questionable direction that trade was taking during his lifetime.[12] We will examine the extent to which the cloth villages of the West-Quarter had merchant-drapers who were guilty of this same kind of behaviour. In order to do so, the first part of the chapter addresses the issue of demand for products from the rural draperies of the West-Quarter. This is intended to contextualize the link between the production side, and demand and consumption. Leading on from that, the subsequent focus is on who sold these rural fabrics, and how these people related to the local communities of the cloth centres in the Flemish countryside. The third and fourth sections deal with a number of commercial institutions that were important for the cloth trade in the fifteenth and sixteenth centuries, most notably the official intervention of brokers and the use of fairs in the market cities of the Low Countries. Woven throughout the chapter is the issue of how the personal and informal dimension (or the 'social capital') of the traders bore down on the success of commercial transactions, specifically regarding the cloth villages that are central in this book.

International demand for cloth from the West-Quarter

In the fourteenth and fifteenth centuries, a crisis in international trade reshaped the textile economy of the Low Countries. Recent studies have broadened our understanding of this structural change by emphasizing the influence of social and political phenomena on the industrial reorientation within specific cities.[13] Herman Van der Wee has noted that supply factors outweighed the influence of demand during this period of recession in the Netherlandish textile trade.

---

11 Jan Luiten van Zanden, 'Do We Need a Theory of Merchant Capitalism?', *Review (Fernand Braudel Center)*, 20 (1997), 255-67 (pp. 258-60); Jan Luiten van Zanden, *The Rise and Decline of Holland's Economy: Merchant Capitalism and the Labour Market* (Manchester: Manchester University Press, 1993), p. 4.

12 Bas van Bavel, *The Invisible Hand? How Market Economies Have Emerged and Declined since AD 500* (Oxford: Oxford University Press, 2016), pp. 186-87.

13 Peter Stabel, 'The Move to Quality Cloth: Luxury Textiles, Labour Markets and Middle Class Identity in a Medieval Textile City: Mechelen in the Late Thirteenth and Early Fourteenth Centuries', in *Europe's Rich Fabric: The Consumption, Commercialisation, and Production of Luxury Textiles in Italy, the Low Countries and Neighbouring Territories (Fourteenth-Sixteenth Centuries)*, ed. by Bart Lambert and Katherine Anne Wilson (Farnham: Ashgate, 2016), 159-80 (pp. 159-61).

But he also underlined the connections between the two.[14] Much of this book is concerned with the industrial side of the textile trade, and therefore mainly focused on the supply angle. Yet the tricky question of demand is important as well, because it was during the 1300s and 1400s that the *nouvelle draperies* of the West-Quarter first rose to prominence. There was probably a growing market for products of middling quality in this period; or, at the very least, there was a stable demand for these products in the city of Bruges throughout the later fifteenth and sixteenth centuries.[15] The middle segment was also less vulnerable to the worsening market conditions plaguing the trade in cheaper textiles from the late thirteenth century onwards. During that period, the export market for light drapery had contracted because of rising transaction costs – largely because of warfare – on one side, and the relatively growing weight of a domestic market for luxury textiles among urban 'upper middle classes' on the other. As mentioned before, this drove the cities to move away from the lower market segments, leaving rural centres like Hondschoote to fill the vacuum left behind through their wage-competitiveness.[16]

The textile market of the late medieval Low Countries was remarkably diversified. We have only to look at overviews of the different products on sale to get an inkling of how varied the demand was in the fifteenth and sixteenth centuries. Indeed, a price list of the Antwerp market in 1575 reproduced *in extenso* by Alfons Thijs contains a plethora of options, which would astonish even the modern consumer. Apart from linens and silks, there were extremely luxurious fabrics partly woven from gold- and silver thread, the most expensive of which cost 840d. Flemish groats per ell.[17] Most variation could be found among the woollen fabrics, however, which ranged from the so-called *fin fin* cloths of Coggeshall (at 480d. per ell) at the top end of the scale, to low-quality undyed kerseys from Scotland and England at the bottom (at 17.5-30d. per ell), and with

14 Van der Wee, 'Structural changes and specialization', pp. 203, 207-08, 212-16.

15 Isis Sturtewagen, 'All Together Respectably Dressed: Fashion and Clothing in Bruges during the Fifteenth and Sixteenth Centuries' (unpublished doctoral thesis, University of Antwerp, 2016), pp. 119-21.

16 Sturtewagen, pp. 214-15; John Munro, 'The Origins of the English "New Draperies": The Resurrection of an Old Flemish Industry, 1250-1570', in *The New Draperies in the Low Countries and England, 1300-1800*, Pasold Studies in Textile Industry 10, ed. by N. B. Harte (New York: Oxford University Press, 1997), pp. 35-128 (pp. 71-74).

17 Alfons Thijs, 'Les textiles au marché anversois au XVIe siècle', in *Textiles of the Low Countries in European Economic History: Proceedings of the Tenth International Economic History Congress, Leuven August 1990*, Studies in Social and Economic History, ed. by Erik Aerts and John Munro (Leuven: Leuven University Press, 1990), pp. 76-86. For a comparable overview of textile prices in Italian cities in the thirteenth century, see: Patrick Chorley, 'The Cloth Exports of Flanders and Northern France during the Thirteenth Century: A Luxury Trade?', *The Economic History Review*, 40 (1987), 349-79 (pp. 352-53, 356-58). For detailed comparisons between prices of cloth from the Low Countries, as well as technical details, see: John Munro, 'Three Centuries of Luxury Textile Consumption in the Low Countries and England, 1330-1570: Trends and Comparisons of Real Values of Woollen Broadcloths (Then and Now)', in *The Medieval Broadcloth: Changing Trends in Fashions, Manufacturing and Consumption*, ed. by Kathrine Vestergård Pedersen and Marie-Louise Nosch (Oxford: Oxbow Books, 2009), 1-73 (pp. 14-15, 20-25, 27-29, 31-32, 34, 35, 37, 39-41, 42-46, 48-50, 61-63).

Hondschoote's cheapest says bringing up the rear of the light drapery spectrum (10d. per ell).[18] Such a vast array of options must have been mirrored by an equally diverse demand.

Textile consumption was, of course, one of the main markers of social status in medieval and early modern Europe, which explains this variation (although recent research on the city of Bruges indicates that the style and quality of tailoring was equally important).[19] Chroniclers often went out of their way to describe in detail the lavishness of princely and noble dress. And their patrons' generosity was occasionally measured according to endowments of clothes to their officers.[20] In order to maintain the fabric of late medieval society, sumptuary legislations laid down who was allowed to go about in which type of clothes.[21] However, evidence from the Low Countries suggests that this type of legislation was not introduced until the very end of the fifteenth century. Nor was it deployed as often as in other regions. Where it did occur, its purpose was primarily to restrict people from using clothes as an expression of political alliances.[22] Yet, while most clothing was sold by retailers, the bulk of the trade in raw textiles was conducted wholesale. Certainly as regarded fabrics, the Netherlandish cities of Bruges (in the fourteenth and fifteenth centuries) and Antwerp (in the sixteenth century) were the major commercial hubs of Europe. By the seventeenth century, the Dutch city of Amsterdam would come to fill this position, even as the textile centres of the Southern Low Countries became primarily oriented towards the city of Lille for political reasons.[23] All these urban trade centres were gateways for products both from the Low Countries and abroad. And so, the European textile market of this time was mainly characterized by wholesale transactions

---

18 Thijs, pp. 81-84.

19 Sturtewagen, pp. 67-72. See also: Frederik Buylaert, Wim De Clercq and Jan Dumolyn, 'Sumptuary Legislation, Material Culture and the Semiotics of "Vivre Noblement" in the County of Flanders (14th-16th Centuries)', *Social History*, 36 (2011), 393-417.

20 A good example is Olivier de la Marche's description of the attire of the prince and courtiers at the marriage between Charles the Bold and Margaret of York, where his benefactor purportedly spent over 40,000 *francs* to robe his officers: Andrew Brown and Graeme Small, *Court and Civic Society in the Burgundian Low Countries, c. 1420-1530* (Manchester: Manchester University Press, 2007), p. 60.

21 John Munro, 'Necessities and Luxuries in Early-Modern Textile Consumption: Real Values of Worsted Says and Fine Woollens in the Sixteenth-Century Low Countries', in *Cities – Coins – Commerce: Essays Presented to Ian Blanchard on the Occasion of his Seventieth Birthday*, Studien Zur Gewerbe- und Handelsgeschichte der Vorindustriel, ed. by Philipp Robinson Rössner (Stuttgart: Franz Steiner Verlag, 2012), pp. 121-46 (p. 121); Margaret Rose Jaster, '"Clothing Themselves in Acres": Apparel and Impoverishment in Medieval and Early Modern England', in *Medieval Clothing and Textiles*, 2, ed. by R. Netherton and G.R. Owen-Crocker (Woodbridge: Boydell, 2006), pp. 91-100 (pp. 91-92). See also pp. 93-98 for a discussion about the ineffectiveness of these legislations. On that point, compare: H. Doda, '"Saide Monstrous Hose": Compliance, Transgression and English Sumptuary Law to 1533', *Textile History*, 45 (2014), 171-91 (pp. 179-86).

22 Buylaert, De Clercq and Dumolyn, pp., 401-02; Sturtewagen, pp. 186-93.

23 Oscar Gelderblom, *Cities of Commerce: The Institutional Foundations of International Trade in the Low Countries, 1250-1650* (Princeton: Princeton University Press, 2013), p. 167; Johan Dambruyne, 'De hiërarchie van de Vlaamse textielcentra (1500-1750): continuïteit of discontinuïteit?', in: *Qui valet ingenio: liber amicorum aangeboden aan dr. Johan Decavele*, ed. by Leen Charles and others (Ghent: Stichting Mens en kultuur, 1996), pp. 155-72 (p. 166).

with international merchants who subsequently resold these goods in other regions.[24]

The urban markets were also the main commercial outlets for Nieuwkerke and the other larger cloth villages of the West-Quarter. Accordingly, the traders from these places were primarily wholesalers, too. Indeed, an overview of taxation on 'merchandise' (*coopmanscepe*) sold in Nieuwkerke in 1544-45, which we previously encountered in Chapter 1, makes clear that only a small proportion of the production output can have been marketed in the village itself. Unlike other (semi) urban industrial centres, such as Hondschoote and Poperinge, neither Nieuwkerke nor any of the other West-Quarter villages saw the foundation of an annual fair or other kind of periodic textile market, making them dependent upon the larger urban commercial centres.[25] Trade via cities like Bruges, Antwerp, and increasingly Lille, was in any case more efficient, as these places harboured far more prospective buyers than the local rural context could provide.

This is not to say there was no retail trade whatsoever. Among the fabrics produced in Nieuwkerke there were also cheaper fabrics called *eenlijsten* and *doucken*, made from lambswool and other inferior fibres, which were intended for those with smaller purses. And this probably included local customers.[26] But these lower-quality textiles were always produced on a smaller scale than the traditional woollens, and they have to be considered as distinct from them. In fact, it was forbidden to sell chartered drapery simultaneously with these coarser cloths. The latter were even banned from Nieuwkerke's halls in the Brabantine cities of Antwerp and Bergen op Zoom in the sixteenth century.[27] Moreover, the cloth sales that were made within the West-Quarter villages usually concerned linens, or sometimes cheaper woollens, and these transactions were partly conducted by people for whom no direct connection to the chartered drapery is recorded in the extant sources.[28] One exception to this pattern was evidenced in Nieppe, where some people sold and bought more luxurious goods, such as velvet (*flauweele*) and damask (*dammast*). But these would not have been produced locally; presumably, we are dealing with imports for a wealthy minority, such as the lord provost of Nieppe's village-seigneurie. The

24 For instance: two-thirds of all English cloth traded via Antwerp in the mid-sixteenth century were re-exported to Italy and the German Empire: Thijs, p. 84.

25 Gaillard, pp. 195-96; Coornaert, *Un centre industriel d'autrefois*, p. 257.

26 After 1542, *eenlijsten* and cut pieces were listed as one category in the acquittances sent to the Chamber of Accounts. After 1564, *doucken* were also included in this category: GSAB, CA 44562/11, 44562/29. On *doucken*, see: Munro, 'Spanish Merino Wools and the Nouvelles Draperies', p. 432; Soens, Stabel and Van de Walle, 'An Urbanised Countryside?', p. 38; Stabel, '"Dmeeste, oirboirlixste ende proffitelixste let ende neringhe"', pp. 120, 128.

27 RDHDF-2, III, pp. 144-45, 149-50.

28 In Nieuwkerke, the taxes on 'merchandise' are sometimes further denoted as 'of the linen-weavers' (*coopmanscepe van den lywadieren*): GSAB, CA, Acquits en portefeuilles 802bis (loose quire of August-September 1545). In Dranouter, the tax for sales of 'cloth' (*laekenen*) by Willem Wils amounted to 1d. for each 40d., meaning his products belonged to the category of says, *ostades*, and other light textiles: GSAB, CA, Acquits en portefeuilles 802bis (loose quire of April-May 1545); Maddens, II, p. 875.

same goes for the wine and beer imported from Lille that was included in this tax list.[29] Apart from this exception, most people in the West-Quarter bought cheaper textiles for their personal use. Even members of the household of the lady abbess of Mesen wore clothes made from linen.[30]

Because of the lack of references in contemporary documents, it is difficult to determine who were the primary consumers of cloth from Nieuwkerke and the other villages. The most solid evidence to go on are acquisitions by the city aldermen of Bruges in the fifteenth century. Among other things, they bought woollens from Nieuwkerke and *witkins* ('little whites') from Eécke. These textiles were expressly intended 'for dressing the mad and the foundlings, and also the other poor people of this city'. According to another entry in the city accounts, the fabric was principally made into 'habits' – a generic term for clothing.[31] John Munro included these transactions in a series of prices for the fifteenth century, from which it appears that Nieuwkerke's fabrics hovered around £2 Fl. gr. per piece of 30-35 ells for most of that period.[32] The white cloths from Eécke included in these same transactions were a lot cheaper, at roughly a third of this price.[33] It seems they were used to make the inner linings for the garments.[34] So, technically, in this instance, the West-Quarter textiles were made into clothes intended for people who were poor and, in a sense, at the margins of urban society. However, it should not be concluded that the price and quality were therefore low. After all, these purchases were made on the authority of Bruges' magistrates to provide for a specific social group under their care. And the attire of institutionalized poor people would have reflected directly on the city's reputation: the better they looked, the more they supported Bruges' image of prosperity. Indeed, the habits gifted to these poor beneficiaries were embroidered with the letter 'B' to showcase the city's benevolence.[35] In that sense, the use of Nieuwkerke cloth could be considered an act of conspicuous consumption, and therefore rather a testament to the relatively high quality of the village's product.[36] On the other hand, the city of Bruges expressly employed lesser tailors to manufacture the

29 GSAB, CA, Acquits en portefeuilles 802bis (loos quires; the reference to velvet and damask occurs in the quire covering December 1545 to January 1546). The imported beer is variously referred to as 'beer from beyond the Lys river' (*Overleys bier*) and 'beer from the Lille district' (*bijere van Rijsselambacht*).

30 In 1522, the abbess paid £59 6s. par. 'for the spinning of linen, flax, and other yarns, for the use of her household' ('van spinnene lynwaet, vlas, gaerne ende andersins omme den oorboor van hueren huuse'): SAB, Aanwinsten 4186, fol. 35r.

31 'Alle welcke voors. lakenen ghecocht waeren omme de cleedinghe van den dullen ende vondelinghen ende ooc van andere aerme liede van deser stede': CAB, 216, Stadsrekeningen, 1476-1477, fol. 40v. Reference to 'habits' (*habyten*) occur, for instance, on fol. 54r; see also: Sturtewagen, p. 36.

32 Munro, 'Three Centuries of Luxury Textile Consumption', pp. 44-45.

33 In May 1476, for example, three *witkins* from Eécke cost 35s. – or roughly 4.75d. per ell: CAB, 216, Stadsrekeningen, 1475-75, fol. 62v.

34 They were also referred to as *voerlaken* ('lining cloth'): CAB, 216, Stadsrekeningen, 1474-75, fol. 62v.

35 CAB, 216, Stadsrekeningen, 1482-1483, fol. 54r.

36 One might also refer to it as 'conspicuous compassion', although this runs the risk of being anachronistic. See: Patrick West, *Conspicuous Compassion: Why Sometimes it Really Is Cruel to Be Kind* (London: Coronet Books, 2004).

clothes of the institutional poor, probably to achieve just the reverse of outward prosperity: to instil a sense of charity among the wealthier citizens and induce them to give more alms. Still, the type of cloth was perhaps less important than the fit and style of the eventual vestment, in which the skill of the tailor was decisive.[37] Therefore we have to be careful not to attach too much importance as to who wore these clothes as an indication of the quality of the fabric itself.

Now, Nieuwkerke's fabrics may not have been cheap, but they did not really qualified as luxury goods either. Looking at the evolution of market prices for these cloths, their value was fairly consistent throughout the fifteenth and sixteenth centuries (**Figures 3.1a-b**). In fact, although the village's best products (called *kepers*, after the chevrons on Nieuwkerke's coat of arms), rose from around £2 Flemish groats in the first half of the fifteenth century to £6 Fl. gr. in 1575, they actually became cheaper in terms of purchasing power over that period. Still, a master mason always had to spend at least 50 days' worth of wages to buy one entire piece of 30 ells, even slightly more in the case of masons from Antwerp. At the same time, though, the data also reveal that for most of the fifteenth century, a master mason of Bruges only had to work between one and two days to generate enough wages to buy 1 ell of Nieuwkerke cloth (*c.* 0.85 m^2). Assuming one needed about 4 ells (*c.* 3.40 m^2) to manufacture an entire set of clothes, it would have taken around 6 to 8 days' wages to purchase the sufficient amount of cloth for this – excluding potential expenses of a tailor.[38] The lower urban middle groups of the Flemish city could therefore probably afford this rural fabric, and these have indeed been identified as the primary consumers of mid-priced textiles in Bruges. Of course, the more well-to-do town dwellers could afford them as well, and it is not unthinkable that they displayed themselves in garments cut from the same cloth worn by partakers of institutional charity, so long as their style of apparel conformed to the latest fashion.[39] Unfortunately, apart from the expenditures of the Bruges aldermen, no domestic sales of Nieuwkerke cloth have been preserved.

---

37 Sturtewagen, pp. 225-31.

38 In the case of the habits for the receivers of charity in Bruges: in 1483, a mixture of cloth from Nieuwkerke and Mesen amounting to 439.75 ells, combined with 263 ells of cloth from the county of Zeeland for the linings, made 95 large habits and 6 small ones, plus 1 pair of stockings and 1 tunic (*lyfroc*). Therefore, in order to sew one habit, one required around 4.4 ells of Nieuwkerke cloth: CAB, 216, Stadsrekeningen, 1482-1483, fol. 54^r. See also a land transaction of 1564 in the lordship of Spiere in Nieuwkerke, when part of the payment consisted of 4 ells of red cloth (which by then cost £7 par., or 35d. gr. per ell). Perhaps 4 ells were generally considered enough for one whole costume: SAB, Gemeentearchief Nieuwkerke 27, fol. 13^v. See also Munro's assessment that 16 day's wages for the purchase of an entire Hondschoote say in the sixteenth century was 'much more in accordance with our own expenditure patterns on clothing today': John Munro, 'Hanseatic Commerce in Textiles from the Low Countries and England during the Late Middle Ages: Changing Trends in Textiles, Markets, Prices, and Values, 1290-1579', in *Von Nowgorod bis London. Studien zu Handel, Wirtschaft und Gesellschaft im mittelalterlichen Europa*, ed. by Marie-Luise Heckmann and Jens Rörhrkasten (Göttingen: V&R Unipress, 2008), pp. 97-181 (pp. 110-11).

39 Sturtewagen, pp. 119-21, 63-70.

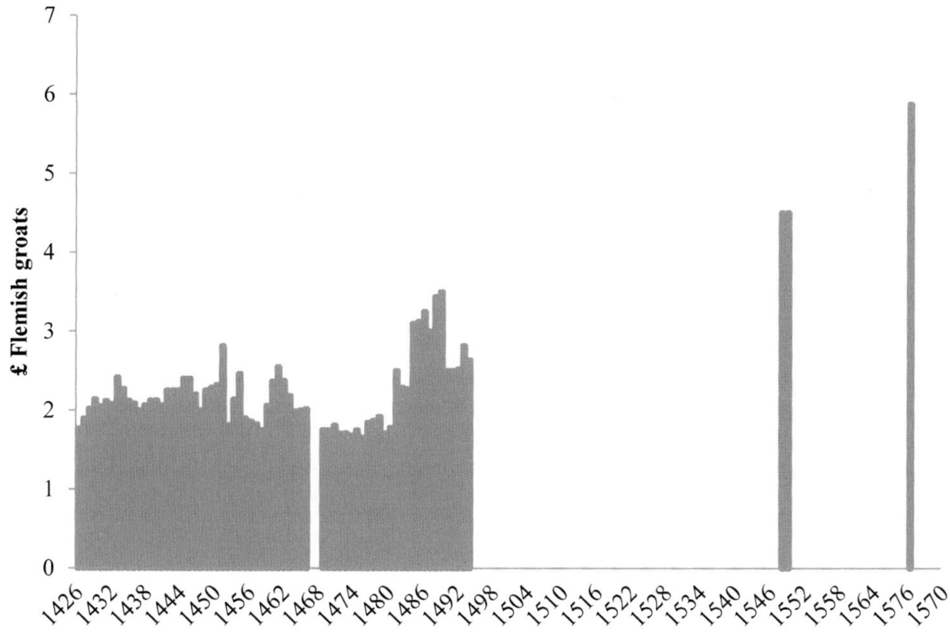

Figure 3.1a. Price of Nieuwkerke cloths (30 ells) in £ Flemish groat

Source: Munro, 'Prices for Cheap Woollens'; 'Antwerp. Annual wages and prices, 1400 – 1700'; 'Prices and Wages in Flanders, 1350 -1500'. Available online: https://www.economics.utoronto.ca/munro5/MedClothPrices.htm; GSAB, CA 23482, 23484; Thijs, 'Les textiles au marché anversois', p. 83.

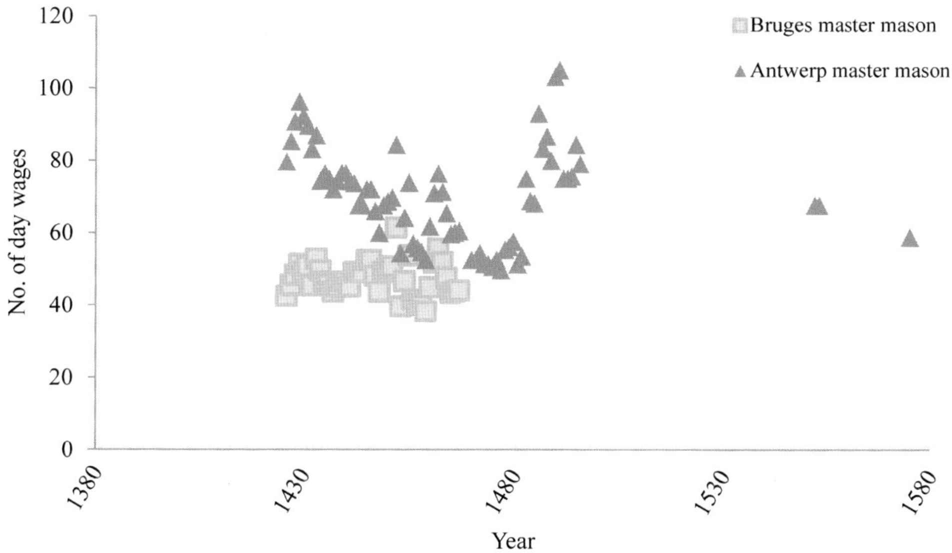

Figure 3.1b. Price evolution of Nieuwkerke cloths (day wages), 15th-16th century

Source: RDHIDF-2, III, pp. 175-76.

Then again, demand for West-Quarter cloth was largely external to the Low Countries. The medium stratum of the woollen market, which also included the products from Nieppe and Dranouter, as well as small Flemish towns like Mesen and Comines, mainly catered to the export market. Many of these younger industrial centres chiefly aimed at merchants from the central and northern German Empire.[40] The best example was the small town of Poperinge, which had an exclusive trading arrangement with the Hansa in the fifteenth century, almost to the point of a monopsony.[41] The earliest reference to 'Nieuwkerke cloth' (*Nigenkerkesch laken*) can also be found in the account book of a merchant from Hamburg, the entry dating from 1384.[42] Furthermore, although Nieuwkerke's fabrics were apparently not yet popular with Hanseatic traders in the fourteenth century, or at least not by their own name, they started to crop up in those parts around 1450.[43] The price of these fabrics was roughly the same as that of the Nieuwkerke woollens bought by the aldermen of Bruges, suggesting that they consisted of the same type and quality.[44] In addition to the German territories, the village's products were exported to the Iberian Peninsula as well, where merchants had fostered trade relations with Ypres since at least the thirteenth century.[45] A Portuguese overview of customs rates for imported fabrics of 1439-48 mentions cloths 'from the village Nieuwkerke' (*E villagem de Hunquerca*).[46] In that sense,

---

40 Van der Wee, 'Structural Changes', pp. 212, 214-15; Hektor Ammann, 'Deutschland und die Tuchindustrie Nordwest-Europas im Mittelalter', *Hansische Geschichtsblätter*, 72 (1954), 1-63.

41 RDHDF-2, III, 257-58; Rudolf Holbach, *Frühformen von Verlag und Grossbetrieb in der gewerblichen Produktion (13.-16. Jahrhundert)* (Stuttgart: Steiner, 1994), pp. 71-72; Rudolf Holbach, 'Some Remarks on the Role of "Putting-Out" in Flemish and Northwest European Cloth Production', in *La draperie ancienne des Pays-Bas: débouchés et stratégies de survie*, ed. by Marc Boone and Walter Prevenier (Leuven: Garant, 1993), pp. 207-49 (p. 211).

42 Vicko von Geldersen, *Das Handlungsbuch Vickos von Geldersen*, ed. by Hans Nirrnheim (Hamburg: L. Voss, 1895), p. 81.

43 In 1364, the Kraków market sold a category of fabrics referred to as 'common [cloth] from Ypres' (*gemeyn Eyprisch*), which Charles Verlinden interpreted as rural manufactures: Charles Verlinden, 'Brabantsch en Vlaamsch laken te Krakau op het einde der XIVe eeuw', *Medeelingen van de Koninklijke Vlaamsche Academie voor Wetenschappen, Letteren en Schoone Kunsten*, 5 (1943), 16-33 (p. 27). Witold von Slaski, *Danziger Handel im XVe Jahrhundert auf Grund eines im Danziger Stadtarchive befindlichen Handlungsbuches gheschildert* (Gdańsk: C.F. Beisel Nachf., 1905), pp. 63-64. Von Slaski erroneously attributed these fabrics to Nijkerk in Holland, but it seems apparent that we are dealing with Nieuwkerke in Western Flanders.

44 In Gdańsk, in 1447, one piece of Nieuwkerke cloth cost 13.5 Mark Lübisch, and in 1449 it cost 12.5 Mark Lübisch. In between 1424 and 1444, the exchange rate averaged at 6.975 Mark Lübisch for each £ Flemish groats: Von Slaski, pp. 23, 25, 64. This roughly corresponds to the rule-of-thumb exchange rate of 6.666 Mark per pound maintained elsewhere: Uwe Ziegler, *Die Hanse: Aufstieg, Blütezeit und Niedergang der ersten Europäischen Wirtschaftsgemeinschaft: Eine Kulturgeschichte von Handel und Wandel zwischen 13. und 17. Jahrhundert* (Bern: Scherz Verlag, 1994), p. 302. The cloths sold in Gdańsk therefore cost respectively £1 18s. 8.5d. and £1 15s. 10d. Fl. gr., or between 14d. and 16d. per ell.

45 Lluís To Figueras, 'Wedding Trousseaus and Cloth Consumption in Catalonia around 1300', *The Economic History Review*, 69 (2016), 522-47 (pp. 532, 536-38).

46 Charles Verlinden, 'Draps des Pays-Bas et du Nord-Ouest de l'Europe au Portugal au XVe siècle', *Annuario de Estudios Medievales*, 2 (1966), 235-61 (pp. 254-55). Verlinden did not connect the entry to Nieuwkerke, but this Flemish village is the only suitable candidate (the passage could technically have referred to Dunkirk, but this was not a village, nor am I aware that it produced cloths for export in this period).

the rural centre stuck to the same pattern as most small urban industries that produced medium-quality woollens, such as Poperinge, Comines, and Wervik. Indeed, the prices of these places all hovered around the same level for most of the fifteenth century.[47]

It seems that little changed on this front in the sixteenth century. The extant administration recording exports from Bruges in the mid-1500s mentions several cargoes of goods destined for Spain containing fabrics from Nieuwkerke.[48] Also, as late as 1563, a spokesmen of the village's drapery corporation pleaded with the Chamber of Accounts for permission to produce shorter pieces of cloth, specifically because of the rising demand for these products among 'the foreign merchants, both from the German countries and elsewhere'.[49] In that regard, the villages of the West-Quarter contrasted with their most prolific contemporaries of Armentières and Hondschoote, the products of which were largely bound for the Italian states.[50] Apart from a consignment of counterfeit Armentières *oultrefins* in 1561 that were really made in Nieuwkerke, there are no recorded trade relations between Italian traders and this or any of the other villages of the region.[51] Even Wouter Ameide of Bruges, who brokered many a deal in fabrics from the Lys region with his Italian clients around 1500, conducted no notable transactions in cloth stemming from the West-Quarter villages.[52] And he would have been in a perfect position to do so, since he oversaw a large number of purchases of raw materials by drapers from Nieuwkerke, Kemmel, Wulvergem, and Dranouter (see below). Apparently, there was no real market for these rural products in the Italian Peninsula. It is unclear why not, because merchants from this region had been buying other mid-priced woollens such as those of Poperinge since the fourteenth century.[53] Perhaps it should be attributed to 'the mysteries of fashion' that seem to have stimulated the consumption of lighter fabrics in the Italian states in this period.[54]

47 Their prices varied between 10 and 16 Lübische Mark, or *c.* 12-17d. per ell: Von Slaski, pp. 61, 63-64, 66.

48 GSAB, CA 23482-85. See below.

49 'Les marchans estrangiers, tant des pays d'Allemainge et d'aultres lieux': RDHDF-2, III, pp. 198-99.

50 John Munro, 'The Low Countries' Export Trade in Textiles with the Mediterranean Basin, 1200-1600: A Cost–Benefit Analysis of Comparative Advantages in Overland and Maritime Trade Routes', *International Journal of Maritime History*, 11 (1999), 1-30 (p. 25); Jeroen Puttevils, '"Eating the Bread out of their Mouth": Antwerp's Export Trade and Generalized Institutions', *The Economic History Review*, 68 (2015), 1339-64 (pp. 1342, 1353, 1356).

51 RDHDF-2, I, pp. 326-32. The expansive correspondence of the Antwerp trading firm of the Van der Molen family with Italian merchants contains no reference to cloth from the West-Quarter villages: Jeroen Puttevils, '*A servitio de vostri sempre siamo*': de effecten van de handel tussen Antwerpen en Italië op de koopmansfamilie Van der Molen (midden zestiende eeuw)' (unpublished Masters-thesis, University of Antwerp, 2007), p. 83. I am indebted to Jeroen Puttevils for allowing me to consult his database on transactions of the Van der Molen.

52 Peter Stabel, 'Entre commerce international et économie locale: le monde financier de Wouter Ameyde (Bruges fin XVe-début XVIe siècle)', in *Finances publiques et finances privés*, ed. by Marc Boone and Walter Prevenier (Leuven & Apeldoorn: Garant, 1996), pp. 75-100 (pp. 85-86).

53 Chorley, pp. 367-68. In the mid-fifteenth century, the fabrics of Poperinge and Nieuwkerke sold in Gdańsk were in the same price range: Von Slaski, pp. 64, 66.

54 Munro, 'The Originis of the English "New Draperies"', p. 87.

The merchant-drapers of the West-Quarter

The main criticism that manufacturers like Cornelis Everaert levelled against the merchants of their time related to their extractive and non-productive approach towards economic enterprise. In another play of Everaert's, the *Play of Unequal Currency* (*'t Spel van d'Onghelycke Munte*), a cast of characters representing the less fortunate working masses discuss the wrongful conduct of merchants during periods when the currency of one place was disproportionate to that of the next. In these circumstances 'the merchant manages to profit doubly' (*Den coopman weet tweesins proffyt te beleuene*), buying goods where his coins have a higher value and selling them where the currency is weak, and back and forth.[55] I would interpret the play as an exposition of the skewed relations between merchants and workers in general in this period. Everaert's opinion is highly understandable: within the merchant capitalism that took hold of European commerce in the sixteenth century, traders were primarily a redistributive link between the production centres and the international urban market place.[56] Moreover, for merchants of the late medieval and early modern Low Countries, the ability to intervene in the production process of commodities that they sold was highly beneficial, as it allowed them to lower costs and adapt more efficiently to market demand. In the case of sixteenth-century Antwerp, the commercial metropolis *par excellence* at the time, this was an area where traders from the city itself clearly had the edge over foreign competitors, who were unable to establish the same ties with production centres. Hondschoote has already been noted as an example in previous chapters; the Brabantine village of Duffel offers another illustration.[57]

Broadly speaking, this interconnection between industry and trade was a departure from the fourteenth and fifteenth centuries, when textile industries in the Southern Low Countries were often controlled by merchant capital from foreign trading nations, mainly by Italian and German firms.[58] As noted in the previous chapter, however, these forms of commercial enterprise are unrecorded for Nieuwkerke, Dranouter, Kemmel, or the other main cloth centres of the Flemish West-Quarter.[59] Indeed, in the fifteenth century, we encounter a group of people in Nieuwkerke who were explicitly called 'merchant-drapers' (*marchans drappiers*), which strongly suggests that they engaged in the commercial

55 Muller and Scharpé, *Spelen*, line 94 (entire passage: lines 80-121).

56 Van Zanden, 'Do We Need a Theory of Merchant Capitalism?', pp. 258-62.

57 Jeroen Puttevils, *Merchants and Trading in the Sixteenth Century: The Golden Age of Antwerp*, Perspectives in Economic and Social History (London: Pickering and Chatto, 2015), pp. 57-59, 169; Michael Limberger, *Sixteenth-Century Antwerp and its Rural Surroundings: Social and Economic Changes in the Hinterland of a Commercial Metropolis (ca. 1450-ca. 1570)* (Turnhout: Brepols, 2008).

58 Van Werveke, p. 8. Having said that, in Hondschoote, the fourteenth- and fifteenth centuries were mainly different in that the local traders had more influence; something that gradually changed from the late-1400s: Coornaert, *Un centre industriel d'autrefois*, p. 356.

59 A notable exception was Flêtre: its charter evidences the importance of merchants, presumably external ones from Lille: RDHDF-2, II, 283 (n. 2).

process as well as in cloth production.[60] There are similar references elsewhere, sometimes also to 'cloth salesmen' (*lakencoopere*); and occasionally, the drapers were simply referred to as 'traders' (*cooplieden*) or 'merchants' (*coopmannen*).[61] Needless to say, this issue of nomenclature is highly dependent upon context, and it comes as no surprise that drapers were often defined in these broader terms within the setting of urban markets – where they came to trade, after all. Yet this confirms the point: clearly, there was a group of cloth entrepreneurs stemming from the production centres who were also directly involved in the sale of fabrics in the market towns.

We mainly catch glimpses of these merchant-drapers, not through records of cloth sales, but in documents of their wool purchases from other traders. This is unfortunate, because it is therefore hard to establish their individual sales volumes. Likewise, although the amount of raw materials they consumed might equally serve as an indication of the scale of their operations, there are problems to this as well. The reason is that it is far from certain that merchant-drapers limited themselves to only one supplier. And so, the volumes of raw materials they purchased could have been substantially bigger than suggested by the transactions for which records happen to survive. Nor can we rule out the possibility that they bought more wool than they required for themselves in order to sell it on to their fellow drapers and artisans in the villages (think of the example of Christiaan Baelde, whom we have encountered in the previous chapter).

What the wool transactions do reveal, however, is which individuals were directly involved in the market for raw materials, and how they conducted their businesses. Two such sources that have proved particularly useful are the account book of the Bruges-based broker Wouter Ameide, which dates from around the turn of the fifteenth century, and the records of the Castilian firm of Juan Castro de Muxica from the 1530s.[62] It should be noted that these two trading contacts were fundamentally different. Ameide was merely a go-between who brokered deals between the rural drapers and the wool-merchants who supplied them with fleeces.[63] De Muxica, on the other hand, who was a member of the Spanish Nation in the city of Bruges, was himself such a supplier.[64] The records of both of these men reveal that the traders of Dranouter, Kemmel, and Nieuwkerke belonged to the same families as those that feature heavily in the documents produced by the rural cloth corporations, as well as those occurring in Nieuwkerke's production overview of 1564-65.

60 RDHDF-2, III, p. 103.

61 For example, Cornelis Liebaert was referred to as *marchant-drappier* during a trial in the sixteenth century: Vandamme, p. 127 (n. 1); GSAB, CA, Dozen van de Rekenkamer 261; CAA, Certificatieboeken 19 (1563), fol. 213^{r}; 24 (1564), fol. 366.

62 CAB, Reeks 305, Wouter Ameyde, Grootboek A, Journaal B; CAB, Archief van het Spaanse Consulaat, Juan Castro de Muxica, Grootboek 1534-1535 (*libro de cajas*); Journaal 1535-1538 (*libros diarios*).

63 Stabel, 'Entre commerce international et économie locale'.

64 Raymond Fagel, *De Hispano-Vlaamse wereld: de contacten tussen Spanjaarden en de Nederlanders, 1496-1555* (Brussels: Archief- en bibliotheekwezen in België, 1996), pp. 56-66.

Underrepresented, however, were female entrepreneurs: Ameide's administration contains no reference to draperesses from the West-Quarter, and the only woman occurring in the Castilian transactions was identified – in typical fashion – as the 'widow of Pieter Ente' (*la biuda de Pieter Entra*).[65] The latter clearly acted as a replacement for her deceased husband, who still figured in the account book (*libro de cajas*) of 1534-35 but no longer occurred in the daily register (*libros diarios*) of 1535-38.[66] We have already seen that women were not excluded from commercial ventures in the same way that they were banned from certain crafts. A city like late medieval Ghent was riddled with female retailers, for instance.[67] Still, based on this evidence, it seems that the commercial dealings of the West-Quarter merchant-drapers were dominated by men, or at least on the record. This particular draperess, for instance, still had her own account with the Castilians in 1537, and she bought no fewer than 8 sacks (more than 700 kilograms) of wool that year.[68] But she continuously featured together with 'Pieter De Keersgieter and company' (*Pietre Quesquitre & conpañia*).[69] Technically, this could have entailed some form of guardianship by a male relative over what were considered the affairs of the late Pieter Ente. Indeed, a Pieter De Keersgieter had married one Jakemine, daughter of Daniel Ente in 1536, so a family connection to Ente's estate is plausible.[70] Yet this is unlikely because female traders in the Flemish cities had a far-reaching level of juridical independence, which was manifested in the specific legal statute of 'saleswoman' (*coopwyf*).[71] Therefore, the wives of male merchant-drapers were probably deeply involved in the commercial part of the entrepreneurial process, even more so than in manufacture. This isolated example certainly indicates that the widow of Pieter Ente was up to speed concerning the acquisition of wool: she had to have been personally present when deals were conducted, and it was she who was held accountable for the debts. Nevertheless, the records of the Castilian form identified her in terms of her relationship to her late husband, perhaps for the sake of continuity (that is, to carry on a pre-existing account).

Overall, the sources do not allow for a comprehensive insight into the stratification of merchant-drapers in the same way as the figures for 1564-65

65 For instance: CAB, Archief van het Spaanse Consulaat, Juan Castro de Muxica, Grootboek (*libro de cajas*), 1534-1535, p. 40 (right side), p. 89 (left side).

66 CAB, Archief van het Spaanse Consulaat, Juan Castro de Muxica, Journaal, 1535-1538, two entries for 15 June 1537, and one for 14 November 1537.

67 Marianne Danneel, *Weduwen en wezen in het laat-middeleeuwse Gent* (Leuven: Garant, 1996), pp. 377-82.

68 The journal of the De Muxica firm contains cross-references to a corresponding main account book, of which the *libro de cajas* is an earlier example. Unfortunately, the two surviving books are not connected in this way. See: Fagel, pp. 56-63 (esp. n. 197 on p. 56).

69 Amsterdam, Leiden, Haarlem, Ypres, Nieuwkerke, Nieppe, Armentières, Saint-Omer, Kemmel, Bruges, Douai, Lille, Bailleul, Dranouter, Menen, Poperinge, Oudenaarde, Antwerp, Breda, Enghien, 's-Hertogenbosch, Mechelen, Tournai, Liège, as well as some unidentified places: Fagel, p. 60.

70 RLB, Fonds Merghelynck, M 18/22, p. 8. Unfortunately, Pieter Ente's marriage was not recorded by the Ypres records or we might have traced the activities of his widow further via her maiden name.

71 Danneel, pp. 377-78.

Table 3.1. Wool sold to West-Quarter drapers by Juan Castro de Muxica, 1535-38

	Wool (*sacas*)	Approximate weight (kg)	Total sum (£-s.-d. Fl. gr.)
Dranouter	127	11,312	768-2-7
Kemmel	100	8907	535-18-2
Nieuwkerke	336	29,927	2038-0-4
Nieppe	3	267	24-2-4
Total	566	50,413	3367-3-7

Source: CAB, Archief van het Spaanse Consulaat, Juan Castro de Mu*xica*, Journaal, 1535-1538.

allowed on the level of cloth production in Nieuwkerke (see Chapter 2). Wouter Ameide's attentions were mainly absorbed by the draperies of the Lys region; in contrast, his records offer far from a complete picture of the West-Quarter's wool imports.[72] The records of Juan Castro de Muxica also offer no more than a partial insight into the total trade volumes of these rural cloth centres. To be sure, his firm mainly traded in wool, and with traders from a variety of places in the Low Countries.[73] Out of the West-Quarter villages, Kemmel, Dranouter, and Nieuwkerke are most prominently represented in the firm's trade register covering the period 1535-38 (**Table 3.1**). Based on these records, it even seems as if the Castilian company supplied a sizeable chunk of the villages' total wool imports. However, it was clearly only one out of several suppliers. This is evident from the scattered references to other wool-merchants who traded with the rural drapers.[74] More so than that, and in spite of the large volume of these traded fleeces, the numbers prove that the cloth industries of the West-Quarter must have sourced raw materials in diverse places. To take Nieuwkerke as an example: between 1535 and 1538, its artisans produced 35,969.5 pieces of cloth, which would weigh around 561,448 kilograms in total (**Table 3.2**). Most of that weight should be attributed to the wool (although how much was water or grease is hard to establish).[75] However we calculate it, the approximate 30,000 kilograms of wool provided by Juan Castro's firm can only have been a minor proportion of this total. Even more so, because medieval Mediterranean fleeces lost about half their mass after the lanolin had been removed.[76] Another part consisted of impurities in the fibre. In fact, this was a bone of contention between Spanish wool-merchants and Netherlandish drapers: the cloth entrepreneurs of Armentières, Nieuwkerke, and Poperinge jointly sued the Spanish Nation in Bruges before the Privy Council in 1522 over just this issue.[77]

72 Stabel, 'Entre commerce international et économie locale', p. 89.

73 Fagel, p. 60.

74 Among others, the Suarez firm and the wool merchant Lopes de la Coroña (*Louppes de la Couronne*) traded with Nieuwkerke, Kemmel and Dranouter: Fagel, pp. 131, 133 (n. 578).

75 Nieuwkerke's fabrics were allowed a maximum of 2 lbs (0.852 kg) of butter per piece: RDHDF-2, III, pp. 169-76.

76 This was a notable contrast with English wool, which lost only about 20 per cent: Dominique Cardon, *La draperie au Moyen Âge. Essor d'une grande industrie Européenne* (Paris: CNRS, 1999), p. 151.

77 Fagel, p. 129.

Table 3.2. Technical details of Nieuwkerke cloth

Drapery: city/region	NIEUWKERKE	ARMENTIÈRES	HONDSCHOOTE
Date of ordinance	1462, 1485	1510, 1546	1553
Name of textile	Kepers	Oultrefins	Single say
Origins of wools	Spain, Scotland, Flanders	Spain, England	Flanders, Friesland, Scotland, Pomerania
Wool types	n.s.	Spanish Merino (2/3) English Cotswolds (1/3)	n.s.
Length on loom (ells)	n.s.	42.000	40.000
Length on loom (metres)	n.s.	29.400	28.000
Width on loom (ells)	2.875	3.000	n.s.
Width on loom (metres)	1.992	2.100	n.s.
Weight on loom (kg)	n.s.	88.000	n.s.
Final length (ells)	32.000	30.000	35.000
Final length (metres)	22.176	21.000	24.500
Final width (ells)	1.750	2.000	0.875
Final width (metres)	1.213	1.400	0.613
N° of warps	1200	1800	n.s.
Warps per cm (fulled)	10.108	12.857	n.s.
Area (m^2)	26.899	29.400	15.006
Final weight (lb)	n.s.	52.000	11.000
Final weight (kg)	*15.609**	24.123	5.103
Weight per m^2 (g)	*580.278**	820.503	340.052

Source: Munro, 'Three centuries of luxury textile consumption', pp. 10-11; RDHIDF-2, I, pp. 63-69; III, pp. 112-20.

* Based upon the mean value between the weight of an Armentières' *oultrefin* and a Hondschoote *say*. This is slightly arbitrary, but in 1575, the price of Nieuwkerke's *kepers* (46-48d. per ell) was almost exactly midway between that of an Armentières' *oultrefin* (60-85d. per ell) and a single *say* from Hondschoote (10-12d. per ell).

Nevertheless, these sources allow some crucial observations about the merchant-drapers of the cloth villages. First of all, the Castilian accounts identify several people as cloth traders for whom other evidence already attested that they were also engaged in local commercial activity, especially in the village of Dranouter. Seventeen drapers from that cloth centre were taxed for selling meat in 1545, though none of them sold more than 5 animals in total.[78] A number of the cloth entrepreneurs from Nieuwkerke who occur in the Castilian administration traded in livestock as well, and some of them were also active in the local beer trade (see Chapter 1). Second, it is clear that some of these merchants had

78 GSAB, CA, Acquits en portefeuilles 802bis (loose, non foliated quires).

substantial enterprises. In Dranouter, such a family with extensive mercantile activity were the Moenin: Jan Moenin bought 18 *sacas* of wool (over 1600 kg) from Juan Castro between 1535 and 1538, and Frans Moenin even purchased as many as 30 sacks (*c.* 2672 kg). Of all the West-Quarter cloth centres, it was the drapers of Nieuwkerke who bought the most wool, however. Chief among them was Michiel Beutack, with no fewer than 42 sacks (or 3741 kg) to his name in this four-year period.

Third, it is interesting to note that the majority of these purchases were made by trading partnerships, which the Spanish wool merchants referred to as 'companies' (*conpañia*). In the case of the Moenin and Beutack enterprises, these partners consisted of their family members. But in other cases the connections were less clear-cut. Joris De Corte of Nieuwkerke, for instance, bought the lion's share of his 34 sacks together with his fellow parishioner Willem De Brouckere. The latter was noted as ex-warden and 'notable' draper in 1553, and still produced 54 cloths in 1564-65.[79] In theory, these joint ventures may have been created to link a merchant's capital to the industrial 'service' of a draper.[80] But all partnerships in the West-Quarter cloth corporations apparently consisted of drapers, which suggests that the partnerships were chiefly a method of pooling resources. The drapers may either have done this to offer extra security to the wool sellers, or to expand their budgets and sales volumes, or probably a combination of both. This seems logical enough when only small volumes were traded – the implication being that these entrepreneurs were not wealthy enough to secure large enough sums on their own.[81] However, several *conpañia* bought more than 10 sacks all at once, even as many as 24 in one instance, which means that the individual partners could have easily bought wool on an individual basis.[82] This, coupled with the recurrent nature of most alliances, suggests that these were all-in partnerships of entrepreneurs.

One family of merchant-drapers which merits extra attention is the Mortier family from Dranouter. Their entrepreneurial activities were centred in this village, where already in 1481, a Willem Mortier was the largest draper on record: his workshop was in the process of producing 28 woollens when he was audited by Ypres' town council for acting in violation of the city's cloth privilege.[83] In the early sixteenth century, a Reinoud Mortier held a small fief from the lord of Dranouter, and he would go on to buy several properties in Nieuwkerke as well in 1533-34.[84] Probably the same Reinoud was one of the local traders of livestock

79 RDHDF-2, III, p. 176; GSAB, CA, Acquits en portefeuilles 1367/34.

80 For the different types and inspirations behind partnerships or *societas*, see: Michael Postan, 'Partnerships in English Medieval Commerce', in *Medieval Trade and Finance*, ed. by Michael Postan (Cambridge: Cambridge University Press, 1973), pp. 65-91 (esp. p. 66).

81 For example, Mathieu De Raedt *&* *conpañia*, who usually bought only 1 to 4 sacks: CAB, Archief van het Spaanse Consulaat, Juan Castro de Muxica, Journaal, 1535-1538, entries for 28 November 1535, 31 March, 8 April 1536.

82 CAB, Archief van het Spaanse Consulaat, Juan Castro de Muxica, Journaal, 1535-1538, entries for 31 July, 15 October, and 16 November 1537.

83 RDHDF-2, I, pp. 24-28.

84 ADN, J 431/5, fol. 20^v; SAB, Aanwinsten 504, fol. 12^r.

in 1545, as was a man called Karel Mortier, who also bought 12 sacks of wool from Juan Castro de Muxica.[85] Most noteworthy, however, are peculiar references to a type of cloth called *mortiers* in the export overviews of the Spanish Nation via the port of Bruges. On May 19th, 1552, a merchant called Melchior de Vega brought along 4 of these fabrics, in a sarpler that also contained *rougelijsten* (from Menen), and 'cloths from Kemmel' (*draps de Kemele*).[86] At that time, the *mortiers* cost £4 18s. 11d. per piece, which places them firmly in the same category as the products of Kemmel (£4 1s. 1d.) and Nieuwkerke (£4 10s.).[87] It appears we are dealing with something like an actual brand: a product identified by casting the provenance in terms of the family that produced it.[88] This is less far-fetched than it seems, considering that the same source mentions Nieuwkerke's *draps kepers* and *ennekins* ('little Ns') without explicit reference to that locality. Similarly, Armentières' *oultrefins*, Kortrijk's *bellaerds* and Menen's *rougelijsten* were often traded without specifying the town from which they came.[89] Quality was the yardstick, and although it was linked to provenance, the worth of a fabric was determined through a minute inspection, particularly of the depth of colour.[90] It is for this same reason that, when Nieuwkerke's drapers rented the cloth hall in Bergen op Zoom, their contract included the clause that they had to 'make all such light necessary to assist and serve them to display their cloths'.[91] Indeed, a medieval cloth merchant worth his salt could identify anywhere between 30 and 60 different kinds of textiles from memory, and this recognition was mainly based on outward characteristics like the selvages (the edges of the weave).[92]

That said, this kind of association, between a type of fabric and its maker, was largely unheard of in this period. The notable exception was John Winchcombe II of Newbury, whose products were marketed as 'Winchcombe kerseys' in Antwerp.[93] Of course, Winchcombe's was an enterprise operating on an unprecedented scale for the time period. Generating over 500 cloths each month, this cloth entrepreneur's reputation was such that a fictionalized story of his life was printed in the 1590s.[94] There is no way that the Mortier operated on a scale that came

85 Between them, they sold 2 cows and 3 pigs that year: GSAB, CA, Acquits en portefeuilles 802bis.

86 GSAB, CA 23482, fol. 21^v.

87 GSAB, CA 23482, fol. 29^v.

88 Bert De Munck, 'The Agency of Branding and the Location of Value: Hallmarks and Monograms in Early Modern Tableware Industries', *Business History*, 54 (2012), 1-22 (pp. 10-13).

89 GSAB, CA 23482, e.g. on fols 11^v, 14^v; Stabel, '"Dmeeste, oirboirlixste ende proffitelixste let ende neringhe"', p. 136.

90 Puttevils, *Merchants and Trading*, p. 59; David Peacock, 'Research Note: Dyeing Winchcombe Kersies and other Kersey Cloth in Sixteenth-Century Newbury', *Textile History*, 37 (2006), 187-202 (p. 189).

91 'Te makenen alle alzulcken nootlick licht als henlieden sal bedienen ende behoeffelick zyn in 't thoonen van hueren lakenen, ende anders nyet': City Archives Bergen op Zoom (subsequently CABZ), Protocol van rentebrieven en recognities, 1511-1512, fol. 66^v.

92 Carsten Jahnke, 'Some Aspects of Medieval Cloth Trade in the Baltic Sea Area', in *The Medieval Broadcloth*, ed. by Pedersen and Nosch, pp. 74-89 (p. 76).

93 David Peacock, 'The Winchcombe Family and the Woollen Industry in Sixteenth-Century Newbury', (unpublished doctoral thesis, University of Reading, 2003), p. 18.

94 Peacock, 'The Winchcombe Family', p. 15; Thomas Deloney, 'The Most Pleasant and Delectable Historie of Iohn Winchcombe, Otherwise Called Iacke of Newberie: And First of his Loue and Pleasant Life', in *The Works of Thomas Deloney*, ed. by Francis Mann (Oxford: Oxford Clarendon Press, 1912), pp. 1-68.

even close to Winchcombe's. But there is little doubt that wholesale traders in the market cities would have had a preference for certain cloth makers. These traders could identify the source of the products they liked through the 'cloth marks' that had to be woven into each piece of fabric. It is only a small step from such identification based on the draper's mark to a connection between a family name (or brand) and an exceptional level of quality.[95]

Shopping around: networks and commercial institutions

While fabrics such as *kepers*, *oultrefins*, and indeed *mortiers* enjoyed a good reputation in the mid-sixteenth century, it would have taken some time before their reliability had become established. The imbalanced foreknowledge of what was exchanged between sellers and buyers in a commercial transaction, or what is referred to as 'information asymmetry', was a main concern of medieval and early modern trade. Trust remained all-important.[96] The previous chapter has shown how several urban governments tried to woo the cloth entrepreneurs of Nieuwkerke, and, as suggested, one reason for this headhunting was the rural drapers' ability to dominate the entire local manufacturing process. But another reason why these cities were interested in the rural drapers was their 'social capital', their networks.[97] These operated on the local, the interregional, and the international level, because the drapers were the middlemen between industrial supply and commercial demand. As regarded the raw materials, the drapers also fulfilled the same function in reverse: they brought the wool, dyestuffs and other goods that were only available on the urban market to the West-Quarter villages. And so, their key role in overseeing the production process was mirrored in their pivotal position in all things commercial. Their 'non-specialization' on this point was the secret behind their driving role in the world of merchant capitalism that they inhabited.[98] They went about this by using the accessible commercial institutions of the Netherlandish urban markets, in combination with their personal connections to other traders. Indeed, despite the increased officialdom of trade transactions, Cornelis Everaert's 'merchant who kissed goodbye to five pound groats' confirmed this importance of socializing with business associates: the protagonist at one point proclaims that 'a pretty penny, to engage with good men, I have always at the ready'.[99]

---

95 See also: John Oldland, 'The Clothiers' Century, 1450-1550', *Rural History*, 29 (2018), 1-22 (p. 9).

96 Gelderblom, 'The Governance of Early Modern Trade', pp. 606-07, 612-14; Alfani and Gourdon, pp. 1009, 1012-13, 1025-26.

97 Pierre Bourdieu, 'The Forms of Capital', in *Handbook of Theory and Research for the Sociology of Education*, ed. by John Richardson (New York: Greenwood, 1986), pp. 246-58 (pp. 251-53).

98 The term was coined in this context by Fernand Braudel, but the reference(is from: Immanuel Wallerstein, 'Merchant, Dutch, or Historical Capitalism?', *Review (Fernand Braudel Center)*, 20 (1997), 243-54 (p. 252).

99 'Jc hebbe altoos eenen pennync moylic / Om met goe mannen te vertheerren': Muller and Scharpé, *Spelen*, p. 107, lines 96-97.

Fortunately for them, when the merchant-drapers from the West-Quarter first began to sell their cloths in cities like Bruges around the year 1400, there was already a useful commercial infrastructure in place. The urban government gave merchants the opportunity to safeguard their investments through a system of contract enforcement via the city's aldermen.[100] This enabled any traders to deal with people with whom they were personally unfamiliar. A good example was Lopes de la Coroña, a merchant of the Spanish Nation in Bruges, who sold wool to many different drapers, usually in small volumes.[101] De la Coroña also traded with a number of cloth entrepreneurs from the West-Quarter, mainly from Kemmel. His trade deals, which were formally certified by the Bruges magistrates, record how much his customers still owed, as well as when they had to pay their outstanding debt, usually in reference to one of the urban fairs in the Low Countries.[102] The benefit of this course of action was that both parties were bound to the agreement by an official court of law, which meant that it was safer to commit to a particular deal. This facilitated the omnipresence of credit, which was especially important for smaller operators. Indeed, in their deals with the De Muxica firm, without exception the traders of Nieuwkerke, Kemmel and Dranouter operated through postponed payment.[103] This applied equally to the larger and the minor transactions. Thus, the rural cloth entrepreneurs were able to buy raw materials on credit, use them to produce textiles in their village, and pay their creditors with the proceeds of those products. As the terms of the transaction usually specified a certain fair as the deadline for payment, the drapers probably used these occasions to offload their fabrics and immediately repay what they owed. Of course, as we saw in the previous chapter, they may not have been left with much of a surplus afterwards, given the meagre level of liquidity of even the wealthier entrepreneurs in 1566-68. In a way, then, this credit system was skewed in favour of the wool-merchants, who stood at the top of the food chain where the actual pay-out was concerned.

On occasion, however, the West-Quarter drapers directly settled their financial obligations in kind. So, a merchant called Diego de Tordomar sold several bales of wool to certain cloth traders from Kemmel in 1538, but he also possessed around 50 half-cloths from Nieuwkerke in 1552, which may indicate that he accepted payment for his raw wool in the form of finished fabrics.[104] Pieces of cloth were also used as sureties between cloth-salesmen, for instance when a draper from Dranouter received a load of English woollens in exchange for his own in 1537 (although that may have been a loan posing as a sales transaction).[105] But

100 Gelderblom, *Cities of Commerce*, pp. 123-24.

101 Fagel, pp. 132-35.

102 CAB, Procuraties, 1538-39, fols 142^{v}-143^{r}; Procuraties, 1539-40, fols 12^{v}-13^{v}, 24.

103 CAB, 304, Archief van het Spaanse Consulaat, Juan Castro de Muxica, Journaal (libros diarios), 1535-1538.

104 CAB, 304, Archief van het Spaanse Consulaat, Juan Castro de Muxica, Journaal (libros diarios), 1535-1538, e.g. on 29 November and 13 December 1538; GSAB, CA 23482, fol. 15^{r}.

105 The trader had sold cloths worth £40 15s. gr. Fl. and received English cloth with an estimated worth of £51 gr. Fl.: Corneel Slootmans, *Paas- en koudemarkten te Bergen op Zoom, 1365-1565*, Bijdragen tot de geschiedenis van het Zuiden van Nederland, 64-66, 3 vols (Tilburg: Stichting Zuidelijk historisch

even people who were not involved in the textile trade frequently used pieces of cloth as pledges for payments of goods in their daily transactions. All over Europe, these everyday transactions were safeguarded by urban law courts.[106] In addition, overarching legal institutions, such as the Council of Flanders in Ghent, protected long-range trade as well.[107] In 1533, for example, a Spanish merchant sued his own agent in Ypres, who was charged with collecting debts from drapers in Kemmel, because this agent had abused his powers to extort the debtors and pocket the extra proceeds.[108] Recourse to an institution like the Council of Flanders was therefore in the general interest of long-distance trade. In the aforementioned example, both the drapers and the wool seller could claim back the damages they had incurred through the illegal actions of the loan shark from Ypres. Urban law courts like that of the city of Bruges served a similar purpose: to witness and notarize trade contracts between foreign traders. At times, these courts even adopted the laws and customs of the merchants' place of origin.[109] There are several recorded instances in the sixteenth century where drapers from the West-Quarter used these formal channels when they purchased wool from Spanish merchants.[110]

As regarded their personal relationships, the merchant-drapers of Nieuwkerke could often be encountered vouching for each other or collecting one another's debts in the market cities. And they did not only do this for their 'companions'. One could argue that this behaviour denotes a certain 'collective spirit', which will be delved into more extensively in Chapter 5. Sometimes these relationships transcended the boundaries of the individual parish, however. For instance, in 1537, a group of drapers from Nieuwkerke and Dranouter jointly purchased 4 bales of Spanish wool from the firm of Juan Castro de Muxica.[111] On another occasion that same year, two wealthy traders from Nieuwkerke redeemed part of a debt owed to that same Spanish firm by a Daniel Voet from Dranouter.[112] Of course, it was highly practical for local traders to combine forces in this way, and even more so for merchant-drapers of the smaller industrial villages, who did not have the same foothold in the market cities as Nieuwkerke. Dranouter,

---

contact, 1985), III, pp. 1399-400. For a discussion of loans disguised as normal transactions, or so-called 'sale credits', see: Michael Postan, 'Credit in Medieval trade', in *Medieval Trade and Finance*, ed. by Postan, pp. 1-27 (pp. 5-11).

106 Elizabeth Gemmil, 'Debt, Distraint, Display and Dead Men's Treasure: Material Culture in Late Medieval Aberdeen', *Journal of Medieval History*, 46 (2020), 350-72 (p. 357).

107 Jan Dumolyn and Bart Lambert, 'Cities of Commerce, Cities of Constraints: International Trade, Government Institutions and the Law of Commerce in Later Medieval Bruges and the Burgundian State', *TSEG – The Low Countries Journal of Social and Economic History*, 11 (2014), 89-102 (pp. 90-92).

108 SAG, Raad van Vlaanderen, Enkwesten 3756.

109 Dumolyn and Lambert, p. 93.

110 CAB, Procuraties, 1538-39, fols 142^{v}-143^{r}; Procuraties, 1539-40, fols 12^{v}-13^{v}.

111 'Antonio Lupe [Antoon Leupe], Franze & Christian Droguebrot [Frans and Christiaan Drogebroot], Clais Erman [Klaas Herman], vezinos de Niuquerca & Darnutra': CAB, 304, Archief van het Spaanse Consulaat, Juan Castro de Muxica, Journaal (*libros diarios*), 1535-38, entry dated 15 June 1537.

112 CAB, 304, Archief van het Spaanse Consulaat, Juan Castro de Muxica, Journaal 1535-38, entry dated 27 October 1537.

for example, was a solid production centre with an annual output of 1500-2000 cloths in between 1500 and 1566.[113] And as mentioned before, its best fabrics, which were made using similar kinds of wool to those of Nieuwkerke, also sold at a similar price. So they attracted the same customers as well.[114] Under such circumstances, there must have been a significant overlap between the trading connections that were useful for drapers from the two villages. In fact, although this is unrecorded, certain drapers from Dranouter who also owned real estate in Nieuwkerke may have sold chartered cloths from both places. This would have been perfectly legal, so long as they did not sell any fabrics that were produced in Dranouter in Nieuwkerke's cloth hall.[115] That the drapers of these places came in frequent contact with each other is further confirmed by a 1539 document, wherein an Olivier Moenin of Dranouter drafted a list of people he commissioned to collect his outstanding debts. Out of the 31 named individuals, three came from Nieuwkerke. The others came from various different places, ranging from cities with an obvious connection to the West-Quarter cloth trade, such as Ypres and Antwerp, to less evident ones like Ghent and the Brabantine town of 's-Hertogenbosch.[116] Clearly, Moenin placed enough confidence in these agents to entrust them with his financial transactions. His network demonstrates that, while the contacts of rural entrepreneurs may not have been as wide-ranging as those of some urban merchants, the West-Quarter drapers were not inconsequential players in the mercantile game either.[117]

In spite of the highly regulated context of urban commerce, therefore, a level of familiarity between fellow traders was nonetheless the rule rather than the exception.[118] During the fairs in the Netherlandish market towns, trade interactions took place within more or less fixed circles of merchants. And the more frequent the contact, the stronger these bonds of acquaintance grew.[119]

There is an important cultural element to be considered here as well. The residents of the market cities in the Low Countries predominantly spoke Middle-Dutch, as did the traders from the Flemish West-Quarter. This would

113 RDHDF-2, II, pp. 264-65.

114 In 1564, 'Reynoutersche zwarte met de waepene van mynen heere' cost 40d. gr. per ell in Bruges. The cloths of Dranouter also contained a higher warp-count than those of Nieuwkerke (60-64 versus 50): *Précis analytique des documents, que renferme le dépot des archives de la Flandre-occidentale à Bruges*, ed. by Octave-Joseph Delepierre and Frédéric-Pierre Priem, 12 vols (Bruges, 1840-1858), III (1842), pp. 243-44; RDHDF-2, III, pp. 605-08.

115 A potential candidate was the already mentioned Reinoud Mortier, who bought some property in Nieuwkerke in 1534: SAB, Aanwinsten 504, fols 11^v-16^v.

116 Slootmans, III, p. 1400.

117 As a point of reference: in 1540, the Spanish wool merchant Lopes de la Coroña commissioned 57 *procureurs* to collect his debts: CAB, 199, Procuraties, 1539-1540, fol. 231. On this merchant, see also: Fagel, pp. 132-35.

118 For a discussion about shifts between 'public' and 'private' trade, see: Peter Stabel, 'Public or Private, Collective or Individual? The Spaces of Late Medieval Trade in the Low Countries', in *Il mercante patrizio: palazzi e botteghe nell'Europa del Rinascimento*, ed. by Donatella Calabi and Silvia Beltramo (Milan: B. Mondadori, 2008), pp. 37-54 (pp. 44-46).

119 Evelyn Welch, *Shopping in the Renaissance: Consumer Cultures in Italy, 1400-1600* (New Haven & London: Yale University Press, 2005), pp. 169, 171-72.

have aided them in striking up relationships with local traders, and vice versa.[120] But their connection went beyond language. These merchants shared a common 'urban' Netherlandish culture that will have acted as a social lubricant.[121] The fairs were not just platforms of trade; they coincided with cultural festivities corresponding to the Christian liturgical year. And so, the fairs often became a stage for theatrical performances, which, in the fifteenth- and sixteenth-century Low Countries, were mainly performed by the so-called 'Chambers of Rhetoric'.[122] The village of Nieuwkerke had two of these Chambers, one of which took part in a competition in Ghent in 1539 – a controversial event because of the evangelical leanings expressed in several of the submissions, including that of Nieuwkerke's association.[123] While very little is known about the composition of the village's theatrical organization, it stands to reason that its performers came from the community's literate elite. In the case of this cloth centre, the members will have largely consisted of drapers.[124] Even if this were not the case, the fairs were also accompanied by less sophisticated forms of celebration, both spiritual and civic, thereby cementing bonds within the interregional trading community.[125] So, one of the account books of Wouter Ameide contains two rather curious insertions that are essentially unconnected to his business. These insertions are made up of haphazard lists, which Ameide or one of his associates drew up in relation to a Rhetoricians' competition in Bruges, in 1517.[126] Apparently, one of Nieuwkerke's Chambers of Rhetoric, entitled 'Benevolent in the heart' (*Goetwillich in 't herte*), was inaugurated at this event. In fact, it was in the running for a (consolation) prize that was awarded to the literary association that 'came from farthest away'.[127] What is mainly interesting, however, is that this list was

120 Some people certainly also spoke French, but the greater part must have solely known Middle-Dutch, as evidenced by the request to translate certain documents into that language in 1553 because many people involved in the industry were ignorant of French: RDHDF-2, III, p. 167. See also: Puttevils, *Merchants and Trading*, pp. 168-69.

121 Dumolyn and Haemers, pp. 170-71.

122 Anne-Laure Van Bruaene, '"A Wonderfull Tryumfe, for the Wynnyng of a Pryse": Guilds, Ritual, Theater, and the Urban Network in the Southern Low Countries, ca. 1450-1650', *Renaissance Quarterly*, 59 (2006), 374-405 (pp. 384-85).

123 Anonymous, *De Gentse Spelen van 1539*, ed. by B. H. Erné and L. M. van Dis, 2 vols (The Hague: Martinus Nijhoff, 1982), I, pp. 177-203; Anne-Laure Van Bruaene, *Om beters wille: rederijkerskamers en de stedelijke cultuur in de Zuidelijke Nederlanden (1400-1650)* (Amsterdam: Amsterdam University Press, 2008), pp. 100-01.

124 One of these was devoted to Saint Sebastian. In 1533-34, one of its 'governors' (*gouverneurs*) was a draper called Jan De Raedt. The other was devoted to Saint George, and one of its governors was a barber named Jacob De Hollander (*Jaques de Hollandre*): SAB, Aanwinsten 504, fol. 19^{v}.

125 In Italy, the fairs even had an aspect of pilgrimage attached to them: Welch, p. 168.

126 In the first entry there is a reference to 'the year 1517, in May' (*anno 1517, in mayo*). Also, it notes the winners: Kortrijk and Ypres. The second entry (in the same hand) contains something like a short-list of the best performers, which includes those of Kortrijk and Ypres. Thus, it probably concerned one and the same event: CAB, Reeks 305, Wouter Ameyde, Journaal B, fols 200^{v}, 227^{v}.

127 It was listed among those Chambers who 'appeared for the first time' (*nieu verscenen sin*) and came in third in the competition for most far-flung participant (*van verst commende*). The person who wrote down this overview also noted that Nieuwkerke was number one of the groups that 'sang best' (*best singende*): CAB, Reeks 305, Wouter Ameyde, Journaal B, fols 200^{v}, 227^{v}. This is the earliest

inserted in the commercial register of a broker known to have maintained trade relations with Nieuwkerke's drapers. It is therefore a physical manifestation of the interconnection between trade and civic ritual.

Continuing on this theme of informality, Everaert's *Farce of the Merchant who Kissed Goodbye to Five Pounds Groats* was not that far off the mark when it discussed the influence of drink. Hosteller-brokers such as Wouter Ameide were a vital link in trade transactions involving 'foreigners' (in other words, all people who did not live in the market city in question).[128] Taverns were a common location for trade, hence the importance of hostellers as brokers in the fifteenth and sixteenth centuries.[129] For foreign merchants, the larger hostels of Bruges were 'one-stop shops' for storage and brokerage, as well as accommodations for food, drink and sleep.[130] On the one hand, this meant that urban governments meddled intensively in the affairs of hosteller-brokers. On the other hand, the sheer number of foreign traders in the city also stimulated the emergence of unauthorized inns, and encouraged deals on the side by the established hostellers.[131] Therefore, commercial transactions were largely conducted within the confines of these watering holes. The same circumstances prevailed in villages like Nieuwkerke, incidentally, both as regarded land transactions and for the various dealings of the cloth industry. Local taverns were a common venue for such official meetings.[132] In fact, transfers of land were traditionally ratified through a symbolic wine toast (*lyfcoop*), for which purpose a specific sum was continuously included in the deal.[133] This is not to say that traders were often inebriated while conducting business, but it does underline the tension between the informal and personal aspects of trade on the one hand, and the formalized rules and regulations on the other. The role of brokers and hostellers in late medieval trade therefore centred on personal networks, as much as (if not more

---

reference to *Goetwillich in 't herte*. Nieuwkerke's other Chamber (*Blyde van sinne*) was baptized in 1520 by *Alpha et Omega*, its Head-Chamber in Ypres: Edmond Vander Straeten, *Le théâtre villageois en Flandre*, 2 vols (Brussels: Claassen/Tillot, 1874/1880), II (1880), p. 170.

128 Ameide began his brokering enterprise by working in the inns of established hostellers. By 1500, he had acquired his own premises, and in 1503 he bought the renowned tavern called *de Halle van Valenchiennes*: Botho Verbist, 'Traditie of innovatie? Wouter Ameyde, een makelaar in het laatmiddeleeuwse Brugge, 1498-1507' (unpublished doctoral thesis, University of Antwerp, 2014), pp. 52-54.

129 Octaaf Mus, 'De verhouding van de waard tot de drapier in de Kortrijkse draperie op het einde van de 15e eeuw', *Handelingen van het Genootschap voor Geschiedenis, gesticht onder de benaming 'Société d'Emulation', te Brugge*, 99 (1961), 156-218 (esp. pp. 159-60); Stabel, 'Entre commerce international et économie locale', pp. 77-78; Verbist, pp. 85-89.

130 Gelderblom, *Cities of Commerce*, pp. 48-49.

131 James Murray, *Bruges, Cradle of Capitalism, 1280-1390* (Cambridge: Cambridge University Press, 2005), pp. 183-85.

132 A good example is the inn called *het Schaeck*, where new regulations were drafted in 1563: RDHDF-2, III, pp. 199-200. An inn of the same name was used in Nieppe for the ratification of land deals: SAB, Gemeentearchief Nieuwkerke 8, fol. 18^{v}.

133 References to *lijfcoop* occur continuously in sixteenth-century registers of land transactions in Nieuwkerke, but they are expressed in money, and it is unclear whether they were actually spent to drink the deal's good fortune or were solely a symbolic additional sum. See, for example, the transactions in: SAB, Gemeentearchief Nieuwkerke 27.

than) on institutions. Merchants used the services of a particular broker, both because they trusted him personally, and because urban governments and the guilds of broker-hostellers could be relied upon to enforce regulations.[134]

Overall, the influence of brokers as go-betweens may have begun to dwindle by the sixteenth century, as traders increasingly set up premises in the market towns and started to create networks of their own. However, Ameide is an example of a broker whose business was still alive and kicking in a period when most trading nations already had a permanent foothold in Bruges. His success showcases how merchants continued to use multiple means to solve their problems.[135] However, with regards to the West-Quarter drapers (as with those of the Lys draperies), Ameide's role seems to have been more encompassing still. His virtual monopoly on cloth from Menen is a good example of this. The merchants from Flemish cloth centres like this one were not represented locally by their own people to the same degree that traders from the Spanish and German nations were – even though a handful of villagers from Nieuwkerke did attain citizenship of Bruges in the 1480s and 1490s.[136] Perhaps Ameide was able to monopolize the commercial link between the drapers from these rural centres and the Spanish wool merchants on whom they relied. After all, he also managed to gain this kind of monopolistic access to the drapers of Menen. Or perhaps he merely acquired a position as the dominant intermediary between the West-Quarter and its wool suppliers, much as he did with the drapers of Kortrijk.[137] Because of this, if anybody in this system of exchange was a merchant-entrepreneur, it was Wouter Ameide: his function was purely one of redistribution. Regardless of whether his clients got a good deal, he was always entitled to his fixed commission. The institutional framework of trade paid dividends here, because the laws of Bruges obliged foreign traders without a go-to residence in the city to employ the services brokers like Ameide.[138]

The cloth entrepreneurs from Nieuwkerke, Dranouter and Nieppe, but mainly those from Kemmel and Wulvergem, did, in fact, buy sizeable amounts of wool through Wouter Ameide in 1505-06. Within the space of that one year, they purchased 268 bales (22,379 kg) via his business.[139] Note that this was proportionally more than all the West-Quarter drapers combined bought from the De Muxica firm in 1535-38 (**Table 3.1**). But of course, Ameide brought the

134 Stabel, 'Entre commerce international et économie locale', p. 77.

135 Stabel, 'Entre commerce international et économie locale', p. 80; Gelderblom, *Cities of Commerce*, p. 42.

136 In this period, five people from Nieuwkerke became citizens of Bruges. One of them, Colart Baelde *fils* Walraam, may have had connections to the drapery, since a Walraam Baelde was listed as merchant-draper in 1455. But there is no other evidence to support this notion: Alfred Jamees, *Brugse poorters: opgetekend uit de stadsrekeningen*, 4 vols (Bruges: Flandria Nostra, 1974-80), III (1980), pp. 28, 35, 57, 64; De Sagher, *Recueil*, III, 100-02.

137 Stabel, 'Entre commerce international et économie locale', pp. 88-89, 98.

138 Verbist, pp. 86-89.

139 These 268 bales were traded between October 1505 and June 1506. With an average weight of 30 naghel per bale (i.e. 180 lbs, or 83.502 kg, per bale), the total comes at 22,378.536 kg: CAB, Reek 305, Wouter Ameyde, Journaal B, fol. 179^{r}-223^{v}; Anonymous, *Handel Buch*, fol. 13.

drapers into contact with not one, but several different wool-merchants. There is also evidence that the drapers of Kemmel used the services of another broker in Bruges, a man called Jacob Voet, in this same period.[140] Clearly, brokers continued to play an important role in the West-Quarter cloth trade. Nieuwkerke even employed a broker explicitly referred to as the 'hosteller of the drapery of Nieuwkerke' (*werd van de draperie van Nieukercke*) in their commercial dealings with Ypres in 1522, a man by the name of Jan Kanin. His house on the Ypres-IJzer Canal served as a storage facility for raw materials imported from Antwerp.[141] Just like Wouter Ameide, this broker also traded cloth on his own account, and from the same market segment as Nieuwkerke's products no less.[142] It is worth noting that at this time, the village's drapers already rented cloth halls in Antwerp as well. This means that they continued to use the expertise of brokers while they already had a permanent marketing outlet in the city. This could have been part of a holistic commercial strategy, but it may have also been a necessary evil, resulting from the fact that Nieuwkerke lacked direct lines of transportation to the market cities in the form of navigable waterways (let alone well-kept roads). Even though they rented halls in Antwerp, to transport bulky goods, the rural drapers still depended upon go-betweens in cities with better infrastructural connections to the urban network. Another explanation for their continued use of brokers may have been that Nieuwkerke's drapery corporation was not opulent enough to establish a permanent trading post in every market city frequented by its members. Indeed, we find no traces of brokers being employed in Antwerp and Bergen op Zoom, where the drapers had their own premises in the sixteenth century (see below).

Of course, the West-Quarter drapers also developed their own personal networks. Yet they may have built up this contact base through the initial introductions of their brokers, whereafter they cut out the middlemen. One such example is the wealthy merchant Fernando de Bernuy, who traded cloth via Ameide in the early sixteenth century, but from whom the drapers of Nieuwkerke would go on to rent their cloth hall in the Hoogstraat in Antwerp directly.[143] Incidentally, in 1556, his son and successor lent the substantial sum of £2500 Fl. gr. to Count Lamoraal van Egmont, who was lord of Nieuwkerke

140 Verbist, pp. 70-71.

141 'Ten huuse [...] op de Leet': RDHDF-2, III, pp. 130-31.

142 In 1510, a *Jan Canin* sued a certain Andries Langhebaert for short-changing him on a load of fabrics from Poperinge (*brunblaeu lakene*) sent to Bruges: RDHDF-2, III, pp. 274-76.

143 The De Bernuy were a wealthy *marano* family of traders who were active in the Low Countries in the sixteenth century. See in general: Alonso Casado, 'Finance et commerce international au milieu du XVIe siècle: la compagnie des Bernuy', *Annales du Midi*, 103 (1991), 323-43. Fernando de Bernuy bought several woollens from the Lys town of Menen in 1506: CAB, Reeks 305, Wouter Ameyde, Journaal B, fol. 124^{r}. His son was still the landlord of the cloth hall of Nieuwkerke's drapers in Antwerp when those same premises were confiscated on the authority of the king in 1573: CAA, Halle van Nieuwkerke, Documenten 4675. The financial worth of this Fernando II de Bernuy was around £5,760,000 Fl. gr. in 1567: Johan Dambruyne, *Corporatieve middengroepen: aspiraties, relaties en transformaties in de 16e-eeuwse Gentse ambachtswereld* (Ghent: Academia Press, 2002), pp. 427-28.

at that time.[144] Another prominent merchant with whom the rural traders had dealings was Thomas Bombelli of Genua, who was treasurer to Margaret of Austria while she governed the Low Countries, and who was also based in Antwerp.[145] Bombelli was a trader in silk cloth and dyestuffs, selling 6 bales of the tincture called 'woad' to three drapers from Nieuwkerke in 1508.[146] Like De Bernuy, Bombelli was a commercial heavy-weight: in 1523, he supervised a massive loan of £117,000 made out to Emperor Charles V by a partnership consisting of fellow merchants.[147] Strikingly, both De Bernuy and Bombelli seem to have flirted with evangelical beliefs, as did many drapers from the West-Quarter.[148] Passing by the idea that something like a 'Protestant ethic' directly influenced their entrepreneurial successes, such shared religious sentiments may have acted as a reinforcement of the bonds that existed between traders in Antwerp in this period (and vice versa).[149]

Fairs and cloth halls

Apart from hosteller-brokers, the merchant-drapers of the West-Quarter used a number of other commercial institutions that existed in their time. Perhaps foremost were the aforementioned fairs in the market cities of the Low Countries. Ever since the 1990s, historians have consistently begun to reject the view that the European fairs witnessed a general decline and diminishing scope after the downfall of the important Champagne fairs in the late thirteenth century.[150] Scholars like Larry Epstein and John Munro have shown that these periodic markets resurfaced in the late 1300s; first as regional outlets, but as population

---

144 Cornelis Dekker and Roland Baetens, *Geld in het water: Antwerps en Mechels kapitaal in Zuid-Beveland na de stormvloeden in de 16e eeuw* (Hilversum: Verloren, 2010), p. 264.

145 ADN, B 19014; Gerrit IJssel de Schepper, *Lotgevallen van Christiern II en Isabella van Oostenrijk, koning en koningin van Denemarken; voornamelijk gedurende huere ballingschap in de Nederlanden* (Zwolle: De Erven J. J. Tijl, 1870), pp. 177-79 (n. 5).

146 Slootmans, I, p. 451.

147 Richard Ehrenberg, *Capital and Finance in the Age of the Renaissance: A Study of the Fuggers and their Connections*, trans. by H. M. Lucas (New York: Augustus H. Kelley, 1928), pp. 260-61.

148 Bombelli was part of a network of people that were more or less openly involved in the new beliefs. Others included Albrecht Dürer and Cornelius Grapheus: Thomas Sturge Moore, *Albert Dürer* (London & New York: Duckworth and company, 1911), pp. 171-72; De Bernuy was charged by the Council of Troubles in 1567: Dambruyne, *Corporatieve middengroepen*, p. 428. See also: Van der Wee, 'Structural Changes and Specialization', pp. 217-18.

149 Guido Marnef, *Antwerpen in de tijd van de Reformatie* (Amsterdam & Antwerp: Meulenhoff Kritak, 1996), p. 56; Anne Kint, 'The Community of Commerce: Social Relations in Sixteenth-Century Antwerp' (doctoral dissertation, Columbia University, 1996), esp. pp. 398-99. See also: Max Weber, *The Protestant Ethic and the Spirit of Capitalism*, trans. by Talcott Parsons (1930; London & New York: Routledge, repr. 2005), pp. x-xiii of the introduction by Anthony Giddens. For a discussion: John Munro, 'Tawney's Century, 1540-1640: The Roots of Modern Capitalist Entrepreneurship', in *The Invention of Enterprise: Entrepreneurship from Ancient Mesopotamia to Modern times*, ed. by David Landes (Princeton: Princeton University Press, 2010), pp. 107-155 (pp. 107-12, 135-37).

150 See: S. R. Epstein, 'Regional Fairs, Institutional Innovation, and Economic Growth in Late Medieval Europe', *The Economic History Review*, 157 (1994), 459-82 (pp. 459-60; with an overview of relevant literature in notes 8 and 9).

levels began to rise, as commercial institutions expanded, and as transportation costs decreased, the fairs once again turned into potent platforms for international trade.[151] In this regard, the city of Antwerp gradually took over Bruges' position of prime commercial hub in north-western Europe in the course of the fifteenth century.[152] This takeover did not so much relate to the sale of products from the city's hinterland, but to the redistribution of imported goods from a much wider radius. And one of the main commodities that was decisive in Antwerp's triumph over Bruges was English cloth.[153] The growing primacy of these fabrics drew German and Italian cloth resellers towards the Brabantine city; merchants specializing in other textiles simply followed suit. Meanwhile, the Antwerp fairs began to form a natural cycle with those of Bergen op Zoom, pulling the cloth trade ever more towards the duchy of Brabant in the early sixteenth century.[154]

But the evidence for the cloth trade of Nieuwkerke slightly qualifies this view. The drapers from this village probably frequented fairs from the later fourteenth century onwards, and certainly from the early fifteenth. So, in 1428, the bailiff of Ypres noted that he had confiscated 'four carts of cloths near Wervik [belonging to] the people of Nieuwkerke, which they brought to the fair of Bruges', suggesting that this was a not inconsiderable load of goods.[155] By the later fifteenth century and in the sixteenth century, the village's drapers were trading cloth at the fairs of Bruges, Ypres, Antwerp, Bergen op Zoom, and Kortrijk.[156] And in the 1530s, the rural merchant-drapers also visited most of the major fairs in the Low Countries to buy wool.[157] This is somewhat late, because Bruges had supposedly given up its leading position to the growing primacy of the Brabantine cities of Bergen op Zoom and especially Antwerp around the

151 Epstein, 'Regional Fairs', pp. 470-71, 476-77; John Munro, 'The "New Institutional Economics" and the Changing Fortunes of Fairs in Medieval and Early Modern Europe: The Textile Trades, Warfare, and Transaction Costs', *Vierteljahrschrift für Sozial- und Wirtschaftsgeschichte*, 88, (2001), 1-47 (pp. 24-26).

152 John Munro, 'Bruges and the Abortive Staple in English Cloth: An Incident in the Shift of Commerce from Bruges to Antwerp in the Late Fifteenth Century', *Revue belge de philologie et d'histoire*, 44 (1966), 1137-59; Gelderblom, *Cities of Commerce*, pp. 174-76; J. L. Bolton and F. Guidi Bruscoli, 'When Did Antwerp Replace Bruges as the Commercial and Financial Centre of North-Western Europe? The Evidence of the Borromei Ledger for 1438', *The Economic History Review*, 61 (2008), 360-79 (pp. 376-78).

153 These formed a 'tripod' with South German metals and Portugese spices: Puttevils, *Merchants and Trading*, pp. 15-16, 67-70.

154 Thijs, pp. 85-86; Charles Verlinden, 'Markets and Fairs', in *The Cambridge Economic History of Europe*, ed. by Michael Postan and others, 8 vols (Cambridge: Cambridge University Press, 1966-1989), III, *Economic Organisation and Policies in the Middle Ages*, 119-53 (p. 150). In fact, the German fustian trade also came to be concentrated in Antwerp. German merchants would offload these products in the city and take English textiles back to the German markets: Munro, 'The Origin of the English "New Draperies"', p. 84.

155 'Quatre carees de draps empres Wervy de ceulx de Neufveglise, que les menoient a la feste de Bruges': GSAB, Acquits de Lille 192-93; GSAB, Rekening Zaal Ieper, 1445-1458, (loose, non foliated document of 1428; no month mentioned).

156 Mus, 'Pieter Lansaem', p. 87; RDHDF-2, III, 130-31, 134-36; Slootmans, I, p. 303; CAB, Stadsrekeningen, 1483-84, fol. 54^{r}.

157 CAB, Archief van het Spaanse Consulaat, Grootboek van Juan Castro (de Muxica), 1534-1535, pp. 20 (*feria de Bergas*), 204 (*feria de Coutray*; *feria de Brujas*), 227 (*feria de Turote*), 324 (*feria de Ypre de Ascenzion*).

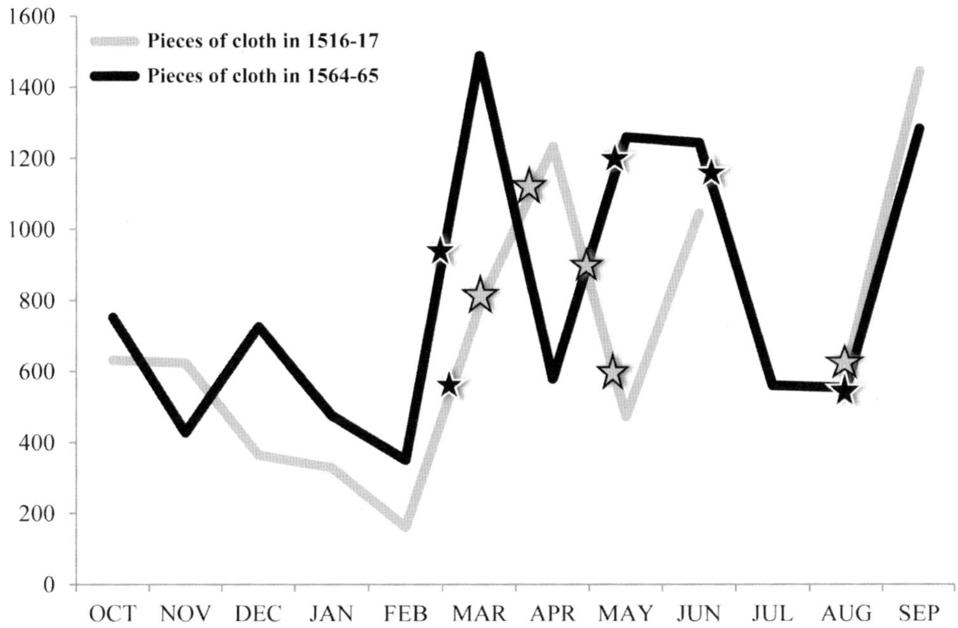

Figure 3.2. Nieuwkerke's production rhythm and the fair cycle (★), 16th century

Source: RDHIDF-2, III, p. 209; GSAB, CA, Acquits en portefeuilles 1367/34; Gaillard, 'Les foires'.

turn of the sixteenth century.[158] Towards the middle of that century, moreover, Antwerp transformed into a permanent commercial outlet, to the detriment of the fair-cycle of the Low Countries.[159] Yet the drapers of Nieuwkerke still maintained their orientation towards Bruges, Ypres, and the other Flemish fairs.

To be sure, the village's drapers increasingly popped up in Antwerp from around 1500 onwards.[160] But if we look at the village's monthly production outputs in 1516-17 and 1564-65, and we entertain the notion that these output levels were linked to commercialization, the export market for Nieuwkerke cloth can consistently be tied to the various Netherlandish fairs. Of course, it is possible that the drapers produced their stock well in advance of these markets. If we take the figures at face value, however, the main seasons for manufacture in both 1516-17 and 1564-65 were early springtime, early summer, and early autumn (**Figure 3.2**). In 1517, the first great peak in production was in April and was followed by a slump directly afterwards. This coincided with the Bruges fair of that year, which would have

158 Gelderblom, *Cities of Commerce*, pp. 28-31.

159 Gelderblom, *Cities of Commerce*, pp. 30-33; Puttevils, *Merchants and Trading*, pp. 51-53; Bruno Blondé, *De sociale structuren en economische dynamiek van 's-Hertogenbosch, 1500-1550* (Tilburg: Stichting Zuidelijk historisch contact, 1987), pp. 131-36.

160 Alfons Thijs, 'Van "werkwinkel" tot "fabriek". De textielnijverheid te Antwerpen van het einde der vijftiende tot het begin der negentiende eeuw' (unpublished doctoral thesis, University of Ghent, 1978-79), pp. 39-43. I am grateful to Jeroen Puttevils for letting me borrow his copies of this voluminous work.

been held from 21 April to 31 May.[161] Also, the Pentecost fair in Antwerp, the Easter market in Bergen op Zoom, and the Ascension fair of Ypres all occurred roughly in the same period.[162] It is likely that the industry aimed at finishing as many fabrics as possible before these important marketing occasions, which would have been followed by a quieter period immediately afterwards. Indeed, during the 1480s, when the urban government of Ypres demanded from several drapers and weavers of the West-Quarter villages that they tie up their current affairs before ceasing production altogether, many of these people stated their intentions to stop manufacturing after a deadline that they explicitly connected to one of these fairs.[163] This is interesting in its own right, because it supports the idea that manufacture and trade were closely integrated via the figure of the draper, who apparently timed the monthly rhythm of production according to the available commercial occasions.

The monthly outputs of the West-Quarter cloth manufacturers are harder to account for in terms of their harmony with the fairs for the year 1564-65. For the most part, however, these links can be established. At this time, the production apexes came in March, May-June, and September (**Figure 3.2**). This pattern was still largely in concert with the Netherlandish fair-cycle. The Lent market of Ypres, for example, was held between 18 March and 29 April, which may account for the village's first production peak in March. Also, the subsequent peaks in May and June more or less preceded two fairs in Antwerp and Ypres. To some degree, they also harmonized with the periodic market of Bruges (which began on 1 May but lasted all the way until 10 June).[164] It is not altogether surprising that there was no spike in production leading up to the annual fair in the city of Lille, which started on 29 August: Lille would grow steadily more important as a gateway for Flemish cloth, but it only became a hub for the West-Quarter's rural fabrics towards the end of the sixteenth century.[165] More difficult to explain are the production peaks in September – which can be witnessed both in 1516 and in 1565. With the exception of the purportedly minor fairs of Bailleul and Mesen, no connection with any of the major Netherlandish fairs is evident for this spike in production in early autumn.[166] The clear slumps in October and

---

161 This fair commenced the second day after *Quasimodo* (the eighth day after Easter, which in that year was 12 April). All the date calculations are based on: Hermann Grotefend, *Zeitrechnung des deutschen Mittelalters und der Neuzeit*, 2 vols (Hannover: Hahn, 1891-98).

162 *Sinxen* in Antwerp: 16 May-27 June; *Assencioensmarct* in Ypres: 25 May – 4 June; Easter fair in Bergen op Zoom: 9 April-7 May.

163 Along the lines of 'such and such declares that he/she is working on X number of cloths, which will be finished by this or that specific fair' (for example, *die vulreet werden te Sinxen*). They refer to *Sinxen* (the Pentecost market of Antwerp), *Brugmarct* (the Bruges fair), and *Assencioensmarct* (the Ypres fair following the Feast of the Ascension): RDHDF-2, I, pp. 24-28.

164 *Sinxen* in Antwerp: 26 May-14 July; *Assencioensmarct* in Ypres: 4 June-12 July. In 1565, 22 April was Easter Sunday.

165 The Lille fair began on the feast of the Beheading of St. John the Baptist: Gaillard, 'Les foires', 210-212. On the city's rising commercial importance, see: Dambruyne, 'De hiërarchie van de Vlaamse textielcentra', p. 157.

166 Mesen's fair was held on 14 October, Bailleul's from 9 through 11 September: Gaillard, 'Les foires', pp. 200, 213; *Documents inedits relatifs à la ville de Bailleul*, ed. by Ignace De Coussemaker, 3 vols (Lille: Quarré du coulombier, 1877-78), I (1877), CXIX.

November are somewhat surprising as well; especially in 1516, when the winter fair of Bergen op Zoom would still have been a major outlet for the fabrics of Nieuwkerke (see below). On the whole, though, there was an obvious correlation between the monthly cadence of cloth manufacture and the periodic marketing opportunities in the Netherlandish cities. We have seen in Chapter 1 that the production rhythm did not really align to the agricultural year. And apparently, the supply of foreign wool was not a limiting factor either, since the important Spanish fleeces arrived in Bruges in March and October. As a consequence, there was a greater trade in this commodity during those months, but this does not show up in the production figures of Nieuwkerke.[167]

The importance of the fairs of Antwerp and Ypres is further attested by independent references. The audits of West-Quarter drapers and artisans by the city government of Ypres in the 1480s indicate the primacy of these markets at that time: 22 people were preparing for Antwerp's Pentecost fair, 19 for Ypres' own Ascension market, and a mere 3 for the Bruges fair.[168] Of course, the latter was the earliest upcoming event; consequently, most fabrics intended for it may have already been finished. However, the inspection took place between 15 April and 8 May, while the Bruges fair had only started on 1 May, so this does not entirely account for its scant occurrence.[169] Meanwhile, the frequent references to Ypres' own fair also occur because the people that were interviewed were external citizens or 'outburghers' of that city, so they were naturally more inclined to attend this 'home match' as it were. Yet, as already indicated in Chapter 2, even in a bad year like 1476, the drapers from the West-Quarter villages still sold a total of 1118 pieces of cloth during the city's fair.[170] The resilience of Ypres' market is further evidenced by the total of 34,720 woollens sold there in 1517.[171] The large number of references to the Antwerp market are also striking, as they occur at an earlier stage than might be expected.[172] The drapers of Nieuwkerke, in particular, showed an interest in this distant fair, whereas those of Kemmel still focused more on the nearby event in Ypres.[173]

That the merchant-drapers of the West-Quarter maintained their affiliation with Bruges throughout the sixteenth century was probably a question of their supply of raw materials. After all, this city held the Spanish wool staple from 1493

167 Fagel, p. 134.

168 RDHDF-2, I, pp. 24-28.

169 Easter Sunday was 22 April in 1481, and the fair started the 2nd day after the Octave of Easter.

170 Mus, 'Pieter Lansaem', p. 87.

171 Jean-Jacques Lambin, *Mémoire sur les questions proposées par la Société des Antiquaires de la Morinie, établie a Saint-Omer: 1. sur l'origine de la Halle aux draps, à Ypres; 2. sur les causes qui ont donné lieu à sa construction; 3. sur les institutions, source de l'ancienne prospérité des habitants; 4. sur l'époque de la fondation de l'église de Saint-Martin* (Ypres: Lambin, 1836), p. 17.

172 Alfons Thijs noted how Flemish textile centres were reluctant to make the switch from Bruges to Antwerp before the sixteenth century, possibly out of loyalty to the former, Flemish city: Thijs, 'Van "werkwinkel" tot "fabriek"', p. 42.

173 Nieuwkerke: 10 people prepared for *Sinxen*, 7 for *Assencioensmarct*, 2 for *Brugmarct*; Kemmel: 2 for *Sinxen*, 11 for *Assencioensmarct*, 1 for *Brugmarct*; the rest: 10 for *Sinxen*, 1 for *Assencioensmarct*, 0 for *Brugmarct*.

onwards, which some historians have considered as its only saving grace at that time.[174] Indeed, connections between the West-Quarter draperies and traders in Bruges usually revolved around wool purchases. The wool deals recorded in Ameide's administration of 1505-06 are a testament to this. Most of these transactions took place during the Lent market of Ypres, but the drapers also attended the Bruges spring fair in 1506.[175] That said, Ameide's administration contains little information about sales of finished cloth from these villages. The same can be said for the merchant-drapers' dealings with the Castilian firm of Juan Castro de Muxica. The division of this firm that was specifically concerned with trade in the Low Countries was based in Bruges, so the city held some gravitational pull on the traders of Nieuwkerke and the other villages.[176] Yet there are no indications that Juan Castro's business associates in Bruges bought fabrics from the West-Quarter. A few years later, some Spanish merchants can be established as having imported cloth from Nieuwkerke and the other villages via Bruges, but it is far from certain that they actually bought these products in the city.[177] This probably means that the rural merchant-drapers were not limited to any one market, instead spending their itinerant lives in various places throughout the Southern Low Countries. These 'travelling salesmen' did occasionally touch base, or kept track of their industrial affairs via a partner, however. One such example was a merchant-draper called Gillis Tayspil, who was active in Antwerp but whose name also occurs in the production records of Nieuwkerke's wardens.[178] Entrepreneurs like these probably used different markets towards different ends. And so, in the sixteenth century, Bruges became more a centre for their supply of wool than an outlet for their cloth.

This is where the fairs of Brabant came in. If the West-Quarter drapers stayed active in Bruges because of the wool supply, from the late 1400s onwards, the marketing of their finished products came to be centred in the markets of Antwerp and Bergen op Zoom. And, during this same period, Nieuwkerke's cloth industry was rapidly expanding. On the commercial level, this was expressed in their collective efforts to establish trading posts in these Brabantine towns. As mercantile outposts, these 'cloth halls' were an important commercial institution in late medieval trade. Already in the fifteenth century, several production centres in the Low Countries established such permanent footholds in Antwerp and Bruges; Hondschoote being a prime example.[179] To Nieuwkerke, the renting

174 Munro, 'Bruges and the Abortive Staple', pp. 1149, 1159.

175 CAB, Reeks 305, Wouter Ameyde, Journaal B, fols 206^{v}-216^{r} (Ypres fair), 217^{r}-223^{v} (Bruges fair). There is also a reference to payment of a debt by Klaas Baelde at the Torhout fair (*Thoroutmert*; fol. 223^{v}) to a certain *Thomaes*, probably Ameide's representative Thomas Goetghebuer: Verbist, p. 32.

176 Fagel, p. 56.

177 GSAB, CA 23482, e.g. fols 10^{r}, 11^{v}, 12^{r}, 14^{r}, 14^{v}, 15^{r}, 17^{r}, 19^{v}. On the interconnection of Spanish merchants between Antwerp and Bruges, see: Fagel, pp. 163-64.

178 CAA, Certificatieboeken 24 (1565), fol. 366; GSAB, CA, Acquits en portefeuilles 1367/34 (he produced 57.5 cloths in 1564-65).

179 Coornaert, *Un centre industriel d'autrefois*, p. 16; Stabel, 'Marketing Cloth', pp. 24-25; Thijs, 'Van "werkwinkel" tot "fabriek"', p. 39; Puttevils, *Merchants and Trading*, pp. 50-52.

of cloth halls was an important step in its commercial development: a mark of the maturity of its woollen industry. Permanence was the key word here, and the all-year-round character of the Antwerp market must have facilitated the cloth centre's economic expansion. This type of continuous trade was not really a sixteenth-century novelty, as the city of Bruges had been harbouring trading communities since 1300.[180] It was a new step for Nieuwkerke, however. In that sense, the village's premises in Bergen op Zoom marked an intermediate stage towards becoming permanently established as a trading nation, since the 1511 contract between Nieuwkerke's drapery corporation and the stewards (*rentmeesters*) of the Brabantine town still specified that the cloth hall was only rented for the duration of the fairs.[181] For the rest of the year, they were used to store the town's unused market stalls.[182]

True permanence for the rural drapers came in Antwerp, where they rented a trading facility from the first decade of the sixteenth century onwards.[183] Apparently, these premises were taken over by Armentières in 1534, because in that year the drapers of the Lys town bought the buildings 'that were previously called "the hall of Nieuwkerke"'.[184] Through the finer points of the sales contract, we learn that the merchants and drapers of Armentières primarily used the hall to display and sell their fabrics, while a backroom on the first floor served as a warehouse (*pachwus*) for cloths and parcels of goods (*fardeaux*). It is likely that Nieuwkerke's drapers had used the location in a similar fashion, and that their new premises further down the road went on to function in the same way.[185] That is to say: very much like a shop and permanent storage facility. This in contrast to their periodic sales venue in Bergen op Zoom, which they only used during the fairs. For Armentières, this permanence is confirmed by the explicit distinction between woollens sold 'during fairs and deliveries, or outside fairs or deliveries'.[186] The latter's hall was clearly an extension of the town's industry: an outpost in Antwerp, where the hall masters (*halliers*) played a role akin to that of the wardens back home, keeping an extensive administration of expenses in the process.[187]

---

180 Gelderblom, *Cities of Commerce*, p. 42; Stabel, 'Marketing Cloth', p. 35. Compare: Van der Wee, *The Growth of the Antwerp Market*, I, pp. 328-30; Puttevils, *Merchants and Trading*, pp. 50-51.

181 'Gheil der natien van der draperien van Nyeukercke': CABZ, Archief van de stadssecretarie van Bergen op Zoom (stadsarchief voor 1810), Protocol van rentebrieven en recognities, 1511-1512, fol. 65^{v}.

182 In 1527, a steward was paid a salary 'to put the stalls [in the town halls] outside market periods', while the same entry still notes that the Nieuwkerke drapery rented them during the fairs: CABZ, Stadsrekeningen 779 (1527-1528), fol. 5^{r}.

183 The exact date is unknown, but a document that was composed before 17 March 1551 refers to cloth halls in Antwerp rented for the last 36 years: RDHDF-2, III, pp. 149-50.

184 'Que l'on nommoit par ci devant la halle de Noeufveglise': RDHDF-2, I, p. 402.

185 Both buildings were located in Antwerp's Hoogstraat: RDHDF-2, I, p. 402; CAA, Halle van Nieuwkerke, Documenten 4675.

186 'En feste et livrison, ou hors feste ou livrison': RDHDF-2, I, p. 404. These *livrisons* were official, two-week periods of delivery, presumably organized centrally by officers of the hall in Antwerp and of the drapery in Armentières.

187 In fact, 6d. Fl. gr. out of the 2s. in commission that the *halliers* received for each cloth they handled, was subtracted from the wardens' fee: RDHDF-2, I, p. 404. See also pp. 409-30.

But in order to sustain such a permanent shop in a distant city, these drapery corporations needed local agents that were more or less continuously on site. Sure enough, in the first half of the sixteenth century, certain cloth traders from Nieuwkerke began to settle in Antwerp as *oppidani*. In some instances, we can even establish their continued affiliation with drapers from their mother parish. Consider the example of Jan Droogebroot, 'cloth-seller and resident' (*lakencoopere, oppidanus*), who vouched for Gillis Droogebroot and Gillis Tayspil, 'merchants' (*cooplieden*) of Nieuwkerke, when they wanted to complete a large trade transaction in the city.[188] Other people with connections to the village's drapery registered as actual citizens, while this was not a common practice among foreigners in Antwerp.[189] Some of these people may have become hall masters in the store of the rural cloth centre, either supervising sales of their fellow traders who showed up infrequently, or overseeing sales at the behest of those who were unable to personally come over.[190] These local hall masters may have ensured that people and goods found their way safely across the vast distance of well over 100 kilometres. This is also how the West-Quarter drapery corporations with no recorded cloth halls operated. Some cloth merchants from Dranouter, for instance, settled in Antwerp while maintaining contacts with their place of origin. Thus, a certain Jan Van Hove began his career as a shearer, draper and cloth merchant in this village until he migrated to the Brabantine metropolis at the age of forty-five (in 1521 or 1522), where he was still active as a cloth merchant in 1545.[191] His son Karel Van Hove, who was also a merchant, would go on to uphold commercial relationships with drapers in Nieuwkerke, asking one of them to represent him before the village aldermen of Dranouter in 1557.[192]

The main benefit of owning or renting a cloth hall over relying on informal connections, however, was that it allowed for a closer integration of industry and commerce, as well as a greater level of control over trade transactions between village drapers and external merchants. To that end, the wardens of Nieuwkerke

188 CAA, Certificatieboeken 24 (1565), fol. 366. Being a 'resident' (*ingezetene*) was a special status awarded to people who lived in the city for more than one year. An ordinance of 1563 specified that these residents enjoyed the same privileges as citizens, excepting freedom from tolls and protection against external juridical authorities: Kint, p. 284.

189 Kint, pp. 275-78. New citizens who immigrated from Nieuwkerke and had a connection to the cloth industry: *Jan Goedscalck* (1539), *Joris De Keesschietere* (clothseller, 1545), *Roelant Godtschalck* (shearer, 1556), and *François Fagiel* (merchant, 1579). The *poortersboeken* for the period 1533 to 1608 are published in: J. Van Roey, *Antwerpse poortersboeken*, 8 vols (Antwerp: Stadsarchief, 1977). Jan De Meester has put this published source into an MS Excel spreadsheet which he kindly granted to Jeroen Puttevils. I am indebted to both Dr. De Meester and Dr. Puttevils for providing me with this spreadsheet. See also: Jan De Meester, 'Gastvrij Antwerpen? Arbeidsmigratie naar het zestiende-eeuwse Antwerpen' (unpublished doctoral thesis, University of Anwerp, 2011).

190 This was certainly the role of the *concierge* of Armentières' hall: RDHDF-2, I, pp. 404-05.

191 RDHDF-2, III, pp. 608-10. A Jan Van Hove was also active as a draper in Nieuwkerke, producing 30 pieces of cloth in 1564-65. But it is unlikely that this was the same individual, as he would have been in his eighties.

192 A 'Karel Van Hove Janssone, coopman, oppidanus' commissioned the services of one 'Jacope Priem, drapier woonende tot Nyeukercke, omme te gane ende te compareren voer schepenen ende wethouders van Dranouter in Vlaenderen': CAA, Certificatieboeken 12 (1557), fol. 140[r].

inserted a bylaw in their cloth charter, which stated that no cloth from other places could be transacted on the common premises in Antwerp and Bergen op Zoom. Nobody was allowed to sell cloth from the village outside the hall either.[193] Thus, these industrial officials extended their authority over commercial affairs. The wardens of Armentières even went so far as to order a wooden chest for holding the corporation's commercial bookkeeping, which was destined for the parish church back home. The chest bore a padlock for which only two keys were made: one for the hall masters, and one for the town's aldermen back in Flanders.[194] How effective these measures were, or whether they were also in place in Nieuwkerke, we can only guess. The careful management of Armentières' trading accounts is reminiscent of the town's scrupulously choreographed industrial organization; a characteristic that Nieuwkerke's drapery certainly did not share (see Chapter 2). More important, perhaps, was that in both of these successful Flemish cloth centres, the same people who ran the production process were also the ones who stood in contact with the trading hubs; if not personally, then certainly via their family members or through partnerships of another nature.

Conclusion

Shakespeare's Shylock exclaimed 'I'll have my bond, I will not hear thee speak', while Cornelis Everaert's burgomaster affirmed 'assent makes legality' (possibly with a loud hiccough for comical effect).[195] These fictional characters of the sixteenth century stood firm on the letter of commercial law. As we have seen, the trade in cloth from the Flemish West-Quarter was indeed structured along the lines of formal legal institutions in the fifteenth and sixteenth centuries. Of course, given that the drapers from these textile villages traded on an international level, with foreign merchants, and in cities where they themselves were also strangers, dictated that they used this highly developed legal infrastructure. The urban courts of cities like Bruges were eager to provide assistance in contract enforcement, as was the Council of Flanders. In doing so, these courts facilitated easy exchange by reducing certain risks of commerce, so that merchants did not have to fear that their debtors would renege on a deal. This was important to the business contacts of drapers from villages like Nieuwkerke, Dranouter, and Kemmel, as the entrepreneurs from these places hardly ever paid in full for their wool straight away.

At the same time, however, both the master-fuller and playwright from Bruges, and the famous Bard from Stratford-upon-Avon were well aware of the personal,

193 RDHDF-2, III, pp. 134-36, 149-50.

194 'Ung coffre à double serure pour mettre en la tresorie de l'eglise du dict Armentières, affin de y enfermer les lettraeges et comptes de la dicte halle': RDHDF-2, I, p. 414. On the use and significance of chests in medieval trade: Katherine Anne Wilson, 'Commerce and Consumers: The Ubiquitous Chest of the Late Middle Ages', *Journal of Interdisciplinary History*, 51 (2021), 377-404.

195 Shakespeare, *The Merchant of Venice*, Act III, Scene 3, line 13; Muller and Scharpé, *Spelen*, p. 116 ('consent maect wet').

informal aspects of commerce which existed side-by-side with the formal elements; a tension that they masterfully exploited in their plays. On various levels, personal networks were invaluable to the cloth traders of the rural textile economies that are central to this book. First of all, partnerships between drapers from the same village gave the individuals involved the opportunity to buy larger quantities of raw materials all at once. Second, these partnerships sometimes extended to multiple cloth centres of the West-Quarter, so that traders from a neighbouring village could collect debts, or stand surety in commercial matters. Third, the merchant-drapers that we have encountered in this chapter had connections to Spanish wool suppliers, and probably also to German cloth merchants, who were prominent resellers of their products. Finally, their interregional networks were greatly expanded through the mediation of brokers such as Wouter Ameide. In fact, people such as Ameide were the embodiment of the tension between formal and informal aspects of trade, since all foreign merchants without recourse to a lodging of their own in trading cities like Bruges were obliged by the urban government to employ a broker (but, by default, had to share the informal space of the tavern with their host and the other traders boarded there). The commercial connections between these merchants were further cemented during the fairs in the market cities, which were not only key platforms for trade, but also for cultural festivities where personal bonds were strengthened. That being said, the increasing primacy of Antwerp's permanent market may have drawn the cloth trade of Nieuwkerke (and, to a lesser extent, its neighbours) ever closer towards this particular city. This encouraged the merchant-drapers, who had to remain abreast of the latest trade opportunities and developments in fashion, to secure their constant presence in the urban market through renting cloth halls; a very successful strategy, as we shall see in Chapter 5.

At the same time, the 'merchant-capitalist' attitude that Cornelis Everaert despised so much, was apparently paramount to the success of Nieuwkerke's drapery. The top-layer of the industry consisted of entrepreneurs who harboured connections to the production process but were also immersed in marketing the products. This integration of industry and trade enabled the drapers to keep track of the specific demand of their customers and directly translate these wishes into their own, or possibly a partner's, industrial output. At the same time, we may wonder whether the wealthier traders with the best connections (or the most 'social capital') attempted to exploit these advantages exclusively for their own benefit. The large volumes of wool imported by groups of drapers do hint at collaboration, but only in small groups. Yet even if the merchant-drapers were primarily chasing their own interests – for instance, by capitalizing on their exclusive access to high-quality wool through reselling it at a higher price to their less well-to-do colleagues in the village – this may ultimately have benefited everyone. Their actions certainly secured a smooth flow of raw materials to, and steady trickle of, finished products from the rural cloth centres. And, as we are about to see in the next two chapters, there are strong hints that at least in Nieuwkerke, the drapery was endowed with a certain collective spirit, a sense that the good of the community outweighed that of the individual.

CHAPTER 4

Town and countryside in the Flemish West-Quarter

In 1502, the drapers of the rural cloth centres in the Flemish West-Quarter were once again embroiled in a legal dispute with those of Ypres over their right to produce cloth for the export market on a large scale. During the court proceedings before the Council of Flanders, the accusers from the city complained about damages to their own industry, and to the general prosperity of the urban populace. However, they also invoked what they considered a fundamental opposition between town and countryside: 'rural villages are dedicated to the performance of labour and agriculture, and transactions of trade and industrial undertakings are given to the good towns'.[1] As will be clear by now, the rural population in this part of the county of Flanders did not hold entirely the same view, since a proportion of the villagers were entirely committed to manufacturing and selling fabrics. This begs the question to what extent these settlements should then still be considered rural, as opposed to actual towns, or even whether such a distinction between different zones should not be qualified altogether. Indeed, around the middle of the sixteenth century, Marcus Van Vaernewijck, a historian from Ghent, professed that the villages in the Western part of Flanders *almost* qualified as towns because they were so 'impressive' (in which he probably referred to their population size and architectural scope); that is to say, if it were not for their lack of 'gates and fortifications'.[2] Clearly, contemporaries of this period were gradually coming to terms with changes in the urban landscape, and they struggled with what exactly defined the urban-rural divide. The present chapter zeroes in on this gradual shift, both in terms of political, cultural and socio-economic aspects. The underlying thesis is that larger industrial villages, such as Nieuwkerke, were hardly distinguishable from towns, both in terms of their occupational structure, their cultural expressions, and their ideology. However, their 'urbanity' was dependent upon ephemeral initiatives that were not crystallized into the legal framework of the time. As a result, the urban status

1 'Les villaiges champestres estoient dediez à l'exercice de labeur et d'agriculture et les negociacions de marchandise et des euvres mecanicques estoient adonnees aux bonnes villes': RDHDF-2, I, p. 83. The term *labour* in Middle French is usually associated with agricultural work, although strictly speaking *labeur* (as opposed to *labour*) had the wider meaning that closer resembles the modern English equivalent.

2 'Alle die Westcant is [...] soo voorsien van treffelicke dorpen ende repassen datter wonder om seggen ware, de welcke om steden te sijne niet en ghebreken dan poorten ende vesten, ende zouden vele ander stedekens beschamen': Marcus Van Vaernewijck, *De historie van Belgis diemen anders noemen mach: den spieghel der Nederlantscher oudtheyt* (Antwerp: H. Verdussen, 1619), Chapter 61.

of the West-Quarter cloth centres could not withstand the economic shift and political turmoil of the later sixteenth century.[3]

The ambiguity over what separated town from countryside in the late Middle Ages originates with the predominant attitudes of the period itself. The passage from Van Vaernewijck quoted above demonstrates the especial importance of the military function of cities and towns for contemporaries, who could not help but notice their strategic (dis)advantage at times when their dwelling places were threatened by outside forces. Indeed, during periods of military upheaval, both the villages of the West-Quarter and its unfortified towns, such as Bailleul, knew many inhabitants who took their refuge in 'closed cities' (*besloten steden*).[4] Yet Van Vaernewijck's confusion on what distinguished town from countryside is evident from an earlier passage in the same book, where he enumerates Flanders's fortified urban centres, but also lists the county's 'open towns'.[5] Beyond this impressionistic account, the legal correspondences in connection to Nieuwkerke's cloth industry breathe the same ambivalence over what divided town from country. In the original cloth charter of 1359, for example, Nieuwkerke was referred to as 'village' (*doorp*), while in the 1450s it was called a 'town', or sometimes 'town and parish' (*ville et paroisse*), and then in 1461 it was a 'village' again. The latter apparently remained the preferred term for the cloth centre into the sixteenth century.[6] This muddled picture of the period itself has, among other reasons, driven historians to uphold present-day criteria and project them backwards in time.[7]

It is perhaps because rural history and urban history (or indeed urban studies) are predominantly separate disciplines, but the idea of distinct urban and rural zones has lingered in the historiography. Writing in the early twentieth century, the Belgian historian Henri Pirenne still followed the antagonistic discourse of the late medieval period: he framed the development of rural cloth centres in the Flemish West-Quarter during this period in terms of a clear *opposition* between the urban and the rural. Apart from the socio-economic aspect, Pirenne asserted that the political context of the mid-fourteenth century was also important in

3 On the relative resilience of the Flemish cloth centres (urban and rural) in this period: Johan Dambruyne, 'De hiërarchie van de Vlaamse textielcentra (1500-1750): continuïteit of discontinuïteit?', in: *Qui valet ingenio: liber amicorum aangeboden aan dr. Johan Decavele*, ed. by Leen Charles and others (Ghent: Stichting Mens en kultuur, 1996), pp. 155-72 (pp. 166-67).

4 See, for instance: ADN, B 4821, fol. 11r: 'dat meest de drapiers hem hilden in besloten steden' (1481-82). See also: *Cartulaire de l'ancien Grand Tonlieu de Bruges faisant suite au cartulaire de l'ancienne Estaple: recueil de documents concernant le commerce intérieur et maritime, les relations internationales et l'histoire économique de cette ville*, ed. by Louis Gilliodts-Van Severen, 2 vols (Bruges: Plancke, 1908-09), I (1908), p. 244 (no. MMDCCCXC): 'Alsoo midts den afloop vanden platten lande ende verwoesten van alle onbeslotene steden, hebben heurlieder vertreck binnen der stede van Brugghe ghenoomen verscheyden drapiers van Belle, Meenen, Nieukerke, Poperinghe, Hondschote ende andere opene plaetsen' (1582).

5 Van Vaernewijck, Chapter 37.

6 RDHDF-1, III, pp. 59-60; RDHDF-2, III, pp. 100-02, 109-11, 131-33.

7 Alain Derville, 'L'urbanisation de la Flandre Wallonne d'après les enquêtes fiscales (1449-1549)', *Revue du Nord*, 79 (1997), 295-302 (pp. 298-301).

this regard. Between the middle of the thirteenth century and the mid-1300s, the counts of Flanders pursued a policy whereby they granted charters to village industries in order to break the power of the ever more dominant cities. Places like Hondschoote, Langemark, and Mesen are examples of this. Meanwhile, the counts benefited themselves financially through the direct and indirect taxes they levelled on these manufacturing centres.[8] This conception of socio-economic and political struggles within a 'triangle' of princes, rural aristocracy in the countryside, and towns has lingered in studies of the late medieval Low Countries.[9] While this thinking in separate power blocks seems convenient for analytical purposes, however, the separation is no longer generally accepted, as neither the dichotomy of nobility-towns, nor that of towns-countryside has held up to closer scrutiny.[10] The recognition that the boundaries between the urban and rural spheres were fluid mainly hinges on the mobility of people, which will be an important theme in this chapter.

At the same time, it is neither helpful nor credible to maintain that there was no separation whatsoever between urban society and the countryside. In any case, downplaying the conceptual framework of a specific historic context may be problematic, because that framework undoubtedly influenced the behaviour of contemporary people and, by extension, affected the nature of urban and rural society. In our own case study, for example, the ideological opposition between the city of Ypres and the West-Quarter countryside features heavily in the legal sources relating to their industrial competition. Some historians even claim that 'in order to understand an age whose way of thinking is different from our own, we must operate only with the concepts of that age'.[11] Yet I do not subscribe to that view. The clear advantage of constructing a common vocabulary that cuts across temporal and geographical boundaries is that it allows historians of different periods and regions to study a phenomenon like urbanization within a diachronic, comparative framework.[12] This is useful, among other things because urbanization rates are considered an important indication of a society's level of development (the idea being that when more people live in towns, more complex economic and political structures evolve, and cultural expressions can

8 Henri Pirenne, *Histoire de Belgique*, 7 vols (Brussels: H. Lamertin, 1900-1932), II (1903), pp. 182-83, 389-90.

9 Raymond Van Uytven, 'Vorst, adel en steden: een driehoeksverhouding in Brabant van de twaalfde tot de zestiende eeuw', *Bijdragen Geschiedenis Hertogdom Brabant*, 59 (1976), 93-122. The tenacity of this idea can be evidenced, among others, in: Wim Blockmans, *Metropolen aan de Noordzee: de geschiedenis van Nederland, 1100-1560* (Amsterdam: Bert Bakker, 2012), pp. 372-80.

10 Frederik Buylaert, 'Lordship, Urbanization and Social Change in Late Medieval Flanders', *Past & Present*, 228 (2015), 31-75 (pp. 32-33).

11 Otto Brunner, *Land and Lordship: Structures of Governance in Medieval Austria*, trans. by Howard Kaminsky and James Van Horn Melton (Philadelphia: Penn Press, 1992), p. xlix, n. 23 (the quote is originally from Otto von Gierke).

12 See the discussion about the application of the concept 'state' by medieval historians: Rees Davies, 'The Medieval State: The Tyranny of a Concept?', *Journal of Historical Sociology*, 16 (2003), 280-300; and especially the response: Susan Reynolds, 'There Were States in Medieval Europe: A Response to Rees Davies', *Journal of Historical Sociology*, 16 (2003), 550-55 (esp. p. 554).

also flourish freely). In other words, towns act like particle accelerators for the development of societies.[13]

The town-country divide has been variously framed in terms of demography, legal status, and economic or political function. Of these, the functional approach has surfaced as the most prominent in recent years.[14] Still, the defining characteristic is largely determined by the goal of the historical enquiry. Alain Derville, for instance, excluded certain small towns from his assessment of urbanization in late medieval Walloon Flanders because he considered their population levels too low.[15] In contrast, Emmanuel Le Roy Ladurie underlined what he called the 'rurban' character of Romans (now in the French Drôme department) in 1580, even though this walled town counted some eight thousand inhabitants at the time. The reason is that Ladurie was principally interested in 'class conflict' during the town's carnival, in which the high proportion of resident agricultural labourers (37 per cent) was of relevance.[16] The aim of this chapter, however, is to move beyond a single determining attribute. And so, I will instead explore several different criteria to gauge the extent to which late medieval cloth centres like Nieuwkerke merit the label 'urban'. The underlying purpose is not to offer a static answer to the question whether these were in effect towns, but rather to further problematize the supposed town-country divide in order to advance the scholarly debate.

The chapter begins with an examination of the degree in which the West-Quarter cloth villages were vested with certain cultural elements that would traditionally be deemed urban, but that, on closer inspection, were largely shared by town and countryside (although, to be fair, they mainly flowed from urban society outwards). In the second part of the chapter, the connections of late medieval countryfolk to the city are further explored by focusing on the legal status of 'external citizen' or 'outburgher'. As will become clear, many people involved in the rural cloth industries in the hinterland of Ypres had close ties to the city by virtue of their institutional statute of external citizen. This further demonstrates the blurred boundaries between urbanites and country residents. The subsequent section of this chapter is an attempt to distinguish the urban aspirations that the local village elite of the cloth centre of Nieuwkerke expressed through a certain 'spatial discourse', as well as the impact of those ambitions on urbanization. The final section lays the groundwork for the fifth and last chapter,

---

13 Charles Tilly, *Coercion, Capital, and European States, AD 990-1990* (Cambridge MA & Oxford: Basil Blackwell, 1990), pp. 47-51. For a nuanced assessment of the link between urbanization rate and long-term economic performance: S. R. Epstein, 'Introduction: Town and Country in Europe, 1300-1800', in *Town and Country in Europe, 1300-1800*, ed. by S. R. Epstein (Cambridge: Cambridge University Press, 2001), pp. 1-29 (pp. 9-11).

14 Epstein, 'Introduction: Town and Country in Europe', pp. 1-4; Christopher Dyer, 'Conclusion: Making Sense of Town and Country', in *Town and Country in the Middle Ages: Contrasts, Contacts and Interconnections, 1100-1500*, ed. by Kate Giles and Christopher Dyer (Leeds: David Brown Book Company, 2005), pp. 313-21 (pp. 314-15).

15 Derville, 'L'urbanisation de la Flandre Wallonne', p. 298.

16 Emmanuel Le Roy Ladurie, *Het carnaval van Romans: van Maria-Lichtmis tot Aswoensdag, 1579-1580*, trans. by Frans de Haan and Barbara Herklots (Amsterdam: Bert Bakker, 1985; 1st French ed. 1979), pp. 12-13, 15-20.

by introducing the ideology of the 'Common Good', and associated themes, which had a great influence on the prosperity of the local cloth industry of Nieuwkerke. That village, which was in many ways the leading textile centre of the Flemish West-Quarter, will be the main protagonist in this chapter.

The urban culture of Nieuwkerke

The goal of the first section of this chapter is twofold: to elaborate on the flourishing cultural life in Nieuwkerke, but to simultaneously qualify the notion that late medieval urban culture stood in clear opposition to a rural counterpart. Cultural life in the medieval countryside has become something of a neglected topic in historical studies of the last three decades, making way for a focus on urban culture instead. This 'urban turn' may be attributed to the 'intellectual exhaustion of rural studies' by the earlier members of the *Annales* school (Marc Bloch, Lucien Fèbvre), as well as a re-found optimistic outlook on modernity and its association with city life.[17] But even those earlier works were mainly devoted to social, political, and economic aspects of the countryside, as opposed to distinctly rural cultural phenomena.[18] One of the reasons for this lack of research is a dearth of sources. Also, where good materials do survive, their representativeness is questionable.[19] Yet it remains uncertain whether there even was such a thing as a strict separation between rural and urban culture in general, especially towards the end of the medieval period. Some studies certainly emphasize that the self-image of premodern urban elites was defined in terms of antagonism to 'uncivilized' and 'peasant-like' behaviour.[20] Then again, the tight urban web in Flanders and the Low Countries in general meant that countryfolk always lived in close proximity to a town, which may have led to the omnipresence of an 'urban way of life'.[21] And there we face the crux of

---

17 Marc Boone, 'Cities in Late Medieval Europe: The Promise and the Curse of Modernity', *Urban History*, 39 (2012), 329-49 (pp. 335-37).

18 A notable exception is, of course, Emmanuel Le Roy Ladurie, *Montaillou: village occitan de 1294 à 1324* (Paris: Éditions Gallimard, 1975).

19 Again, Le Roy Ladurie's *Montaillou* is a good example, as are other micro-studies such as: Carlo Ginzburg, *The Night Battles: Witchcraft and Agrarian Cults in the Sixteenth and Seventeenth Centuries*, trans. by John Tedeschi and Anne Tedeschi (Baltimore: Routledge & Kegan Paul PLC, 1983; 1st Italian ed. 1966); Carlo Ginzburg, *The Cheese and the Worms: The Cosmos of a Sixteenth-Century Miller*, trans. by John Tedeschi and Anne Tedeschi (Baltimore: Routledge & Kegan Paul PLC, 1980; 1st Italian ed. 1976).

20 Herman Pleij, 'Restyling "Wisdom", Remodelling the Nobility, and Caricaturing the Peasant: Urban Literature in the Late Medieval Low Countries', *Journal of Interdisciplinary History*, 32 (2002), 689-704 (pp. 690-91, 695-96); Herman Pleij, *De sneeuwpoppen van 1511: literatuur en stadscultuur tussen middeleeuwen en moderne tijd* (Amsterdam: Bert Bakker, 1988), pp. 121-50. For a critique of Pleij's emphasis on elites: Jan Dumolyn and Jelle Haemers, '"Let Each Man Carry on with his Trade and Remain Silent": Middle-Class Ideology in the Urban Literature of the Late Medieval Low Countries', *Cultural and Social History*, 10 (2013), 169-89 (pp. 170-71).

21 Peter Stabel, 'Urbanization and its Consequences: Spatial Developments in Late Medieval Flanders', in *Raumerfassung und Raumbewußtsein im späteren Mittelalter*, Vorträge und Forschungen, 49, ed. by Peter Moraw (Stuttgart: Jan Thorbecke Verlag, 2002), pp. 179-202 (pp. 181-82).

the matter: cultural exchange is usually presented as a one-way street in this regard, proceeding from the town outwards to a passively receptive (uncultured) countryside. Rural historians naturally reject this notion, because it discounts the internal dynamics of rural society and the agency of people living in the countryside – who still constituted the vast majority of the general population throughout the pre-industrial period. Furthermore, in a predominantly rural world, the urban way of life retained a lot of rural characteristics, such as the importance of land possession, food production, and the household economy.[22] In fact, a proportion of pre-industrial town dwellers were engaged in land cultivation themselves. One could hypothesize, therefore, that the cultural life of the industrial manufacturers in the villages of the Flemish West-Quarter was more urban than that of these 'rurban' town dwellers.[23]

John Decavele's 1992 study on cultural developments in fifteenth- and sixteenth-century Flanders certainly confirms that this was a period of cultural blooming for the West-Quarter. According to the criteria he selected, namely the presence of Latin schools, humanists, 'Protestants', Chambers of Rhetoric, and graduates of the university of Leuven, the West-Quarter emerges as one of the leading cultural regions of Flanders at the close of the Middle Ages.[24] In terms of literary societies alone, the region vied for first place with the Franc of Bruges, with a marked upsurge of rural Chambers towards the middle of the sixteenth century. Even smaller cloth villages such as Steenwerck and Flêtre founded literary associations, in addition to more obvious places like Eécke and Nieuwkerke.[25] The latter cloth centre was once again unusual: it saw the official recognition, or 'baptism', of not just one but two literary societies by the Head Chamber of Rhetoric in Ypres. The first one was called *Goetwillich in 't Herte* ('Benevolent in the Heart') and was baptized before 1517, the other was called *Blijde van Sinnen* ('Of Happy Sense') and was baptized in 1520.[26] In fact, Nieuwkerke ticked all the boxes of Decavele's study, with at least 26 students at

---

22 Tim Soens, Eline Van Onacker and Kristof Dombrecht, 'Metropolis and Hinterland? A Comment on the Role of Rural Economy and Society in the Urban Heart of the Medieval Low Countries', *BMGN – Low Countries Historical Review*, 127 (2012), 82-88 (pp. 86-87). See also: Buylaert, 'Lordship, Urbanization and Social Change', esp. pp. 32-33.

23 In the small English town of Rugeley, for instance, 16 per cent of the population were 'cultivators' in 1380-81: Richard Goddard, 'Small Boroughs and the Manorial Economy: Enterprise Zones or Urban Failures?', *Past & Present*, 210 (2011), 3-31 (p. 6).

24 Johan Decavele, 'Het culturele en intellectuele netwerk: middeleeuwen en 16e eeuw', in *Het stedelijk netwerk in België in historisch perspectief (1350-1850): een statistische en dynamische benadering: 15de Internationaal Colloquium, Spa, 4-6 september 1990: Handelingen* (Brussels: Gemeentekrediet, 1992), pp. 155-90 (p. 382).

25 Anne-Laure Van Bruaene, *Om beters wille: rederijkerskamers en de stedelijke cultuur in de Zuidelijke Nederlanden (1400-1650)* (Amsterdam: Amsterdam University Press, 2008), pp. 87, 97-98.

26 There is no actual information on the baptism of *Goetwillich in 't herte*, but Anne-Laure van Bruaene considers the dove in the Chamber's sigil a clear sign that it *was* baptized. Another source makes clear that this literary association was present at a literary event in Bruges in 1517 (see also Chapter 3): Anne-Laure Van Bruaene, 'Repertorium van rederijkerskamers in de Zuidelijke Nederlanden en Luik, 1400-1650' (2004), online resource at: www.dbnl.org [accessed 23 March 2021] CAB, Reeks 305, Wouter Ameyde, Journaal B, fol. 200^{v}.

university, two known humanists, and a Latin school, in addition to the already-mentioned Chambers of Rhetoric.[27] We might further add that the village counted two archery confraternities in 1533: one devoted to Saint Sebastian (archers), the other to Saint George (crossbowmen).[28] Little information survives about these rural shooting- and literary associations.

There are, however, plenty of recorded instances where rural Chambers of Rhetoric participated in urban competitions and vice versa during the sixteenth century. This clearly demonstrates that the urban-rural cultural opposition sometimes identified for the earlier fifteenth century did not persist into the Early Modern Period.[29] Nieuwkerke's *Goetwillich in 't Herte*, for example, took part in urban events in Bruges (1517) and Ghent (1539), while a Chamber from the small town of Wervik took place in a competition held in Nieuwkerke itself in 1565.[30] Apparently, the interregional network of literary associations in the Low Countries cut across the supposed town-country divide. And part of the explanation is that the members of these associations shared identities that were defined by their occupation and socio-economic position, rather than by their place of residence.[31] This link between line of work and cultural identity suggests that the expansion of cloth production led to a kind of 'cultural urbanization' in the Flemish West-Quarter. Indeed, the Chambers of Rhetoric have been noted as key advertisers of the corporate middle-class ideology of working commoners in the late medieval Low Countries.[32] Meanwhile, the relatively high rate of literacy in the Flemish countryside, combined with the literary associations' low admission fees and contributions, facilitated membership among the rural artisans.[33]

But it was most likely the wealthier entrepreneurs and traders who provided the main impetus behind the spread and assimilation of these cultural expressions. As attested in the previous chapter, they were the people who interacted with city dwellers on a frequent basis. The fragmentary evidence in surviving sources related to the Flemish literary associations confirms this notion. For instance, at the baptism of Flêtre's Chamber of Rhetoric in 1548, a Frans Van Der Meulen was baptized along with it 'in the name of the same guild and general community'.[34]

27 Decavele, 'Het culturele en intellectuele netwerk', pp. 374-76.

28 SAB, Aanwinsten 504, fol. 19ᵛ; Laura Crombie, *Archery and Crossbow Guilds in Medieval Flanders, 1300-1500* (Woodbridge: Boydell, 2016), pp. 4-5.

29 Van Bruaene, *Om beters wille*, pp. 101-06; Crombie, p. 174, 177-78; Pleij, 'Restyling "Wisdom"', pp. 695-96.

30 CAB, Reeks 305, Wouter Ameyde, Journaal B, fol. 200ᵛ; Anonymous, *De Gentse Spelen van 1539*, ed. by B. H. Erné and L. M. van Dis, 2 vols (The Hague: Martinus Nijhoff, 1982), I, pp. 177-203; Van Bruaene, 'Repertorium van rederijkerskamers'.

31 Van Bruaene, *Om beters wille*, pp. 106-08.

32 Dumolyn and Haemers, pp. 182-84.

33 In 1567, Lodovico Guicciardini asserted the near-universal literacy of the Flemish population in town and countryside. Although this was an exaggeration, around 80 per cent of the Flemish lease-farmers could apparently write their own names: Decavele, 'Het culturele en intellectuele netwerk', p. 373. In the small town of Steenvoorde, admission to the Chamber cost 2d. Fl. gr. in 1518 (and the yearly contribution amounted to an additional 1d. Fl. gr.): Van Bruaene, *Om beters wille*, pp. 94-95.

34 Van Bruaene, 'Repertorium van rederijkserskamers'.

According to the records of the wardens of Flêtre's textile industry, this man was a draper with an annual output of 27 pieces of fabric in the course of the year 1551-52, placing him among the more productive cloth entrepreneurs of that village.[35] In a similar vein, in 1533-34, the governors of Nieuwkerke's Confraternity of Saint Sebastian were Jan and Gillis De Raedt, both of whom were drapers of some note in the village.[36] In the end, the lack of evidence about memberships makes it hard to gauge the accessibility or exclusivity of these cultural associations. On the one hand, the shooting guilds in the Flemish towns were apparently quite open during the fourteenth and fifteenth century; they even forged communities that cut across different socio-economic backgrounds.[37] However, in the neighbouring principality of Brabant, these lay clubs had come to exclude poorer members of society by the seventeenth century.[38]

In that sense, it could be significant that in Nieuwkerke, both the literary and the archery associations showed signs of division; for starters, there were two of each. This may simply have been a consequence of the steady growth of the local population between the late fifteenth and mid-sixteenth century (see Chapter 1). But it is not inconceivable that the village's cultural associations were split along socio-economic fault lines. So, while the shooting confraternity of Saint Sebastian was ruled over by drapers, a barber and a brewer governed its counterpart devoted to Saint George in 1533.[39] This occupational or socio-economic division is further suggested by the fact that members of the guild of Saint Sebastian practiced their crossbow skills on a plot of land they rented from a man named Joris De Hane: yet another draper.[40] Alternatively, given the emergence of evangelical beliefs in the West-Quarter during this very period, there is the possibility that the division followed religious lines. In that case, there would have been no direct link with occupation or socio-economic position, because adherents of the new faith came from various different professions, financial capacities, and even socio-political estates.[41]

---

35 GSAB, CA, Acquits en portefeuilles 1367 (booklet beginning with 'Dit zyn de lakins die gheloyt zyn van dess. jaere XV^c LI ...').

36 Jan De Raedt was one of the drapers who bought wool from the Castilian firm of Juan Castro de Muxica in the 1530s. In 1564-65, a Jan De Raedt still produced 57 whole pieces of cloth. That same year, there were four men called Gillis De Raedt, but the most likely candidate was Gillis De Raedt 'the elder'. This man only produced 18 pieces that year, but his son Daniel was warden of the high perch in 1562 and 1563: CAB, Archief van het Spaanse Consulaat, Juan Castro de Muxica, Journaal (1535-38); GSAB, CA, Acquits en portefeuilles 1367/33 (non foliated quires); RDHDF-2, III, pp. 191-93, 199-200.

37 Crombie, pp. 221-22, 100-14.

38 Maarten Van Dijck, 'Het verenigingsleven op het Hagelandse platteland: sociale polarisatie en middenveldparticipatie in de 17e en 18e eeuw', *TSEG – The Low Countries Journal of Social and Economic History*, 2 (2005), 81-108 (pp. 95-102).

39 The governors of the latter were *maistre Jaques De Hollandre, baerbier* and *Jaques Hueghebaert* (who occurs in a document of 1545 as a *brauwer*): SAB, Aanwinsten 504, fol. 19^v; GSAB, CA, Acquits en portefeuilles 802bis (loose, non foliated quire of June-July 1545).

40 In 1564-64, Joris De Hane produced a total of 49 pieces of cloth: GSAB, CA, Acquits en portefeuilles 1367/33; SAB, Aanwinsten 504, fol. 4^r.

41 Marcel Backhouse, *Beeldenstorm en bosgeuzen in het Westkwartier (1566-1568): bijdrage tot de geschiedenis van de godsdiensttroebelen der Zuidelijke Nederlanden in de XVIe eeuw* (Kortrijk: Koninklijke Geschied- en Oudheidkundige Kring, 1971), p. 46. Compare: Johan Decavele, *De*

Still, although the spread of the new belief in the West-Quarter may have been caused by an initial outflow of religious sentiments from urban society, the fact that these ideas took hold so successfully was probably a consequence of the specific rural context. Certainly, through their frequent visits to the city of Antwerp (that 'centre of Protestant reform'), the merchant-drapers of Nieuwkerke would have been among the first to be exposed to evangelical Christianity.[42] At the same time, though, the rising demand for manual labour meant that the village itself attracted migrants from urban society. In 1529, for example, the law court of Bailleul executed a 'native of the town of Kortrijk [...] of the Lutheran sect, living in Nieuwkerke', amongst other things because he had in his possession 'certain forbidden books'.[43] Although Nieuwkerke did not have its own printing press, there are two recorded instances in the 1560s where bookbinders from the village were suspected of sympathizing with the new faith. One of them had apparently learned his trade in the city of Antwerp, as another bookbinder, who was *oppidanus* of the city, vouched for him: 'having held him, and still holding him, and also knowing him, for a journeyman of good repute and fame, and also for a person in no way being tainted with, or suspected of, any heresy'.[44]

While these examples still seem to underscore the linear urban-rural trajectory of ideas, we should not forget that it was in the West-Quarter that the Iconoclastic Fury of 1566 first ignited, in the small cloth town of Steenvoorde. The growing, and increasingly poor, textile proletariat in this region was especially susceptible to the evangelical teachings. Only twenty per cent of the population of Nieuwkerke went to get their Holy Communion during Easter of 1566.[45] Meanwhile, the local cloth entrepreneurs testified to the grim atmosphere that had taken hold of the village at this point. In 1533, a group of drapers from Nieuwkerke complained to the Chamber of Accounts in Lille that they feared their children's minds would be poisoned if they let them wander about freely in the village, 'where they often learn the way of the tavern, keep bad company, wander around at

---

dageraad van de reformatie in Vlaanderen (1520-1565), 2 vols (Brussels: Paleis der Academiën, 1975), II, pp. 562-64.

42 Guido Marnef, *Antwerpen in de tijd van de Reformatie* (Amsterdam & Antwerp: Meulenhoff Kritak, 1996), p. 11; Decavele, *De dageraad van de reformatie*, I, p. 240.

43 'Ung nomme Willem Cousture dict "Lerfekin", natif de la ville de Courtray demourant en la paroisse de Neufeglise, avoit renomme d'estre de la secte Lutherane, et qu'il se advanchoit de lire aulcuns livres deffendus par les placcatz de l'empereur notre seigneur publies au pays dudit seigneur empereur': ADN, B 5669 (1529-1530), fol. 6ᵛ.

44 The first was Jan De Vick, who had fled to Sandwich in England before 1563 to escape persecution. The second was 'Henricke Fossaert, van Nyenkercke in Westvlaenderen, boekbindere'. A certain 'Peter Wils, boekbindere oppidanus' testified 'dat hy den voirseit Henricke Fossaert altyt hebben gehouden ende alnoch houdende zyn ende oock alsmede hebben weten houden voir een gezelle van eenen staende tott goeden name ende faem, ende oock voer een persoon gheenssins wesende besmet oft suspect van eenige heresien oft ketteryen': Marcel Backhouse, 'De Vlaamse vluchtelingenkerk in Sandwich in 1563: twee manuscripten uit het British Museum', *Bulletin de la Commission Royale d'Histoire / Handelingen van de Koninklijke Commissie voor Geschiedenis*, 147 (1981), 75-113 (p. 112); CAA, Certificatieboeken 20 (1564), fol. 41ʳ.

45 Decavele, *De dageraad van de reformatie*, II, pp. 562-63.

night, play at dice, whore around, and utter blasphemies'.[46] Indeed, it was the populations of the rural and small-town cloth centres of the West-Quarter that re-exported the evangelical sentiments to urban society, plundering convents and destroying religious images along the way before converging on towns like Bailleul and larger cities such as Ypres. This marked a contrast with the regions around Ghent and Antwerp, where the iconoclasm proceeded from the towns outwards.[47] In the end, though, the swift exchange of the new faith throughout Flanders is primarily a testament to the interconnectedness of the network of the Flemish cities. This supports the idea that at least Nieuwkerke, but probably other large cloth villages such as Dranouter, Eécke, and Kemmel should be considered a part of this urban web.[48]

Citizens of the countryside

In a rather concrete sense, the boundaries between the rural West-Quarter of Flanders and Netherlandish urban society were leaky as a sieve. As demonstrated in the previous chapter, the cloth entrepreneurs from villages such as Nieuwkerke, Kemmel, and Dranouter had commercial ties to various market cities in the Low Countries. Perhaps more striking is that many of them actually sought to acquire a legal status that gave them access to the same privileges as citizens. They were able to do this through the statute of 'outburgher'. Variously known as *buitenpoorters* or *hagepoorters* in Middle Dutch, *Ausbürger* or *Pfahlbürger* in the German Empire, and *bourgeois foraines* in French-speaking regions, outburghers occurred in many urbanized regions in Western Europe from about the thirteenth century onwards. While the finer details were subject to regional variation, in essence an outburgher was a person who bore some or all of the same privileges and responsibilities connected to full citizenship of a distinct town or city, but who lived outside that settlement for extended periods of the year.[49] Presumably, the statute originally came about because certain citizens felt hampered by the fact that they lost their legal privileges every time they briefly vacated the city to pursue their ventures in other places. For these people, outburghership was a way to take a licensed leave to trade or pursue other interests as they saw fit. However, the most recurrent type of outburghership came to be the reverse procedure: where people who were external to urban society acquired the privileges of citizenship while continuing to live outside a town's jurisdictional

46 'Alwaer zy dicwyle leeren de taverne ende quaet gheselscap antieren, als by nachte lopen, tuuschen ende speylen, hoerieren ende putieren ende quaede eeden sweren': Decavele, *De dageraad van de reformatie*, II, p. 561.

47 Backhouse, *Beeldenstorm en bosgeuzen*, p. 78-86.

48 Peter Stabel, *Dwarfs among Giants: The Flemish Urban Network in the Late Middle Ages* (Leuven: Garant, 1997), pp. 203-04.

49 Jan Verbeemen, 'De buitenpoorterij in de Nederlanden', *Bijdragen voor de Geschiedenis van de Nederlanden*, 12 (1957), 81-97 (pp. 81-83).

zone.[50] The cloth entrepreneurs of the West-Quarter were generally of the latter type. This is relevant to the present discussion, because in a sense their close relationship with the urban sphere effectively dissolved the barriers between rural and urban society.

There has been some debate about the abilities of urban governments in different European regions to extend jurisdiction over their hinterlands by attracting outburghers. Their success in this regard generally depended upon the prevailing power relations between city, prince, and nobility.[51] Indeed, the count of Flanders apparently instituted the statute of outburgher in many small towns to counterbalance the all-too-powerful cities in the thirteenth century.[52] In the longer term, however, it was mainly the small Flemish towns and big cities alike that profited from their outburghers, first through taxation and other financial contributions, and second because the institution stimulated the inflow of labour from the countryside.[53] The party that consistently lost out were the lords in the countryside, whose juridical hold over their local subjects was eroded through the institution. Unsurprisingly, there are examples where Flemish lords' frustration with these limitations spilled over into violent retributions against members of the city government that enfranchised their subjects.[54] At the other end of the spectrum, the party that mainly benefited from the institution were the outburghers themselves: their legal and economic options were expanded, yet they could also revoke their citizenship at any time they wanted. In sixteenth-century Geraardsbergen, for example, the outburghers cleverly switched between appealing to the urban court and appealing to their rural lord's jurisdiction, alternately revoking and reinstating their statute. This is reminiscent of the way in which the merchant-drapers of Nieuwkerke could 'shop around' the different commercial institutions available to them as and when they pleased in the market cities of the Low Countries (see Chapter 3).[55]

50 Erik Thoen, 'Rechten en plichten van plattelanders als instrumenten van machtspolitieke strijd tussen adel, stedelijke burgerij en grafelijk gezag in het laat-middeleeuwse Vlaanderen: buitenpoorterij en mortemain-rechten ten persoonlijken titel in de kasselrijen van Aalst en Oudenaarde vooral toegepast op de periode rond 1400', *Machtsstructuren in de plattelandsgemeenschappen in België en aangrenzende gebieden: Handelingen van het 13de Internationaal Colloquium Spa, 3-5 sept. 1986*, Gemeentekrediet, Historische Reeks in-8°, 77 (Brussels: Gemeentekrediet van België, 1986) pp. 469-90 (pp. 484-85).

51 Tom Scott, 'Town and Country in Germany, 1350-1600", in *Town and country*, ed. by Epstein, pp. 202-28 (pp. 207-09); Guy Marchal, 'Pfahlbürger, bourgeois forains, buitenpoorters, bourgeois du roi: Aspekte einer zweideutigen Rechtsstellung, in *Neubürger im späten Mittelalter: Migration und Austausch in der Städtelandschaft des Alten Reiches (1250-1550)*, ed. by Rainer Christoph Schwinges, Barbara Studer, and Roland Gerber (Berlin: Duncker und Humblot, 2002), pp. 333-67 (pp. 337-38); Marie-Jeanne Dankaart, 'De Gentse buitenpoorters en poorters tijdens het laatste kwart van de 15de eeuw: een sociale analyse en een topografische benadering (unpublished Masters-thesis, University of Ghent, 1989), p. 20.

52 Thoen, 'Rechten en plichten', pp. 484-85.

53 Stabel, *Dwarfs among Giants*, pp. 94-106.

54 Buylaert, 'Lordship, Urbanization and Social Change', pp. 40-41.

55 Bas van Bavel, *Manors and Markets: Economy and Society in the Low Countries AD 500-1600* (Oxford: Oxford University Press, 2010), pp. 114-15; Marchal, pp. 346-47.

There were, in fact, several reasons why a resident of a cloth village might wish to acquire external citizenship of a nearby town. First and foremost was the right to appeal to the urban law court for legal procedures, even when the crime or conflict occurred outside the city's physical jurisdiction. In Flanders, this also applied to capital offences. In 1516, for example, the Council of Flanders ruled in favour of a murder suspect's demand for a retrial before the urban court of Ypres, thereby overruling the prosecution's assertion that the defendant was 'only an outburgher'.[56] In a broader sense, outburghers effectively fell within the town's jurisdiction, which was particularly useful when they were in conflict with their rural lord. But formally belonging to the urban jurisdiction also meant that certain economic claims that the lord held over his subjects could be evaded, such as the so-called *mortemain*. This Flemish death duty was broadly similar to the English 'heriot' and consisted of collecting the 'best chattel' (usually the best piece of livestock) upon the death of the head of the family.[57] As we have seen, some of the drapers of Nieuwkerke also held livestock, so they certainly stood to benefit from being absolved of this duty.[58] It is unlikely that this was their prime motivator, yet we should not directly dismiss the *mortemain* as an out-dated institution. Consider that the seigneurial accounts of the village lordship of Nieuwkerke still contained a separate entry devoted to such levies in 1534, and also consider that the lord of Spiere effectively claimed a load of wool-yarn based on similar entitlements in 1539 (see Chapter 2).[59] Becoming an outburgher meant foregoing these seigneurial levies. Of course, lords and village aldermen often attempted to tax residents in spite of their citizenship, but the advanced legal institutions of Flanders ensured that the external citizens were protected. Both the Great Council in Mechelen and the Council of Flanders could be called upon in such cases, while they also protected outburghers from any additional taxes the cities tried to impose upon them illegally.[60]

In theory, however, to become an outburgher of Ypres was a bit of a double-edged sword for the drapers of the rural West-Quarter. On the one hand, it was certainly an attractive option because the statute exempted traders from certain tolls and excises when offloading their merchandise within the city's

56 Verbeemen, pp. 82-83. On Ypres see: Isidore Diegerick, *Inventaire analytique et chronologique des chartes et documents appartenant aux archives de la ville d'Ypres*, 6 vols (Bruges, 1853-1868), DCXLVII, MCCCCLXXIV.

57 Thoen, 'Rechten en plichten',pp. 472, 474-77; Michael Postan and Jan Titow, 'Heriots and Prices on Winchester Manors', in *Essays on Medieval agriculture and General Problems of the Medieval Economy*, ed. by Michael Postan (Cambridge: Cambridge University Press, 1973), pp. 150-85 (p. 151).

58 Joris Leupe, for instance, with an output of 32.5 pieces of cloth in 1564-65, sold two cows in the winter of 1544-45. Leupe had been an outburgher of Ypres since before 3 February 1531, because on that day his wife registered as an outburgher by virtue of her marriage to him. Another draper-outburgher, called Jan Lammen, can be connected to the farming of livestock through his lease of pastureland within the parish of Nieuwkerke: GSAB, CA, Acquits en portefeuilles 802bis; CAY, Kasselrijarchief, Eerste Reeks 2665, fol. 22^{v}; RLB, Fonds Merghelynck, M 18.

59 In the village seigneurie, it concerned 'bastard-, stranded-, heriot-, and strangers' goods' (*bien bastars, lagans, espaneez, estragiers*): SAB, Aanwinsten 504, fol. 10^{v}. The episode with the lord of Spiere occurred in 1539: RDHDF-2, III, pp. 137-39.

60 Diegerick, MCLXXII; CAY, Kasselrijarchief, Tiende Reeks 1424.

boundaries. Thus, rural cloth entrepreneurs who became outburghers of Ypres could sell cloth and buy raw materials in the city, or transport goods via its waterways, without having to await the fairs.[61] On the other hand, the external citizens had to pay a yearly contribution to the town, were taxed for any real estate they possessed within the urban jurisdiction, and sometimes even had to contribute additional sums for the renovation of city architecture. And all these sums came on top of the taxes they had to pay in their rural home parish for any landholdings they possessed there.[62] Furthermore, as mentioned in previous chapters, the government of Ypres undertook many repressive measures towards the rural draperies in the city's vicinity. This makes it all the more interesting that the city gates were apparently wide open to external citizens. In 1465, the city numbered a total of 1465 outburghers, 86 of whom lived in Nieuwkerke; quite a high number, considering that the city's total population fell below the 10,000 mark in this period.[63] This means that Ypres still had a much smaller number of outburghers than the city of Ghent, as the latter counted around 5000 external citizens in 1432 and accepted no fewer than 1805 new outburghers in the period 1477-88. Proportionally, however, the external citizens of the two Flemish cities hovered around the same level, as Ghent had a resident population of between 45,000 and 60,000 people. But several other Flemish towns had a considerably larger proportion than these prominent cities. Perhaps most notable in this regard are the town of Geraardsbergen (which had 4621 outburghers in 1398, while the town's total resident population only amounted to 3817 in 1469) and the city of Kortrijk (which counted 8333 outburghers in 1440, against a total of 9517 inhabitants in 1469). In fact, no less than 70 per cent of people living in the castellany of Kortrijk were external citizens of the city in the fifteenth century.[64] Tellingly, there is evidence that drapers from the surrounding countryside of Kortrijk became outburghers as a means to have their rural fabrics recognized as city cloth by the wardens. In that case, the institution was a tool for rural drapers to gain entry to the urban drapery corporation, but it may also have offered a legal basis for cloth entrepreneurs from other towns to sell the products from their hometown simultaneously with fabrics of Kortrijk.[65]

The question is whether the drapers of Nieuwkerke similarly exploited the institutional framework of Ypres. Certainly, quite a few cloth entrepreneurs

---

61 Diegerick, DCCCXLVII; Marchal, p. 335; RDHDF-2, III, pp. 130-31.

62 Diegerick, DCCCCXXX; Stabel, *Dwarfs among Giants*, p. 98.

63 Émile De Sagher, *Notice sur les archives communales d'Ypres et documents pour servir à l'histoire de Flandre du XIIIe au XVIe siècle* (Ypres: Callewaert-De Meulenaere, 1898), pp. 160-62; Henri Pirenne, 'Les dénombrements de la population d'Ypres au XVe siècle (1412-1506)', *Vierteljahrschrift für Sozial- und Wirtschaftsgeschichte*, 1 (1903), 1-32 (pp. 10-11); Walter Prevenier, 'La démographie des villes du comté de Flandre aux XIIIe et XVe siècles; état de la question: essai d'interprétation', *Revue du Nord*, 65 (1983), 255-75 (pp. 257-60).

64 Stabel, *Dwarfs among Giants*, pp. 31, 101-05; Peter Stabel, 'Demography and Hierarchy: The Small Towns and the Urban Network in Sixteenth-Century Flanders', in *Small Towns in Early Modern Europe*, ed. by Peter Clark (Cambridge: Cambridge University Press, 1995), pp. 206-28 (pp. 210-11).

65 Bertrand Haquette, 'Des lices et des joncs: rivière et draperies de la vallée de la Lys à la fin du Moyen Age', *Revue du Nord*, 79 (1997), 859-82 (pp. 871-75).

acquired outburghership of Ypres in the sixteenth century. At least 28.9 per cent of the drapers who were active in Nieuwkerke in 1564, became outbughers of the city at some point during their lifetime.[66] This figure is based on nineteenth-century transcriptions of contemporary records that listed the admissions of those people who entered the external citizenry through their marriage to an already-registered citizen or outburgher.[67] The city government allowed partners to register within a certain designated period after the wedding – a custom still in use in 1769, when the incubation period was six days.[68] That it truly concerned outburghers and not regular citizens can be inferred from the original documents of the same nature, which are extant for the period 1639-1796.[69] This 28.9 per cent is an absolute minimum of the village's total, since it solely accounts for the drapers, and then only those who acquired the statute through their marriage with a citizen, or those whose spouses received it by marrying them. What is more, these were only the outburghers of Ypres, while other towns in the wider region also offered the statute to countryfolk (Mesen, for one, and probably Bailleul as well).[70] Therefore, the total number of outburghers may have been a lot higher. As mentioned, these rural outburghers benefited from their status by having recourse to the urban court, but another major boon for rural drapers was the ability to use the city's commercial infrastructure. There is clear evidence, for example, that drapers of Nieuwkerke with real estate in Ypres imported raw materials via the city during the sixteenth century.[71]

One of Ypres' motives for attracting external citizens, apart from the prospect of financial revenue, was to revitalize the city's dwindling population during the economic downturn of the fifteenth and sixteenth centuries – which throws into sharp relief the urban government's exclusionist policy during the more prosperous fourteenth century, when outburghers were actively warded off.[72] This is supported by specifications such as 'wealthy' (*weildich*) and 'very rich'

66 RLB, Fonds Merghelynck, M 18. These are partial transcriptions from contemporary accounts listing people who registered as outburghers by virtue of their marriage to a current (out)burgher of the city: Kristof Papin, 'Gids voor het Fonds Merghelynck', Westhoek – Jaarboek, 9 (1994), 133-45, pp. 137-38. Out of the 270 checked drapers, 78 registered as outburghers. A cross-reference was considered a positive match when the first and last names of the individual were the same, registration took place in between 1505 and 1595, and Nieuwkerke was either listed as place of origin, as place of marriage, or both. See also: Simon Deschodt, 'De Ieperse buitenpoorterij in de 15de tot begin 16de eeuw: Studie naar de conflictueuze relatie tussen de stad Ieper en haar hinterland' (unpublished Masters-thesis, Ghent University, 2019).

67 RLB, Fonds Merghelynck, M 18.

68 *Wetten, costumen, keuren ende usantien van de Zale ende casselrye van Ipre*, ed. by Laureyns Van den Hane (Ghent: Petrus de Goesin, 1769), Rub. 6, IX-X.

69 Papin, pp. 137-38.

70 Johan Beun, *De costume van de stad Mesen, 1547: originele tekst met overzetting in het modern Nederlands* (Ypres, 2004), VIII, LX, CCXXIX, CCXXXII. All of these bylaws refer to *haghepoorters*. See also: Verbeemen, pp. 197-98. Families like De Brune and Liebaert had ties of kinship to the castellany capital of Bailleul: RLB, Fonds Merghelynck, M 18/15, p. 43.

71 RDHDF-2, III, pp. 130-31.

72 David Nicholas, *Town and Countryside: Social, Economic, and Political Tensions in Fourteenth-Century Flanders* (Bruges: De Tempel, 1971), pp. 222-49.

(*over rike*) behind the names of certain people from Dranouter, Kemmel, and Nieuwkerke in the registers listing the city's new outburghers.[73] Incorporating people like that into the city was a way to stimulate the concentration of capital and enterprise, as well as to raise revenues from consumption taxes. Another potential advantage was the chance to break the supposed rural competition to Ypres' cloth industry. After all, the city magistrate was in a better position to punish rural drapers who acted against the privileges of Ypres' drapery when they (the drapers) were formally subject to the urban judiciary. One might even interpret the city's privileges against rural cloth production (most notably in 1428, 1482, 1502, and 1545) as a sign that the draper-outburghers we find in the sources were not originally from the villages, but were in fact cloth entrepreneurs from Ypres who had branched out to the countryside.[74] This might explain the zeal with which the aldermen and urban council of Ypres kept up their legal battle against rural cloth production even though the city's own industry produced for an entirely different market segment.[75] In that scenario, the damage would not have been to the urban cloth trade itself, but to Ypres' resident cloth manufacturers, who were passed over in favour of the cheaper rural labour force (see Chapter 2). However, if this were the case, then the city government could easily have solved the problem on its own: the aldermen could simply have locked up the perpetrators, fined them, confiscated their goods, and so forth, as was their legal right to do when dealing with citizens.

Of course, this was a lot harder to achieve when the offending party's presence in the city essentially only existed on paper and there was not necessarily any property to be seized. The fact alone that the aldermen of Ypres appealed to the counts and the Council of Flanders to combat rural cloth production, confirms that the rural drapers whom they sought to prosecute were either non-citizens, or they were outburghers without concrete physical ties to the city (who could swiftly revoke their external citizenship when they faced litigation).[76] Curiously, some draper-outburghers of the cloth villages did allow themselves to be prosecuted by the judiciary of Ypres during the 1480s, even though they could technically have laid down their statute to avoid this. They may have been unable to do so at this point in time because Ypres exerted a firmer control over its countryside during the political unrest of the early co-rule of Mary of Burgundy and Maximilian of Austria (1477-92) – when the city's textile guilds temporarily gained in political clout as well.[77] Alternatively, these were drapers that owned

---

73 RLB, Fonds Merghelynck, M 23, e.g. on pp. 5, 27, 111, 127.

74 RDHDF-2, I, pp. 3-7, 78-86; RDHDF-2, III, pp. 122-23.

75 Alfons Thijs, 'Les textiles au marché anversois au XVIe siècle', in *Textiles of the Low Countries in European Economic History: Proceedings of the Tenth International Economic History Congress, Leuven August 1990*, Studies in Social and Economic History, ed. by Erik Aerts and John Munro (Leuven: Leuven University Press, 1990), pp. 76-86 (pp. 82-83); RDHDF-2, III, pp. 139-44.

76 RDHDF-2, I, pp. 3-7, 78-86; RDHDF-2, III, pp. 122-23.

77 RDHDF-2, I, pp. 24-28. On Ypres' political power in this period see: Jelle Haemers, *For the Common Good: State Power and Urban Revolts in the Reign of Mary of Burgundy, (1477-1482)*, Studies in European Urban History (1100-1800), 17 (Turnhout: Brepols, 2009), pp. 250-60.

real estate in the city, and as such they would have suffered too much financial losses if their goods were confiscated by the urban magistrate.

On the whole, the city government of Ypres was not lastingly successful in its attempts to extend power over the countryside via its external citizens, nor is there a clear indication that the rural cloth entrepreneurs of the West-Quarter used the outburgher-statute to the detriment of the urban textile industry or the city's interests in general. In essence, the relationship was mutualistic. From the perspective of the rural draperies, there were potential benefits both to the individual entrepreneur and to the corporation. On the individual level, access to the urban infrastructure gave entrepreneurs a slight edge on their local competitors who lacked this connection. That said, the production figures for 1564-65 only show a slight positive correlation between external citizenship and a higher average cloth output per enterprise, which suggests that the commercial edge on the individual level was negligible.[78] Also, it was not expensive to become and remain outburgher of Ypres. This meant that, in contrast to distant trade connections via remote cities like Bruges and Antwerp, a link to Ypres' commercial infrastructure was relatively easy to establish for all drapers. In fact, outburghership was even attainable for textile artisans such as weavers and fullers.[79] On the collective level, then, the links to Ypres provided the drapery corporation with an advantage because of the aforementioned access to the city's waterways, as well as to storage facilities.

But the outburghers' ties to the urban sphere went beyond simple economic interests. From the addresses they had to provide as proof of periodic residence within the urban limits ('fictitious domiciles'), it appears that about half of the West-Quarter outburghers had family members living in the city.[80] Already in the early fifteenth century, there were apparently daily contacts between the people of Ypres and those of the textile villages.[81] Nieuwkerke also hired musicians from Ypres to sing during the important feast of the Assumption of Mary in the 1540s.[82] This great degree of mobility between the rural and the urban spheres must have fed into the urban aspirations of the village's socio-political elite.

78 On average, the draper-outburghers of 1564-65 produced 31.43 pieces, against the 27.30 pieces of those who could not be connected to outburghership using the same source.

79 For outburghership of Ypres, one had to pay an entrance fee of 2d. par, plus the same amount as an annual contribution: *Costumen van Ipre*, Rub. 6, x. Convictions of outburghers in the 1480s include several weavers and fullers: RDHDF-2, I, pp. 24-28.

80 These fictitious domiciles were not listed in all cases, but they were recorded for 27 of the outburgher registrations of people from West-Quarter cloth villages; 11 of those people registered on the address of somebody with the same last name, and 2 with a *neveu* (which could either refer to a 'grandson' or a 'nephew'; in this context, the latter seems the more likely option): RLB, Fonds Merghelynck, M 23.

81 A fifteenth-century chronicler reported that the craftsmen of Ypres 'heard daily from those of Nieuwkerke and the other aforementioned villages' ('daghelicx hoorden van die van Nieukerke ende anderen van den vorseiden dorpen'): Olivier van Dixmude (?), *Merkwaerdige gebeurtenissen, vooral in Vlaenderen en Brabant, en ook aengrenzende landstreken, van 1377 tot 1443: letterlyk gevolgd naer het oorspronkelyk onuitgegeven en titelloos handschrift van Olivier van Dixmude*, ed. by Jean-Jacques Lambin (Ypres: Lambin, 1835), pp. 119-22.

82 P. J. Vandendorpe, *Het handboek van P. J. Vandendorpe, pastoor van Nieuwkerke (1730-1806)*, ed. by Jozef Geldhof (Bruges: Genootschap voor Geschiedenis, 1974), p. 33.

Urban aspirations

The question is to what extent the urban aspirations of Nieuwkerke's residents manifested themselves in the village's physical development and spatial outlay. Of course, the spatial and architectural make-up of a settlement are chief indicators of its urbanity in any period. In the Middle Ages, the ultimate outward marks of the city were arguably its gates and walls.[83] However, as evidenced by the remarks of Marcus Van Vaernewijck quoted in the introduction to this chapter, by the sixteenth century, Flemish contemporaries upheld a distinction between walled and unwalled towns. This implies that fortifications were not the decisive criterion of a settlement's urban status at that time. Indeed, unfortified towns like Bailleul were still able to serve as capital of a castellany. Also, city limits and jurisdictions usually extended beyond the physical walls, across a zone of influence known as the *banmijl* (or *banlieu* in French), the size of which differed from one case to the next.[84] (Not to mention the fact that the physical and jurisdictional boundaries between town and countryside were regularly crossed by the outburghers.) Nevertheless, the physical development of an expanding industrial centre such as Nieuwkerke provides additional clues about the extent to which its people were, or aspired to be, urbanites. Ever since the 1970s, historians have recognized that the way in which space is organized and negotiated between different power groups within the urban fabric offers crucial insights into the political development of towns and societies in general. This 'Spatial Turn' still has a commanding presence in the current historiography.[85]

Solely judging from what we know of their spatial outlays, the cloth villages of the Flemish West-Quarter hardly qualified as towns between the fourteenth and sixteenth centuries. The earliest cartographic evidence on these places only dates back to Antonius Sanderus's *Flandria Illustrata*, which was published in the first half of the seventeenth century.[86] As a consequence, these images depict the physical appearance of the settlements after the tempestuous period of the Dutch Revolt (1566-1648), during which many buildings in the Flemish West-Quarter were destroyed. One might wonder, therefore, to what extent the

83 Henri Pirenne, *Medieval Cities: Their Origins and the Revival of Trade*, trans. by Frank Halsey (Princeton: Princeton University Press, 1925; repr. 1974), pp. 150-51.

84 In the fourteenth century, it had generally constituted 1 mile in each direction beyond the walls: David Nicholas, 'Town and Countryside: Social and Economic Tensions in Fourteenth-Century Flanders', *Comparative Studies in Society and History*, 10 (1968), 458-85 (pp. 459-60). But in fifteenth-century Bergues-St-Winoc, for example, the *banmijl* was more or less equal to the entire castellany: Émile Coornaert, *L'industrie de la laine à Bergues-Saint-Winoc: une industrie urbaine du XIVᵉ au XVIIᵉ siècle* (Paris: Presses universitaires de France, 1930), p. 34. In Ypres, it apparently constituted 3 leagues (*c.* 18 kilometres) beyond the city walls, (which was one of the reasons why the city felt it could meddle with the rural draperies): RDHDF-2, I, pp. 3-7.

85 The seminal work in this regard is Henri Lefebvre, *La production de l'espace* (Paris: Anthropos, 1974). For a useful handle on Lefebvre's theory and its application for urban historians, see: Peter Arnade, Martha Howell and Walter Simmons, 'Fertile Spaces: The Productivity of Urban Space in Northern Europe', *The Journal of Interdisciplinary History*, 32 (2002), 515-48 (pp. 517-23).

86 Antonius Sanderus, *Flandria illustrata, sive descriptio comitatus istius per totum terrarum orbem celeberrimi, III tomis absoluta*, 2 vols (Amsterdam: Joan and Cornelis Blaeu, 1641-1644).

maps and illustrations by Vedastus du Plouich – a native of the West-Quarter, incidentally – relate to the reality of a century before.[87] The town of Bailleul, for instance, which also suffered greatly during the religious wars of the later 1500s, had apparently changed little between the middle of the sixteenth century and the moment when Du Plouich made an engraving of it around one hundred years later (**Figures 4.1a and 4.1b**).[88] Alternatively, by that time, the town's architectural appearance had been largely restored to its former self of the pre-war period. Of course, this is in itself no evidence that the same had happened in places like Nieuwkerke, so we should be cautious in attributing too much value to the seventeenth-century evidence. But it is hard to square the picture of Nieuwkerke's outlay in the 1640s (**Figure 4.2**) with the village's estimated population level of around 5000 people during the industrial boom of the mid-1500s (see Chapter 1). In fact, the illustration in *Flandria Illustrata* only portrays some 200 houses, which is roughly equal to the 225 houses recorded in 1469; that is, just before the sharp demographic upsurge.[89]

Perhaps this means that in the sixteenth century, Nieuwkerke's cloth workshops and other buildings had sprawled beyond the spatial structure as shown on the seventeenth-century picture. The latter only betrays nucleation around the church and former castle site, with housing primarily ordered along the village's main street. To be sure, that settlement pattern and east-west orientation are still visible on Joseph de Ferraris's map of 1777. But this later source also offers a wider view of the adjoining region and reveals additional clustering around a street that extends southwards from the village square (**Figure 4.3**). Today, this street is called the *Niepkerkestraat*, but in the sixteenth century it was known as the *Lange Horsmolenstraat* (presumably named after a horse-powered mill that was, or had been, a local landmark) and ran from Nieuwkerke to Nieppe by way of the lordship of Inghelant. According to the research of Robert Passchier, who was the parson of Nieuwkerke around the time of the Second World War, the archives of the parish church revealed that this street was crammed with many small houses of weavers during the glory years of the cloth industry (see Chapter 2).[90] I was unable to find the source that Passchier

87 Little is known of this illustrator, but in a letter of 1637, Sanderus reveals that he was a 'mathematician and land surveyor in the castellany of Bailleul, residing in Westouter' (*matematico y geometra en la castellania de Bailloeul, residente a Westoutre*): M. Le Glay, 'Rapport de M. Le Glay sur quelques planches gravées du *Flandria Illustrata*, de Sanderus', in *Bulletin de la Commission Historique du Département du Nord*, 4 (1851), 96-103 (pp. 101-02).

88 Other engravings by Du Plouich support the notion that he composed 'original' and current work and did not simply base himself on his predecessor Jacob van Deventer. This is most evident from his incorporation of military fortifications that were not present in Van Deventer's work, for instance in his map of Armentières: Joan Blaeu, *Novum Ac Magnum Theatrum Urbium Belgicae* (Amsterdam: Joan and Cornelis Blaeu, 1649), p. 74. On Bailleul's tribulations during the war period (including a massive fire): *Documents inedits relatifs à la ville de Bailleul*, ed. by Ignace De Coussemaker, 3 vols (Lille: Quarré du coulombier, 1877-78), I (1877), CLXVI.

89 I count 194 houses and 80 sheds on the picture in *Flandria Illustrata* (see **Figure 4.2**). For the 1469 hearth tax: M. Le Glay, 'Tableaux de la population des châtellenies de Cassel, Bergues et Bailleul, en 1469', *Bulletin du Comité Flamand de France*, 1 (1857), 344-47.

90 Robert Passchier, *Memorieboek Nieuwkerke* (Nieuwkerke, 1943), manuscript

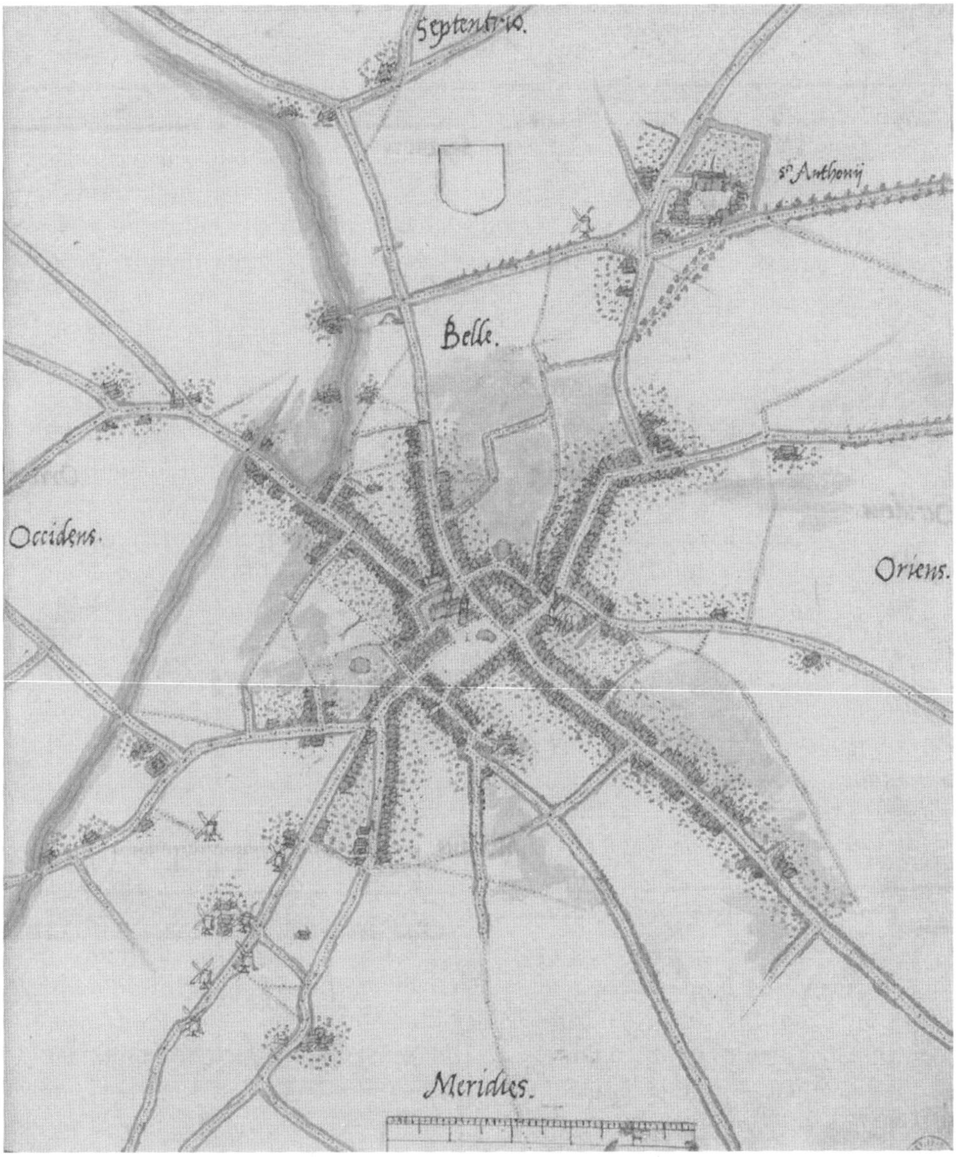

Figure 4.1a. Map of Bailleul, mid-sixteenth century (Jacob van Deventer)

Source: Jacob Van Deventer, *Planos de ciudades de los Países Bajos. Parte II* (manuscript, 1545), p. 54, Biblioteca Nacional d'España, Madrid, online at: bdh.bne.es (Creative Commons License 4.0).

used, but it seems likely that some physical expansion born of the growing textile economy occurred in the 1500s. Admittedly, the seventeenth-century birds-eye view of the village does not support this idea. Yet this discrepancy might well be a consequence of the destructions due to the ravages of war in the interim period. Du Plouich's engraving could also be misleading because it does not extend to the southernmost part of the settlement. Another possibility is that Nieuwkerke's demographic expansion was either absorbed through the

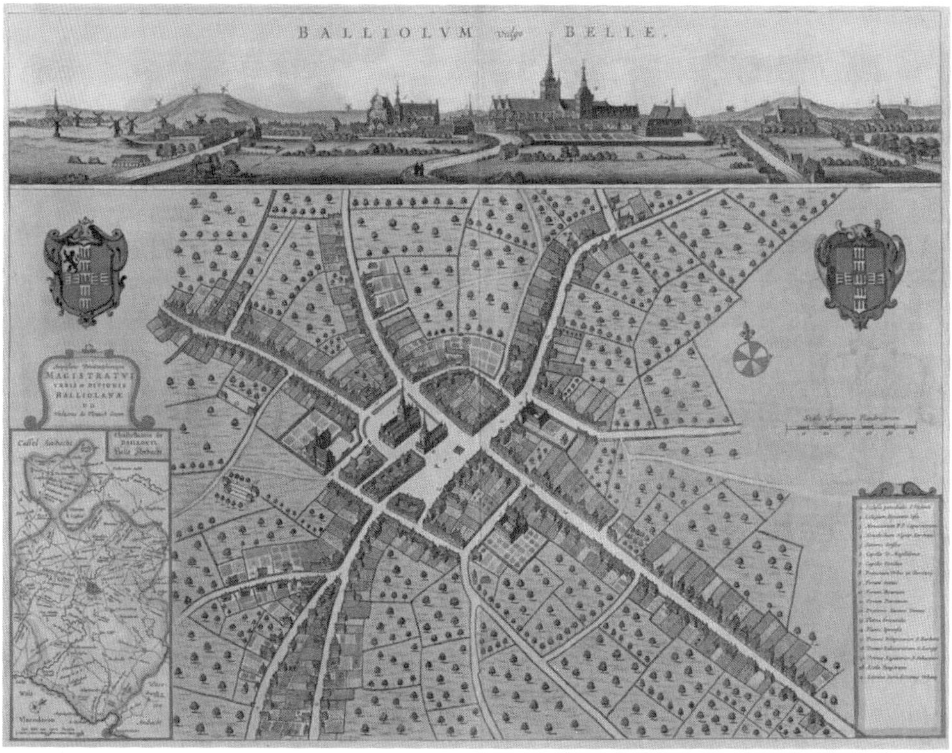

Figure 4.1.b. Birds-eye view of Bailleul, 1641-1644 (detail)

Source: Sanderus, *Flandria illustrata*, I, pp. 554-55, Ghent University Library, BIB.G.005840, online at lib.ugent.be (Creative Commons License 4.0).

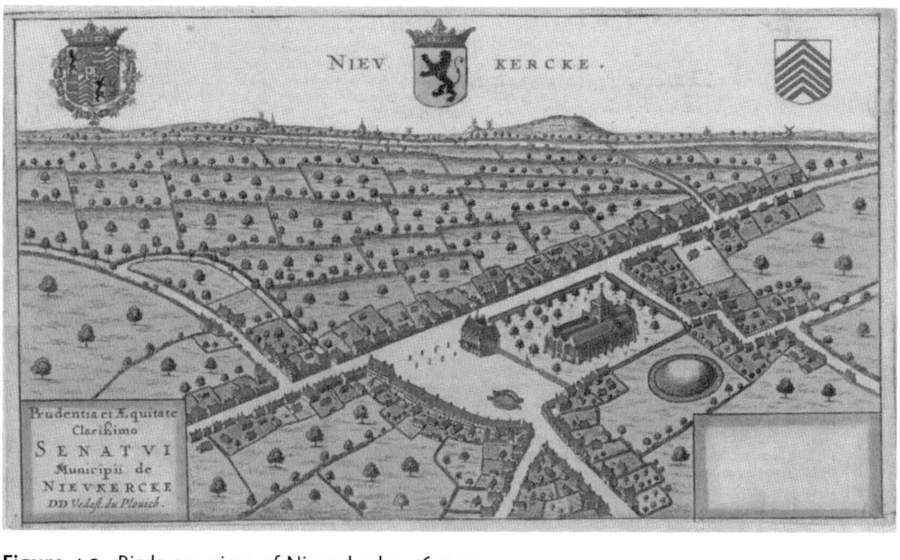

Figure 4.2. Birds-eye view of Nieuwkerke, 1641-44

Source: Antonius Sanderus, *Flandria illustrata*, I, p. 560, Ghent University Library, BIB.G.005840, online at lib.ugent.be (Creative Commons license 4.0).

Figure 4.3. Map of Nieuwkerke, 1777 (detail)

Source: Joseph de Ferraris, *Carte de cabinet des Pays-Bas autrichiens levée à l'initiative du comte de Ferraris*, The Royal Library of Belgium (Brussels), online at: www.kbr.be.

construction of ephemeral architecture or through forms of clustered living; locals hosting workers as temporary lodgers, for instance, or more extreme situations where entire families had to live in single, rented rooms. These are only speculations, of course. But the aforementioned description of Nieuwkerke as a hotbed of social deviance, where things like prostitution and public inebriation ran rampant in the 1530s, would suggest scenarios that are reminiscent of the 'shanty towns' that shape the face of so many urban areas in the Global South in the present day.[91]

However, the absence of a more complex street pattern around the village square still calls into question whether Nieuwkerke's potential physical expansion conformed to a pattern of nucleated settlement, such as we would associate with urban centres in the (late) medieval period. Indeed, small Flemish towns like Hondschoote, or even Bailleul (which was less populous than Nieuwkerke during its heyday), conformed to a star-shaped model that one would sooner define as urban purely in spatial terms (**Figures 4.1a-b,**

91 Mike Davis, *Planet of slums* (Londen & New York: Verso Books, 2005), pp. 45-51.

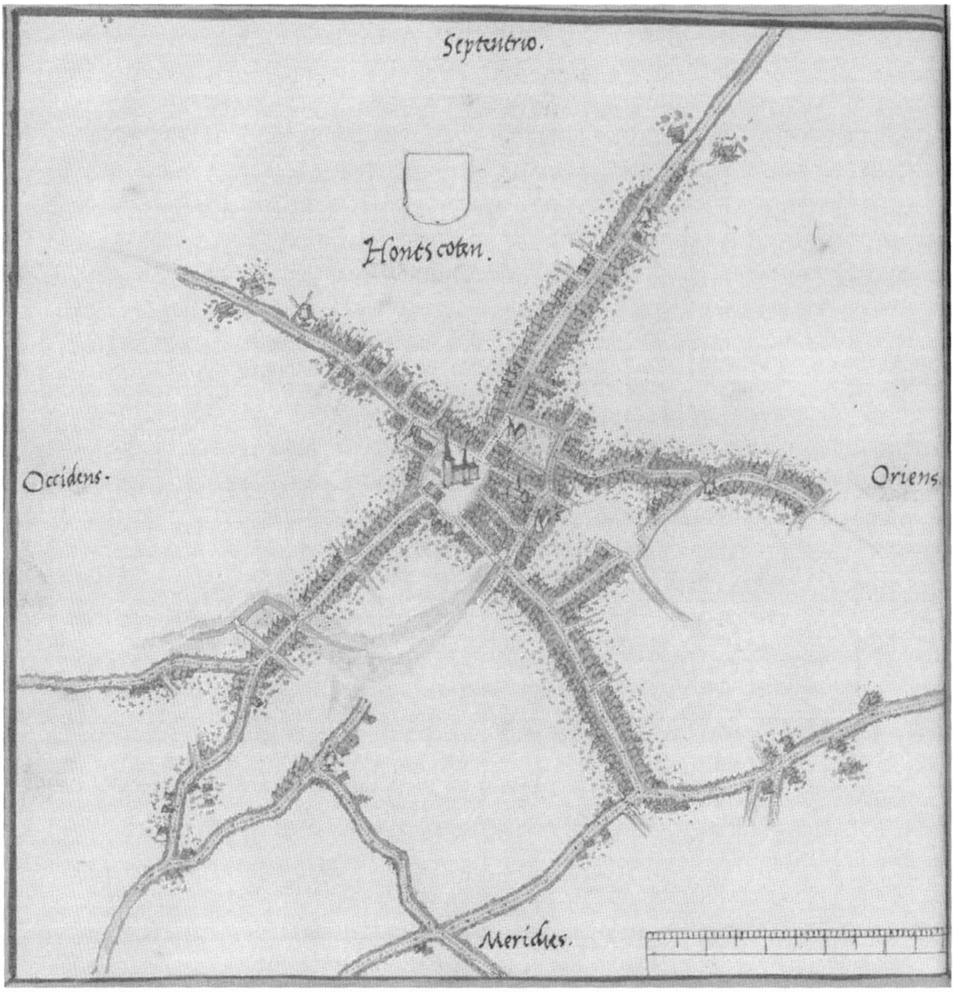

Figure 4.4. Map of Hondschoote, mid-sixteenth century

Source: Jacob Van Deventer, *Planos de ciudades de los Países Bajos. Parte II* (manuscript, 1545), p. 61. Biblioteca Nacional d'España, Madrid, online at: bdh.bne.es (Creative Commons License 4.0).

Figure 4.4).[92] It appears that Nieuwkerke's architecture was not lastingly affected by demographic expansion, if it ever was. The same probably applies to the other cloth villages of the West-Quarter. Du Plouich's seventeenth-century engravings of the villages of Westouter and Flêtre, for example, show only minor clusters of habitation around the moated sites and churches of these places.[93] The ordering of houses along Nieuwkerke's central street gave

92 See also: Henri Pirenne, 'Une crise industrielle au XVIe siècle: la draperie urbaine et la "nouvelle draperie" en Flandre', *Bulletin de l'Académie royale de Belgique, Classe des Lettres*, 5 (1905), 489-521 (p. 509).

93 Sanderus, I, pp. 460, 465.

villagers easy access to public amenities like the market square, the well, and the church, which may have strengthened the ties between villagers. Yet this cannot really be interpreted as a sign of urbanity, since the same applied to many medieval villages.[94]

That said, Nieuwkerke clearly became the subject of a spatial discourse betraying aspirant urban status during the fifteenth and sixteenth centuries. A first, tentative example of this was the village's empty motte, a result of the castle's destruction through the incendiary efforts of French troops in the second half of the fifteenth century. In 1488, Isabel de la Douve, lady of Nieuwkerke, sold all the remaining stones and ironwork to the village churchwardens, probably to construct the eastern part of the parish church.[95] Although the villagers were obviously not responsible for the removal of the local seigneurial residence, they nevertheless experienced the psychological consequences of its absence. Castles were the most visible symbol of the power and authority of lords and princes; a means of communicating their ability to rule over and control their subjects.[96] That this vital node in the spatial power discourse was taken out of the equation in Nieuwkerke must have stimulated a certain feeling of independence among the villagers, especially because the empty motte-and-bailey lingered as a physical reminder of that independence, even well into the seventeenth century (**Figure 4.2**). After 1488, there is also no longer any evidence of a lordly residence whatsoever in the village. The only *maison* of the lord that was left in the village in the sixteenth century was the one used by the wardens to inspect and seal cloth.[97] This is somewhat paradoxical given Ypres' complaints that the drapers from Nieuwkerke operated 'in the shadow of' (*soubz umbre*) their lord's protection from the early sixteenth century onwards.[98] As we shall see in Chapter 5, the drapery corporation thereby enjoyed a double advantage. First, they benefited from the outward protection by their lords; but second, given that those lords were not even physically present in the village and only meagrely represented by local agents, the cloth entrepreneurs were able to operate largely autonomously (see also Chapter 2). And the bricks and other materials that had made up the physical manifestation of seigneurial power in Nieuwkerke were used to improve the most important architectural structure

94 Stephen Mileson, 'Opennes and Closure in the Later Medieval Village', *Past & Present*, 234 (2017), 3-37 (pp. 13-16).

95 The destruction of the castle probably occurred in 1477: Geldhof, p. 31.

96 Oliver Creighton, 'Castles and Castle Building in Town and Country', in *Town and Country*, ed. by Giles and Dyer, pp. 275-92 (pp. 275, 280-83). See also: Marc Boone, 'From Cuckoo's Egg to "Sedem Tyranni": The Princely Citadels in the Cities of the Low Countries, Or: The City's Spatial Integrity Hijacked (15th – Early 16th Centuries)', in *The Power of Space in Late Medieval and Early Modern Europe: The Cities of Italy, Northern France and the Low Countries*, Studies in European Urban History (1100-1800), 30, ed. by Marc Boone and Martha Howell (Turnhout: Brepols, 2013), pp. 77-95 (pp. 77-78, 91-95).

97 SAB, *Aanwinsten*, Nr. 504, fol. 17r.

98 RDHDF-2, I, p. 93.

of communal interest: the church edifice.[99] In 1533, the lord rented out the land that had formerly featured the castle to a group of local inhabitants, including some drapers. The village's Confraternity of Saint Sebastian also held a stake in this land plot. The archery guild used this location for practice rounds: the record specifies that the Confraternity was allowed to keep its targets (*berchaulx*) on this plot, and that members were free to use it day and night for shooting.[100] And so, what had previously hosted a symbol of seigneurial control now featured an important pillar of civic identity.[101]

Still, communal independence and civic identity do not a town make; these elements could simply have strengthened the bonds within a rural, village community.[102] However, another episode in the fifteenth century further demonstrates that at least some inhabitants of Nieuwkerke had urban aspirations for their place of residence. In 1465, the town government of Bailleul, supported by its overlord Charles of Burgundy (the future count of Flanders), litigated against the villagers of Nieuwkerke, who were in turn backed by their overlord, Lady Isabel de la Douve. The point of contention was a weekly market that the people of Nieuwkerke had been trying to install for some time. This market was mainly intended for the sale of agricultural produce such as 'corn, beans, oats, peas, butter and other dairy' but also of 'meat, fish, shoes, silverware, gloves, woodwork [and] ironwork'.[103] The magistrates of Bailleul raised their complaint because the village market purportedly damaged the town's venders. By their account, Bailleul's own, twice-weekly market had become poorly attended ever since Nieuwkerke created its rival commercial platform, luring traders and customers away from town to countryside. This had already resulted in losses estimated at £300 par. in a single year.[104] Thus, while there is an argument to be made that this initiative on the part of the people of Nieuwkerke to institute a weekly market bespeaks their urban ambitions, at first glance, the ensuing conflict mainly appears as economic competition between town and countryside.

99 A. J. A. Bijsterveld, 'De kerk in het midden: de parochiekerk als centrum van de middeleeuwse dorpsgemeenschap', *Noordbrabants Historisch Jaarboek*, 17-18 (2000-2001), 91-119 (pp. 91-92); Eamon Duffy, *The Stripping of the Altars: Traditional Religion in England, 1400-1580* (New Haven & London: Yale University Press, 2005), pp. 123-26, 153-54.

100 SAB, Aanwinsten 504, fols 4^{v}, 5^{v} ('A condicion qu'il et ses hoyrs seront tenu souffrir tant de jour que de nuyct aller et venir les Confreres de la Confrarie de l'Arbalestre audit Neufeglise y jouer et tirer').

101 Crombie, pp. 221-23.

102 Albrecht Claassen, 'Introduction: Rural Space in the Middle Ages and Early Modern times: A Significant Domain Ignored for Too Long by Modern Research?', in *Rural Space in the Middle Ages and Early Modern Age: The Spatial Turn in Premodern studies*, Fundamentals of Medieval and Early Modern Culture, 9, ed. by Albrecht Claassen (Berlin & Boston: De Gruyter, 2012), pp. 1-192 (p. 93). On the role of parish churches in constructing rural communal ties: Monique Bourin and Robert Durand, *Vivre au village au Moyen Age: les solidarités paysannes du XIe au XIIIe siècle* (Paris: Temps actuels, 1984), pp. 57-63.

103 The casefiles mention 'coorne, boonen, evene, haerweten, botere ende andere zuvele': SAG, Raad van Vlaanderen, Enkwesten 8606, quire of 20 November 1565, fol. 2^{v}; and also 'vleesch, visch; scoen, platinen, hanscoen, houtinwerc, yserinwerc': De Coussemaker, I, XCIX.

104 De Coussemaker, I, XCIX.

But there was another side to this conflict; one that we may describe as 'urban rivalry'. Apparently, there were two things that the citizens of Bailleul deemed particularly troublesome. The first was the regional scope of Nieuwkerke's market, which attracted people not just from the village itself but also from 'other lordships and parishes in the vicinity who used to frequent the market of Bailleul'.[105] As such, it may not have been purely a question of lost revenue but also one of lost prestige. The capital of the castellany would not brook trespasses against its commercial pre-eminence, especially from a settlement that lacked an urban charter and depended upon the law court of Bailleul for criminal prosecutions.[106] Second, and more important for the present argument, is that the town government of Bailleul was specifically opposed to the foundation of a market in Nieuwkerke that was *fixed in time and place*. They did not oppose the exchange of products for money per se, which had apparently been ongoing for more than fifty years (albeit on an irregular basis and directly from the homes of the larger farmers).[107] It was the weekly nature that rubbed the plaintiffs the wrong way; but also, and emphatically, the construction of a semi-permanent, physical space that was specifically designated as a marketplace (*plaetse propice*). The town dwellers unceasingly complained that the churchwardens and lady of Nieuwkerke had given the people of the village permission to fill up the church ditches that ran along the village's main street towards Bailleul.[108] This initiative undertaken by the villagers can be seen as a form of collective action intended to allocate space that was more or less 'public' to serve the local community. In terms of a contemporary spatial discourse, however, the villagers' actions also communicated a sense of independence and self-governance; and, as such, their initiative was a renunciation of Bailleul's authority. In a more abstract sense, the allocation of a specific commercial space can also be seen as an expression of urban ideology and power by the people of Nieuwkerke. After all, in the late medieval Low Countries, marketplaces were the 'main carriers for symbols of urbanity', and therefore the *sine qua non* for aspiring towns.[109]

---

105 'Groote menichte van der inghesetenen persoonen van der heerlichede van Nieukerke ende anderen heerlicheden ende prochien daerontrent, die te Belle er maerct van ouden tijden gheust hebben': SAG, Raad van Vlaanderen, Enkwesten 8606, quire of 26 March 1565, fol. 6r.

106 SAG, Raad van Vlaanderen, Enkwesten 8606, quire of 26 March 1565, fols 4v-5r, 6v.

107 SAG, Raad van Vlaanderen, Enkwesten 8606, quire of 20 November 1565, fol. 2v.

108 'Zeker grachten te vullene ende plaetse propice te makene ende den volk te bewijsene bij der kerke van der voors. prochie van Nieukerke, up een mile naer der voors. stede van Belle, ende hebben die wekemaerct ghehouden in elke welke [sic], up den zaterdach'. And also: 'In de voors. prochie van Nieukerke an 't kerchof, daer de zelve verweerers plaetse propice omme wekemaerct te houdene ghemaect, ende de grachten van der kerchove omme de plaetse te makene, ghevult hadden.': SAG, Raad van Vlaanderen, Enkwesten 8606, quire of 26 March 1565, fols 3r, 4r.

109 Peter Stabel, 'Markets and Retail in the Cities of the Late Medieval Low Countries: Economic Networks and Socio-Cultural Display', in *Fiere e mercati nella integrazione delle economie europee, secc. XIII-XVIII*, ed. by Simonetta Cavaciocchi (Florence: Le Monnier, 2001), pp. 797-817 (p. 800). See also: Chloé Deligne, 'Powers over Space, Spaces of Powers: The Constitution of Town Squares in the Cities of the Low Countries (12th-14th Centuries)', in *The Power of Space*, ed. by Boone and Howell, 21-28 (pp. 21-22).

Having said that, these ambitions were at least partly thwarted by Bailleul's lawsuit. The Council of Flanders ultimately ruled in favour of the town, thereby prohibiting the official foundation of a weekly market in the village of Nieuwkerke.[110] Also, and perhaps unsurprisingly given that no rural cloth centre in the West-Quarter ever received a town charter, even during the industrial peak period of the 1540s, none of them apparently boasted a town hall. This can be inferred from the way in which agents of the city of Ypres publicized a privilege they acquired in 1545, which reiterated the restrictions on cloth production in the city's hinterland. The officer charged with proclaiming the contents of this charter recorded how he proceeded in the various places. While he referred to all these places as *villaiges*, he noted that in Warneton, Comines, Bailleul, Wervik, Poperinge, and Mesen he delivered his broadcast from the balcony of the town hall (*la bretesque*). In contrast, he explicitly stated that in Nieuwkerke, Wulvergem, Kemmel, Dranouter, Méteren, Loker and Nieppe, he posted himself before the church entrance during Sunday mass to spread the word (*à l'heure de la grand messe, devant les huys d'église sur l'atre*).[111] Tellingly, this division carries through into the present day, because the settlements in the first group are currently still recognized as towns, whereas those of the second have all remained villages.

Of course, Nieuwkerke had another building that arguably carried urban status on a similar level to that of a town hall. Even in the middle of the seventeenth century, when the textile centre had apparently acquired a town hall, it was still dwarfed by the village cloth hall (**Figure 4.2**). Within the urban landscape of the Low Countries, such commercial and industrial structures continued to dominate public space, even when town halls became ever more important in terms of communicating political power during the fifteenth and sixteenth centuries.[112] In fact, the construction of cloth halls in rural area has been previously interpreted as reflecting 'proto-urban' aspirations.[113] Note that the cloth hall pictured in *Flandria Illustrata* is not the one that concerns us here, because it was only built in 1608. But a nineteenth-century local historian of Nieuwkerke provides some useful information on its sixteenth-century predecessor. He refers to a 'poorly drawn picture' of the village's 'oldest' hall, which burned down in 1582 during the religious wars, and which he estimated to have been built in the early 1500s.[114] This picture has not come down to us, but we do have this

110 De Coussemaker, I, XCIX.

111 RDHDF-2, I, pp. 97-98.

112 Stabel, 'Markets and Retail', pp. 801-02.

113 Kate Giles, 'Public Space in Town and Village', in *Town and Country*, ed. by Giles and Dyer, pp. 293-311 (pp. 301-02).

114 Whether he was correct is not entirely clear. For one thing, I presume Nieuwkerke already had some kind of hall in the fifteenth century, so this may not have been the oldest version. Also, the picture he was referring to sported the year '1598', which the author explained as either an error on the part of the illustrator or a reference to the year in which the picture was drawn. This would make it less reliable. Yet drawings are, in any case, a subjective representation of reality, and it is quite certain that the picture depicts the cloth hall that Nieuwkerke used in the sixteenth century, making it suitable for the present discussion. W. Verhelst, *West-Nieuwkerke. Beschrijving en geschiedenis* (Bruges, 1877), pp. 10-13.

nineteenth-century historian's description. According to his assessment, the cloth hall was 65 feet long, or around 28 metres, with a stone-arched double staircase and four entrances. The central doorway on top of the staircase probably led to the actual cloth hall; a door below it ended in the 'law court' (*wetkaemere*); the one on the right of the stairs was the 'door of the hall keeper' (*de duere van de consirgerie*); and the door on the left was 'to enter the meat hall' (*om in 't vleeshuus te gane*). The staircase also contained a window above which the coat of arms of Nieuwkerke was cut out in stone.[115]

Several elements are of interest here. For starters, the hall must have been an imposing structure, after the destruction of the castle even the second-grandest building in the village (the largest still being the parish church). As it was presumably located on the same location as its seventeenth-century successor – that is, right in the middle of the market square – the cloth hall, along with the church, dominated the 'skyline' of Nieuwkerke. And just like the church, it was a symbol of the local community; not just of the religious community but also of the body politic, as the cloth hall bore the village's coat of arms. Because of this, the interests of local industry were symbolically tied to those of the villagers in general. For the drapers, this was further mirrored in the display of Nieuwkerke's heraldic *kepers* ('chevrons') on the leaden cloth seals affixed to their products. In fact, the better fabrics were themselves colloquially known as *keperkins* or *kepers*.[116] Such daily usage of the coat of arms strengthened the connection between cloth production and community for those involved in the industry, much like coins bearing the coat of arms or the likeness of a ruler reminded people of the authority of the state.[117] But the rest of the parishioners were also reminded of the connection between the cloth trade and the local community every time they saw their heraldic ensign on the hall's facade, which they would have passed on at least a weekly basis to attend mass (always supposing they still did this; see above).

Of course, one might argue that the prominence of Nieuwkerke's coat of arms was first and foremost a reminder of the authority of the lords from whose personal ensign it derived.[118] The custom of new lords from another lineage to incorporate the heraldic sigil of recently acquired possessions into their coats of arms can be interpreted as a way to appropriate this symbol of authority and communal interest.[119] But it is safe to assume that, over time, inhabitants of the

115 Verhelst, pp. 11-12.

116 See, for instance: RDHDF-2, I, pp. 75-77; GSAB, CA 23484, fols 5ʳ, 17ʳ.

117 See also: Michel Pastoureau, *Une histoire symbolique du Moyen Âge occidental* (Paris: Seuil, 2004), pp. 286-91. On coins: Deborah Valenze, *The Social Life of Money in the English Past* (Cambridge: Cambridge University Press, 2006), p. 51.

118 The heraldic device of the De la Douve family, which held the seigneurie in the fifteenth century, contained four 'chevrons' or *kepers*: Jean Théodore De Raadt, *Sceaux et armoriés des Pays-Bas et des pays avoisinants (Belgique-Royaume des Pays-Bas-Luxembourg-Allemagne-France): recueil historique et héraldique*, 4 vols (Brussels: Société belge de librairie, 1898-1901), I (1898), pp. 393-94.

119 Lords even attempted to establish their links to the mythological origins of the settlement they ruled: Jean-Baptiste Delzant, 'Instaurator et fundator: édification de la seigneurie urbaine et présence monumentale de la commune (Italie centrale, fin du Moyen Âge)', in *The Power of Space*, ed. by Boone and Howell, pp. 97-112 (pp. 98-106).

village came to associate personally with this symbol, much like they would have felt a connection with their parish church's patron saint.[120] Coupled with the otherwise physical absence of the castle and the lord, this suggests that if anybody appropriated the chevrons of Nieuwkerke's coat of arms it was the village community itself. Indeed, the emblem of one of Nieuwkerke's Chambers of Rhetoric, *Goetwillich in 't herte*, also featured the heraldic device.[121] Returning to the architectural elements of the cloth hall: in terms of a physical hierarchy, the cloth business was literally placed above the level of the butchers' professional dwellings, and even above that of the law court.[122] In a more tangible sense, the building was simply a dominant feature of public space, even more so because it straddled the boundaries of the local churchyard – the public space *par excellence* in this period. Thus, the cloth hall was also a powerful tool to emphasize the power of the local cloth entrepreneurs: its construction and location symbolized their 'ability to appropriate and reconstruct existing spaces'.[123]

In fact, the urban element of Nieuwkerke as a settlement was inextricably linked to its industrial and commercial elite. Ironically, their efforts to secure industrial autonomy and political independence benefited the community as a whole, even though they may have been primarily motivated by prospects of personal gain.[124] The attempts to establish a weekly market in the village, for example, could have been a strategic ploy on the part of prominent landowners to raise the value of their real estate that surrounded the newly designated market space. The people of Bailleul, for one, thought that a man called Jacob Ente (who had close ties to the cloth industry) had this strategy in mind, because he owned 'many plots of land' around Nieuwkerke's market square.[125] During the trial before the Council of Flanders in 1465, however, the defendants of Nieuwkerke objected that they were solely acting out of concern for the poor artisans of the village. Under the current circumstances, these people paid more than a third extra for their food – which they bought straight from the farm – than they would if they had access to a local market. Moreover, the remote locations of these farms, let alone the long distance to the urban market of Bailleul, supposedly meant that the industrial workers had to neglect their handiwork for hours on end to get their groceries.[126] Evidently, both of these

120 Duffy, pp. 160-63.

121 Dis and Erné, *De Gentse Spelen van 1539*, p. 177.

122 On the use of 'high' and 'low' places to create and reinforce hierarchies: Giles, p. 304. On the screening off of butchers' activities for the general public in multipurpose halls: Deligne, p. 28.

123 Giles, p. 303.

124 Katherine Giles refers to the 'spatial paradox' of guildhalls: they were both a 'symbol of egalitarian principles of fraternity, but also deeply hierarchical': Giles, pp. 304-05.

125 'Ende hebben vele plecken van lande ligghende (ende zonderlinghe vors. Jacop Hente) omtrent der plaetse': SAG, Raad van Vlaanderen, Enkwesten 8606, quire of 20 November 1565, fol. 3v. In 1483, this Jacob Ente held the office of receiver of the village: RDHDF-2, I, p. 37 (the transcription erroneously reads 'Jacop Heute').

126 'Indien dat men 't t'hueren huuse halen moeste, vercoopen d'een derde dierdere ende hoghere dan men 't nu coopt te Nieukerke ter place, bij dat den aermen volke te lastich wezen zoude om zulke cleene provanche te gane te Belle of eldere ontrent Nieukerke, want zij daermede huerlieder

matters were also damaging to the entrepreneurial elite. One might therefore argue that, in the end, it all came back to economic advantages for individual or clan. The same went for the involvement of the lord of Bailleul and the lady of Nieuwkerke, both of whom had financial stakes in the outcome of the trial.[127] That said, the influence of ideological considerations for the prosperity of the general community should not be underestimated either.

The Common Good

In late medieval Christendom, concerns of collective prosperity for the community of a specific town or of an entire principality were contained within the ideology of the 'Common Good'. By the early sixteenth century, princes, lords, and town governments recurrently and easily invoked this concept of the Common Good (*utilitas publica, bonum commune* or *ghemene orbore* in Middle Dutch). Although we should not discount their genuine concerns for equality, from a slightly more sceptical outlook, the concept was also conveniently vague enough to exploit to one's own advantage.[128] In the Netherlandish principalities of Flanders and Brabant, the concept of the Common Good was developed further within urban society in particular. It became an expression of the self-governance of towns, but also a rallying cry for collaboration within the Netherlandish urban network. Then again, the Valois dukes of Burgundy appropriated the concept while they ruled the greater part of the Low Countries in the fifteenth century; they increasingly applied it independently from the cities, primarily as a means to justify such things as new taxes to finance wars.[129]

Accordingly, the inhabitants of the rural cloth centres in the Flemish West-Quarter could have become familiar with the Common Good through either of these channels. Indeed, when the lord of Kemmel accorded a charter to the

---

ambacht ende neeringhe verletten zouden.': SAG, Raad van Vlaanderen, Enkwesten 8606, quire of 20 November 1565, fol. 2v.

127 On lords' benefits of markets in general, see: Terry Slater, 'Plan Characteristics of Small Boroughs and Market Settlements: Evidence from the Midlands', in *Town and Country*, ed. by Giles and Dyer, pp. 23-43 (p. 27). More specifically, market attendance came with increased consumption of commodities such as beer in taverns, which was subject to seigneurial taxes. The issue over tavern visitors was explicitly mentioned in the legal file: SAG, Raad van Vlaanderen, Enkwesten 8606, quire of 20 November 1565, fol. 2v. The entitlement of the lords and ladies of Nieuwkerke to a tax on beer consumption is apparent in 1533: SAB, Aanwinsten 504, fol. 10r.

128 Jan Dumolyn, 'Privileges and Novelties: The Political Discourse of the Flemish Cities and Rural Districts in their Negotiations with the Dukes of Burgundy (1384-1506)', *Urban History*, 35 (2008), 5-23 (pp. 13-17); Minne De Boodt, ''How One Shall Govern a City': The Polyphony of Urban Political Thought in the Fourteenth-Century Duchy of Brabant', *Urban History*, 46 (2019), 1-19 (pp. 2-5).

129 Robert Stein, Anita Boele and Wim Blockmans, 'Whose Community? The Origin and Development of the Concept of *Bonum Commune* in Flanders, Brabant and Holland (12th-15th Century)', in *De Bono Communi: The Discourse and Practice of the Common Good in the European City (13th-16th Century)*, Studies in European Urban History (1100-1800), 22, ed. by Élodie Lecuppre-Desjardin and Anne-Laure van Bruaene (Turnhout: Brepols, 2010), pp. 149-70.

drapery corporation of his village seigneurie in the second half of the fifteenth century, he felt the need to insert that the regulations were intended to serve the interests of 'the Common Good' (*le bien publicque*). In a similar fashion, the 1473 cloth charter of Dranouter specified that comital agents of the Chamber of Accounts were to ensure that the village's industrial regulations did not harm *la chose publicque* of the principality (nor the interests of the counts of Flanders).[130] In contrast, a few decades earlier, Duke Philip the Good had still defied textile production in the West-Quarter's countryside precisely because it 'went against the Common Good of [our land of Flanders]'.[131] The fact that all these rulers justified their decisions in terms of this ideological *topos*, however, reveals its primacy and tenacity in late medieval and early modern thought, even if its interpretation was open to debate.[132]

Often, the connections between the Common Good and a given settlement's main economic activity were explicitly invoked in contemporary rhetoric. In the city of Antwerp, for instance, commerce was frequently hailed as the foundation stone of welfare for all its inhabitants.[133] Likewise, in the cloth villages of the West-Quarter, the links between public prosperity and industrial success were a powerful ideological theme beyond simple self-interest. Associations such as craft guilds and confraternities also played an important role in 'socializing' and moulding good Christian behaviour among their members, among other things by appealing to the concept of the Common Good.[134] As recounted above, Nieuwkerke had several of these organizations, which could instil a sense of shared responsibility for public welfare. To be sure, there were no craft guilds as such, while these were usually vital institutions for safeguarding public interests (or, more accurately, for balancing competing interests within the body politic). The village of Nieuwkerke, and to a lesser extent the other cloth centres of the West-Quarter as well, did have archery guilds and Chambers of Rhetoric. But the more crucial associations in terms of guarding the interests of the community were the mercantile-*cum*-industrial corporations of the 'draperies'. So, when a number of wealthy cloth entrepreneurs of Nieuwkerke enlisted 'strangers' (*estraingiers*) to work in their workshops in 1532, it caused a small uproar within the corporation. By doing so, these rich entrepreneurs were passing over the local workforce, which was 'to the detriment of the greater good of the community and the preservation of the village'.[135] Once again, self-interest probably provided some of the impetus behind the subsequent complaint filed with the Chamber

130 RDHDF-2, III, pp. 611-14; RDHDF-2, II, pp. 253-56.

131 'Contre le bien de la chose publicque [de nostre dict pays de Flandres]': De Coussemaker, I, CXXIII.

132 Linguistically, there were even subtle differences in meaning and application between *pro bono comuni* (for the public good) and *pro bono comunis* (for the good of the commune): Delzant, pp. 97-98.

133 Anne Kint, 'The Community of Commerce: Social Relations in Sixteenth-Century Antwerp' (doctoral dissertation, Columbia University, 1996), p. 399.

134 Gervase Rosser, 'Guilds and Confraternities: Architects of Unnatural Community', in, *De Bono Communi*, ed. by Lecuppre-Desjardin and Van Bruaene, pp. 29-46 (pp. 22-23).

135 'Au grant prejudice d[u] plus grand prouffit de la dite communaulté et pour l'entretenement d'icelluy villaige': RDHDF-2, III, p. 132.

of Accounts. Yet the person who entered this suit was a mid-level draper named Steven Wemare, who claimed that he was acting on behalf of 'the larger part of the village of Nieuwkerke'.[136] Clearly, some cloth entrepreneurs considered their interests bound up with those of the local artisans, and these two parties jointly felt the need and inclination to connect their wellbeing to that of the entire village. And so, if Antwerp was a 'community of commerce', then Nieuwkerke was first and foremost a 'community of industry'.[137] As we shall see in the final chapter of this book, care for the general welfare of this vital branch of the local and regional economy were inextricably bound up with one another – in a positive, but also in a negative sense.

Conclusion

In the year 1545, the urban government of Ypres once again managed to have its regional monopoly on *grande draperie* reinstated through careful lobbying with the Privy Council of the Low Countries. The West-Quarter villages of Dranouter, Kemmel, and Wulvergem were unable to successfully defend their own industrial privileges, but the towns that were also targeted by Ypres could not be detained. Probably because its representatives had entered into a coalition with the small towns of Mesen and Poperinge to secure a favourable verdict, Nieuwkerke was deemed to have belonged to the latter category at this point.[138] And so, it appears the village was finally on the brink of upgrading its status to that of a town. Not coincidentally, this occurred during the most successful period of its cloth industry. With the onset of the Religious Troubles in 1566, however, Nieuwkerke's industrial vitality soon collapsed. One reason for this was that the persistent state of war cut the region off from the northern markets, most notably in Antwerp. Another reason for the decline was a demographic drain due to vast waves of emigration, mainly to the Northern Low Countries and England.[139] Even when things had quietened down at the end of the century, and the cloth centres of the Southern Low Countries had re-oriented towards the city of Lille for their trade in textiles, the West-Quarter villages were never

---

136 'Estienne Wemare, drappier, tant pour luy que pour la plus saine partie du villaige de Neufeglise': RDHDF-2, III, p. 132. In 1564-65, a draper named Steven Wemare still produced 37.5 pieces of cloth: GSAB, CA, Acquits en portefeuilles 1367/34.

137 See also: Jim van der Meulen, 'Get Rich and Try Dyeing: Cloth Production and Social Inequality in Town and Countryside (Sixteenth Century)', in *Inequality and the city in the Low Countries (1200-2020)*, Studies in European Urban History (1100-1800), 50, ed. by Bruno Blondé and others (Turnhout: Brepols, 2020), 45-62 (pp. 54-55).

138 The towns were: Warneton, Wervik, Poperinge, Comines, and Mesen: J. Th. De Smidt and others, *Chronologische lijsten van de geëxtendeerde sententiën (dossiers) berustende in het archief van de Grote Raad van Mechelen*, 6 vols (Brussels: Koninklijke Commissie voor de Uitgave der Oude Wetten en Werordeningen van België, 1966-88), III (1979), p. 743; RDHDF-2, I, pp. 96-97; RDHDF-2, III, p. 285.

139 John Desreumaux, *Leidens weg op* (Roeselare: Familia et Patria, 1992), pp. 295-311; Backhouse, 'De Vlaamse vluchtelingenkerk', pp. 78-79.

restored to their former glory.[140] Thus, this chapter cannot help but conclude by repeating Marcus Van Vaernewijck's claim quoted in the introduction: in the sixteenth century, the West-Quarter villages were *almost* towns, but not quite.

However, there is little doubt that the people working in the cloth industry in this region during the fifteenth and sixteenth centuries were largely indistinguishable from town dwellers. As we have seen, at least 28.9 per cent of the cloth entrepreneurs in Nieuwkerke actually 'infiltrated' urban society by becoming external citizens of Ypres. In essence, they were countryfolk and town dwellers all at once. Quite apart from disproving the strict separation between town and countryside in the late medieval period, this also explains why these rural societies became impregnated with urban ideology and probably (although this is harder to prove) vice versa as well.

Expressions of civic culture through Chambers of Rhetoric, shooting guilds, and institutions of higher education are only one side of this story; quite another are the ambitions of 'urban' independence that were most clearly apparent in fifteenth- and sixteenth-century Nieuwkerke. Led by the socio-political elite of the village, the local community pursued a degree of autonomy from the towns in its vicinity. Among other things, this bout for urban-like enfranchisement manifested itself in attempts to create a periodic market for agricultural produce and manufactured goods (though not cloth, which is interesting). The villagers even tried to specifically designate a space for weekly commerce. In a broader sense, certain key architectural landmarks of the village, most notably the cloth hall, were designed to reflect communal interests and subtly connect them to those of the trade and manufacture of fabrics. Together, these elements undermine the notion of a strict separation between urban and rural spheres in the pre-industrial period. Antagonism between towns and cities like Bailleul and Ypres, and the wider rural region mainly occurred because of a perceived economic competition, in the course of which urban governments pleaded for the preservation of what was in fact becoming an outdated ideological distinction. Ultimately, however, these urban competitors – helped along by external circumstances such as the Religious Troubles of the later-1500s – managed to forestall the urban enfranchisement of the West-Quarter cloth centres.

140 Henri De Sagher, 'Une enquête sur la situation de l'industrie drapière en Flandre à la fin du XVIe siècle', *Études d'histoire dédiées à la memoire de Henri Pirenne par ses anciens élèves*, ed. by Hans Van Werveke (Brussels: Nouvelle société d'éditions, 1937), pp. 471-500 (pp. 490-91).

CHAPTER 5

Collective action and industrial expansion*

Throughout the fourteenth, fifteenth, and sixteenth centuries, the textile centres of the Flemish West-Quarter all knew periodic rises and falls in their productivity. Even the village of Nieuwkerke, which was always the longest pole in the tent, saw lean years during which its annual output slowed down to a mere trickle of a few hundred pieces of cloth. Wherein Nieuwkerke differed from its neighbours, however, was its spectacular industrial growth between 1500 and 1550. During the opening years of the sixteenth century, the village's production output rose to double the volume of its best years in the anterior period. After 1515, it rose to still greater heights (see Chapter 1, **Figure 1.2**). And around the middle of the sixteenth century, Nieuwkerke alone produced as many pieces of cloth as the other West-Quarter centres combined. As has been recounted in the first chapter of this book, in the fifty years leading up to the production boom of the mid-sixteenth century, Nieuwkerke's economic expansion was accompanied by a demographic explosion unrivalled by any of its neighbouring cloth centres. During these same decades, cultural life in the village flourished on the same level as that of a town. The question is what set Nieuwkerke apart from most other villages of this time period. The village's economic and demographic trajectory was not only exceptional within the context of late medieval Europe, but also within the Low Countries, the county of Flanders, even within the West-Quarter – while the latter assuredly produced very similar products and were embedded in the same regional social and political structure.

This final chapter explores the enigma of this peculiar expansion of the West-Quarter's most successful cloth centre, right from its genesis up until its demise after the Iconoclastic Fury of 1566. I will argue that Nieuwkerke's economic trajectory shows signs of a cyclical pattern, with upsurges corresponding to periods of successful collective action and social cohesion within the top ranks of the drapery, while downturns can be connected to discord and polarization within the village's cloth corporation. More specifically, there was a correlation between the village's glory period between 1500 and 1550, and the collective approach adopted by its cloth entrepreneurs, who managed to unite their peers towards a common goal; in their own words: 'together, without exception, and one for all'.[1]

---

* An alternative version of this chapter has been previously published as: Jim van der Meulen, 'Corporate Collective Action and the Market Cycle in Nieuwkerke, Flanders, 1300-1600', *Social History*, 43 (2018), pp. 375-99.

1 'Gesamende [...] overgesonders ende elckeen voir al'; literally: 'held together, without exceptions, and each for everybody else'. CABZ, Protocol van rentebrieven en recognities, 1511-1512, fol. 65^{v}.

This entrenches the current chapter in two different, although related, debates in social and economic history. First, it has an affiliation with the recent work of Bas van Bavel, specifically his book *The Invisible Hand: How Market Economies Have Emerged and Declined Since AD 500* (2016). Van Bavel posits that market economies follow a fixed cycle of rise and fall, which is ingrained in their very being. Put simply, the cycle is characterized by initial economic growth due to the commodification of land, labour and capital. But this commercialization chiefly benefits a small 'market elite', which subsequently seeks to freeze the system responsible for its exalted position, which leads to increasing social polarization and 'institutional sclerosis', and thence to economic stagnation and decline.[2] As we shall see, something similar took place in the late medieval West-Quarter, although I will question the unilinear nature of these developments. The second debate that is aligned to the present analysis, attributes a beneficial role to social cohesion (the inverse of Van Bavel's polarization) as a stimulating force on socio-political change, specifically through processes of 'collective action'. Ever since the seminal historical work devoted to this subject by Charles and Louise Tilly in 1981, collective action has been primarily treated in direct relation to class struggle.[3] Studies about the late medieval Low Countries and beyond also mainly connect collective action to popular protest, most often in urban society.[4] More recently, however, Tine De Moor has created a *Collective Action Network* at Utrecht University in the Netherlands in order to address the long-term effects of organized forms of collective action on societal development. According to De Moor, units of collective action, such as guilds, were paramount in the formation of an 'institutional infrastructure for socio-political change'; or even part of a 'silent revolution' that laid the groundwork for the leading economic position of Western Europe up until the present day.[5] This chapter will show that the case of the rural cloth industry of Nieuwkerke partly supports this idea. Upon closer inspection, however, the village's socio-economic development belies the wider pattern identified by De Moor.

The upcoming analysis will therefore integrate Van Bavel's focus on cyclical socio-economic development with De Moor's focus on the positive influence of organized collective action; the common core is the relationship between social

2 Bas van Bavel, *The Invisible Hand? How Market Economies Have Emerged and Declined since AD 500* (Oxford: Oxford University Press, 2016), pp. 2, 19-20.

3 See the contributions in: *Class Conflict and Collective Action*, ed. by Louise Tilly and Charles Tilly (Beverly Hills & London: Sage, 1981).

4 Jelle Haemers, 'Révolte et requête: les gens de métiers et les conflits sociaux dans les villes de Flandre (XIIIe-XVe siècle)', *Revue historique*, 677 (2016), 27-56; Samuel Cohn Jr., *Lust for Liberty: The Politics of Social Revolt in Medieval Europe, 1200-1425, Italy, France and Flanders* (Cambridge MA: Harvard University Press, 2006), p. 8; Jan Dumolyn, 'Guild Politics and Political Guilds in Fourteenth-Century Flanders', in *The Voices of the People in Late Medieval Europe: Communication and Popular Politics*, ed. by Jan Dumolyn and others (Turnhout: Brepols, 2014), pp. 15-48; Jan Dumolyn, 'Les "plaintes" des villes flamandes à la fin du XIIIe siècle et les discours et pratiques politiques de la commune', *Le Moyen Âge*, 121 (2015), pp. 383-407.

5 See: http://www.collective-action.info/; Tine De Moor, 'The Silent Revolution: A New Perspective on the Emergence of Commons, Guilds, and Other Forms of Corporate Collective Action in Western Europe', *International Review of Social History*, 53, Supplement 16: The Return of the Guilds (2008), 179-212 (pp. 179-80).

cohesion and economic expansion. Nieuwkerke is the primary case study, partly because it is the best documented cloth centre of the West-Quarter, but also because its pre-industrial economic trajectory fits the patterns laid out by De Moor and Van Bavel surprisingly well. To that end, the chapter is divided into three sections, which correspond to different phases in the development of Nieuwkerke's cloth industry, both in terms of collective action and economic success. As will become clear, the 'golden age' of Nieuwkerke's industrial economy (*c.* 1500 – *c.* 1550) was marked by industrial expansion, which coincided with what we might call a collective spirit among the village's cloth entrepreneurs. I will contend that at the heart of this take-off lay the combined effort of the village's cloth entrepreneurs. First, by organizing themselves as a collective, they were able to protect their industry against exogenous, extra-economic incursions, mainly from their urban rival: the city of Ypres. In order to achieve this security, the entrepreneurs manipulated the legal-political framework that was characteristic of their region, and that we have become familiar with in the previous chapters. Second, around the year 1500, the drapers of Nieuwkerke also adopted a collective approach towards marketing their finished product. Most importantly, they created a shared commercial platform to sell their fabrics in the market cities of the Low Countries, which improved the general efficiency of their trade. Put together, these collective, bottom-up initiatives helped Nieuwkerke's cloth corporation achieve a level of economic expansion beyond the level of any other village in the Flemish West-Quarter. Tellingly, when the industry began to decline from around 1550 onwards, it coincided with a breaking down of the collective spirit among the village's traders and entrepreneurs. Conflicts within the industry tore apart the joint initiative, while at the same time the region witnessed increasing social and religious tensions that culminated in the destructive Iconoclastic Fury of 1566. The subsequent period of Religious Troubles would be the kiss of death for Nieuwkerke's already enfeebled textile economy.

Some issues need to be addressed right from the start, the first being the definition of 'collective action'. Social and political historians have often used this term simply as a synonym for sudden outbursts of organized political protest.[6] De Moor's analytical framework, however, removes these elements of abruptness and protest; as such, she implicitly endorses a definition that is closer to the broad one formulated by Charles Tilly in 1981. According to that definition, collective action refers to 'all occasions on which sets of people commit pooled resources, including their own efforts, to common ends'.[7] It is in this way that the term will be used here as well. The question *why* collective action came about *when* it did in this specific context will be briefly assessed as well. Yet, lacking a comparative framework, I want to chiefly examine and problematize the inner workings of collective action in connection with questions of social cohesion and (in)equality, rather than offer general conclusions about so broad

6 Bert Klandermans, 'Collective Action', in *International Encyclopedia of the Social and Behavioral Sciences*, ed. by James Wright (Oxford: Oxford University Press, 2015), pp. 145-50.

7 Charles Tilly, 'Introduction', in *Class Conflict and Collective Action*, ed. by Tilly and Tilly, pp. 13-25 (p. 17).

a phenomenon.[8] On a final note, let me reiterate that where this chapter refers to 'drapers' or cloth entrepreneurs, these groups should not be confused with weavers or craftsmen, but neither should they be automatically equated with merchants. Certainly, many drapers engaged in weaving, and most had a craft background, but 'draping' in its most basic definition simply meant ownership of the raw materials and the cloth while it was being processed (see Chapter 2). Drapers stood at the intersection between industrial and mercantile activities, and it was this two-sided capacity that gave them the interesting position that we continue to explore in this final chapter.

Phase one: strained beginnings (1358-*c.* 1500)

To begin with, it is worth to consider that the rise of large-scale production of mid-priced woollens in the Flemish West-Quarter – the start of the 'cycle' – emerged from the smouldering ashes of another cloth centre: the city of Ypres. Indeed, textile production was an important pillar of the West-Quarter's wider regional economy well before the ascension of the rural industries central to this study. From the eleventh to the late thirteenth century, the pronounced urbanization of the county of Flanders had been accompanied by distinct economic specialization in the largest cities of Ghent, Bruges, Lille, Douai, Arras, and Ypres. The latter city rose to a veritable industrial metropolis through the mass-scale production of textiles, especially woollen cloth. Towards the end of the thirteenth century, Ypres' woollen industry faced commercial problems, however. The city's entrepreneurs and manufacturers were confronted with a reduced supply of English fleeces, which were an essential component of their product. From around the same time, they faced increasing competition from other regions. And to make matters worse, one of their main commercial platforms – the Champagne fairs – also went into decline in this period.[9] These commercial problems manifested themselves in several decades of political turmoil on the home front, starting with the so-called 'Cokerulle revolt' of 1280-85. The Cokerulle was an uprising against the power of the city's aldermen, merchant elites, and wealthy cloth entrepreneurs; the aggrieved parties being the poorer

---

8 Luis Fernando Medina, *A Unified Theory of Collective Action and Social Change* (Michigan: University of Michigan Press, 2007), pp. 7-19. See also: Tine De Moor, 'Three Waves of Cooperation: A Millennium of Institutions for Collective Action in Historical Perspective (Case-Study: The Netherlands)', in *Oxford Handbook on International Economic Governance*, ed. by Eric Brousseau and Jean-Michel Glachant (Oxford: Oxford University Press, 2021; forthcoming). I am grateful to Tine De Moor for providing me with a digital copy of this chapter.

9 Gustave Doudelez, 'La revolution communale de 1280 a Ypres', in *Prisma van de geschiedenis van Ieper: een bundel historische opstellen*, ed. by Octaaf Mus and Jan Van Houtte (Ypres: Stadsbestuur, 1974), pp. 188-294 (pp. 201-03); Jan Van Houtte, 'Ieper door de eeuwen heen', in *Prisma van de geschiedenis van Ieper*, ed. by Mus and Van Houtte, pp. x-xxi (pp. xiii-xiv); John Munro, 'The "New Institutional Economics" and the Changing Fortunes of Fairs in Medieval and Early Modern Europe: The Textile Trades, Warfare, and Transaction Costs', *Vierteljahrschrift für Sozial- und Wirtschaftsgeschichte*, 138 (2001), 1-47 (pp. 14-20).

cloth entrepreneurs and craftsmen. But the conflict also involved artisans from outside the city, as the drapers of Ypres had tapped into the labour supply of the city's suburbs (*faubourgs*) and the neighbouring countryside.[10] Dissatisfied cloth entrepreneurs from Ypres' hinterland joined in the protests as well. Much like the poorer and less privileged entrepreneurs from the city itself, these drapers were completely dependent upon the merchants and wealthier urban drapers for access to the city's market.[11]

The Cokerulle uprising had important ramifications for Ypres' political economy. For one thing, after 1289, the drapers acquired the legal right to purchase their own wool directly on the city's market and sell their fabrics in the cloth hall; and so, they were partly able to assimilate with the city's merchants.[12] For another, the count of Flanders granted the weavers, fullers, and shearers the right to elect their own people as industrial overseers, while it had previously been city officials that were charged with this task.[13] This meant that the manufacturers got a say in the contents of their industrial regulations. They also received permission to organize professional gatherings; that is, after an initial ban on any assembly larger than ten people, which had been temporarily instated to prevent another Cokerulle.[14] This process led to the formation of artisanal corporations, the craft guilds. Following on from the Battle of the Golden Spurs (1302), these craft guilds gained access to the city's bench of aldermen. At this point, we can see the beginnings of a progressive rift between artisans and cloth entrepreneurs, because the drapers joined the merchants in opposing this political emancipation of the craft guilds – to no avail, however.[15] But in practice, real power continued to reside with a network of elite families which effectively formed an oligarchy. And so, the 'democratic thrust' of the early fourteenth century did enable the craftsmen of Ypres to secure that their wages stayed at a fixed level (and above that of some competing centres).[16] Yet, in a bout of bitter irony, the relatively high cost of these artisans' wages led the cloth entrepreneurs to reorient towards the market for expensive, luxury woollens. In doing so, they ensured that they could still compete on the international cloth market through the high skill-level of the

10 Filip Hooghe, 'De Cokerulle (1280-1285): een conflict tussen Ieper en zijn hinterland over de lakennijverheid', *Handelingen van het Genootschap voor Geschiedenis*, 143 (2006), 293-448; Marc Boone, 'Social Conflicts in the Cloth Industry of Ypres (Late 13th-Early 14th Centuries): The Cockerulle Reconsidered', in *Ypres and the Medieval Cloth Industry in Flanders: Archaeological and Historical Contributions*, ed. by Marc De Wilde, Anton Ervynck, and Alexis Wielemans (Zellik: Instituut voor het archeologisch patrimonium, 1998), pp. 147-55.

11 Doudelez, p. 224.

12 Jules Demey, 'De Vlaamse ondernemer in de middeleeuwse nijverheid: de Ieperse drapiers en "upsetters" op het einde der XIIIe en in de XIVe eeuw', *BMGN – Low Countries Historical Review*, 4 (1949), 1-15, reprinted in *Prisma van de geschiedenis van Ieper*, ed. by Mus and Van Houtte, pp. 143-56 (p. 146).

13 Haemers, 'Révolte et requête', pp. 42-44.

14 Carlos Wyffels, *De oorsprong der ambachten in Vlaanderen en Brabant* (Brussels: Koninklijke Vlaamse academie voor wetenschappen letteren en schone kunsten van België, 1951) pp. 85-87, 92-97.

15 Van Houtte, 'Ieper door de eeuwen heen', pp. xiii-xiv.

16 Doudelez, p. 195; Peter Stabel, 'Guilds in Late Medieval Flanders: Myths and Realities of Guild Life in an Export-Oriented Environment', *Journal of Medieval History*, 30 (2004), 187-212 (pp. 189-91).

city's manufacturers. But this shift from quantity towards quality lowered the demand for labour, and put a lot of artisans out of a job.[17] This was the turning point for Ypres' economy, which had peaked in the late thirteenth century and would never fully recover afterwards, as evidenced by the city's decline in cloth output and its decimated population.[18]

With the exception of luxury woollens, then, the late thirteenth and early fourteenth centuries marked what we might call the 'end cycle' to the greater part of Ypres' textile sector. However, one element is at odds with Bas van Bavel's thesis: in this case, the move towards a more egalitarian socio-political structure was actually one of the key factors underlying economic stagnation. Through their collective action, the craft workers were able to push for more inclusive political institutions, enabling them to press for the preservation of relatively high wages. But in the end, this only contributed to toppling their own economic bargaining power. In other words, more inclusive political institutions paradoxically led to greater economic inequality in this case.[19] Furthermore, it is very much the question whether the Cokerulle and subsequent uprisings were sparked by actual *increasing* inequality, as Van Bavel's theory would suggest. The all-round worsening of Ypres' position on the international cloth market might have been unequally distributed across the various layers of society, but it is more likely that the crucial element was an absolute reduction of prosperity in the city in general. Of course, a drop in income brought the craftsmen and poorer entrepreneurs a lot closer to the bottom than the richer town dwellers, thereby raising their *perception* of unequal opportunities. This is in accordance with a recent study, which found no clear correlation between rising sentiments of unequal opportunity – potentially leading to revolt – and objectively measurable increases in societal inequality.[20] There is even evidence to suggest that economic decline diminishes a society's potential for inequality, as the surplus that can be extracted by elites becomes smaller under these circumstances.[21] In a similar vein, the Brabantine city of 's-Hertogenbosch, for example, witnessed increasing socio-political polarization and revolt in the first quarter of the sixteenth century, even as the actual distribution of wealth became more egalitarian in this period. In that instance as well, it was the economic 'pie' in general that shrank, bringing the less well-to-do closer to,

17 Pieter Boussemaere, 'De Ieperse lakenproductie opnieuw berekend aan de hand van de lakenloodjes', *Jaarboek voor Middeleeuwse Geschiedenis*, 3 (2000), 131-61 (pp. 154-57).

18 The city's textile economy had slightly recovered by the eighteenth century through product diversification: Johan Dambruyne, 'De hiërarchie van de Vlaamse textielcentra (1500-1750): continuïteit of discontinuïteit?', in: *Qui valet ingenio: liber amicorum aangeboden aan dr. Johan Decavele*, ed. by Leen Charles and others (Ghent: Stichting Mens en kultuur, 1996), pp. 155-72 (p. 166).

19 Daron Acemoglu and James Robinson, *Why Nations Fail: The Origins of Power, Prosperity, and Poverty* (London: Profile Books, 2012), pp. 364-67.

20 Paolo Brunori, 'The Perception of Inequality of Opportunity in Europe', *Review of Income and Wealth*, 63 (2016), 1-28 (pp. 25-26).

21 Branko Milanovic, Peter Lindert and Jeffrey Williamson, 'Pre-Industrial Inequality', *The Economic Journal*, 121 (2011), 255-72 (pp. 267-68).

or across, the brink of poverty.[22] Therefore, the key endogenous variable appears to be heightened social polarization as a consequence of perceived inequality, which is tied to the exogenous element of worsening market conditions.

We might call these developments in Ypres the 'prehistory' of the cloth industry in the rural West-Quarter, because they indirectly led to the shift of large-scale production of cheaper and medium-priced fabrics from city to the countryside. In the first instance, export-oriented cloth production in the countryside was a consequence of outsourcing by urban entrepreneurs, which is proven by the participation of craft workers and entrepreneurs from places like Kemmel and Westouter in the Cokerulle uprising of the 1280s.[23] This gradually evolved into a medieval equivalent of present-day 'offshoring', wherein the manufacturing stages were increasingly outsourced to workers in the countryside. The period between the late thirteenth and late fourteenth century was crucial in this transition, because the conflicts in Ypres came with periodic bursts of emigration by urban artisans. This urban outflow boosted both the numbers and the technical abilities of the rural labour force.[24] And so, as the greater part of Ypres' textile economy came to the end of its cycle, the rural West-Quarter essentially arose as its worthy successor.

A pivotal moment in this process of relocation occurred in the year 1358, when Nieuwkerke first acquired the cloth franchise that gave its villagers a formal licence to produce woollen fabrics for the export market.[25] In a way, this fits into a more general pattern during this period, when the counts of Flanders expanded the privileges of many small towns and villages as a buffer against the growing power of the Flemish cities.[26] However, Nieuwkerke resided under the authority of Louis of Namur, a member of a cadet-branch of the Flemish comital family that ruled independently over the lordship of Bailleul between 1305 and 1421.[27] Louis of Namur may have copied the strategy of his cousin, the count of Flanders, in this regard. But in his case, the expanded privilege of Nieuwkerke was more of a means to insulate rural manufacturers against incursions from outside Louis of Namur's territory. Indeed, the phrasing of the document indicates that the people of Nieuwkerke had probably requested this legal document from their

---

22 Bruno Blondé, *De sociale structuren en economische dynamiek van 's-Hertogenbosch, 1500-1550* (Tilburg: Stichting Zuidelijk historisch contact, 1987), pp. 76-80, 135-40.

23 Jules Demey, 'De Ieperse lakennijverheid: haar ontstaan, ontwikkeling en verval' (unpublished doctoral thesis, University of Leuven, 1947-48), p. 98.

24 Jules Demey, 'Proeve tot raming van de bevolking en de weefgetouwen te Ieper van de XIIe tot de XVIIe eeuw', *Revue belge de philologie et d'histoire*, 28 (1950), 1031-48 (pp. 1036-37); Van Houtte, 'Ieper door de eeuwen heen', pp. xiv-xv.

25 RDHDF-1, III, pp. 58-61.

26 Henri Pirenne, *Histoire de Belgique*, 7 vols (Brussels: H. Lamertin, 1900-1932), II (1903), pp. 182-83, 389-90.

27 Jan Dumolyn and Kristof Papin, 'La révolte paysanne à Cassel (1427-1431): lutte d'une communauté rurale contre la centralisation Bourguignonne', in Haro sur le seigneur! *Les luttes anti-seigneuriales dans l'Europe médiévale et modern: Actes des XXIXes journées internationales d'histoire de l'abbaye de Flaren, 5 et 6 octobre 2007*, ed. by Ghislain Brunel and Serge Brunet (Toulouse: Presses universitaires du Midi, 2009), pp. 79-92 (p. 81); *Documents inedits relatifs à la ville de Bailleul*, ed. by Ignace De Coussemaker, 3 vols (Lille: Quarré du coulombier, 1877-78), I (1877), xc.

overlord to protect themselves against harassment from their rivals from the city of Ypres. And understandably so, since as recently as 1352, the 'bastard of Flanders' had led 55 citizens of Ypres on an armed expedition to the village to stop the manufacture of cloth in the countryside.[28] Apparently, the lord of the village, Bernard Van Nieuwkerke, was incapable of fending off Ypres' punitive expeditions without the official support of his overlord Louis of Namur.

The decline of Ypres' drapery probably provided the impetus behind the expanding draperies, first in nearby smaller towns and thereafter in the villages. The city's industry had already been shrinking in the late thirteenth century, which allowed competition from small towns like Poperinge, Langemark and Wervik.[29] But the real watershed came with the war of 1380-83, when Ypres picked the side of the count of Flanders during an uprising of Ghent, resulting in the destruction of Ypres' suburbs (*buitenparochies*). Curiously, after the war, the count and the aldermen of the city signed an official agreement that these suburbs were never to be rebuilt. In the aftermath, Ypres may have lost as much as half of its population (or 10,000 people).[30] This caused a sudden outflow of human capital over the surrounding region that can be inferred from the 200 per cent increase in the cloth output of Langemark and Wervik in the years following 1383.[31] The villages of the West-Quarter were apparently slower to attract this surplus of labour and technical expertise from Ypres. The only known figure for the lease price of Nieuwkerke's cloth seal in this period dates from the year 1384-85, when a certain Pieter Willaert and Jan Martin paid £13 par. for the right to collect the duty of 12d. par. per cloth. This means that they estimated the village hand workers to process at least 260 pieces that year. While we cannot equate this to earlier figures, it hardly hints at a large influx of capital or labour. Likewise, the court of Bailleul leased out the seal duty of the village of Eécke for £6 par. in that same year, which implies an expected minimum of 240 pieces of cloth, as Eécke's duty was only 6d. par. for each piece.[32] And so, it was probably the small towns that were the chief beneficiaries of the early wave of emigration from the city of Ypres. By the early fifteenth century, though, these smaller urban industries began to face problems of their own. The production levels of Langemark, for example, had significantly dropped by the 1420s and the town's cloth trade all but disappeared around the middle of the century.[33] It was in this same period that the villages of the region asserted themselves

28 Probably Robert, burgrave of Ypres, who was a bastard son of Count Louis of Male: Jean-Joseph Carlier, 'Robert de Cassel, seigneur de Dunkerque, Cassel, Nieppe, Warneton, Gravelines, Bourbourg', *Annales du Comité Flamand de France*, 10 (1870), 17-248 (p. 165); Jean-Jacques Lambin, *Revue succincte de quelques comptes de la ville d'Ypres des 13ᵉ, 14ᵉ et 15ᵉ siècles* (Ypres, 1st half of the 19th century), p. 189.

29 RDHDF-2, II, pp. 626-34.

30 Pieter Boussemaere, 'De Ieperse poorterijregisters tussen 1250 en 1468: reconstructie, analyse en bespreking', *Westhoek. Tijdschrift voor geschiedenis en familiekunde in de Vlaamse en de Franse Westhoek*, 15 (1999), 147-61 (pp. 152-53).

31 Boussemare, 'De Ieperse poorterijregisters', pp. 153-54.

32 ADN, B 1333 (formerly B 18586).

33 During the 1385 production peak, the minimum output had been 2000 pieces, which dropped to 860 in 1422 and to 30 in 1449: De Sagher, *Recueil*, II, 631-33.

as heir apparent to the former market position of Ypres, especially as regards mid-priced woollens. This is perhaps most evident from Ypres' renewed attempts to dismantle rural cloth production in its hinterland.

In fact, the city of Ypres was one of the inhibitors of industrial development in the burgeoning cloth centres of the West-Quarter. Clearly, there was a strong political faction in Ypres which looked after artisanal interests. And this faction could not abide competition from industrial villages in the city's hinterland.[34] It was presumably through their lobbying that the city of Ypres acquired a charter from Duke Philip 'the Good' of Burgundy, count of Flanders, in 1428. The charter forbade any rural cloth centres from producing woollens for anything but local consumption. This ban dated back to a privilege that had been granted by Count Louis of Nevers in the early fourteenth century, which protected the Flemish cities from competition within a certain radius of their walls (with the exception of towns with a cloth charter).[35] By establishing a similar charter, Philip the Good gave Ypres the ammunition to ban export-oriented cloth manufacture in its rural hinterland through punitive measures. Indeed, prosecutions of several rural drapers followed, and in June 1429, the Duke ordered his officers to arrest drapers from Nieuwkerke while they were on their way to a fair in the Flemish town of Torhout, despite their right of safeguard.[36]

So began a long-winded legal battle during which the West-Quarter villages, Nieuwkerke chief amongst them, tried to have this prohibitive charter nullified. Right from the start, they were supported in their attempts by Lady Jeanne de Harcourt, who was dowager-countess of Namur and in that capacity also lady of Bailleul. Through her help, emissaries of Nieuwkerke were sent to the Parlement of Paris, where they sought to bypass the decision of the count of Flanders through an appeal. This was a way of circumnavigating comital authority which the Flemish cities often used during this period.[37] And the Parlement did in fact lift the ban on rural cloth production; it even fined the city of Ypres for its unlawful confiscations and prosecutions. However, Philip the Good simply overturned the Parlement's decision: in 1431, he reaffirmed his previous ruling and obstructed Nieuwkerke's industry once again.[38] This put the village's champion, Jeanne de Harcourt, in a difficult position, because Philip had bought the county of Namur in 1421 and was technically her feudal overlord.[39] Fortunately for Nieuwkerke, Philip the Good largely stopped interfering in

34 RDHDF-2, I, pp. 24-69.

35 David Nicholas, 'Town and Countryside: Social and Economic Tensions in Fourteenth-Century Flanders', *Comparative Studies in Society and History*, 10 (1968), 458-85 (p. 465).

36 RDHDF-2, I, pp. 7-14; Isidore Diegerick, *Inventaire analytique et chronologique des chartes et documents appartenant aux archives de la ville d'Ypres*, 6 vols (Bruges, 1853-1868), DCCCLXIV.

37 Serge Dauchy, 'Introduction historique', in *Les arrets et jugés du Parlement de Paris sur appels flamands conservés dans les registres du Parlement*, ed. by Serge Dauchy and others, 3 vols (Brussels: Ministère de la justice, 1966-2002), I (1966), pp. 96-105.

38 Diegerick, DCCCLXXV.

39 Frederik Buylaert, *Repertorium van de Vlaamse adel (ca. 1350-ca. 1500)* (Ghent: Academia Press, 2011), p. 737.

matters pertaining to the Kingdom of France after 1435. And so, in 1441, the procurator of the reinstated king of France ensured that the issue was brought before the Parlement of Paris yet another time. Finally, in 1449, the Parlement determined that the village industries were to be respected. The only stipulation was that they refrained from using English wool, and did not produce the same styles of fabrics as their colleagues in Ypres.[40] Thereafter followed a few decades when the rural centres were apparently left alone by their urban rival, and Philip the Good's son and successor Charles the Bold did not reinstate Ypres' privilege during his reign (1467-77) either.

But the 1480s and 1490s were again marked by crisis, as a consequence of the renewed political power of Ypres, and the continuous state of war in the West-Quarter. First, the region was invaded by the king of France; later it became the stage of civil war within Flanders, when the Flemish cities rose up against Archduke Maximilian while he co-ruled the county with Mary of Burgundy.[41] As a consequence of this urban uprising, Ypres briefly ruled supreme in the West-Quarter in the early 1480s. The city used its newly found power to come down hard on the rural draperies in its hinterland again, prosecuting many cloth entrepreneurs from the various villages, and often exiling them from Flanders altogether.[42] The hardships faced by Nieuwkerke's cloth industry in the 1480s are reflected in the village's irregular production during this period. Annual outputs dropped from 1757 pieces in 1480 to 517 in 1481, followed by a few years when the cloth tax was not collected at all because of Ypres' hegemony, only to come in at an all-time low of 258 pieces in 1489. Then, in 1501, Philip 'the Fair' of Habsburg reinstated Ypres' charter as count of Flanders. Once again, textile production in the West-Quarter was restricted along the lines laid down in the city's privilege of 1428. When a number of cloth traders from Nieuwkerke and some other villages continued to sell their prohibited fabrics in Antwerp and Bergen op Zoom, the urban authorities were forced to publish a placard that forbade merchants from having any commercial dealings with these places.[43] Joost Godeschalck, a weaver who had lived in Nieuwkerke in this period, would later remark that at that time 'the trade broke down entirely'.[44] (In fact, in due course, the industry would begin to flourish like it never had before.)

All in all, this first phase of formally organized industry in the West-Quarter villages was marked by strain due to the opposition from Ypres. And while the city was not wholly successful in defeating the rural competition, there is little doubt that its efforts had a negative effect on the potential growth of the

40 *Les arrêts et jugés du Parlement de Paris*, I, pp. 576-78.

41 In 1477, during the campaign of King Louis XI into Flanders, the castle of Nieuwkerke had been destroyed: Ferdinand Van de Putte, 'Notes et analectes devant servir à une histoire complète de Neuve-Église', *Annales de la société d'émulation pour l'étude de l'histoire et des antiquités de la Flandre*, 8 (1850), 254-90 (p. 257). Apparently, the situation was still so severe in 1481 that many of the village's inhabitants had to temporarily reside in walled towns: AND, B 4821, fol. 11^r.

42 Dauchy, 'Introduction historique', pp. 120-21.

43 RDHDF-2, III, p. 124; RDHDF-2, I, pp. 75-77, 88-90.

44 'De neeringhe verviel gheheel al': RDHDF-2, I, p. 92.

industries. That said, Ypres' own economic and political position in the county was on the wane in this period, with the temporary exception of the 1480s. So why were the villages unable to overcome this obstacle? The answer seems to be twofold. First, the rural cloth centres depended upon the political support of their lords and princes. Strictly speaking, this should not have been the case with regards to Nieuwkerke at least, because it had a formal charter, which should have protected the village's cloth manufactures and entrepreneurs. But Philip the Good had no scruples about overturning privileges that had been accorded by previous lords of Bailleul. While Countess Jeanne de Harcourt defended the interests of the cloth villages she held in usufruct, her efforts were probably ineffective because she was not on the same political level as her feudal overlord. The same can be said for the village lords of Nieuwkerke in this period. In 1484, the lord of the seigneurie had tried to protect his village industry, and with temporary success, backed by the decrees of the Parlement of Paris. Yet these were overturned one year later by the administration of the new count of Flanders.[45] Generally speaking, the counts were on Ypres' side throughout the fifteenth century. This was partly because they had enjoyed close ties with the city's oligarchy ever since the late fourteenth century.[46] Political allegiances aside, princely support also required careful lobbying and the allocation of large amounts of money. Consider, for instance, that the city of Ypres had to pay a sum of no less than £8875 par. before it acquired its important privilege of 1428.[47]

But there may have been another reason why the rural cloth centres were unable to throw off the yoke of Ypres in this period, namely a lack of collective action. The legal proceedings before the Parlement of Paris in 1443 note that 'a *small number of inhabitants* of the parishes [of Nieuwkerke, Nieppe, and Eécke]' initiated the legal objections (my emphasis).[48] In fact, Ypres' solicitor used this as a legal argument to try and refute the villages' claim before the Parlement. He claimed that the 77 people who filed the suit had no right to declare themselves representatives of a community of some 6000 people in total.[49] Obviously, this point should not be taken too far, since one could hardly expect entire village communities to drop everything they were doing and lend nominal support to such a lawsuit. That said, there are traces in the sources which suggest the cloth entrepreneurs of Nieuwkerke may have indeed lacked unity at this point in time. In the 1450s, there were clear

---

45 Diegerick, MCXXII, MCXXIX, MCXXXI. These legal battles continued for some time, but ultimately resulted in a reinstatement of Ypres' privilege in 1501: Diegerick, MCCCLXIII.

46 Jelle Haemers, *For the Common Good: State Power and Urban Revolts in the Reign of Mary of Burgundy, (1477-1482)*, Studies in European Urban History (1100-1800), 17 (Turnhout: Brepols, 2009), pp. 248-51, 256-61.

47 Octaaf Mus, 'Pieter Lansaem, promotor van de nieuwe draperie te Ieper in de tweede helft van de 15e eeuw', *Handelingen van het Genootschap voor Geschiedenis, gesticht onder de benaming 'Société d'Émulation' te Brugge*, 130 (1993), 61-88 (p. 74).

48 'Au pourchas et instance d'aucuns particuliers habitans en icelles paroisses [des Neufeglise, Niepeglise et Ecque]': RDHDF-2, I, p. 16.

49 *Les appels flamands au Parlement de Paris: regestes des dossiers de procès reconstitués d'après les registres du Parlement et les sources conservées dans les dépôts d'archives de Belgique et du Nord de la France*, ed. by Serge Dauchy (Brussels: Ministère de la justice, 1998), DXLVII.

signs of factional struggle within the village's cloth industry. Most notably, there was a group of merchant-drapers who were perceived to have acted against the interests of the *commun pueple* by combining several craft stages in their workshops and hiring workers from outside the local community.[50] Through its relative lack of regulation, Nieuwkerke may have fallen victim to exploitation by a small group of dominant entrepreneurs. Similar to what had happened in Ypres in the late thirteenth and fourteenth centuries, these skewed relations within the village industry could have undermined social cohesion within the community of drapers.

And so, the lack of unity within Nieuwkerke's drapery may have factored into its failure to reach common accord in the battle against Ypres. The corollary was that in the 1450s and 1460s – the very period when the village was relatively free from the meddling of Ypres – these conflicts over inequality led to the expansion and tightening of the textile bylaws. The administration of Charles the Bold of Burgundy, who was lord of Bailleul at the time, laid the institutional groundwork for more 'egalitarian' conditions, mainly by countering vertical integration and electing an officer to guard over regulations that were expanded considerably in 1462 (see Chapter 2).[51] After his demise in 1477, the political turmoil shifted conditions to the detriment of the West-Quarter cloth villages. But Nieuwkerke's recently redacted cloth charter was the first building block for its golden age in the first half of the sixteenth century.

Phase two: collective action and 'golden age' (*c.* 1500 – *c.* 1550)

The early sixteenth century marked the beginning of a new phase in the economic development of Nieuwkerke. As already recounted, the preceding period was marked by setbacks for which Ypres' extra-economic pressure was partly responsible. Tellingly, the village's reversal of fortune began when a new lord arrived on the scene in 1503. In a legal document of 1545, the drapers of Ypres complained that the village lord's protection had prevented their reinstated cloth charter of 1501 from going into effect in Nieuwkerke:

> Under cover of being subjects of the late count of Gavere, and before that of his father the late lord of Fiennes, who were both grand governors in our land and county of Flanders and feared accordingly, [... the people of Nieuwkerke] have meddled with and acted against the aforesaid decree and bylaw.[52]

The new lord did indeed look after the interests of his villagers on several occasions, interfering on their behalf against Ypres.[53] Of course, he had a vested interest

50 RDHDF-2, III, pp. 100-07.

51 RDHDF-2, III, pp. 100-02, 109-20.

52 'Soubz umbre qu'ilz estoient subgectz et appartenoient à deffunct le conte de Gavre et auparavant au feu le seigneur de Fiennes son père, lesquelz successivement avoient esté grandz gouverneurs de nostre pays et conté de Flandres et partant cremuz, [...] s'estoient ingérez et avanchez de contrevenir à la susdicte sentence et arrest.' RDHDF-2, III, p. 93.

53 Diegerick, MCCCLXXIV, MCCCXCII.

in the survival and success of the rural drapery, because he was entitled to 6d. par. for each cloth that was produced and sealed within the parish.[54] This is not the whole story, because even a production level of 5000 pieces would merely contribute £125 par. to the lord's coffers – not a very large sum, considering that it was only 1.5 times the yearly wage of a master-mason in Antwerp in 1503.[55] However, although the lords of Nieuwkerke did not hold high jurisdiction over their village, they did have the right to collect all fines up to £3 par., as well as the right to certain taxes such as excises on beer and land transfers. Therefore, they stood to benefit from a flourishing population and, by extension, of a blooming textile industry.

To be sure, these same interests had already existed in the fifteenth century. But at that time, the lords of Nieuwkerke had predominantly been local nobles without much political clout.[56] Up until the late fourteenth century, it was the toponymic 'Van Nieuwkerke' family that held the village seigneurie. It appears that the powers of most of these lords were limited to this single lordship; which does not necessarily mean that they were ineffective political players, but it does suggest that they were not members of the high nobility. In the fifteenth century, the lords of the village belonged to the slightly more influential De la Douve family. After his marriage to the seigneurie's heiress Isabel de la Douve, Lord George d'Escornay briefly ruled over Nieuwkerke, whose highest political office was that of alderman in the Franc of Bruges.[57] In contrast, in 1503 lordship reverted to Jacques II de Luxembourg-Fiennes. This man was a knight of the Order of the Golden Fleece, and one of the most eminent aristocrats of the Low Countries; so much so, that he became the Habsburg government's regional representative, or 'stadtholder', of Flanders and Artois from 1504 onwards. According to Hans Cools, De Luxembourg and his fellows 'determined the appearance of the Burgundian-Habsburg court for several decades' from around 1490 onwards.[58] As he was stadtholder of Flanders and Artois, his authority was perhaps not 'feared' by the people of Ypres, or at least not in the crude sense of the word. But his high position at court would definitely have been known in the city.[59] Furthermore, after the redaction of Nieuwkerke's cloth charter in 1462, the count of Flanders came to share the spoils and financial responsibilities of

---

54 GSAB, CA, Acuits en portefeuilles 1367 (unnumbered, non foliated document of 3 October 1558).

55 In 1503, a master-mason in Antwerp earned £10.2 Brabant groats: John Munro, 'Prices and Wages in Brabant, 1400-1700', Excel-spreadsheet (based on data compiled by Herman Van der Wee), online on: www.economics.utoronto.ca/munro5/PricesandWages.htm. This was equivalent to £81.4 par., or 1.5 times less than the £125 par.

56 See the entry in the Egmont archives: 'Confirmation du don d'un gros sur la drapperie a Neuffeglise, joinct la Seigneurie dudit lieu par le Ducq Philippe en l'an 1433': NAP, Papiers de comte d'Egmont-Pignatelli, émigré, T 159/05, fol. 19^{v}.

57 Buylaert, *Repertorium*, pp. 523, 206-08, 248.

58 Hans Cools, *Mannen met macht: edellieden en de moderne staat in de Bourgondisch-Habsburgse landen, ca. 1475 – ca. 1530* (Zutphen: Walburg pers, 2001), pp. 217, 358.

59 At various times, Jacques de Luxembourg interfered in issues between Ypres' city government and other parties. The same went for his successor. See: Diegerick, MCCCCXXXIII, MDVII, MDXXVII, MDXXVIII, MDLXXVII, MDXCII.

Nieuwkerke's industry with the village lord. And so, for the first time, lord and prince were united in their investment in its wellbeing.[60]

It is worth to pause for a moment and emphasize that Nieuwkerke was not an isolated case of a late medieval village where the lord intervened to the benefit of the local industry. In the first half of the sixteenth century, the lord of Roubaix also tried to protect the textile manufacturers of that small town against extra-economic pressures from the city of Lille.[61] Similar to Ypres, Lille unceasingly strove to combat textile production in its wider hinterland, but many of the rural industries in its vicinity 'enjoyed the protection of powerful seigneurs', much like Roubaix.[62] In the county of Holland in the Northern Low Countries, village lords also had some successes in throwing off the efforts of urban governments to impose their general authority over the surrounding countryside (although most of them held their seigneuries with high jurisdiction, whereas Nieuwkerke's final jurisdiction rested with the court of Bailleul).[63]

Notwithstanding the importance of these aristocratic backers, it should be stressed that it was the drapers of Nieuwkerke who exploited the fearsome quality of their lord. According to the testimony of one Frans De Lopere, a former resident of the village, the drapers had initially obeyed Ypres' prohibitive privilege of 1501. That is to say, 'until *they* bought the lordship of Nieuwkerke *and bequeathed it to the lord of Fiennes*' (my emphases). From that moment onwards, the drapers had apparently resumed their production of cloth in violation of the city's privilege.[64] Unfortunately, the original document of sale or infeudation is not extant, so it is unclear what to make exactly of this curious statement. An entry in the inventory of the archives of the lords of Egmont – who inherited the seigneurie of Nieuwkerke after 1550 – contains an entry on the *achapt faict par le seigneur de Fiennes de la terre et seigneurie dudit Neuffeglise*, yet it does not mention the involvement of the villagers.[65] Another source sheds some more light on the event, however. It concerns a now lost document of 14 July 1503, which Isidore Diegerick, nineteenth-century archivist of the city archives of Ypres, summarized as followed in 1868:

60 Both gained 6d. par. for each cloth, and they shared the costs for the lead and the lodgings of the bailiff fifty-fifty: GSAB, CA 44562/25.

61 Michel Baelde, 'Un conflit économique entre Lille et Roubaix, 1553', *Revue du Nord*, 66 (1984), 1071-74 (pp. 1071-72).

62 Robert DuPlessis, 'One Theory, Two draperies, Three provinces and a Multitude of Fabrics: The New Drapery of French Flanders, Hainaut and the Tournaisis, *c.* 1500-*c.* 1800', in *The New Draperies in the Low Countries and England, 1300-1800*, ed. by N. B. Harte (Oxford: Oxford University Press, 1997), pp. 129-72 (p. 139).

63 Peter Hoppenbrouwers, 'Town and Country in Holland, 1350-1550', in *Town and Country in Europe, 1300-1800*, ed. by S.R. Epstein (Cambridge: Cambridge University Press, 2001), pp. 54-79 (pp. 76-77).

64 'Tot zy de heerlichede van Nieukerke cochten ende daermede beghifteden myn heere van Fiennes. De heerlichede in handen wesende van myn heere van Fiennes, begonsten die van Nieukerke te reedene lakenen ghecammet 60 ende 64.' RDHDF-2, I, p. 92.

65 NAP, Papiers de comte d'Egmont-Pignatelli, émigré, T 159/05, fol. 19^{v}.

> The aldermen and inhabitants of the lordship of Nieuwkerke have committed themselves, in the name of the community, to pay Jacques de Luxembourg […] their lord, the sum of £1200 par., to be employed for the redemption of a claim held on the aforementioned lordship by Jean Sauvage.[66]

The inventory of the Egmont family archives does indeed mention an annual rent of £95 15s. *au proffit de Messire Jean Sauvage.*[67] It is unclear how this claim had come to rest upon the lordship. Most likely, it ensued from a loan made out by Le Sauvage to one of the village's former lords or even to Jacques de Luxembourg himself, probably a lump sum in exchange for a yearly annuity. Much like De Luxembourg, Jean le Sauvage was a key figure at the Burgundian-Habsburg court, also a knight of the Golden Fleece, lord of Escobecques near Lille, and president of the Council of Flanders since 1497.[68] This would have placed him very close to Jacques de Luxembourg. In fact, in 1508 the two men joined a party of nobles who stood surety for a sum of 50,000 crowns that the future Emperor Charles V would have to pay if he reneged on his marriage contract with Mary Tudor of England.[69] The wealth of Le Sauvage is further illustrated by his generous patronage of Desiderius Erasmus, whom he paid out of his own pocket.[70] Put together, these facts make it probable that Le Sauvage had lent a large sum to the lord of Nieuwkerke at some point, whether this was De Luxembourg or not.

In any case, the joint effort by the people of Nieuwkerke to either purchase the lordship or to buy off such a massive debt resting on it would have been an impressive form of collective action. The £1200 par. (or £100 Flemish groats) was a high sum by any standard; ten times higher, in fact, than the annual gross income that the lord of Nieuwkerke stood to gain from the tax on cloth production. Accepting for the moment that these funds were effectively raised, the episode denotes a clear eagerness among the population to tie their fate to a

---

66 'Les échevins et les habitants de la seigneurie de Neuve-Église, s'engagent, au nom de la communauté, à payer à Jacques de Luxembourg […] leur seigneur, la somme de douze cents livres parisis, monnaie de Flandre, afin de les employer au rachat d'une charge qui pesait sur ladite seigneurie en faveur de Jean Savage': Diegerick, MCCCLXXIV (14 July 1503). I am grateful to Ludo Vandamme for pointing out an erratum in my original translation of this passage.

67 NAP, Papiers de comte d'Egmont-Pignatelli, émigré, T 159/05, fol. 19v. The full entry reads: 'Rente heritiere de £95 15s. l'an, au proffit de maitre Jean Sauvage, et a la charge de Jean Teremonde, laquelle est cassee'. It is unclear how this *Jean Teremonde* (Jan Van Dendermonde) had acquired responsibility for the annuity. In 1516, a *Jean Tenremonde* was mayor (*maieur*) of the city of Lille, but that does not bring us a whole lot further: RDHDF-2, I, pp. 324-25. He may have taken on this debt at the behest of the lord of Nieuwkerke, or its people, in exchange for certain perquisites, but we simply do not know.

68 Maarten Vermeir, 'Chancellor Jean le Sauvage/Ioannes Sylvagius: Erasmus' *Princeps Christianus* and a Prince of Utopia for Thomas More', *Moreana*, 53 (2017), 269-82; Peter Bietenholz and Thomas Deutscher, *Contemporaries of Erasmus: A Biographical Register of the Renaissance and Reformation*, 3 vols (Toronto: University of Toronto, 1995), III, pp. 325-26.

69 *Calendar of Letters, Despatches and State Papers Relating to the Negotiations between England and Spain Preserved in the Archives at Simancas and Elsewhere* (London: Longman etc., 1862-1954), II (1862), DLXXXIII.

70 Vermeir, p. 277.

mighty protector. This was not unheard of elsewhere. In the neighbouring cloth village of Dranouter, for example, the Chamber of Accounts in Lille contested the right of the lord to 6d. par. per cloth produced in the parish in 1519. The local drapery corporation responded by supporting the lord's claim to the duty.[71] Of course, the latter case did not concern one large sum but a periodic duty that would otherwise simply have been claimed by the prince. Nieuwkerke's £100 Fl. gr. would have required a more considerable common effort to obtain. Unfortunately, there are no references as to how and if this money was ever raised.

While it is not hard to accept that the drapers of Nieuwkerke would have wanted to throw off the prohibitive restrictions imposed upon them by Ypres, the question is how it would have been possible for such a sum to be raised. And also: why would anyone pay it, given that there were no solid guarantees that a new, more powerful, lord would act in favour of the cloth corporation? Let us begin by answering the first question. Departing from a conservative profit margin of 10 per cent of the sales price, to raise the £100 Flemish groats would require the profits of some 350-400 pieces of Nieuwkerke cloth.[72] From everything we have seen of individual production outputs and fortunes of the drapers up to this point, it is most unlikely that any single draper would have been able raise this sum on their own. However, even a relatively small group of them could have managed it. Assuming the drapers acted as a team, the task of raising £100 was demonstrably feasible, as in 1506, the total sum for all the wool bought by drapers from Nieuwkerke via the broker Wouter Ameide already amounted to £269 9s. 1d. (see Chapter 3).[73] And so, if everyone joined in, the sum was highly attainable.

This leads us to the question why it would be worthwhile to 'bail out the lord', when individual cloth entrepreneurs could have just as easily set up shop in any one of the Flemish cities that were apparently so eager to accommodate them (see Chapter 2). This only makes sense if the drapery already knew some kind of corporate organization, possibly even with access to a common fund. Evidently, this corporate collective would have been a lot harder to uproot than an individual enterprise. And, as will become clear, the redacted cloth charter of 1462 contained the elements necessary for such a corporation. Even though the drapery had not been able to function properly in the last decades of the fifteenth century (what with all the political and military turmoil), the leaders of the industry would still have been aware of the potential outputs and proceeds that a collective could stand to gain. The reason why they needed a powerful

71 RDHDF-2, II, 258-61.

72 There is little information on the average profit margins in the premodern cloth trade. In Francesco di Marco Datini's fourteenth-century cloth enterprise, 9 per cent of the proceeds were profits: Francesco Ammanniti, 'Francesco di Marco Datini's Wool Workshops', in *Francesco di Marco Datini: The Man, the Merchant*, ed. by Giampiero Nigro (Florence: Firenze University Press, 2010), pp. 489-514 (p. 492). According to John Munro's overview of cloth prices for Nieuwkerke (see Chapter 3, **Figure 3.1**), the village's fabrics cost £2 12s. 8d. per whole piece in 1496, which would give (100: 0,2633 =) 379.7 pieces.

73 CAB, Reeks 305, Wouter Ameyde, Journaal B, fols 187^{r}-223^{r}.

aristocrat as their lord, was not so much his ability to scare off the competition, as his capacity to negotiate on their behalf with the magistrates of Ypres and with the count of Flanders. In fact, the original document specifying that the people of Nieuwkerke would pay the £100 Fl. gr. was joined to two letters addressed by Jacques de Luxembourg to the aldermen of Ypres, inviting them to discuss the long-standing disagreement between the city and the cloth village.[74]

Of course, a powerful lord was mainly useful as an *external* shield. Internally, the less involved he was, the better it suited the aldermen and cloth entrepreneurs of Nieuwkerke. Luckily for them, although the lords officially ruled over the industry, in practice, their engagement was superficial at best. There are no traces of the active involvement of the lords of Nieuwkerke in the affairs of the village's cloth corporation. This is noteworthy, because these same lords also held the seigneurial town of Armentières in fief and there are plenty of indications that they did interfere in the cloth industry of this town.[75] Perhaps there is a connection with the fact that the lords of Nieuwkerke did not hold high jurisdiction in their village seigneurie, which meant that their purview did not extend to higher fines, corporal punishments, or banishments: these rights rested with the princely government of Flanders.[76] This jurisdictional fragmentation may have benefited industrial expansion because entrepreneurs had more freedom to improvise.[77] Then again, if individual entrepreneurs escaped the inspection of the wardens, this was not a good thing for the general reputation of Nieuwkerke's products.

This is where the expanded regulations of the later fifteenth century came in. For one thing, as we saw in Chapter 2, the charter of 1462 introduced the office of 'bailiff of the drapery' to uphold the industrial bylaws and supervise the wardens. For another, this charter contained a new bylaw, which stated that all fabrics would henceforth require the 'draper's mark' (*'t maerc van den drapier*) to be woven into them; a rule that became a common feature in rural cloth centres throughout the Low Countries (and beyond) in this period.[78] This measure was designed to increase the accountability of the entrepreneur, as the cloth charter articulated that customers could return substandard cloth to sender via the wardens, who were now able to identify the responsible party by his or her mark. By that same token, these individual marks were primarily used for purposes of internal control and not so much for outward 'branding'; a task sooner fulfilled by the corporation's cloth seal, to which the draper's

74 Diegerick, MCCCLXXIV.

75 RDHDF-2, I, pp. 99-100.

76 In 1529-30, for example, the bailiff of Bailleul interfered in criminal cases in the villages. The records explicitly note that this was 'a cause que icelle seigneurie de Neufeglise ne a que justice viscontiere': ADN, B 5669, fol. 6v.

77 Another example of such a cloth centre consisting of several different seigneuries is Langemark: RDHDF-2, II, pp. 626-27.

78 RDHDF-2, III, pp. 112-20; RDHDF-2, II, 253-56; John Oldland, 'The Clothiers' Century, 1450-1550', *Rural History*, 29 (2018), 1-22 (p. 9).

personal 'signature' was subordinated.[79] But this also meant that the industrial officials would have kept some kind of written administration to list which mark belonged to which draper. The marks of new drapers would have been entered into this ledger upon their acceptance into the corporation, while the marks of former entrepreneurs would have been removed from it. This strongly suggests that the entry into the drapery came with some procedure of admission, even though the charters never explicitly mention this.

The draper's mark therefore constituted a two-pronged approach to safeguard the quality and reputation of Nieuwkerke's fabrics: it raised individual accountability within the corporation, but it also enabled the wardens to monitor the performance of (new) members. Although there is little empirical ground to support the idea that this created a situation of outright exclusion, the implied membership and shared initiation rite probably increased the sense of cohesion among the drapers. Additionally, as we have already seen, there was a kind of educational period that the drapers of Nieuwkerke had to fulfil before they were accepted into the corporation. The sense of unity this created was further facilitated by the periodic public inquests (*waerheden*), which were also instituted in 1462. At these occasions, the wardens and bailiff of the drapery passed judgment on offenders of the regulations. This led to a sense of collective responsibility, because all drapers and master-artisans could be summoned to attend these proceedings. The public inquests originated in an old, inclusive legal tradition in the county of Flanders: the so-called *franches vérités* or *waerheden*. These juridical assemblies were periodically organized by an officer of the count, who invited ordinary people to bear testimony in local legal matters, usually based on customary law.[80] Indeed, during the *waerheden* of Nieuwkerke's drapery, any attendant could be prompted to give testimony concerning the contents of the bylaws. Because of this, all the attendants had to swear an oath.[81] This ensured that people were more involved with their fellows and reinforced the general knowledge about the regulations, while it also served to ratify the verdicts of the wardens. Meanwhile, the more detailed records of the cloth industry in the small Flemish town of Estaires (Stegers) – at about 15 kilometres distance from Nieuwkerke – indicates that these *waerheden* were also the occasions where the wardens officially recorded the names (and presumably the marks) of new drapers.[82] Together, the official registration of the draper's mark and the oath that

79 Bert De Munck, 'The Agency of Branding and the Location of Value: Hallmarks and Monograms in Early Modern Tableware Industries', *Business History*, 54 (2012), 1-22 (pp. 5-6).

80 Egied Strubbe, 'Het houden van de doorgaande waarheid in het Vrije van Brugge', *Annales de la Société d'Émulation de Bruges: revue trimestrielle pour l'étude de l'histoire et des antiquités de la Flandre*, 66 (1923), 249-53; Léo Verriest, 'Une institution judiciaire en action: les "franches vérités" du bailliage de Flobecq Lessines en la seconde moitié du XIVe siècle', *Revue du Nord*, 40 (1958), 411-21 (pp. 414-17).

81 RDHDF-2, III, p. 119.

82 Georges Espinas, 'Une draperie rurale dans la Flandre française au XVe siècle: la draperie rurale d'Estaires (Nord) (1428-1434)', *Revue d'histoire des doctrines economiques et sociales*, 11 (1923), 1-44 (p. 18).

had to be sworn at the *waerhede* functioned as a stand-in for the entry barrier of citizenship which most urban guilds used to control their membership base.[83] And so, in the run up to the sixteenth century, the institutional framework of Nieuwkerke's textile industry was already stimulating a sense of collective responsibility, even though the turbulent period of the 1470s until around 1500 had precluded these facets from coming to fruition.

Starting in 1503, then, Nieuwkerke drew up its lordly 'cover', while the drapery corporation effectively maintained its independence and strengthened internal control over its members. It was around this same time that the village entrepreneurs started a new collective approach towards marketing their cloth. As we saw in Chapter 3, the cloth industry of Nieuwkerke, like many others, continuously depended upon the markets of gateway cities. In the fifteenth century, Bruges had been the main commercial outlet for their products. But when that city began to founder in the late 1400s, the fairs in the duchy of Brabant became the pre-eminent channel to market cloth from the Low Countries. The cities of Bergen op Zoom, and Antwerp in particular, were the new platforms for the trade in Nieuwkerke's fabrics.[84] Yet the real commercial shift for the village only occurred when the drapery corporation decided to collectively rent cloth halls in these fair towns, for the benefit of 'the entire nation of the drapery of Nieuwkerke'.[85] In 1511, the drapers jointly rented premises in Bergen op Zoom. This suggests that some type of common fund had probably been created before that moment; after all, the yearly rent of £120 par. had to come from somewhere.[86] Around the same time, the drapers also started to rent lodgings in the Hoogstraat in Antwerp, from a private trader named Fernando de Bernuy (see Chapter 3). By 1573, the annual rent for these premises amounted to no less than £720 par.[87] As with the joint effort to provide the £100 Fl. gr. to buy out a claim on the seigneurie of Nieuwkerke, the management of these rental sums would have required a commonly controlled treasury of some sort. In keeping with the collective take-off in Nieuwkerke, the phrasing in the original contract with the city government of Bergen op Zoom conjures up an image of an actual trading 'nation'. This terminology could be noteworthy in itself, as some trading nations had special legal arrangements with the courts of market cities concerning their trade transactions. Furthermore, if Nieuwkerke's corporation was seen as resembling the formally instituted trading nations of other places, this would have increased the sense of community among its members even more.[88]

83 See, for example: Émile Coornaert, *L'industrie de la laine à Bergues-Saint-Winoc: une industrie urbaine du XIVe au XVIIe siècle* (Paris: Presses universitaires de France, 1930), p. 47.

84 John Munro, 'Bruges and the Abortive Staple in English Cloth: An Incident in the Shift of Commerce from Bruges to Antwerp in the Late Fifteenth Century', *Revue belge de philologie et d'histoire*, 44 (1966), 1137-59 (pp. 1143-44).

85 'Gheil der natien van der draperien van Nyeukercke': CABZ, Protocol van rentebrieven en recognities, 1511-1512, fol. 65^{v}.

86 CABZ, Protocol van rentebrieven en recognities, 1511-1512, fols 65^{v}-66^{r}.

87 CAA, Halle van Nieuwkerke, Documenten 4675, fol. 1^{r}.

88 Jeroen Puttevils, *Merchants and Trading in the Sixteenth Century: The Golden Age of Antwerp*, Perspectives in Economic and Social History (London: Pickering and Chatto, 2015), pp. 144, 150-53.

Of course, the creation of the village's trade collective might seem to be a consequence, and not a cause, of Nieuwkerke's economic efflorescence – simply a necessary outcome of scale-enlargement. But the output figures of the industry reveal that the collective initiative predated the actual boom, which only occurred after 1516 (see Chapter 1, **Figure 1.2**). The corporation also chose to abandon the cloth hall in Bergen op Zoom three years *before* the production peak of 1549.[89] Therefore, it is more likely that the opposite was true: that Nieuwkerke's corporate collective was brought on by the period of adversity in the last decades of the fifteenth century. In fact, other textile industries of the period instated similar collective efforts precisely at times when their fortunes were on the wane. The city magistrate of the town of Leiden in Holland, for example, organized a common 'purse' (*beurs*) in 1530: a joint venture that sold cloth in large quantities in order to maintain a firmer control on the price level of Leiden's fabrics.[90] In fifteenth-century Bergues-Saint-Winoc in Flanders, a similar common fund (*burse*) was set up to support the town's newly founded branch of light textiles.[91] In both cases, the collective spirit was aimed at countering a situation of crisis. Nieuwkerke's inspiration may have likewise derived from its losses in the final decades of the fifteenth century. Ironically, then, the external pressures from the government of Ypres probably contributed to the collaboration between Nieuwkerke's cloth entrepreneurs, and so the city was complicit in the village's economic success.

As we saw in the previous chapter, the idea of acquiring a permanent foothold in urban markets was not a new one: foreign trading nations had been doing so since the early fourteenth century.[92] But from the fifteenth century onwards, draperies from throughout the Low Countries also began to obtain such a foothold in the market cities. By the sixteenth century, the tactic was pretty common. It was especially popular with small settlements that produced fabrics of medium-high quality. So, when the drapers from Nieuwkerke frequented the fairs at Bergen op Zoom, they could plainly see how places like Diest and Turnhout (from the duchy of Brabant), and Weert (in the duchy of Guelders) also rented common warehouses and stores.[93] Successful commercial methods such as this were imitated to and fro in this period because of the continuous interactions between traders stemming from different regions.[94] Sometimes

---

89 CABZ, Stadsrekeningen, 1547-48, unnumbered folio. See also: CABZ, Stadsrekeningen, 1552-53, fol. 13^{r}.

90 N. W. Posthumus, *De geschiedenis van de Leidsche lakenindustrie*, 3 vols (The Hague: M. Nijhoff, 1908-1939), I (1908), pp. 258-59.

91 Peter Stabel, 'Marketing Cloth in the Low Countries: Manufacturers, Brokers and Merchants (14th-16th Centuries)', in *International Trade in the Low Countries (14th-16th Centuries): Merchants, Organization, Infrastructure. Proceedings of the International Conference Ghent-Antwerp, 12th-13th January 1997*, ed. by Peter Stabel, Bruno Blondé and Anke Greve (Leuven: Garant, 2000), pp. 15-36 (p. 30).

92 Rolf Hammel-Kiesow, 'The Early Hansas', in *A Companion to the Hanseatic League*, ed. by Donald Harreld (Leiden: Brill, 2015), pp. 15-63 (pp. 61-63).

93 Corneel Slootmans, *Paas- en koudemarkten te Bergen op Zoom, 1365-1565*, Bijdragen tot de geschiedenis van het Zuiden van Nederland, 64-66, 3 vols (Tilburg: Stichting Zuidelijk historisch contact, 1985), I, pp. 345-53.

94 Oscar Gelderblom, *Cities of Commerce: The Institutional Foundations of International Trade in the Low Countries, 1250-1650* (Princeton: Princeton University Press, 2013), p. 204.

it was even possible to swoop into a recently vacated lodging that had already been used as a cloth hall by traders from another settlement. The drapers of the successful cloth town of Armentières, for instance, employed this tactic on two occasions: in 1529, they took over the 'old hall of Weert' in Bergen op Zoom; and a few years later, they took up lodging in the city of Antwerp, this time in the house 'formerly known as the hall of Nieuwkerke'.[95]

Nieuwkerke's drapers appear to have used their urban cloth halls as the commercial extension of their collective village corporation. The main benefit of this shared trading post was that it lowered the transaction costs per individual trader. This further supports the idea that the common initiative came about because of a period of general slump that drove the entrepreneurs to collaboration. After all, the richest drapers were presumably the people most apt to influence industrial policy. And so, they must have felt the need (or opportunity) to lower their expenses by installing a public venture. But it stands to reason that they were the ones who had to front a larger proportion of the rent sum and that they were well aware of this. They must also have been aware that they would have to contend with an increased level of control by the wardens, and that they (like everybody else) would face additional levies per piece of cloth that was processed via the hall.[96] In other words, the need would have had to be dire for them to accept such an arrangement. Having said that, even though the cloth halls were technically open to 'all those of the (parish of Nieuwkerke) carrying or transporting cloth into said cities', in practice, the enterprise could have benefited the wealthier drapers in particular.[97] In order to make use of the cloth halls, one had to cross the vast distance of about 175 kilometres between the Flemish West-Quarter and the north of the duchy of Brabant. While the expenditures of such a journey little affected the eventual cost of the fabric, the undertaking did require a considerable investment of time, during which the draper was absent from his or her workshop.[98] This potentially put drapers with smaller operations at a disadvantage. Then again, the example of the *beurs* of Leiden belies this notion. In that case, the co-operative venture was intended to support poorer drapers who could not travel to the market towns.[99] To that end, their cloth was sold on a common account. The drapers of Nieuwkerke may have done this as well (although there are no records to support this idea).

And so, there are two opposing possibilities. Either the rich drapers of Nieuwkerke played a role similar to that of the merchants in the boomtown of Hondschoote, who primarily advanced their own interests by buying large quantities of woollens from their poorer colleagues and selling them on in the

95 'Que l'on nommoit par ci devant la halle de Noeufveglise': RDHDF-2, I, 402; Slootmans, I, p. 347.
96 This was the case in Armentières, for example: RDHDF-2, I, p. 404.
97 'Tous ceulx de la dicte paroiche aporteroyent ou amenroyent draps es dictes villes': RDHDF-2, III, pp. 149-50.
98 Stabel, 'Marketing cloth', pp. 34-35.
99 Posthumus, I, p. 258.

market towns.[100] Or, quite the contrary, the village's drapery corporation followed a procedure akin to that of Armentières, where the wardens appointed official hall masters to sell the fabrics of everybody who could not travel to the market cities in exchange for a small fee.[101] Given the other evidence presented here, the latter seems the more likely scenario. As to this potential common account of Nieuwkerke's cloth corporation: the sixteenth century was marked by a remarkable price uniformity of the village's fabrics. Woollens of the type called *kepers* which were sold to Spanish merchants in 1552 and 1553 always cost £4 10s. Fl. gr.[102] This evidence may be distorted somewhat because it comes from excise records (and, as such, the numbers were possibly rounded off, or the customs officials used a rule of thumb). Yet this in itself would be proof of the relative uniformity of the Nieuwkerke's fabrics, since either system was predicated upon a degree of consistency between the products. This uniformity is particularly noteworthy because the woollens that the city government of Bruges bought from drapers of Nieuwkerke in the last quarter of the fifteenth century had still shown remarkable price fluctuations. Of course, these fluctuations were partly a consequence of varying dimensions, and possibly also of different colours, but it appears that the price differences were chiefly based on quality. This is best illustrated by a transaction of May 1477, when one draper from Nieuwkerke sold two black cloths measuring 70 ells for 14.5d. per ell, while another sold two black pieces of 68 ells in total for 13d. per ell, and a third sold yet another black piece, also 34 ells long, for 13.7d. per ell.[103]

The corporate commercial spirit in Nieuwkerke extended into local politics. First of all, the village aldermen were probably involved in the peculiar collective attempts to buy off the claim held on the lordship by Jean le Sauvage in 1503. And they certainly interfered for the protection of the corporation's industrial interests: in 1522, the aldermen pressured the magistrate of Ypres to make restitutions for a shipment of raw materials which had never been delivered to the drapers of Nieuwkerke.[104] Apparently, these raw materials were purchased collectively, too, and the village officials were involved in its protection. This is not altogether surprising, considering that the aldermen often engaged in cloth enterprises themselves, or were related to drapers.[105] But the drapers of Nieuwkerke were also well-versed in the game of political lobbying, as apparent

---

100 In Hondschoote, there was also a gradual merging of the 'notable' drapers and the merchants around the middle of the sixteenth century: Émile Coornaert, *Un centre industriel d'autrefois: la draperie-sayetterie d'Hondschoote (XIVe-XVIIIe siècles)* (Paris: Presses universitaires de France, 1930), pp. 378-79.

101 RDHDF-2, I, pp. 402-04.

102 See, for example: GSAB, CA 23482, fols 10^r-22^r; CA 23484, fols 40^v-43^v.

103 'Item, Pieter van der Donc van Nieukerke, van twee zwarte lakenen t'samen lanc LXX ellen, costen £4 4s. 5d. Item, Dieric Godscalc van Nieukerke van twee zwarte lakenen lanc t'samen LXVIII ellen, costen £3 13s. 8d. Item, Jan Priem van een zwart laken, lanc 34 ellen ende een vierendeel, coste 39s. 4d. gr.': CAB, Stadsrekeningen, 1476-77, fol. 40^v.

104 RDHDF-2, III, pp. 130-31.

105 Recurrent families on the bench of aldermen were, amongst others: Ente, De Hane, De Raedt, De Quekere: RDHDF-2, I, pp. 32-53, 65-69; RDHDF-2, III, pp. 169-76; GSAB, CA, Acquits en portefeuilles 802bis (loose, non foliated quires of 1544-45).

from their collaboration with the cloth towns of Poperinge and Mesen in 1545. At that time, Ypres was once again launching a legal assault on the draperies in its hinterland; and, in an attempt to bribe their way to a favourable verdict, the entrepreneurs of the village and the two towns pooled their resources to buy the governor of Flanders a new horse.[106] Incidentally, this again implies some kind of shared fund that could be used in such cases.

These close interconnections between local politics and industry and trade benefited the drapers of Nieuwkerke as a collective from around 1500 to 1550. Of course, the foundations for this collective action had been laid in the second half of the fifteenth century, as the village drapers united against the external threat of Ypres (meanwhile battling the overly ambitious fellows within their own ranks). Perhaps it is no coincidence that this prologue to effective collective action was paralleled in increased references to the Common Good during the same period, as recounted in the previous chapter. That common spirit was clearly visible in 1484, when the draping 'community' (*'t ghemeente*), consisting of some 160 people, conferred for three hours in Nieuwkerke's parish church to reach common accord about the terms that had been presented to them by the city of Ypres.[107] References to acts for the 'benefit of the community of drapers' (*proufict du commun des drapiers*) and the 'entire nation' on the commercial level were a rhetorical reiteration of this collective action.[108] Even if one were sceptical about how genuine the richer drapers were in looking after general interests (as opposed to their own), there is little doubt that their outward stance promoted internal cohesion. And this was reflected in the most pronounced expansion of industrial productivity that Nieuwkerke ever reached. Also, the collective strategy of this rural cloth centre was mirrored by its more urban counterpart of Armentières, which rose to prominence simultaneously with Nieuwkerke. When the drapers of that town rented their cloth hall in Antwerp in 1534, no fewer than 93 of them adjoined their names to the contract.[109] In terms of the economic cycle identified by Bas van Bavel, this period in the development of Nieuwkerke's textile economy was marked by a relatively 'closed' system, in the sense that the corporation monitored commercial exchange through the intervention of industrial agents. And the social stability within the ranks of the cloth entrepreneurs which accompanied this supervision was apparently conducive to the industry's flourishing.[110] Yet it was the deep breath before the plunge, as the gradual breaking down of internal cohesion over the subsequent period went hand in hand with the industry's overall decline.

---

106 The horse cost 100 guilders (*eenen peerde van hondert ghuldens*) and each cloth corporation would contribute one-third: RDHDF-2, III, p. 285.

107 RDHDF-2, I, pp. 60-61.

108 RDHDF-2, III, 149; CABZ, Protocol van rentebrieven en recognities, 1511-12, fol. 65^v.

109 RDHDF-2, I, p. 406.

110 Van Bavel, *The Invisible Hand*, pp. 177-88.

Phase three: bang or whimper (> *c.* 1550)?

In 1593, the Chamber of Accounts in Lille held an inquest to determine the current state of the textile industries in the western part of Flanders and in the region of Hainaut. While many traditional cloth centres had faltered in recent years, in most places there were signs of recovery and renewed growth.[111] Nieuwkerke, however, was found to be a mere shadow of its former self. The village counted no more than 106 looms, 28 of which had fallen in disuse. Moreover, there were no longer traces of any dyeing operations, and the remaining drapers operated small-time operations, with none among them possessing more than eight pieces of cloth at the time.[112] It is tempting to lay these events at the door of the religious wars that took hold of the wider region after 1566. The destruction of the village cloth hall, along with a large part of Nieuwkerke's buildings in 1582, coupled with a mass emigration from the West-Quarter, ended the glory period for good.[113] The fall of Antwerp a few years later was a huge commercial blow as well. Yet, if truth be told, King Philip II of Spain, formal ruler of the Habsburg Low Countries, had already confiscated Nieuwkerke's premises in Antwerp in 1573, more than a decade before the Brabantine city fell before Spanish troops.[114] The Revolt against the King and his religious policies caused large-scale emigrations of artisans from many cloth centres in the Southern Low Countries. And in the course of this massive outflow of people, foreign industries were more than eager to absorb the human capital, and to fill the market vacuum that was left behind.[115]

If this goes some way towards explaining the decline of Nieuwkerke's cloth industry, it cannot have been all-encompassing, because these same conditions hit other Flemish textile centres, and some of these were able to rebuild their industrial economy. Hondschoote, for example, which had been almost completely burned to the ground by marauding troops and rebels in 1582, made a spectacular comeback after 1600. Likewise, the town of Armentières, whose industrial boom had run parallel to that of Nieuwkerke, saw a renewed upturn during the final decades of the sixteenth century.[116] One way in which Nieuwkerke differed from these centres may have been a permanent exodus of

---

111 Henri De Sagher, 'Une enquête sur la situation de l'industrie drapière en Flandre à la fin du XVIe siècle', *Études d'histoire dédiées à la memoire de Henri Pirenne par ses anciens élèves*, ed. by Hans Van Werveke (Brussels: Nouvelle société d'éditions, 1937), pp. 471-500 (pp. 471-500).

112 De Sagher, 'Une enquête', pp. 490-91. For the sources, see: De Sagher, RDHDF-2.

113 RDHDF-2, III, p. 98; Ludo Vandamme, 'Calvinisme, textielindustrie en drapeniers te Nieuwkerke in de 16e eeuw', in: *Westhoek – Jaarboek*, 1 (Ypres: Westhoek, 1984), 114-30 (p. 127); John Desreumaux, *Leidens weg op* (Roeselare: Familia et Patria, 1992), pp. 295-311.

114 CAA, Halle van Nieuwkerke, Documenten 4675; Oscar Gelderblom, 'The Organization of Long-Distance Trade in England and the Dutch Republic, 1550-1650', in *The Political Economy of the Dutch Republic*, ed. by Oscar Gelderblom (Farnham and Burlington: Ashgate Publishing, 2009), pp. 223-54 (p. 227).

115 DuPlessis, 'One theory, two draperies, three provinces', p. 134.

116 Coornaert, *Un centre industriel d'autrefois*, 35-43, Annexe V; DuPlessis, 'One theory, two draperies', pp. 132-36; De Sagher, 'Une enquête', pp. 481-83, 500.

its capital-rich entrepreneurs. This is evidenced by the inquest of 1593. By that time, dyeing operations had completely disappeared from the village, which was probably a consequence of the capital-intensive nature of this production stage. In fact, the 1593 inquest suggests that the dyeing of Nieuwkerke cloth was entirely relocated to Armentières.[117] Although the dyers of Armentières had already processed some of Nieuwkerke's fabrics during the village's industrial boom, at that time the cloth had still been predominantly dyed within the local parish.[118] The industrial textile centres of Western Flanders and Hainaut which showed signs of economic recovery around the turn of the seventeenth century all either harboured their own population of merchant-drapers, or were closely tied to merchant capital from other towns. Hondschoote, for one, which was no longer financed by trade firms from Antwerp, saw a swift transition wherein rich drapers from the local community increasingly filled the role of merchants.[119]

Of course, this is not the whole story. After all, during the 1550s, the output of Nieuwkerke's fabrics had already begun to gradually drop, never again to reach the level of the 1540s. This downturn coincided with increased polarization and factional struggles within the community of drapers. A series of conflicts ensued in the 1550s, between the rich drapers on one side and the poor and 'common' (*commun*) drapers on the other. Members of the latter faction wanted to curb scale-enlargement of their richer colleagues, because they were increasingly less able to compete with them. As such, their discontent echoed that of their predecessors in the 1450s, with references to the Common Good (*le prouffit du commun*) by the faction that felt they lacked equal opportunities. Around this same period, the wardens acted on complaints from within the drapery that certain traders were bypassing the joint cloth halls in Antwerp and Bergen op Zoom, renting private premises to market their products instead.[120] In terms of collective action, this constituted a form of free-riding, since the wardens could not monitor sales outside the common halls. And so, these traders were theoretically able to fly the colours of Nieuwkerke's chartered drapery while selling substandard fabrics. This not only gave them a competitive advantage, but it was also damaging to the industry's general reputation. As renting private stores must have been a costly affair, the drapers in question were supposedly at the wealthier end of the spectrum. It appears, therefore, that in the course of Nieuwkerke's blooming, this group had pulled away from their fellows in terms of prosperity, and now sought to undermine the collective in their own interest. This corresponds closely to what Oliver Volckart concluded about village co-operation in the marketing of agricultural produce in the later Middle Ages: these

117 RDHDF-2, I, p. 438.

118 This is proven by the references to dyers and dyeing in the cloth regulations. See, for example: RDHDF-2, III, pp. 151-52. For the processing of Nieuwkerke cloth by the dyers of Armentières: RDHDF-2, I, pp. 189, 240-41.

119 De Sagher, 'Une enquête', p. 483; Coornaert, *Un centre industriel d'autrefois*, pp. 295-97.

120 RDHDF-2, III, pp. 156-76, 149-50. For a comparison with Hondschoote: van der Meulen, 'Get Rich and Try Dyeing', p. 58.

collectives only lasted while there was a relatively small group of rich participants. Internal stratification within the community was not a problem, so long as the affluent did not become too numerous, in which case they stood to gain more from stepping outside of – and thereby disintegrating – the collective.[121] In other words, none of the stake-holders had been powerful enough to completely push their own interests in the first half of the sixteenth century, which had resulted in an equilibrium. However, as a small group gained dominance after 1550, the ensuing imbalance disrupted the smooth operation of the textile industry.

These developments conform to Van Bavel's prediction about the connection between rising social polarization and economic decline. Yet it would be wrong to label the Nieuwkerke case a unilateral question of 'the rich' parasitizing on the industry. Rather, it comes back to the growing *perception* of inequality, which we previously encountered in Ypres. In the second half of the sixteenth century, Nieuwkerke's cloth industry was facing massive challenges, both in terms of international competition and a shift in market demand. The problem was made worse by an overall increase in food prices, and a downturn in real wages.[122] In dealing with these external developments, the industrial officers were wedged in between opposing factions on the home front. As they were trying to rein in the merchant-drapers who had set up private shop in Antwerp, so they also had to contend with inferior cloth from poor or impoverished producers at the other end of the spectrum. This is apparent from the wardens' attempts to enforce stricter regulations on the types of wool allowed for use, which they began doing around the year 1553. The professed reason was that they wished to guarantee more uniformity in the finished fabrics.[123] Although a useful strategy in an increasingly competitive international textile market, this constituted an indirect assault upon those drapers who were unable to afford materials of the required standards.

Yet it is difficult to determine what would have been the right or wrong decision in economic terms, even with hindsight. After all, if subpar fabrics were indeed damaging the commercial reputation of Nieuwkerke's product, this undermined the collective interests just as strongly as individual trade transactions outside the halls did. However that may be, the new wool regulations must have fuelled the flames of factional friction within the cloth corporation. It is also worth considering that, as we have seen, leniency as regards the types of wool that could be used in the production of Nieuwkerke's fabrics was probably a key factor in the cost-competitiveness of the village's product (see Chapter 2). In any case,

121 Olivier Volckart, 'Die Dorfgemeinde als Kartell: Kooperationsprobleme und ihre Lösungen im Mittelalter und in der frühen Neuzeit', *Jahrbuch für Wirtschaftsgeschichte / Economic History Yearbook*, 45 (2004), 189-204 (p. 201).

122 Particularly the English and Dutch fabrics caused strong competition in the lower segment of the traditional woollen cloth industry: Peter Stabel, '"Dmeeste, oirboirlixste en proffitelixste let ende neringhe": een kwantitatieve benadering van de lakenproductie in het laatmiddeleeuwse en vroegmoderne Vlaanderen', *Handelingen van de Maatschappij voor Geschiedenis en Oudheidkunde te Gent*, 51 (1997), 113-53 (p. 138); van Bavel, *The Invisible Hand*, p. 186.

123 RDHDF-2, III, pp. 156-76.

while the initial, crippling fines were brought down to a more acceptable level through the intercession of the Chamber of Accounts, the stricter requirements remained in place. As a consequence, many drapers must have been unable to maintain their own enterprises. Instead, they were forced to work for their richer colleagues, either as subcontractors or as wageworkers.[124] Indeed, the available data for the 1560s suggest that more than half of the village's drapers had annual outputs that were probably too small to constitute a successful enterprise without additional economic activities (see **Table 2.1**).

Still, it remains unclear to what extent the cracks in the collective were a cause, rather than a consequence, of the recession. After all, Nieuwkerke was not the only textile centre that faced conflicts about inequality between drapers in this period. In Hondschoote, the *commun drapiers* were also protesting against attempts at scale-enlargement by the richer entrepreneurs in 1557. The difference was that Hondschoote was almost entirely driven by capital inputs from external merchant firms; in the fifteenth century mainly from Bruges, in the sixteenth from Antwerp.[125] These merchants bought finished cloth off the drapers and took care of the marketing process. In Nieuwkerke, by contrast, it was the drapers who oversaw both the production process and the marketing of fabrics.[126] While things were going smoothly, this integration on the collective level may have given the drapers a self-image of belonging to an undivided community. Yet when their own tradesmen started openly pursuing selfish gain (and even enriching themselves at the expense of others), this was interpreted as a subversion of public interest, causing 'great scandal and damage' to the entire parish.[127] This was different in Hondschoote, with its occupational division between drapers and merchants. There, the agitation among the poorer drapers followed attempts at assimilation between some of the rich entrepreneurs and the (mostly external) merchants. In the seventeenth century, this process of assimilation would crystallize into a 'capitalist' division, between merchants and 'notable' drapers on the one hand, and 'ordinary' drapers and all the rest of the labour force on the other.[128] In terms of such capitalist relations of production, the organization of Nieuwkerke's industry and trade were less advanced. As industrial and commercial activities were merged, both at the level of the

124 RDHDF-2, III, pp. 169-76. For a similar stratification of drapers, see: Jos Vermaut, 'De textielnijverheid in Brugge en op het platteland, Westelijk Vlaanderen voor 1800: konjunktuurverloop, organisatie en sociale verhoudingen' (unpublished doctoral thesis, Ghent University, 1977), pp. 480-89. See also the related analysis based on Vermaut's findings: Catharina Lis and Hugo Soly, 'Subcontracting in Guild-Based Export Trades, Thirteenth-Eighteenth Centuries', in *Guilds, Innovation and the European Economy, 1400-1800*, ed. by S. R. Epstein and Maarten Prak (Cambridge: Cambridge University Press, 2008), pp. 81-113 (p. 100).

125 Coornaert, *Un centre industriel d'autrefois*, pp. 375-77, 234, 237-40.

126 In all of the sources that I have been able to find, there is only a single mention of an external merchant dealing in Nieuwkerke cloth: RDHDF-2, I, pp. 326-32. All the other traders (be they in Bruges, at the fairs of Bergen op Zoom, or in Antwerp), are referred to as stemming from Nieuwkerke itself.

127 'Contourner au grand scandalle, dhommaige et interest de la dicte paroiche': RDHDF-2, III, p. 150.

128 Coornaert, *Un centre industriel d'autrefois*, pp. 375-77.

individual enterprise and at the level of the corporation, the village's individual entrepreneurs were unable to operate on the same scale as those of the external merchant firms that were active in places like Hondschoote.

That said, one cannot exclude the possibility that the polarization in Nieuwkerke's cloth corporation arose at least in part because of actual rising levels of economic inequality. Indeed, another complaint levelled against the village's richer drapers was that they traded in 'foreign cloth' (*draps estrangiers*); which is to say, any textiles that were not produced in the local parish.[129] This could suggest that these cloth entrepreneurs tried to hedge their bets commercially, as a tactical response to deteriorating market conditions for the fabrics of Nieuwkerke. From the perspective of the integrated industrial-trade collective, this was base treachery; because, in doing so, these traders were diverting mercantile capital away from potentially productive use in the village itself.[130] These merchant-drapers had one foot inside and one outside of the door, as they obviously also had ties to the market cities. Then again, other evidence suggests that this top layer of the drapery corporation was still of relatively humble means when the religious wars broke out, certainly in comparison to the more prosperous merchants from cities such as Antwerp (see Chapter 2). And so, even Nieuwkerke's 'rich' drapers would have been less able to recover from temporary economic adversity than traders from these other places.[131] They were also more dependent upon pooling their resources, both to buy the expensive raw materials and to come up with the rent for their commercial outlets in the market cities. Even as the drapery still rented the cloth hall in Antwerp shortly before it was seized in 1573, the ratio between overhead and income would have been increasingly off keel because of falling production levels. Of course, it is possible that the confiscation records on which these insights are based are unreliable, because the richer traders of Nieuwkerke had already departed the village before the invading troops descended on their village after 1566 (possibly because they were already more or less permanently residing in the market cities). The less well-to-do drapers may further have been over-represented in the sources because the confiscation registers only list people prosecuted for their evangelical beliefs. However, previous studies have found no neat correlation between economic position and sympathy with the new faith in the county of Flanders at this time. Thus, the evidence we have of the wealth of Nieuwkerke's drapers is not necessarily unrepresentative.[132]

Nevertheless, this exposes an interesting interconnection between the economic developments analysed in this chapter, and the so-called Dutch Revolt (1566-1648): the uprising against the Habsburg government of King Philip II of Spain, which swept through various regions of the Low Countries,

129 RDHDF-2, III, p. 150.

130 Van Bavel, *The Invisible Hand*, pp. 200-07.

131 Coornaert, *Un centre industriel d'autrefois*, p. 364.

132 Johan Decavele, *De dageraad van de reformatie in Vlaanderen (1520-1565)*, 2 vols (Brussels: Paleis der Academiën, 1975), II, pp. 543-50.

but first ignited in the West-Quarter. On the one hand, the increasing state of war after the Iconoclastic Fury of 1566 might seem a *deus ex machina* that extinguished Nieuwkerke's cloth industry with a bang. The massive emigrations from the general region, coupled with the fall of Antwerp in 1585, were certainly instrumental in the downfall of the West-Quarter cloth industries.[133] However, it is very much the question whether the village would have recovered from the industrial decline that had already set in by this time, even without these external circumstances. In fact, we may wonder to what extent the Religious Troubles of this period should not be considered a partial consequence of the underlying social tensions.[134] According to that interpretation, the increased gap between poor and rich within the cloth industry of Nieuwkerke – whether imagined or real – would have been merely indicative of a social rift that was impacting upon society as a whole. Indeed, some historians have interpreted the Iconoclastic Fury of 1566 as the aftermath of harvest failures that simply brought pre-existent social tensions to breaking point.[135] To be sure, in the West-Quarter – where the iconoclasm began – there were increasing signs of poverty in this period. One inhabitant of Nieuwkerke was even so plagued by hunger in 1556 that he robbed the parish church of its silver chalice, but not before eating the sacramental bread it contained. A weaver from the nearby village of Flêtre was also exiled for committing larcenies in the town of Bailleul.[136] At the other end of the spectrum, two men, one of whom a draper from Nieuwkerke, were convicted for abusing their powers as deputies to the judicial bailiff to extort money from their fellow parishioners.[137]

Within this context of worsening social conditions, the people who had access to extra food via the urban markets were first and foremost the richer drapers. It so happened that, in 1565, two merchant-drapers (*cooplieden*) of Nieuwkerke bought 38,000 litres of wheat in Antwerp to peddle in their home parish.[138] What with the rising food prices at this time, grain speculation by wealthy merchants was becoming a real problem. In fact, it was probably one of the main instigators of the social unrest that would spill over into revolt the following year.[139] This does not automatically mean that the two drapers of Nieuwkerke had such intentions in mind when they bought the wheat in Antwerp. It is slightly suspicious, however, that neither one of them reported

---

133 The earliest industrial source after 1566 is of the year 1585. Its contents imply that there had hardly been activity in the interim: RDHDF-2, III, pp. 212-13. On the destruction of the cloth hall, see: W. Verhelst, *West-Nieuwkerke. Beschrijving en geschiedenis* (Bruges, 1877), p. 11.

134 Decavele, *De dageraad van de reformatie*, II, pp. 556-66.

135 See, in general: Erich Kuttner and J. M. Romein, *Het Hongerjaar 1566* (Amsterdam: Amsterdamsche boek- en courantmaatschappij, 1949).

136 ADN, B 5688, fols 40^r, 19^r (1556-57).

137 ADN, B 5692, fol. 27^v (1568-69).

138 'Dat alsulcke vierhondert tachtentich veertelen terwen als zy alhier gecocht hebben ende in meyningen zyn te voeren naer Nieukercke voers., dat alle de selve terwe binnen des v.s. prochie van Nieukercke ende daeromtrent uytvercocht ende gepennenckweert sal worden': CAA, Certificatieboeken 24 (1565), fol. 366.

139 Kuttner and Romein, pp. 228-38.

back within two months after they had made their purchase in the city, which they should have done as per the recent royal placard.[140] They were therefore in a position to behave very much like the 'market elites' characteristic of the end-cycle in Van Bavel's model: these drapers could potentially enrich themselves at the expense of ordinary people, whose collective efforts in industry and trade had advanced the primacy of the market but who had thereby concomitantly advanced their own market-dependence. At this juncture, the development of Nieuwkerke's cloth industry fits the model quite well. After all, the cloth centre's sixteenth-century expansion was buttressed by workers without (strong) ties to the land, who consequently relied on trading their labour via the market. A small elite of employers could well have been able to exploit these people's productive efforts for their own betterment, and it is far from inconceivable that this caused their economy to stagnate or decline in the end.[141]

Some pronounced differences do catch the eye, however. Perhaps most importantly, the elite in this case was only an 'economic' elite. Around the time that Nieuwkerke's output began a downturn (*c.* 1550), the wardens of the cloth industry were apparently not in cahoots with the wealthy drapers who sought out private trading opportunities in Antwerp and Bergen op Zoom. Quite the contrary: they openly opposed the 'market elitism' of these drapers. Furthermore, one cannot really hold the actions of this small group of drapers responsible for the 'institutional sclerosis' that would underly the eventual stagnation of Nieuwkerke's textile economy (the idea being that this blocked the formation of new, more efficient institutions). Strictly speaking, if we apply Van Bavel's theory to Nieuwkerke's textile industry and trade, the market elite would actually consist of people within the industry who attempted to *maintain* the collective, which is to say: the wardens and 'common drapers'. They were the ones who tried to inhibit market conditions from running their course, after all. The wardens also acted as the corporation's gatekeepers, among other things through monitoring the drapers' marks. And so, the small group of rich entrepreneurs who sought individual betterment cannot be held wholly responsible for Nieuwkerke's economic stagnation. But their actions did add to the breaking down of communal sentiments, and, by extension, they harmed the social cohesion that had existed within the higher ranks of the industry for some fifty years. Perhaps it would be more accurate to say that, after 1550, Nieuwkerke fell victim to a deadly cocktail of rising social inequality, growing religious antagonism, and the breaking up of collective action in the cloth industry. These elements were all interlinked, forming a vicious triangle that would have engendered stagnation to the cloth trade in any case but wherein the military pressure acted as a final catalyst.

---

140 This was the reason why the contract was included among Antwerp's 'certified transactions' ('ende dat sy daer aff selven bringhen behoorlicke certificatie binnen twee maenden naercommende, achtervolghende den voers. placate'): CAA, Certificatieboeken 24 (1565), fol. 366^{v}.

141 Van Bavel, *The Invisible Hand*, pp. 256-59, 18-24.

Conclusion

Early in 2017, the economic historian Peer Vries wrote an in-depth review essay of Bas van Bavel's book *The Invisible Hand? How Market Economies have Emerged and Declined Since AD 500* (2016). A central claim of Vries's essay is that Van Bavel 'does not show *what* exactly causes inequality, *how* inequality causes decline, and how important it is compared with other causes'.[142] I will not allege that the present chapter sufficiently answers these questions; certainly not on the encompassing scope of Van Bavel's study or on the general level that Vries envisioned. Yet, by peeling apart the case study of Nieuwkerke's textile industry between 1300 and 1600, this chapter nevertheless contributes to this debate, as well as to the more general discussion on what drives long-term economic developments.

Born amidst the rubble of its crumbling predecessor, the urban woollen industry of Ypres, Nieuwkerke's rural cloth industry initially rose to prominence through 'leftovers' of economic capital, human capital, and social capital from the anterior period, when the village had still primarily functioned as a cheap labour pool for the dominant merchants and industrial entrepreneurs of the city. Over the next two centuries, the fabrics of this rural production centre gained a certain reputation on the international cloth market. But it was not until its cloth entrepreneurs were able to wrest themselves free of the formal restrictions imposed by the city of Ypres that, from around the year 1500, Nieuwkerke grew into one of the foremost centres of woollen cloth production in all of Flanders. Ironically, the village's cloth entrepreneurs may have achieved this feat precisely because Ypres' bullying forced them to form a united front. And so, it is not entirely surprising to find that, when the cloth industry gradually fell into decline around the middle of the sixteenth century, this coincided with factional strife and a faltering of internal cohesion within the village's drapery corporation. In keeping with the framework of Van Bavel, the disputes that broke out were primarily related to a sense of rising inequality within the corporate ranks.

But perhaps the chief point of this chapter is that inequality in itself does not cause decline, which relates to the second question posed by Vries. In Ypres, it was probably the *perception* of rising inequality which precipitated a process of collective (political) action, which resulted in institutional protection of a disadvantaged group of poor cloth entrepreneurs and artisans. In a somewhat paradoxical reversal of Van Bavel's thesis, it may have been this extra-economic insulation through collective action which caused the industry's decline and disappearance, because wage-privileges obstructed the operation of the market for labour. As a consequence, the dominant merchants and industrial entrepreneurs in the city of Ypres – the employers, in other words – reoriented towards a luxury industry that required fewer labour-inputs. And so, they drove out a large number of former cloth workers, who suddenly saw their jobs evaporate. In a similar

142 Peer Vries, 'Inevitable Decline? A Review of Bas van Bavel, *The Invisible Hand? How Market Economies Have Emerged and Declined since AD 500* (Oxford: Oxford University Press, 2016)', *International Review of Social History*, 62 (2017), 131-47 (p. 145).

vein, in Nieuwkerke, the increased social polarization after 1550 stimulated the local woollen industry's decline. But this was mainly because polarization had a detrimental effect on internal cohesion, which was necessary for the smooth operation of the village's particular form of industrial organization. That system also chiefly revolved around the *perception* of equal opportunities, and a united corporate community. Thus, in a seeming reversal of what had happened in Ypres two centuries previously, the collective action of Nieuwkerke's cloth entrepreneurs was conducive to the expansion of their industry – despite the fact that the drapers were a markedly differentiated occupational group in terms of production output, as demonstrated for the year 1564-65.

Of course, the two contexts were quite different: as opposed to what happened in Ypres from the fourteenth century onwards, Nieuwkerke never showed any sign of craft guilds. Instead, the village only developed a sort of homegrown mercantile-*cum*-industrial corporation, namely the drapery. This corporation sooner resembled a 'proto-guild' of the type that city elites had used to dominate urban textile industries prior to the late thirteenth century, rather than a craft guild.[143] Throughout the fourteenth, fifteenth and sixteenth centuries, the artisans of Nieuwkerke were largely subjected to the authority of the cloth entrepreneurs. Presumably, it was partly the rhetoric of communal solidarity and the Common Good which kept them in check. In the same way, this ideology acted as a kind of social mortar between drapers of different levels of wealth. Still, Nieuwkerke's collective action should not be dismissed as empty rhetoric. Together, the villagers effectively dealt with the threat of Ypres by attracting a powerful lord as an external shield in 1503. This required the creation of some kind of common fund to pay off the enormous rent resting on their seigneurie. Around the same time, the village entrepreneurs began to adopt a collective approach to marketing cloth, renting premises in the market towns of Bergen op Zoom and Antwerp for the benefit of all the drapers of the village. Meanwhile, the wardens began to guard more strenuously over the uniformity of Nieuwkerke's fabrics, while the individual marks and public inquests (*waerheden*) boosted individual accountability and a sense of collective responsibility. And so, collective action was a key variable in bringing about Nieuwkerke's golden age of 1500-50. After all, this period was 'book-ended' before and after by phases when the coordination of common interests was unsuccessful. In other words, during these periods of industrial downturn, the key missing element was collective action.

This still leaves the question how important inequality was, compared to other causes of economic decline. Of course, the contingent element of war was arguably more damaging still.[144] Consider that, in Nieuwkerke, it was the

143 Peter Stabel, 'Labour Time, Guild time? Working Hours in the Cloth Industry of Medieval Flanders and Artois (Thirteenth-Fourteenth Centuries)', *TSEG – The Low Countries Journal of Social and Economic History*, 11 (2014), 27-54 (pp. 31-32).

144 Vries also mentions this as an often-hailed variable in studies of economic decline: Vries, p. 146. Compare: Walter Scheidel, *The Great Leveler: Violence and the History of Inequality from the Stone Age to the Twenty-First Century* (Princeton: Princeton University Press, 2018), wherein the author argues just the opposite: that warfare has historically created more equal opportunities within societies.

religious conflict later known as the Dutch Revolt which had a particularly adverse influence after 1550. Similarly, in thirteenth-century Ypres, the problems with the cloth industry began after rising political conflicts had precipitated a crisis over English wool, and incessant warfare caused the decline of the Champagne fairs.[145] That said, the religiously charged military conflict that hit sixteenth-century Nieuwkerke and its neighbours, was connected to rising socio-economic inequality. But the polarization within the village's drapery corporation was largely caused by the increasing *perception* of this inequality. And this perception of unequal opportunity was connected to another external variable: a worsening position in the international marketplace. The internal equilibrium of the industry may not have been distorted all that much, but, as overall prosperity took a turn for the worse, the poorer entrepreneurs were brought closer to the bottom than the rich. Thus, if the case of Nieuwkerke suggests one thing, it is that these different elements – internal and external – were interconnected. Now. it would be hard, and slightly subjective, to argue which one was more important than the others. Chronologically speaking, however, the inequality probably predated the worsening market conditions, and the latter principally served to illuminate and exacerbate the former, pre-existing condition, which only then led to the onset of political conflicts that disrupted the local economy. And so, the unequal economic opportunities were always lying in wait as a *casus belli* for social and political turmoil, ready to topple the textile economy as and when enough ordinary people were no longer able to support themselves financially.

145 Wim Blockmans, *Metropolen aan de Noordzee: de geschiedenis van Nederland, 1100-1560* (Amsterdam: Bert Bakker, 2012), pp. 205-07.

Conclusion

Around the year 1300, European cloth entrepreneurs began a process of what we might call 'medieval offshoring': they outsourced cloth manufacturing to the countryfolk that lived in the rural hinterlands of the cities they inhabited. Demographic pressure and subdivision of landholdings had created a large labour reserve among these people in the countryside. And they accepted lower payment because they were not wholly dependent upon wages for their subsistence. These late medieval developments resemble 21st-century offshoring, in the sense that modern companies based in the Western world also turn to foreign regions for their cheaper labour, their less-rigid work regulations, and often for their tax exemptions. As we have seen, however, in the case of the late medieval West-Quarter, the tail began to wag the dog at some point. In the course of the fourteenth and fifteenth centuries, cloth entrepreneurs and artisans based in this rural production zone gained control over the industrial process. What is more, these rural drapers started to outstrip their urban competitors, particularly in the lower market segments where the countryside's cheap labour costs were a critical factor. As a result, urban cloth artisans in the city of Ypres had to plead with their governments – that is, their civic magistrates but also the count of Flanders – to guard over the city's industrial interests. Over the next 120 years or so, the counts of Flanders would concede these desired legal privileges on several occasions, yet to no lasting avail. In doing so, the counts employed a rhetoric based around the distinction between the economic tasks of towns (industry and trade) and countryside (tilling the soil). And so, the urban and the rural were presented as two opposing economic zones. Writing some five centuries later, the Belgian historian Henri Pirenne made a similar distinction. He saw a dividing line between the economically lethargic protectionism of the craft corporations in the Flemish cities, and the potential of unregulated rural industries for capitalist, 'modern' enterprise. And while Pirenne's views on this economic division are no longer generally accepted in the historiography, the town-country divide lingers as a fault line between the sub-disciplines of rural and urban history.

The present book makes clear that this division should be revised even further. During the fourteenth, fifteenth, and sixteenth centuries, the rural cloth centres in the West-Quarter of Flanders, most notably in the village of Nieuwkerke, were gradually woven into the urban fabric of the Low Countries. This process of growing urbanity was caused by a number of factors. All of these factors were tied to the expansion of the regional cloth industry. First of all, as we saw in Chapter 1, the booming textile economy raised the population levels of these villages; Nieuwkerke's even exceeded that of many Flemish towns in the mid-sixteenth century. While not a decisive criterion to be labelled 'urban', the village's demographic growth, from circa 1000 residents in 1469 to around 5000 inhabitants around the middle of the sixteenth century, definitely put Nieuwkerke on the map as a vital member of the urban network in the Low Countries. In this regard, the village followed a trajectory similar to that of other industrial villages and small towns in Flanders; for example, those of the light drapery centre of Hondschoote and of the tapestry town of Oudenaarde.[1]

Second, as shown in Chapter 4, the West-Quarter cloth villages came to resemble their sisters in the urban network more and more on a cultural level as well. The establishment of Chambers of Rhetoric and of archery guilds, the growing education of the rural inhabitants, as well as the spread of humanistic and evangelical beliefs, were all signs of a flourishing urban culture. The encounters with other towns and cities made this acculturation a two-way street. The Rhetoricians of Nieuwkerke attended urban literary contests in Bruges and Ghent, for example, but their fellows in the small town of Wervik also came to Nieuwkerke for the same purpose. One of the main reasons for this integration of town and country was the urban trade connections of the rural merchant-drapers, which we examined in Chapter 3. Their attendance of the festive market fairs, and their informal networks with fellow traders dissolved possible barriers between town dwellers and countryfolk. And so, the drapers of Nieuwkerke, along with those of villages like Dranouter and Kemmel, were essentially cut from the same cloth as their counterparts in the Netherlandish cities. After all, as we saw in Chapter 5, these ostensibly rural entrepreneurs not only had the same profession as their urban counterparts, but they also developed a similar ideology based around the 'Common Good'.

Third, this urbanity manifested itself in the villagers' urban aspirations for their place of residence, as discussed in Chapter 4. The local cloth hall of Nieuwkerke, for one thing, may have functioned much like a town hall. It was certainly one the most imposing architectural structures in the village. Vested with the chevrons (*kepers*) of Nieuwkerke's coat-of-arms, which also adorned the leaden hallmarks attached to the village's woollens, this building occupied a central place in the community. For another thing, the more opulent villagers tried to instate a weekly market, primarily for trading agricultural produce but also for certain manufactured goods. This may be interpreted as an attempt to cut out a commercial function for Nieuwkerke, in direct competition with the towns of the region (primarily the castellany capital of Bailleul). Following a complaint by this urban competition, Nieuwkerke's weekly market was officially banned by the Council of Flanders in 1465. Yet the villagers' attempts to institute it, is a sure sign of their urban ambitions.

Fourth, the villagers of the West-Quarter showed a remarkable mobility between town and countryside. We saw in Chapter 4 that many rural cloth entrepreneurs fostered ties with nearby cities such as Ypres: some of them had family living there, while many others acquired the statute of external citizen or 'outburgher' (*buitenpoorter*). Coupled with their far-reaching commercial networks, which

1 Peter Stabel, 'Demography and Hierarchy: The Small Towns and the Urban Network in Sixteenth-Century Flanders', in *Small Towns in Early Modern Europe*, ed. by Peter Clark (Cambridge: Cambridge University Press, 1995), pp. 206-28 (pp. 214-15).

we established in Chapter 3, this meant that the drapers, in particular, trespassed upon the physical and conceptual borders of the late medieval town with such frequency that the lines between the urban and the rural were blurred. In effect, the outburghers were the ultimate personification of these dissolving boundaries. Not only were they required to be physically present in town from time to time, but their town governments also had juridical claims over their person. And vice versa: the outburghers could request justice from the urban law court. This calls into question whether it is even useful to uphold the distinction between town dwellers and countryfolk in the pre-industrial county of Flanders.

Lastly, the 'village of Nieuwkerke' was simply not a predominantly agricultural settlement. The same applied to cloth centres like Dranouter and Kemmel, albeit to a lesser degree. Farming continued to be an important occupation in these places, of course, but it was largely split off from industry and trade. And so, these villages were not really marked by a 'dual economy', as has been argued for other areas in the Low Countries, where the greater part of the population still owned a small parcel of land in the early twentieth century but supplemented their incomes through additional waged labour.[2] If anything, the reverse happened: manufacture became the primary, agriculture the secondary, economic activity. What occurred in the premodern West-Quarter of Flanders, particularly in the fifteenth and sixteenth centuries, does not comfortably fit the label 'proto-industry' either. As discussed in Chapter 1, the connection between the majority of local artisans and the agrarian economy is tenuous at best. Certainly, demographic pressure and the increasing subdivision of farmland in the later thirteenth century had played its part in the reorientation towards textile manufacture. The regional landholding structure around 1570 was also characterized by a distinct pattern of smallholding. In fact, land plots were more fragmented here than they were in the region known in the scholarship as 'Interior Flanders'. Erik Thoen has shown that most peasant families of the latter region combined subsistence-farming with (proto-industrial) by-employment, most often in linen production.[3] In the West-Quarter, the predominance of holdings that were too small for subsistence-farming similarly resulted in labour surpluses as well. And theoretically, these landless, or land-poor, people could be put to use in the village draperies. However, as shown in Chapter 1, the manufacture of the mid-priced fabrics of Nieuwkerke, Dranouter, Eécke, Nieppe, Kemmel, and Wulvergem required a high level of skill from the workers. The width of the cloths (*c.* 3 metres) also called for at least two people to occupy each loom. This not only required a certain organizational sophistication, but it was furthermore

2 Daniel Curtis, 'A North Sea Coastal Area under Pressure of Land Consolidation: Transition from a Farmer's Republic to an Unequal Polder Society in the Oldambt of Groningen, 1700-1900', in *Coping with Crisis: The Resilience and Vulnerability of Pre-Industrial Settlements*, ed. by Daniel Curtis (Burlington: Ashgate, 2014), pp. 181-222 (p. 184).

3 Erik Thoen, 'A "Commercial Survival Economy" in Evolution: The Flemish Countryside and the Transition to Capitalism (Middle Ages – 19th century)', in *Peasants into Farmers: The Transformation of Rural Economy and Society in the Low Countries (Middle Ages – 19th century) in light of the Brenner Debate*, ed. by Peter Hoppenbrouwers and Jan Luiten van Zanden (Turnhout: Brepols, 2001), pp. 102-57 (pp. 124-25).

unlikely that peasant families could do without all those working hands at once; they would have needed them on the farm. Even more so, because the monthly production rhythms that we were able to reconstruct for the accounting years of 1516-17 and 1564-65 reveal that the high seasons for cloth manufacture coincided with periods when the farm needed all the help it could get. And, inversely, the idle agricultural winter season was mirrored in a slump in monthly cloth outputs. In other words, the opportunity costs to engage in part-time weaving would have been too high for the majority of the farming population.

Then again, as inferred in Chapter 2, the situation may have been entirely different for what was the most time-consuming production stage of all: namely, wool preparation. Particularly the spinning of yarn, but also combing and carding, and other preparatory tasks of all kinds, required vast inputs of labour. And it is conceivable that this occupation was carried out as a form of by-employment by members of local peasant families with a smallholding. Spinning not only required a lower level of skill than weaving, but it was also a solo activity; and one that could be carried out in between other work, at that. In all likelihood, this wool preparing labour force predominantly consisted of women. A crucial common denominator between the West-Quarter draperies was their virtual absence of formal rules concerning these preparatory tasks of woollen production. With a few exceptions, the village cloth entrepreneurs were free to use any type of wool they pleased, so long as the finished products passed the inspection of the wardens. This wiggle room extended to how the spinsters and other wool workers processed the raw fleeces into yarn that was ready to be woven into fabric. From that point onwards, the production process was monitored relatively intensively, although there was still much room for improvisation compared to urban centres like Ypres, or even relative newcomers such as the small town of Armentières.

We can be fairly sure, therefore, that the use of female labour power in wool preparation was a fundamental aspect of the economic success of the West-Quarter draperies. Far less clear is to what extent the wool preparation stages were centralized and market-oriented. The problem here is the fragmented source material. In this case, this scarcity is not specific to the West-Quarter, however, as the historic records are often silent on the initial stages of textile production. Arguably, this meagre evidence implies that these tasks were usually part of the 'informal branch' of the economy. And yet there are examples from elsewhere in Flanders, of urban cloth entrepreneurs who organized the sale of yarn produced by rural spinsters from a wide radius through a central 'yarn market'; in other words: a decentralized yet market-driven form of (proto-industrial) labour organization, with merchant-capitalist overtones at the commercial level. Sadly, this will have to remain a mysterious aspect of the West-Quarter's industrial organization. On the one hand, there is practically no evidence of such commercialization as regards the preparatory stages of cloth production. On the other hand, we do have some evidence of centralized wool warehouses, or 'carding yards', owned by entrepreneurs who bought large shipments of raw fleeces from Spanish merchants (and who we can tentatively connect to the sale of yarns in the city of Ypres as well). And so, it is almost certain that the by-employment of local women in the preparatory stages of cloth production was a key factor in the region's competitiveness, but we know next to nothing about how labour was organized, how commercialized these activities were, nor how dependent these women were on wages to make a living.

The conclusion is that the West-Quarter draperies had some traits of proto-industrialization; but only in the initial production stages, and primarily in terms of the female labour force (which is interesting in its own right, but the lack of detailed records forestalls further investigation at this point). For the remaining craft phases, however, it appears that certainly Nieuwkerke, and probably other villages as well, had already moved beyond proto-industry around the middle of the fifteenth century. Circumstantial evidence suggests that entire families were devoted to manufacturing cloth.[4] To be sure, there may have been another kind of connection between agriculture and the textile industries of this region. We saw in Chapter 1, for example, that some of the drapers of Nieuwkerke and Dranouter also sold livestock. These drapers may have converted their agricultural gains into valuable capital to be used in the cloth industry – a phenomenon that is reported for late medieval English regions as well.[5] Overall, though, the prevailing landholding pattern disproves that this was (still) a common strategy around the middle of the sixteenth century, when the village draperies were at their peak. Also, as the sales of meat by drapers of Nieuwkerke in the 1540s mainly involved sheep, it is altogether more likely that they held a small flock for their fleeces, probably to supplement the higher-grade wool they had to import from Spain. This would have been a clever way to gain control over the supply of raw materials. If so, this is a rare example of vertical integration that has left no explicit signs of resistance in the extant sources – which do reveal forceful protests against the combination of different phases of the cloth production process. Of course, the industrial organization of these craft stages had tenets that some might call proto-industrial, because it appears that decentralized manufacture in workers' own homes predominated. Yet, all in all, I would argue that the woollen cloth industry in the West-Quarter shared more similarities with urban craft production than with rural proto-industry.

The critical insight this study offers into what drove the manufacturing economy of pre-industrial Europe is that the motor of commercialization and capitalist relations of production was alternately located in the urban and rural spheres. Or, more accurately, this was a back and forth which mainly consisted of *negative* constraints. These were largely extra-economic forces. It should be further emphasized that, not only were these urban and rural spheres closely intertwined, but neither one of them was a homogenous block. These entangled zones were

4 Kristof Papin and Arnold Preneel, '*Ne peuis adveniat*: sociale politiek en bevolkingsmigraties in de stad Ieper (1571-1575)', *Westhoek. Tijdschrift voor Geschiedenis & Familiekunde in de Vlaamse & Franse Westhoek*, 15 (1999), 4-52 (pp. 13-14).

5 Michael Zell, *Industry in the Countryside: Wealden Society in the Sixteenth Century* (Cambridge: Cambridge University Press, 2004), pp. 190-93, 176-78.

continuously offset by internal and external pressures that simultaneously boosted and impeded their economic expansion. Thus, the case of the West-Quarter draperies belies the old modernization paradigm of Henri Pirenne; at least, insofar as his thesis was that the rural draperies followed a 'clear course' or linear trajectory. Wherein Pirenne was right, is that the transfer of production stages to the countryside around 1300, at the initiative of urban entrepreneurs, initially resulted in more capitalist relations of production. These urban employers suddenly faced next to no regulations about which kinds of wool had to go into their fabrics. They also encountered a rural workforce whose wages were determined by a 'freer' labour market, because, in contrast to the guildsmen of the cities, these rural artisans were unincorporated and non-politicized. This meant that the superior economic bargaining position of the entrepreneurs was not negated by political forces. However, the urban artisans perceived this medieval version of offshoring as disruptive to their own livelihoods. And, as the political influence of their craft corporations reached beyond the city walls, they were able to acquire formal privileges from the count of Flanders that forbade rival export-oriented woollen production in the countryside. Thus, while the seeds for a capitalist textile economy were planted by urban drapers like those of Ypres, these were subsequently uprooted by another faction within urban society.

This urban impediment was counterbalanced by an immediate rural response, however. As the city government of Ypres came down on manufacturing in the countryside, drapers from the West-Quarter villages took over the position of their urban predecessors. At first, these rural entrepreneurs still operated within a sector characterized by virtually no regulations. Even Nieuwkerke's earliest cloth charter of 1358 preserved an economic environment wherein drapers were free to improvise, and rural handicraft workers had to trade their labour via the market. But as the draperies of the West-Quarter got more and more successful from the mid-fifteenth century onwards, their regulations also became increasingly protectionist. In Nieuwkerke, a local faction of rural drapers pleaded with the regional authorities for a stricter enforcement of the village's bylaws, and for additional rules to ensure a more level playing field between the entrepreneurs. These new bylaws were expressly designed to benefit the less well-to-do drapers and the craftsmen, and they were accepted in 1462. This essentially led to a less market-driven and less capitalist industry, primarily because the redacted charter prevented the formation of larger enterprises which combined different production stages. It also forbade the cloth entrepreneurs from soliciting work from outside the local parish, similar to how Ypres' government had opposed 'offshoring' to the countryside. And yet, while these constraints on capitalist relations imposed from within the rural production zone seem to echo what happened in Ypres less than a century before, the outcome was quite different. In fact, as we have seen in Chapter 5, the 'golden age' of cloth production in Nieuwkerke began right around this period.

Once again, this economic upsurge was caused by a to and fro of rural and urban forces. But at this point, the lines between the two categories became truly blurred. As we have seen, there were several external factors that underpinned Nieuwkerke's industrial efflorescence between around 1500 and 1550. Three components, in particular, were key: first, a successful negation of the adverse pressures exerted by the city government of Ypres. In this case, it was a political force that cancelled out another political force: the village drapers were able to counterbalance the city's pressure by attracting a crucial ally in the form of a powerful new lord. And Nieuwkerke is not an isolated example of this kind of seigneurial barrier, which has been demonstrated for various areas in the premodern Low Countries. Second, a seemingly 'rural' factor that contributed to the success of the village industry was a new-found collective spirit among the local entrepreneurs, who increasingly began to act as a corporation. But this collective action was buttressed by the ideology of the Common Good, which is often associated with urban society, especially in the Low Countries. And it was accompanied by the foundation of other kinds of corporate bodies that are deemed typical of the urban sphere as well (Chambers of Rhetoric, archery guilds). Of course, Nieuwkerke's drapery corporation was further held together by formal rules and institutions which ensured a certain inclusivity and accountability among its members. One example of this was the organization of public inquests (*waerheden*). Third, and closely related to the second factor, the rural textile corporation was able to capitalize on the various commercial platforms that were available to them in the cities of the Low Countries. Despite the city's official bans on rural cloth production, the outburgher-drapers from the West-Quarter had ready access to Ypres' commercial infrastructure. Moreover, the cloth corporation collectively rented premises in the Brabantine cities of Antwerp and Bergen op Zoom. This enabled all the drapers to sell their products on the international market via an appointed agent. The drapers used other commercial channels and institutions as well, such as town-based brokers, and the open platforms of trade that were the Netherlandish fairs.

And so, the evolution of the hybrid rural-urban textile industries in this part of the Low Countries supports the idea that town and countryside were inextricably linked, and largely interdependent, in the pre-industrial European economy. What the case study uniquely shows is just how interwoven these spheres were, to the point that town and country became virtually indistinguishable. At the same time, one could argue that the 'embryonic capitalism' that George Espinas signalled in the case of the thirteenth-century Flemish draper Jehan Boinebroke, did not outgrow its adolescence in the rural West-Quarter.[6] Indeed, in Nieuwkerke, the glorious first half of the sixteenth century occurred during what was arguably the industry's least capitalist period. At the time, the village's cloth charters blocked individual drapers from expanding their enterprises, while the corporation enforced uniform prices and products, and its regulations were becoming altogether tighter. But then, even in the commercial metropolis that was sixteenth-century Antwerp, examples of capitalist entrepreneurship were still aberrations.[7] In his study about Hondschoote, moreover, Émile Coornaert

6 '*Un embryon de capitalisme*': Georges Espinas, *Les origines du capitalisme*, 2 vols (Lille: Raoust, 1933-49), I, *Sire Jehan Boinebroke: patricien et drapier douasien* (1933), p. 216.

7 Hugo Soly, 'De brouwerijenonderneming van Gilbert van Schoonbeke (1552-1562)', *Belgisch Tijdschrift voor Filologie en Geschiedenis*, 40 (1968), 339-92, 1166-1204 (pp. 1203-04).

posited that true signs of capitalism in this textile centre were only apparent for a brief spell between the late sixteenth and early seventeenth centuries. He based this conclusion on the fact that the local merchant-drapers made no productive reinvestments in their enterprises, investing instead in safer options, such as land, real estate, and rents.[8] Then again, other historians have nuanced the idea that capitalist entrepreneurship in this period should be judged in terms of its long-term endurance, especially in the volatile cloth industries.[9]

But perhaps we should reconsider whether capitalist relations of production and unbridled commercialization were optimal goals within the context of the pre-industrial economy, before we can consider if they were realistically attainable. After all, if this book has shown us one thing, it is that economic forces do not exist in a social and political vacuum. Nor are they ahistorical. While many historians have tried to pinpoint a pivotal period when 'capitalism' or 'the modern market economy' first arose, the findings of this study raise the question whether such a perspective is not overly teleological. It may limit us from understanding the true complexity of past societies and their economies. Or, as Martha Howell has put it, the framework that has long dominated the discussion on pre-industrial economic development 'ineluctably gives us a naturalized model of the modern economy with "laws" and a logic so immutable that its only history can be the story of its discovery'.[10] Perhaps this is not the best way forward.

Indeed, the example of the textile economy of the pre-industrial West-Quarter suggests that the contemporary idea that commercial welfare should serve the local community may have outweighed 'economic efficiency' from a present-day perspective. By that same token, there was an apparent resentment of people that sought to carve out larger pieces of the pie for themselves. In Nieuwkerke, this is clear from the corporation's actions to suppress the renting of private shops in the city of Antwerp towards the middle of the sixteenth century. While this restriction was framed as protecting the Common Good, it also has a whiff of trying to forestall individual betterment as such. One may even discern a condescending undertone in the corporation's records on this point, as if there were something indecent about self-interest.[11] Under these circumstances, a kind of 'corporate merchant capitalism' may have been the most efficient economic system within reach. And just because this system only lasted for about a century, and occurred well before the advent of factory industrialization, does not mean it has nothing valuable to tell us about the ways in which humans interact with each other in their continuous search for economic survival.

8 Émile Coornaert, *Un centre industriel d'autrefois: la draperie-sayetterie d'Hondschoote (XIVᵉ-XVIIIᵉ siècles)* (Paris: Presses universitaires de France, 1930), pp. 364-66.

9 Christine Jackson, 'Boom-Time Freaks or Heroic Industrial Pioneers? Clothing Entrepreneurs in Sixteenth- and Early Seventeenth-Century Berkshire', *Textile History*, 39 (2008), 145-71 (pp. 163-64).

10 Martha Howell, *Commerce before Capitalism in Europe, 1300-1600* (New York: Cambridge University Press, 2010), p. 299.

11 'Prendre par louaige et estre es dictes villes en diverses et distinctes maisons, ouvroirs et boutticques indiferement, la ou bon leur semble, [...] de sorte que sur la vente des dicts draps [...] se feroyent icelles ventes tart et tempre, aussy bien sur jours solemnels et festes que autres.': RDHDF-2, III, pp. 149-50.

Sources and bibliography

1. Manuscript sources

Archives Départementales du Nord, Lille (ADN)

B: B 1333 (formerly B 18586), 3898/7, 3898/11a, 4821, 5669, 5688, 5692, 7045, 7050, 18118, 19014.
J: 431/5, 766.

Bishopric's Archives, Bruges (Bisschoppelijk Archief Brugge; BAB)

Klooster Voormezele: C 167/4.

City Archives, Antwerp (Stadsarchief Antwerpen / Felixarchief; CAA)

Certificatieboeken: 12, 19, 20, 24.
Halle van Nieuwkerke: Documenten 4675.

City Archives, Bruges (Stadsarchief Brugge; CAB)

Procuraties: years 1538-39, 1539-40.
Reeks 216, Stadsrekeningen, 1474-75, 1476-77, 1482-83, 1483-84.
Reeks 304, Archief van het Spaanse Consulaat: Juan Castro de Muxica, Journaal (*libros diarios*), 1535-1538; Grootboek, 1534-1535.
Reeks 305, Wouter Ameyde: Journaal B.

City Archives, Bergen op Zoom (Stadsarchief Bergen op Zoom; CABZ)

Archief van de stadssecretarie van Bergen op Zoom (stadsarchief vóór 1810):
Protocol van rentebrieven en recognities, 1511-12.
Stadsrekeningen: 1527-28, 1547-48, 1552-53.

City Archives Ypres (Stadsarchief Ieper; CAY)

Kasselrijarchief: Eerste Reeks, 2655, 2665; Tiende Reeks, 1424.

General State Archives, Brussels (Algemeen Rijksarchief / Archives Générales du Royaume; GSAB)

Chamber of Accounts (Rekenkamer / Chambre des Comptes; CA)
Acquits de Lille: 192-93, 809-14bis.
Acquits en portefeuilles: 802-14, 1367.
Audiëntie van de Rekenkamer 618/20, 618/30, 618/31-32, 618/34.
Chamber of Accounts (Rekenkamer/Chambre des Comptes): 100, 23482-85, 44562/1-16, 44562/25, 44562/29.
Dozen van de Rekenkamer: 261.
Inventaire des comptes en rouleaux : Oudeneem 150-51.
Oorkonden van Vlaanderen: 776.
Rekeningen Zaal Ieper: years 1445-58

National Archives, Paris (Archives Nationales, Paris; NAP)

Papiers de comte d'Egmont-Pignatelli, émigré: T 159/05.

Royal Library, Brussels (Koninklijke Bibliotheek Brussel / Bibliothèque Royale de Belgique; RLB)

Fonds Merghelynck: M 18, M 23.

State Archives, Bruges (Rijksarchief Brugge; SAB)

Aanwinsten: 504, 3640, 3682, 4186.
Gemeentearchief Nieuwkerke: 8, 27.
Proosdij van Sint-Donaas: 1658.

State Archives, Ghent (Rijksarchief Gent; SAG)

Raad van Vlaanderen, Enkwesten: 3756, 8606.
Schenking de Breyne: 106.

2. Printed sources

Anonymous, *De Gentse Spelen van 1539*, ed. by B. H. Erné and L. M. van Dis, 2 vols (The Hague: Martinus Nijhoff, 1982).

Anonymous, *Handel Buch, darin angezeigt wird, welcher Gestalt inn den den fürnembsten Hendelstetten Europa, allerley Wahren anfencklich kaufft, dieselvig wider mit nutz verkaufft, wie die Wechsel gemacht, ßfund, Ellen, unnd Muntz uberal verglichen, und zu welcher Zeit die Merckten gewonlich gehalten werden* (Nuremberg, 1558).

Beun, Johan (ed. and trans.), *De costume van de stad Mesen, 1547: originele tekst met overzetting in het modern Nederlands* (Ypres, 2004).

Blaeu, Joan, *Novum Ac Magnum Theatrum Urbium Belgicae* (Amsterdam: Joan and Cornelis Blaeu, 1649).

Brown, Andrew and Small, Graeme (eds), *Court and Civic Society in the Burgundian Low Countries, c. 1420-1530* (Manchester: Manchester University Press, 2007).

Buylaert, Frederik, *Repertorium van de Vlaamse adel (ca. 1350-ca. 1500)* (Ghent: Academia Press, 2011).

Calendar of Letters, Despatches and State Papers Relating to the Negotiations between England and Spain Preserved in the Archives at Simancas and Elsewhere (London: Longman etc., 1862-1954).

Chaucer, Geoffrey, *The Canterbury Tales: A Retelling*, ed. and trans. by Peter Ackroyd (New York: Viking, 2009).

De Coussemaker, Ignace (ed.), *Documents inedits relatifs à la ville de Bailleul*, 3 vols (Lille: Quarré du coulombier, 1877-78).

Dauchy, Serge and others (eds), *Les arrets et jugés du Parlement de Paris sur appels flamands conservés dans les registres du Parlement*, 3 vols (Brussels: Ministère de la justice, 1966-2002).

Dehaisnes, Chrétien and Finot, Jules (eds), *Inventaire sommaire des archives départementales antérieures à 1790: Nord, Archives civiles, série B: Chambre des Comptes de Lille, art. 653 à 1560*, 8 vols (Lille: Danel, 1877-1906).

Delepierre, Octave-Joseph and Priem, Frédéric-Pierre (eds), *Précis analytique des documents, que renferme le dépot des archives de la Flandre-occidentale à Bruges*, 12 vols (Bruges, 1840-1858).

Deloney, Thomas, 'The Most Pleasant and Delectable Historie of Iohn Winchcombe, Otherwise Called Iacke of Newberie: And First of his Loue and Pleasant Life', in *The Works of Thomas Deloney*, ed. by Francis Mann (Oxford: Oxford Clarendon Press, 1912), pp. 1-68.

De Raadt, Jean Théodore (ed.), *Sceaux et armoriés des Pays-Bas et des pays avoisinants (Belgique-Royaume des Pays-Bas-Luxembourg-Allemagne-France): recueil historique et héraldique*, 4 vols (Brussels: Société belge de librairie, 1898-1901).

Derville, Alain (ed.), *Enquêtes fiscales de la Flandre wallonne, 1449-1549*, 3 vols (Lille: Commission historique du Nord, 1983-2003).

De Sagher, Émile, *Notice sur les archives communales d'Ypres et documents pour servir à l'histoire de Flandre du XIIIe au XVIe siècle* (Ypres: Callewaert-De Meulenaere, 1898).

De Sagher, Henri, and others (eds), *Recueil de documents relatifs à l'histoire de l'industrie drapière en Flandre. Deuxième partie: le sud-ouest de la Flandre depuis l'époque bourguignonne*, 3 vols (Brussels: Kiessling et Imbreghts, 1951-66).

De Smidt, Th. and others (eds), *Chronologische lijsten van de geëxtendeerde sententiën (dossiers) berustende in het archief van de Grote Raad van Mechelen*, 6 vols (Brussels: Koninklijke Commissie voor de Uitgave der Oude Wetten en Werordeningen van België, 1966-88).

Diegerick, Isidore (ed.), *Inventaire analytique & chronologique des chartes et documents appartenant aux archives de l'ancienne abbaye de Messines* (Bruges: De Zuttere, 1876).

Diegerick, Isidore (ed.), *Inventaire analytique et chronologique des chartes et documents appartenant aux archives de la ville d'Ypres*, 6 vols (Bruges, 1853-1868).

Donche, Pieter, 'De haardentelling van Westieperambacht, 1469', *Vlaamse Stam*, 24 (1988), 517-39.

Espinas, Georges and Pirenne, Henri (eds), *Recueil de documents relatifs à l'histoire de l'industrie drapière en Flandre: des origines à l'époque bourguignonne*, 4 vols (Brussels: Kiessling et Imbreghts, 1906-24).

Everaert, Cornelis, *Cornelis Everaert: Spelen*, ed. by Jacob Muller and Lodewijk Scharpé (Leiden: Brill, 1920).

Everaert, Cornelis, *De spelen van Cornelis Everaert*, ed. by Wim Hüsken, 2 vols (Hilversum: Verloren, 2005).

Gilliodts-Van Severen, Louis (ed.), *Cartulaire de l'ancien Grand Tonlieu de Bruges faisant suite au cartulaire de l'ancienne Estaple: recueil de documents concernant le commerce intérieur et maritime, les relations internationales et l'histoire économique de cette ville*, 2 vols (Bruges: Plancke, 1908-09).

Gilliodts-Van Severen, Louis (ed.), *Coutumes des pays et comté de Flandre. Quartier de Bruges: Coutumes des petites villes et seigneuries enclavées*, 6 vols (Brussels: Gobbaerts, 1890-93).

Grotefend, Hermann, *Zeitrechnung des deutschen Mittelalters und der Neuzeit*, 2 vols (Hannover: Hahn, 1891-98).

Jamees, Alfred, *Brugse poorters: opgetekend uit de stadsrekeningen*, 4 vols (Bruges: Flandria Nostra, 1974-80).

Lambin, Jean-Jacques, *Revue succincte de quelques comptes de la ville d'Ypres des 13e, 14e et 15e siècles* (Ypres, 1st half of the 19th century).

Master Fitzherbert, *The Book of Husbandry by Master Fitzherbert: Reprinted from the Edition of 1534*, ed. by Walter Skeat (London: Trübner & Co., Ludgate Hill, 1882).

Miraeus, Aubertus, *Opera diplomatica et historica, in quibus continentur chartæ fundationum ac donationum piarum, testamenta, privilegia, fœdera principum, & alia tum sacræ tum profanæ antiquitatis monumenta, à pontificibus, imperatoribus, regibus, principibusque Belgii edita*, 2 vols (Leuven: typis Ægidii Denique, 1723).

Munro, John, 'Prices and Wages in Brabant, 1400-1700', Excel-spreadsheet (based on data compiled by Herman Van der Wee), online on: www.economics.utoronto.ca/munro5/PricesandWages.htm.

Sanderus, Antonius, *Flandria illustrata, sive descriptio comitatus istius per totum terrarum orbem celeberrimi, III tomis absoluta*, 2 vols (Amsterdam: Joan and Cornelis Blaeu, 1641-1644).

Stabel, Peter and Vermeylen, Filips (eds), *Het fiscale vermogen in Brabant, Vlaanderen en in de heerlijkheid Mechelen: de Honderdste Penning van de hertog van Alva (1569-1572)* (Brussels: Koninklijke academie van België, Koninklijke commissie voor geschiedenis, 1997).

Van Bruaene, Anne-Laure, 'Repertorium van rederijkerskamers in de Zuidelijke Nederlanden en Luik, 1400-1650' (2004), online resource at: www.dbnl.org.

Vandendorpe, P. J., *Het handboek van P. J. Vandendorpe, pastoor van Nieuwkerke (1730-1806)*, ed. by Jozef Geldhof (Bruges: Genootschap voor Geschiedenis, 1974).

Van den Hane, Laureyns, *Wetten, costumen, keuren ende usantien van de Zale ende casselrye van Ipre* (Ghent: Petrus de Goesin, 1769).

Van de Putte, Ferdinand and Van de Casteele, Désiré (eds), *Cronica et cartularium Monasterii de Dunis*, (Bruges: Vandecasteele-Werbrouck, 1864).

van Dixmude, Olivier (?), *Merkwaerdige gebeurtenissen, vooral in Vlaenderen en Brabant, en ook aengrenzende landstreken, van 1377 tot 1443: letterlyk gevolgd naer het oorspronkelyk onuitgegeven en titelloos handschrift van Olivier van Dixmude*, ed. by Jean-Jacques Lambin (Ypres: Lambin, 1835).

Van Roey, J., *Antwerpse poortersboeken*, 8 vols (Antwerp: Stadsarchief, 1977).

Van Vaernewijck, Marcus, *De historie van Belgis diemen anders noemen mach: den spieghel der Nederlantscher oudtheyt* (Antwerp: H. Verdussen, 1619).

Verhulst, Adriaan and Gysseling, Maurits (eds), *Le compte général de 1187, connu sous le nom de "gros brief", et les institutions financières du comté de Flandre au XII*e *siècle* (Brussels Palais des Académies, 1962).

von Geldersen, Vicko, *Das Handlungsbuch Vickos von Geldersen*, ed. by Hans Nirrnheim (Hamburg: L. Voss, 1895).

von Slaski, Witold (ed.), *Danziger Handel im XV*e *Jahrhundert auf Grund eines im Danziger Stadtarchive befindlichen Handlungsbuches gheschildert* (Gdańsk: C.F. Beisel Nachf., 1905).

Wielant, Filips, *Tractaet van den leenrechten na de hoven van Vlaenderen, metgaders de diensten daertoe staende* (Antwerp, 1557).

3. Secondary literature

Acemoglu, Daron and Robinson, James, *Why Nations Fail: The Origins of Power, Prosperity, and Poverty* (New York: Crown Business, 2012).

Adriaenssen, Leo, 'De plaats van Oisterwijk in het Kempense lakenlandschap', *Textielhistorische Bijdragen*, 41 (2001), 27-48.

Alfani, Guido and Gourdon, Vincent, 'Entrepreneurs, Formalization of Social Ties, and Trust Building in Europe (Fourteenth to Twentieth Centuries)', *The Economic History Review*, 45 (2012), 1005-28.

Ammann, Hektor, 'Deutschland und die Tuchindustrie Nordwest-Europas im Mittelalter', *Hansische Geschichtsblätter*, 72 (1954), 1-63.

Ammanniti, Francesco, 'Francesco di Marco Datini's Wool Workshops', in *Francesco di Marco Datini: The Man, the Merchant*, ed. by Giampiero Nigro (Florence: Firenze University Press, 2010), pp. 489-514.

Arnade, Peter, Howell, Martha and Simmons, Walter, 'Fertile Spaces: The Productivity of Urban Space in Northern Europe', *The Journal of Interdisciplinary History*, 32 (2002), 515-48.

Aston, T.H. and Philpin, C.H.E. (eds), *The Brenner Debate: Agrarian Class Structure and Economic Development in Pre-Industrial Europe*, (Cambridge: Cambridge University Press, 1985).

Aubry, Martine, 'Les mortalités lilloises (1328-1369)', *Revue du Nord*, 65 (1983), 327-42.

Backhouse, Marcel, *Beeldenstorm en bosgeuzen in het Westkwartier (1566-1568): bijdrage tot de geschiedenis van de godsdiensttroebelen der Zuidelijke Nederlanden in de XVI*e *eeuw* (Kortrijk: Koninklijke Geschied- en Oudheidkundige Kring, 1971).

Backhouse, Marcel, 'De Vlaamse vluchtelingenkerk in Sandwich in 1563: twee manuscripten uit het British Museum', *Bulletin de la Commission Royale d'Histoire / Handelingen van de Koninklijke Commissie voor Geschiedenis*, 147 (1981), 75-113.

Baelde, Michel, 'Un conflit économique entre Lille et Roubaix, 1553', *Revue du Nord*, 66 (1984), 1071-74.

Bietenholz, Peter and Deutscher, Thomas, *Contemporaries of Erasmus: A Biographical Register of the Renaissance and Reformation*, 3 vols (Toronto: University of Toronto, 1995).

Bijsterveld, A. J. A., 'De kerk in het midden: de parochiekerk als centrum van de middeleeuwse dorpsgemeenschap', *Noordbrabants Historisch Jaarboek*, 17-18 (2000-2001), 91-119.

Blockmans, Wim, 'Constructing a Sense of Community in Rapidly Growing European Cities in the Eleventh to Thirteenth Centuries', *Historical Research*, 83 (2010), 575-87.

Blockmans, Wim, *Metropolen aan de Noordzee: de geschiedenis van Nederland, 1100-1560* (Amsterdam: Bert Bakker, 2012)

Blockmans, Wim, 'The Social and Economic Effects of Plague in the Low Countries, 1349-1500', *Revue belge de philologie et d'histoire*, 58 (1980), 833-63.

Blondé, Bruno, *De sociale structuren en economische dynamiek van 's-Hertogenbosch, 1500-1550* (Tilburg: Stichting Zuidelijk historisch contact, 1987).

Bolton, J. L. and Guidi Bruscoli, F., 'When Did Antwerp Replace Bruges as the Commercial and Financial Centre of North-Western Europe? The Evidence of the Borromei Ledger for 1438', *The Economic History Review*, 61 (2008), 360-79.

Boone, Marc, 'Cities in Late Medieval Europe: The Promise and the Curse of Modernity', *Urban History*, 39 (2012), 329-49.

Boone, Marc, 'From Cuckoo's Egg to "Sedem Tyranni": The Princely Citadels in the Cities of the Low Countries, Or: The City's Spatial Integrity Hijacked (15th – Early 16th Centuries)', in *The Power of Space in Late Medieval and Early Modern Europe: The Cities of Italy, Northern France and the Low Countries*, Studies in European Urban History (1100-1800), 30, ed. by Marc Boone and Martha Howell (Turnhout: Brepols, 2013), pp. 77-95.

Boone, Marc, 'Social Conflicts in the Cloth Industry of Ypres (Late 13th-Early 14th Centuries): The Cockerulle Reconsidered', in *Ypres and the Medieval Cloth Industry in Flanders: Archaeological and Historical Contributions*, ed. by Marc De Wilde, Anton Ervynck, and Alexis Wielemans (Zellik: Instituut voor het archeologisch patrimonium, 1998), pp. 147-55.

Bourdieu, Pierre, 'The Forms of Capital', in *Handbook of Theory and Research for the Sociology of Education*, ed. by John Richardson (New York: Greenwood, 1986), pp. 246-58.

Bourin, Monique and Durand, Robert, *Vivre au village au Moyen Age: les solidarités paysannes du XIe au XIIIe siècle* (Paris: Temps actuels, 1984).

Boussemaere, Pieter, 'De Ieperse lakenproductie opnieuw berekend aan de hand van de lakenloodjes', *Jaarboek voor Middeleeuwse Geschiedenis*, 3 (2000), 131-61.

Boussemaere, Pieter, 'De Ieperse poorterijregisters tussen 1250 en 1468: reconstructie, analyse en bespreking', *Westhoek. Tijdschrift voor geschiedenis en familiekunde in de Vlaamse en de Franse Westhoek*, 15 (1999), 147-61.

Brand, Hanno and Stabel, Peter, 'De ontwikkeling van vollerslonen in enkele laat-middeleeuwse textielcentra in de Nederlanden: een poging tot reconstructie', in: *Peasants and Townsmen in Medieval Europe: Studia in Honorem Adriaan Verhulst*, ed. by Jean-Marie Duvosquel and Erik Thoen (Ghent: Snoeck-Ducaju & Zoon, 1995), pp. 203-22.

Braudel, Fernand, *Civilization and Capitalism, 15th-18th Century*, 3 vols (New York: Harper & Row, 1982-1984).

Brenner, Robert, 'Agrarian Class Structure and Economic Development in Pre-Industrial Europe', *Past & Present*, 70 (1976), 30-75.

Brenner, Robert, 'The Low Countries in the Transition to Capitalism', *Journal of Agrarian Change*, 1 (2001), 169-241.

Brunner, Otto, *Land and Lordship: Structures of Governance in Medieval Austria*, trans. by Howard Kaminsky and James Van Horn Melton (Philadelphia: Penn Press, 1992).

Brunori, Paolo, 'The Perception of Inequality of Opportunity in Europe', *Review of Income and Wealth*, 63 (2016), 1-28.

Buntinx, Willy, 'Het Transport van Vlaanderen (1305-1517): bijdrage tot de geschiedenis van de financiële instellingen van het Graafschap Vlaanderen' (unpublished Masters-thesis, Ghent University, 1965).

Buylaert, Frederik, *Eeuwen van ambitie: de adel in laat-middeleeuws Vlaanderen* (Brussels: KVAB, 2010).

Buylaert, Frederik, 'Lordship, Urbanization and Social Change in Late Medieval Flanders', *Past & Present*, 228 (2015), 31-75.

Buylaert, Frederik, De Clercq, Wim and Dumolyn, Jan, 'Sumptuary Legislation, Material Culture and the Semiotics of "Vivre Noblement" in the County of Flanders (14th-16th Centuries)', *Social History*, 36 (2011), 393-417.

Cardon, Dominique, *La draperie au Moyen Âge. Essor d'une grande industrie Européenne* (Paris: CNRS, 1999).

Carlier, Jean-Joseph, 'Robert de Cassel, seigneur de Dunkerque, Cassel, Nieppe, Warneton, Gravelines, Bourbourg', *Annales du Comité Flamand de France*, 10 (1870), 17-248.

Carpenter, Christine, *Locality and Polity: A Study of Warwickshire Landed Society, 1401-1499* (Cambridge: Cambridge University Press, 1992).

Carus-Wilson, Eleanora, 'An Industrial Revolution of the Thirteenth Century', *The Economic History Review*, 11 (1941), 39-60.

Carus-Wilson, Eleanora, 'Evidences of Industrial Growth on Some Fifteenth-Century Manors', *The Economic History Review*, 12 (1959), 190-205.

Casado, Alonso, 'Finance et commerce international au milieu du XVIe siècle: la compagnie des Bernuy', *Annales du Midi*, 103 (1991), 323-43.

Chen, Martha and Carré, Françoise, 'Introduction', in *The Informal Economy Revisited: Examining the Past, Envisioning the Future*, ed. by Martha Chen and Françoise Carré (London and New York: Routledge, 2020), pp. 1-28.

Chorley, Patrick, 'The Cloth Exports of Flanders and Northern France during the Thirteenth Century: A Luxury Trade?', *The Economic History Review*, 40 (1987), 349-79.

Claassen, Albrecht, 'Introduction: Rural Space in the Middle Ages and Early Modern times: A Significant Domain Ignored for Too Long by Modern Research?', in *Rural*

Space in the Middle Ages and Early Modern Age: The Spatial Turn in Premodern studies, Fundamentals of Medieval and Early Modern Culture, 9, ed. by Albrecht Claassen (Berlin & Boston: De Gruyter, 2012), pp. 1-192.

Cohn, Samuel Jr., *Lust for Liberty: The Politics of Social Revolt in Medieval Europe, 1200-1425, Italy, France and Flanders* (Cambridge MA: Harvard University Press, 2006).

Cools, Hans, *Mannen met macht: edellieden en de moderne staat in de Bourgondisch-Habsburgse landen, ca. 1475 – ca. 1530* (Zutphen: Walburg pers, 2001).

Coornaert, Émile, *Un centre industriel d'autrefois: la draperie-sayetterie d'Hondschoote (XIVᵉ-XVIIIᵉ siècles)* (Paris: Presses universitaires de France, 1930).

Coornaert, Émile, 'Draperies rurales, draperies urbaines: l'évolution de l'industrie flamande au moyen âge et au XVIᵉ siècle', *Revue Belge de Philologie et d'Histoire*, 28 (1950), 59-96.

Coornaert, Émile, *L'industrie de la laine à Bergues-Saint-Winoc: une industrie urbaine du XIVᵉ au XVIIᵉ siècle* (Paris: Presses universitaires de France, 1930).

Creighton, Oliver, 'Castles and Castle Building in Town and Country', in *Town and Country in the Middle Ages: Contrasts, Contacts and Interconnections, 1100-1500*, ed. by Kate Giles and Christopher Dyer (Leeds: David Brown Book Company, 2005), pp. 275-92.

Crombie, Laura, *Archery and Crossbow Guilds in Medieval Flanders, 1300-1500* (Woodbridge: Boydell, 2016).

Curtis, Daniel, 'A North Sea Coastal Area under Pressure of Land Consolidation: Transition from a Farmer's Republic to an Unequal Polder Society in the Oldambt of Groningen, 1700-1900', in *Coping with Crisis: The Resilience and Vulnerability of Pre-Industrial Settlements*, ed. by Daniel Curtis (Burlington: Ashgate, 2014), pp. 181-222.

Curtis, Daniel, 'Trends in Rural Social and Economic History of the Pre-Industrial Low Countries: Recent Themes and Ideas in Journals and Books of the Past Five Years (2007-2013)', *BMGN – Low Countries Historical Review*, 128 (2013), 60-95.

Dalle, D., 'Pogingen tot heropbeuring van de wolnijverheid te Veurne (15e-17e eeuw)', *Handelingen van de Maatschappij voor Geschiedenis en Oudheidkunde te Gent*, 13 (1959), 103-12.

Dambruyne, Johan, *Corporatieve middengroepen: aspiraties, relaties en transformaties in de 16e-eeuwse Gentse ambachtswereld* (Ghent: Academia Press, 2002).

Dambruyne, Johan, 'De hiërarchie van de Vlaamse textielcentra (1500-1750): continuïteit of discontinuïteit?', in: *Qui valet ingenio: liber amicorum aangeboden aan dr. Johan Decavele*, ed. by Leen Charles and others (Ghent: Stichting Mens en kultuur, 1996), pp. 155-72.

Dankaart, Marie-Jeanne, 'De Gentse buitenpoorters en poorters tijdens het laatste kwart van de 15de eeuw: een sociale analyse en een topografische benadering (unpublished Masters-thesis, University of Ghent, 1989).

Danneel, Marianne, *Weduwen en wezen in het laat-middeleeuwse Gent* (Leuven: Garant, 1996).

Dauchy, Serge, 'Introduction historique', in *Les arrets et jugés du Parlement de Paris sur appels flamands conservés dans les registres du Parlement*, ed. by Serge Dauchy and others, 3 vols (Brussels: Ministère de la justice, 1966-2002), I (1966), pp. 96-105.

Davies, Rees, 'The Medieval State: The Tyranny of a Concept?', *Journal of Historical Sociology*, 16 (2003), 280-300.

Davis, Mike, *Planet of slums* (Londen & New York: Verso Books, 2005).

De Boodt, Minne, '"How One Shall Govern a City': The Polyphony of Urban Political Thought in the Fourteenth-Century Duchy of Brabant', *Urban History*, 46 (2019), 1-19.

Decavele, Johan, *De dageraad van de reformatie in Vlaanderen (1520-1565)*, 2 vols (Brussels: Paleis der Academiën, 1975).

Decavele, Johan, 'Het culturele en intellectuele netwerk: middeleeuwen en 16e eeuw', in *Het stedelijk netwerk in België in historisch perspectief (1350-1850): een statistische en dynamische benadering: 15de Internationaal Colloquium, Spa, 4-6 september 1990: Handelingen* (Brussels: Gemeentekrediet, 1992), pp. 155-90.

De Keyzer, Maïka, 'The Impact of Different Distributions of Power on Access Rights to the Common Wastelands: The Campine, Brecklands and Geest Compared', *Journal of Institutional Economics*, 9 (2013), 517-42.

De Keyzer, Maïka, *Inclusive Commons and the Sustainability of Peasant Communities in the Medieval Low Countries* (New York: Routledge, 2018).

Dekker, Cornelis and Baetens, Roland, *Geld in het water: Antwerps en Mechels kapitaal in Zuid-Beveland na de stormvloeden in de 16e eeuw* (Hilversum: Verloren, 2010).

Deligne, Chloé, 'Powers over Space, Spaces of Powers: The Constitution of Town Squares in the Cities of the Low Countries (12th-14th Centuries)', in *The Power of Space in Late Medieval and Early Modern Europe: The Cities of Italy, Northern France and the Low Countries*, Studies in European Urban History (1100-1800), 30, ed. by Marc Boone and Martha Howell (Turnhout: Brepols, 2013), pp. 21-28.

Delzant, Jean-Baptiste, 'Instaurator et fundator: édification de la seigneurie urbaine et présence monumentale de la commune (Italie centrale, fin du Moyen Âge)', in *The Power of Space in Late Medieval and Early Modern Europe: The Cities of Italy, Northern France and the Low Countries*, Studies in European Urban History (1100-1800), 30, ed. by Marc Boone and Martha Howell (Turnhout: Brepols, 2013), pp. 97-112.

De Meester, Jan, 'Gastvrij Antwerpen? Arbeidsmigratie naar het zestiende-eeuwse Antwerpen' (unpublished doctoral thesis, University of Anwerp, 2011).

De Meulenaere, Fabrice, 'Le château d'Oosthove à Nieppe, Neuve-Église et Ploegsteert du XIIIe au début du XXe siècle', *Mémoires de la Société d'Histoire de Comines-Warneton et de la Région*, 19 (1989), 43-72.

Demey, Jules, 'De Ieperse lakennijverheid: haar ontstaan, ontwikkeling en verval' (unpublished doctoral thesis, University of Leuven, 1947-48).

Demey, Jules, 'De Vlaamse ondernemer in de middeleeuwse nijverheid: de Ieperse drapiers en "upsetters" op het einde der XIIIe en in de XIVe eeuw', *BMGN – Low Countries Historical Review*, 4 (1949), 1-15, reprinted in *Prisma van de geschiedenis van Ieper: een bundel historische opstellen*, ed. by Octaaf Mus and J. A. Van Houtte (Ypres: Stadsbestuur, 1974), 143-56.

Demey, Jules, 'Proeve tot raming van de bevolking en de weefgetouwen te Ieper van de XIIe tot de XVIIe eeuw', *Revue belge de philologie et d'histoire*, 28 (1950), 1031-48.

Demo, Edoardo, 'Mercati e manifatture nel Veneto tardomedievale', *Reti Medievali Rivista*, 2 (2001), online publication (https://doi.org/10.6092/1593-2214/225).

Demo, Eduardo, 'Wool and Silk: The Textile Urban Industry of the Venetian Mainland (15th-17th Centuries)', in *At the Centre of the Old World: Trade and Manufacturing in*

Venice and the Venetian Mainland, 1400-1800, ed. by Paola Lanaro (Toronto: CRRS Publications, 2006), 217-44.

De Moor, Tine, 'The Silent Revolution: A New Perspective on the Emergence of Commons, Guilds, and Other Forms of Corporate Collective Action in Western Europe', *International Review of Social History*, 53, Supplement 16: The Return of the Guilds (2008), 179-212.

De Moor, Tine, 'Three Waves of Cooperation: A Millennium of Institutions for Collective Action in Historical Perspective (Case-Study: The Netherlands)', in *Oxford Handbook on International Economic Governance*, ed. by Eric Brousseau and Jean-Michel Glachant (Oxford: Oxford University Press, 2021; forthcoming).

De Munck, Bert, 'The Agency of Branding and the Location of Value: Hallmarks and Monograms in Early Modern Tableware Industries', *Business History*, 54 (2012), 1-22.

Derville, Alain, 'La population du Nord au Moyen Âge, II: de 1384 à 1549', *Revue du Nord*, 81 (1999), 65-82.

Derville, Alain, 'L'urbanisation de la Flandre Wallonne d'après les enquêtes fiscales (1449-1549)', *Revue du Nord*, 79 (1997), 295-302.

Derolez, Albert, 'De valse oorkonde van graaf Arnulf I van Vlaanderen voor het Sint-Donatiaanskapittel te Brugge (961, juli 31)', *Handelingen van de Koninklijke Commissie voor Geschiedenis / Bulletin de la Commission Royale d'Histoire*, 140 (1974), 431-99.

De Sagher, Henri, 'Une enquête sur la situation de l'industrie drapière en Flandre à la fin du XVIe siècle', *Études d'histoire dédiées à la memoire de Henri Pirenne par ses anciens élèves*, ed. by Hans Van Werveke (Brussels: Nouvelle société d'éditions, 1937), pp. 471-500.

de Schepper, Gerrit IJssel, *Lotgevallen van Christiern II en Isabella van Oostenrijk, koning en koningin van Denemarken; voornamelijk gedurende huere ballingschap in de Nederlanden* (Zwolle: De Erven J. J. Tijl, 1870).

Deschodt, Simon, 'De Ieperse buitenpoorterij in de 15de tot begin 16de eeuw: studie naar de conflictueuze relatie tussen de stad Ieper en haar hinterland', (unpublished Masters-thesis, Ghent University, 2019).

Desreumaux, John, *Leidens weg op* (Roeselare: Familia et Patria, 1992).

de Vries, Jan, *The Industrious Revolution: Consumer Behavior and the Household Economy, 1650 to the Present* (Cambridge: Cambridge University Press, 2008).

de Vries, Jan, and van der Woude, Ad, *The First Modern Economy: Success, Failure, and Perseverance of the Dutch Economy, 1500-1815* (Cambridge: Cambridge University Press, 1997; repr. 2010).

Dhondt, Jan, 'Bijdrage tot het cartularium van Meesen (1065-1334)', *Handelingen van de Koninklijke Commissie voor Geschiedenis / Bulletin de la Commission Royale d'Histoire*, 106 (1941), 95-234.

Diegerick, Isidore, 'Le prieuré de Nieppe', *Société des Antiquaires de la Morinie – Bulletin Historique Trimestriel*, 1 (Saint-Omer, 1852), 61-73.

Doda, H., '"Saide Monstrous Hose": Compliance, Transgression and English Sumptuary Law to 1533', *Textile History*, 45 (2014), 171-91.

Doudelez, Gustave, 'La revolution communale de 1280 a Ypres', in *Prisma van de geschiedenis van Ieper: een bundel historische opstellen*, ed. by Octaaf Mus and Jan Van Houtte (Ypres: Stadsbestuur, 1974), pp. 188-294.

Duffy, Eamon, *The Stripping of the Altars: Traditional Religion in England, 1400-1580* (New Haven & London: Yale University Press, 2005).

Dumolyn, Jan, 'Guild Politics and Political Guilds in Fourteenth-Century Flanders', in *The Voices of the People in Late Medieval Europe: Communication and Popular Politics*, ed. by Jan Dumolyn and others (Turnhout: Brepols, 2014), pp. 15-48.

Dumolyn, Jan and Lambert, Bart, 'Cities of Commerce, Cities of Constraints: International Trade, Government Institutions and the Law of Commerce in Later Medieval Bruges and the Burgundian State', *TSEG – The Low Countries Journal of Social and Economic History*, 11 (2014), 89-102.

Dumolyn, Jan, 'Les "plaintes" des villes flamandes à la fin du XIIIe siècle et les discours et pratiques politiques de la commune', *Le Moyen Âge*, 121 (2015), pp. 383-407.

Dumolyn, Jan, 'Privileges and Novelties: The Political Discourse of the Flemish Cities and Rural Districts in their Negotiations with the Dukes of Burgundy (1384-1506)', *Urban History*, 35 (2008), 5-23.

Dumolyn, Jan and Papin, Kristof, 'La révolte paysanne à Cassel (1427-1431): lutte d'une communauté rurale contre la centralisation Bourguignonne', in Haro sur le seigneur! *Les luttes anti-seigneuriales dans l'Europe médiévale et modern: Actes des XXIXes journées internationales d'histoire de l'abbaye de Flaren, 5 et 6 octobre 2007*, ed. by Ghislain Brunel and Serge Brunet (Toulouse: Presses universitaires du Midi, 2009), pp. 79-92.

DuPlessis, Robert, 'One Theory, Two draperies, Three provinces and a Multitude of Fabrics: The New Drapery of French Flanders, Hainaut and the Tournaisis, *c.* 1500-*c.* 1800', in *The New Draperies in the Low Countries and England, 1300-1800*, ed. by N.B. Harte (Oxford: Oxford University Press, 1997), pp. 129-72.

Duplessis, Robert and Howell, Martha, 'Reconsidering the Early Modern Urban Economy: The Cases of Leiden and Lille', *Past & Present*, 94 (1982), 49-84.

Duvosquel, Jean-Marie, 'La villa de Dêulémont partagée par Baudoin V de Flandre entre le chapitre de Lille et l'abbaye de Messines en 1066: cartographie d'un domaine comtal', *Peasants and Townsmen in Medieval Europe: Studia in Honorem Adriaan Verhulsti*, ed. by Jean-Marie Duvosquel and Erik Thoen (Ghent Snoeck-Ducaju & Zoon, 1995), pp. 397-427.

Dyer, Christopher, *A Country Merchant, 1495-1520: Trading and Farming at the End of the Middle Ages* (Oxford: Oxford University Press, 2014).

Dyer, Christopher, 'Conclusion: Making Sense of Town and Country', in *Town and Country in the Middle Ages: Contrasts, Contacts and Interconnections, 1100-1500*, ed. by Kate Giles and Christopher Dyer (Leeds: David Brown Book Company, 2005), pp. 313-21.

Edler, Florence, 'Le commerce d'exportation des sayes d'Hondschoote vers l'Italie d'après la correspondance d'une firme anversoise entre 1538 et 1544', *Revue du Nord*, 22 (1936), 249-66.

Ehrenberg, Richard, *Capital and Finance in the Age of the Renaissance: A Study of the Fuggers and their Connections*, trans. by H. M. Lucas (New York: Augustus H. Kelley, 1928).

Endrei, Walter, 'Manufacturing a Piece of Woollen Cloth in Medieval Flanders: How Many Work Hours?', in *Textiles of the Low Countries in European Economic History:*

Proceedings of the Tenth International Economic History Congress, Leuven August 1990, Studies in Social and Economic History, ed. by Erik Aerts and John Munro (Leuven: Leuven University Press, 1990), pp. 14-23.

Endrei, Walter and Egan, Geoffrey, 'The Sealing of Cloth in Europe, with Special Reference to the English Evidence', *Textile history*, 13 (1982), 47-75.

Epstein, S. R., *Freedom and Growth: The Rise of States and Markets in Europe, 1300-1750* (London: Routledge, 2000).

Epstein, S. R., 'Introduction: Town and Country in Europe, 1300-1800', in *Town and Country in Europe, 1300-1800*, ed. by S. R. Epstein (Cambridge: Cambridge University Press, 2001), pp. 1-29.

Epstein, S. R., 'Regional Fairs, Institutional Innovation, and Economic Growth in Late Medieval Europe', *The Economic History Review*, 157 (1994), 459-82.

Espinas, Georges, *Les origines du capitalisme*, 2 vols (Lille: Raoust, 1933-49).

Espinas, Georges, 'Une draperie rurale dans la Flandre française au XVe siècle: la draperie rurale d'Estaires (Nord) (1428-1434)', *Revue d'histoire des doctrines economiques et sociales*, 11 (1923), 1-44.

Fagel, Raymond, *De Hispano-Vlaamse wereld: de contacten tussen Spanjaarden en de Nederlanders, 1496-1555* (Brussels: Archief- en bibliotheekwezen in België, 1996).

Fuji, Yoshio, 'Draperie urbaine et draperie rurale dans les Pays Bas meridionaux au bas moyen âge: une mise ou point des recherches après H. Pirenne', *Journal of Medieval History*, 16 (1990), 77-98.

Fukuyama, Francis, *The End of History and the Last Man* (New York: Free Press, 1992; 2006 ed.).

Gaillard, Victor, 'Études sur le commerce de la Flandre au Moyen-Âge: les foires', *Messager des Sciences Historiques, des Arts et de la Bibliographie de Belgique* (Ghent: Hebbelynck, 1851), pp. 193-220.

Gelderblom, Oscar, *Cities of Commerce: The Institutional Foundations of International Trade in the Low Countries, 1250-1650* (Princeton: Princeton University Press, 2013).

Gelderblom, Oscar, 'The Governance of Early Modern trade: The Case of Hans Thijs, 1556-1611', *Enterprise and Society*, 4 (2003), 606-39.

Gelderblom, Oscar, 'The Organization of Long-Distance Trade in England and the Dutch Republic, 1550-1650', in *The Political Economy of the Dutch Republic*, ed. by Oscar Gelderblom (Farnham and Burlington: Ashgate Publishing, 2009), pp. 223-54.

Gemmill, Elizabeth, 'Debt, Distraint, Display and Dead Men's Treasure: Material Culture in Late Medieval Aberdeen, *Journal of Medieval History*, 46 (2020), 350-72.

Genicot, Léopold, 'L'industrie dans le comté de Namur à la fin du moyen âge (1350-1430)', *Namurcum*, 21 (1946), 49-57.

Gies, Frances and Gies, Joseph, *Cathedral, Forge, and Waterwheel: Technology and Invention in the Middle Ages* (London: Harper Perennial, 1994; 1995 ed.).

Gies, Frances and Gies, Joseph, *Life in a Medieval Village* (New York: Harper and Row, 1990).

Giles, Kate, 'Public Space in Town and Village', in *Town and Country in the Middle Ages: Contrasts, Contacts and Interconnections, 1100-1500*, ed. by Kate Giles and Christopher Dyer (Leeds: David Brown Book Company, 2005), pp. 293-311.

Gimpel, *The Medieval Machine: The Industrial Revolution of the Middle Ages* (New York: Penguin Books, 1976).

Ginzburg, Carlo, *The Cheese and the Worms: The Cosmos of a Sixteenth-Century Miller*, trans. by John Tedeschi and Anne Tedeschi (Baltimore: Routledge & Kegan Paul PLC, 1980; 1st Italian ed. 1976).

Ginzburg, Carlo, *The Night Battles: Witchcraft and Agrarian Cults in the Sixteenth and Seventeenth Centuries*, trans. by John Tedeschi and Anne Tedeschi (Baltimore: Routledge & Kegan Paul PLC, 1983; 1st Italian ed. 1966).

Goddard, Richard, 'Small Boroughs and the Manorial Economy: Enterprise Zones or Urban Failures?', *Past & Present*, 210 (2011), 3-31.

Grafe, Regina and Gelderblom, Oscar, 'The Rise and Fall of the Merchant Guilds: Re-thinking the Comparative Study of Commercial Institutions in Premodern Europe', *The Journal of Interdisciplinary History*, 40 (2010), 477-511.

Haemers, Jelle, *For the Common Good: State Power and Urban Revolts in the Reign of Mary of Burgundy, (1477-1482)*, Studies in European Urban History (1100-1800), 17 (Turnhout: Brepols, 2009).

Haemers, Jelle, 'Révolte et requête: les gens de métiers et les conflits sociaux dans les villes de Flandre (XIIIe-XVe siècle)', *Revue historique*, 677 (2016), 27-56.

Haemers, Jelle and Dumolyn, Jan, '"Let Each Man Carry on with his Trade and Remain Silent": Middle-Class Ideology in the Urban Literature of the Late Medieval Low Countries', *Cultural and Social History*, 10 (2013), 169-89.

Hallam, Herbert, 'The Life of the People', in *The Agrarian History of England and Wales*, ed. by Joan Thirsk and others (Cambridge: Cambridge University Press, 1981-91), II (1983), 818-53.

Hammel-Kiesow, Rolf, 'The Early Hansas', in *A Companion to the Hanseatic League*, ed. by Donald Harreld (Leiden: Brill, 2015), pp. 15-63.

Haquette, Bertrand, 'Des lices et des joncs: rivière et draperies de la vallée de la Lys à la fin du Moyen Age', *Revue du Nord*, 79 (1997), 859-82.

Haquette, Bertrand, 'Les précurseurs de la délocalisation: entre commerce triangulaire et économie *offshore*: le rôle des financiers italiens dans les villages drapiers de la vallée de la Lys', *Publications du Centre Européen d'Etudes Bourguignonnes*, 49 (2009), 131-58.

Holbach, Rudolf, *Frühformen von Verlag und Grossbetrieb in der gewerblichen Produktion (13.-16. Jahrhundert)* (Stuttgart: Steiner, 1994).

Holbach, Rudolf, 'Some Remarks on the Role of "Putting-Out" in Flemish and Northwest European Cloth Production', in *La draperie ancienne des Pays-Bas: débouchés et stratégies de survie*, ed. by Marc Boone and Walter Prevenier (Leuven: Garant, 1993), pp. 207-49.

Hooghe, Filip, 'De Cokerulle (1280-1285): een conflict tussen Ieper en zijn hinterland over de lakennijverheid', *Handelingen van het Genootschap voor Geschiedenis*, 143 (2006), 293-448.

Hoppenbrouwers, Peter, 'Town and Country in Holland, 1350-1550', in *Town and Country in Europe, 1300-1800*, ed. by S.R. Epstein (Cambridge: Cambridge University Press, 2001), pp. 54-79.

Van Houtte, Jan, 'Ieper door de eeuwen heen', in *Prisma van de geschiedenis van Ieper*, ed. by Mus and Van Houtte, pp. x-xxi.

Howell, Martha, *Commerce before Capitalism in Europe, 1300-1600* (New York: Cambridge University Press, 2010).

Jackson, Christine, 'Boom-Time Freaks or Heroic Industrial Pioneers? Clothing Entrepreneurs in Sixteenth- and Early Seventeenth-Century Berkshire', *Textile History*, 39 (2008), 145-71.

Jahnke, Carsten, 'Some Aspects of Medieval Cloth Trade in the Baltic Sea Area', in *The Medieval Broadcloth: Changing Trends in Fashions, Manufacturing and Consumption*, ed. by Kathrine Vestergård Pedersen and Marie-Louise Nosch (Oxford: Oxbow Books, 2009), pp. 74-89.

Jaster, Margaret Rose, '"Clothing Themselves in Acres": Apparel and Impoverishment in Medieval and Early Modern England', in *Medieval Clothing and Textiles*, 2, ed. by R. Netherton and G.R. Owen-Crocker (Woodbridge: Boydell, 2006), pp. 91-100.

Juma, Calestous, *Innovation and its Enemies: Why People Resist New Technologies* (Oxford: Oxford University Press, 2016).

Keibek, Sebastian and Shaw-Taylor, Leigh, 'Early Modern Rural By-Employments: A Re-examination of the Probate Inventory Evidence', *Agricultural History Society*, 111 (2013), 244-81.

Kint, Anne, 'The Community of Commerce: Social Relations in Sixteenth-Century Antwerp' (doctoral dissertation, Columbia University, 1996).

Klandermans, Bert, 'Collective Action', in *International Encyclopedia of the Social and Behavioral Sciences*, ed. by James Wright (Oxford: Oxford University Press, 2015), pp. 145-50.

Koch, A., 'L'origine et la formation territoriale des châtellenies de Cassel et de Bailleul', *Revue du Nord*, 29 (1947), 5-25.

Koebner, Richard, 'The Settlement and Colonization of Europe', in *The Cambridge Economic History of Europe*, ed. by Michael Postan and others, 8 vols (Cambridge: Cambridge University Press, 1966-1989), I, *The Agrarian Life of the Middle Ages* (1966), pp. 1-91.

Kuttner, Erich and Romein, J. M., *Het Hongerjaar 1566* (Amsterdam: Amsterdamsche boek- en courantmaatschappij, 1949).

Lambin, Jean-Jacques, *Mémoire sur les questions proposées par la Société des Antiquaires de la Morinie, établie a Saint-Omer: 1. sur l'origine de la Halle aux draps, à Ypres; 2. sur les causes qui ont donné lieu à sa construction; 3. sur les institutions, source de l'ancienne prospérité des habitants; 4. sur l'époque de la fondation de l'église de Saint-Martin* (Ypres: Lambin, 1836).

Lambrecht, Thijs, *Een grote hoeve in een klein dorp: relaties van arbeid en pacht op het Vlaamse platteland tijdens de 18de eeuw*, Reeks Historische Economie en Ecologie, 8 (Ghent: Academia Press, 2002).

Lanaro, Paolo (ed.), *At the Centre of the Old World: Trade and Manufacturing in Venice and the Venetian Mainland, 1400-1800* (Toronto: CRRS Publications, 2006).

Lee, John S., *The Medieval Clothier* (Woodbridge: Boydell, 2018).

Lefebvre, Henri, *La production de l'espace* (Paris: Anthropos, 1974).

Le Glay, M., 'Rapport de M. Le Glay sur quelques planches gravées du *Flandria Illustrata*, de Sanderus', in *Bulletin de la Commission Historique du Département du Nord*, 4 (1851), 96-103.

Le Glay, M., 'Tableaux de la population des châtellenies de Cassel, Bergues et Bailleul, en 1469', *Bulletin du Comité Flamand de France*, 1 (1857), 344-47.

Le Roy Ladurie, Emmanuel, *Het carnaval van Romans: van Maria-Lichtmis tot Aswoensdag, 1579-1580*, trans. by Frans de Haan and Barbara Herklots (Amsterdam: Bert Bakker, 1985; 1st French ed. 1979).

Le Roy Ladurie, Emmanuel, *Montaillou: village occitan de 1294 à 1324* (Paris: Éditions Gallimard, 1975).

Le Roy Ladurie, Emmanuel, *The French peasantry, 1450-1660* (Berkeley CA: University of California Press, 1987).

Lesger, Clé and Noordegraaf, Leo (eds), *Entrepreneurs and Entrepreneurship in Early Modern Times: Merchants and Industrialists within the Orbit of the Dutch Staple Market* (The Hague: Stichting Hollandsche Historische Reeks, 1995).

Limberger, Michael, *Sixteenth-Century Antwerp and its Rural Surroundings: Social and Economic Changes in the Hinterland of a Commercial Metropolis (ca. 1450 – ca. 1570)* (Turnhout: Brepols, 2008).

Lim, Walter, 'Surety and Spiritual Commercialism in The Merchant of Venice', *Studies in English literature, 1500-1900*, 50 (2010), 355-81.

Lis, Catharina and Soly, Hugo, *Poverty and Capitalism in Pre-Industrial Europe* (Brighton: The Harvester Press, 1979).

Lis, Catharina and Soly, Hugo, 'Subcontracting in Guild-Based Export Trades, Thirteenth-Eighteenth Centuries', in *Guilds, Innovation and the European Economy, 1400-1800*, ed. by S. R. Epstein and Maarten Prak (Cambridge: Cambridge University Press, 2008), pp. 81-113.

Lopez, Robert, *The Commercial Revolution of the Middle Ages, 950-1350* (New York: Cambridge University Press, 1976).

Maddens, Klaas, 'De invoering van de "nieuwe middelen" in het graafschap Vlaanderen tijdens de regering van Keizer Karel V', *Revue belge de philologie et d'histoire*, 57 (1979), 342-63, 861-98.

Marchal, Guy, 'Pfahlbürger, bourgeois forains, buitenpoorters, bourgeois du roi: Aspekte einer zweideutigen Rechtsstellung, in *Neubürger im späten Mittelalter: Migration und Austausch in der Städtelandschaft des Alten Reiches (1250-1550)*, ed. by Rainer Christoph Schwinges, Barbara Studer, and Roland Gerber (Berlin: Duncker und Humblot, 2002), pp. 333-67.

Marfany, Julie, 'Is It Still Helpful to Speak of Proto-Industrialization? Some Suggestions from a Catalan Case-Study', *Economic History Review*, 63 (2010), 942-73.

Marnef, Guido, *Antwerpen in de tijd van de Reformatie* (Amsterdam & Antwerp: Meulenhoff Kritak, 1996).

Masquelin, Hubert and Vandamme, Ludo, 'De familie Tayspil als spiegel van de geschiedenis van Nieuwkerke tijdens de 16de eeuw', in *Histories van Heuvelland: bijdragen ter herinnering aan Hubert Masquelin*, ed. by Koen Baert and others (Heuvelland: VVV Heuvelland, 2011), pp. 157-68.

Medina, Luis Fernando, *A Unified Theory of Collective Action and Social Change* (Michigan: University of Michigan Press, 2007).

Mendels, Franklin, 'Proto-Industrialization: The First Phase of the Industrialization Process', *The Journal of Economic History*, 32 (1972), 241-61.

Milanovic, Branko, Lindert, Peter and Williamson, Jeffrey, 'Pre-Industrial Inequality', *The Economic Journal*, 121 (2011), 255-72.

Mileson, Stephen, 'Opennes and Closure in the Later Medieval Village', *Past & Present*, 234 (2017), 3-37.

Moscatelli, Umberto, 'Le briciole di Pollicino: vita nascosta delle strade tra età romana e Medioevo', *Il Capitale Culturale – Studies on the Value of Cultural Heritage*, 7 (2013), 211-25.

Munro, John, 'Bruges and the Abortive Staple in English Cloth: An Incident in the Shift of Commerce from Bruges to Antwerp in the Late Fifteenth Century', *Revue belge de philologie et d'histoire*, 44 (1966), 1137-59.

Munro, John, 'Hanseatic Commerce in Textiles from the Low Countries and England during the Late Middle Ages: Changing Trends in Textiles, Markets, Prices, and Values, 1290-1579', in *Von Nowgorod bis London. Studien zu Handel, Wirtschaft und Gesellschaft im mittelalterlichen Europa*, ed. by Marie-Luise Heckmann and Jens Rörhrkasten (Göttingen: V&R Unipress, 2008), pp. 97-181.

Munro, John, 'The Low Countries' Export Trade in Textiles with the Mediterranean Basin, 1200-1600: A Cost–Benefit Analysis of Comparative Advantages in Overland and Maritime Trade Routes', *International Journal of Maritime History*, 11 (1999), 1-30.

Munro, John, 'Medieval Woollens: Textiles, Textile Technology and Industrial Organisation', in *The Cambridge History of Western Textiles*, 2 vols, ed. by David Jenkins (Cambridge: Cambridge University Press, 2003), I, pp. 181-227.

Munro, John, 'Necessities and Luxuries in Early-Modern Textile Consumption: Real Values of Worsted Says and Fine Woollens in the Sixteenth-Century Low Countries', in *Cities – Coins – Commerce: Essays Presented to Ian Blanchard on the Occasion of his Seventieth Birthday*, Studien Zur Gewerbe- und Handelsgeschichte der Vorindustriel, ed. by Philipp Robinson Rössner (Stuttgart: Franz Steiner Verlag, 2012), pp. 121-46.

Munro, John, 'The "New Institutional Economics" and the Changing Fortunes of Fairs in Medieval and Early Modern Europe: The Textile Trades, Warfare, and Transaction Costs', *Vierteljahrschrift für Sozial- und Wirtschaftsgeschichte*, 138 (2001), 1-47.

Munro, John, 'The Origins of the English "New Draperies": The Resurrection of an Old Flemish Industry, 1250-1570', in *The New Draperies in the Low Countries and England, 1300-1800*, Pasold Studies in Textile Industry 10, ed. by N.B. Harte (New York: Oxford University Press, 1997), pp. 35-128.

Munro, John, 'Spanish Merino Wools and the *Nouvelles Draperies*: An Industrial Transformation in the Late Medieval Low Countries', *Economic History Review*, 58 (2005), 431-84.

Munro, John, 'The Symbiosis between Towns and Textiles: Urban Institutions and the Changing Fortunes of Cloth Manufacturing in the Low Countries and England, 1270-1570', *Journal of Early Modern History*, 3 (1999), 1-74.

Munro, John, 'Tawney's Century, 1540-1640: The Roots of Modern Capitalist Entrepreneurship', in *The Invention of Enterprise: Entrepreneurship from Ancient Mesopotamia to Modern times*, ed. by David Landes (Princeton: Princeton University Press, 2010), pp. 107-55.

Munro, John, 'Three Centuries of Luxury Textile Consumption in the Low Countries and England, 1330-1570: Trends and Comparisons of Real Values of Woollen Broadcloths (Then and Now)', in *The Medieval Broadcloth: Changing Trends in*

Fashions, Manufacturing and Consumption, ed. by Kathrine Vestergård Pedersen and Marie-Louise Nosch (Oxford: Oxbow Books, 2009), 1-73.

Murray, James, *Bruges, Cradle of Capitalism, 1280-1390* (Cambridge: Cambridge University Press, 2005).

Mus, Octaaf, 'De verhouding van de waard tot de drapier in de Kortrijkse draperie op het einde van de 15e eeuw', *Handelingen van het Genootschap voor Geschiedenis, gesticht onder de benaming 'Société d'Emulation', te Brugge*, 99 (1961), 156-218.

Mus, Octaaf, 'Pieter Lansaem, promotor van de nieuwe draperie te Ieper in de tweede helft van de 15e eeuw', *Handelingen van het Genootschap voor Geschiedenis, gesticht onder de benaming 'Société d'Émulation' te Brugge*, 130 (1993), 61-88.

Nicholas, David, *Town and Countryside: Social, Economic, and Political Tensions in Fourteenth-Century Flanders* (Bruges: De Tempel, 1971).

Nicholas, David, 'Town and Countryside: Social and Economic Tensions in Fourteenth-Century Flanders', *Comparative Studies in Society and History*, 10 (1968), 458-85.

North, Douglass, *Institutions, Institutional Change and Economic Performance* (Cambridge: Cambridge University Press, 1990).

North, Douglass, 'Institutions', *Journal of Economic Perspectives*, 5 (1991), 97-112.

Ogilvie, Sheilagh, 'The Economics of guilds', *Journal of Economic Perspectives*, 28 (2014), 169-92.

Ogilvie, Sheilagh, *The European Guilds: An Economic Analysis* (Princeton: Princeton University Press, 2019).

Ogilvie, Sheilagh and Cerman, Markus, 'The Theories of Proto-Industrialization', in *European Proto-Industrialization: An Introductory Handbook*, ed. by Markus Cerman and Sheilagh Ogilvie (Cambridge NY: Cambridge University Press, 1996), pp. 1-11.

Oldland, John, 'The Clothiers' Century, 1450-1550', *Rural History*, 29 (2018), 1-22.

Ørberg Jensen, Peter, and Pedersen, Torben, 'Offshoring and International Competitiveness: Antecedents of Offshoring Advanced Tasks', *Journal of the Academy of Marketing Science*, 40 (2012), 313-28.

Pajic, Milan, 'The Fortunes of Urban Fullers in Fourteenth-Century England', *Historical Research*, 93 (2020), 227-51.

Papin, Kristof, 'Gids voor het Fonds Merghelynck', *Westhoek – Jaarboek*, 9 (1994), 133-45.

Papin, Kristof and Preneel, Arnold, '*Ne peuis adveniat*: sociale politiek en bevolkingsmigraties in de stad Ieper (1571-1575)', *Westhoek. Tijdschrift voor Geschiedenis & Familiekunde in de Vlaamse & Franse Westhoek*, 15 (1999), 4-52.

Passchier, Robert, *Memorieboek Nieuwkerke* (Nieuwkerke, 1943), manuscript.

Pastoureau, Michel, *Une histoire symbolique du Moyen Âge occidental* (Paris: Seuil, 2004).

Peacock, David, 'Research Note: Dyeing Winchcombe Kersies and other Kersey Cloth in Sixteenth-Century Newbury', *Textile History*, 37 (2006), 187-202.

Peacock, David, 'The Winchcombe Family and the Woollen Industry in Sixteenth-Century Newbury', (unpublished doctoral thesis, University of Reading, 2003).

Pirenne, Henri, 'Une crise industrielle au XVIe siècle: la draperie urbaine et la "nouvelle draperie" en Flandre', *Bulletin de l'Académie royale de Belgique, Classe des Lettres*, 5 (1905), 489-521.

Pirenne, Henri, 'Les dénombrements de la population d'Ypres au XVe siècle (1412-1506)', *Vierteljahrschrift für Sozial- und Wirtschaftsgeschichte*, 1 (1903), 1-32.

Pirenne, Henri, *Histoire de Belgique*, 7 vols (Brussels: H. Lamertin, 1900-1932).

Pirenne, Henri, *Medieval Cities: Their Origins and the Revival of Trade*, trans. by Frank Halsey (Princeton: Princeton University Press, 1925; repr. 1974).

Pirenne, Henri, 'Note sur la fabrication des tapisseries en Flandre au XVIe siècle : contribution à l'histoire de l'industrie capitaliste', *Vierteljahrschrift für Sozial- und Wirtschafsgeschichte*, 4 (1906), 325-39.

Pleij, Herman, *De sneeuwpoppen van 1511: literatuur en stadscultuur tussen middeleeuwen en moderne tijd* (Amsterdam: Bert Bakker, 1988).

Pleij, Herman, 'Restyling "Wisdom", Remodelling the Nobility, and Caricaturing the Peasant: Urban Literature in the Late Medieval Low Countries', *Journal of Interdisciplinary History*, 32 (2002), 689-704.

Poos, Lawrence, *A Rural Society after the Black Death: Essex, 1350-1525*, Cambridge Studies in Population, Economy and Society in Past Time (Cambridge: Cambridge University Press, 1991).

Postan, Michael, 'Credit in Medieval trade', in *Medieval Trade and Finance*, ed. by Michael Postan (Cambridge: Cambridge University Press, 1973), pp. 1-27.

Postan, Michael, 'Partnerships in English Medieval Commerce', in *Medieval Trade and Finance*, ed. by Michael Postan (Cambridge: Cambridge University Press, 1973), pp. 65-91.

Postan, Michael and Titow, Jan, 'Heriots and Prices on Winchester Manors', in *Essays on Medieval agriculture and General Problems of the Medieval Economy*, ed. by Michael Postan (Cambridge: Cambridge University Press, 1973), pp. 150-85.

Posthumus, N. W., *De geschiedenis van de Leidsche lakenindustrie*, 3 vols (The Hague: M. Nijhoff, 1908-1939).

Prak, Maarten, 'Early Modern Capitalism: An Introduction', in *Early Modern Capitalism: Economic and Social Change in Europe, 1400-1800*, ed. by Maarten Prak (London: Routledge, 2001), 1-20.

Prevenier, Walter, 'La démographie des villes du comté de Flandre aux XIIIe et XVe siècles; état de la question: essai d'interprétation', *Revue du Nord*, 65 (1983), 255-75.

Puttevils, Jeroen, '*A servitio de vostri sempre siamo*': de effecten van de handel tussen Antwerpen en Italië op de koopmansfamilie Van der Molen (midden zestiende eeuw)' (unpublished Masters-thesis, University of Antwerp, 2007).

Puttevils, Jeroen, '"Eating the Bread out of their Mouth": Antwerp's Export Trade and Generalized Institutions', *The Economic History Review*, 68 (2015), 1339-64.

Puttevils, Jeroen, *Merchants and Trading in the Sixteenth Century: The Golden Age of Antwerp*, Perspectives in Economic and Social History (London: Pickering and Chatto, 2015).

Reynolds, Susan, 'There Were States in Medieval Europe: A Response to Rees Davies', *Journal of Historical Sociology*, 16 (2003), 550-55.

Roch, Jean-Louis, 'Artisans ou marchands: la draperie médiévale de l'Italie à la Normandie', *Revue historique*, 695 (2020), 39-58.

Roch, Jean-Louis, *Un autre monde du travail: la draperie en Nordmandie au Moyen Âge* (Rouen: Presses Universitaires du Rouen et du Havre, 2013).

Roch, Jean-Louis, 'Entre draperie rurale et draperie urbaine? La draperie foraine de Rouen à la fin du Moyen Âge', *Annales de Normandie*, 48 (1998), 211-30.

Roch, Jean-Louis, 'De la nature du drapier medieval: l'exemple rouennais', *Revue Historique*, 613 (2000), 3-31.

Rosser, Gervase, 'Guilds and Confraternities: Architects of Unnatural Community', in, *De Bono Communi: The Discourse and Practice of the Common Good in the European City (13th-16th Century)*, Studies in European Urban History (1100-1800), 22, ed. by Élodie Lecuppre-Desjardin and Anne-Laure van Bruaene (Turnhout: Brepols, 2010), pp. 29-46.

Ruffel, A. H. and others., 'Fuller's Earth (Bentonite) in the Lower Cretaceous (Upper Aptian) of Shanklin (Isle of Wight, Southern England)', *Proceedings of the Geologists' Association*, 113 (2002), 281-90.

Scheidel, Walter, *The Great Leveler: Violence and the History of Inequality from the Stone Age to the Twenty-First Century* (Princeton: Princeton University Press, 2018).

Schumpeter, Joseph, *Capitalism, Socialism and Democracy* (New York: Harper & Brothers, 1942; repr. 2008).

Scott, Tom, 'Town and Country in Germany, 1350-1600'', in *Town and Country in Europe, 1300-1800*, ed. by S. R. Epstein (Cambridge: Cambridge University Press, 2001), pp. 202-28.

Slater, Terry, 'Plan Characteristics of Small Boroughs and Market Settlements: Evidence from the Midlands', in *Town and Country in the Middle Ages: Contrasts, Contacts and Interconnections, 1100-1500*, ed. by Kate Giles and Christopher Dyer (Leeds: David Brown Book Company, 2005), pp. 23-43.

Slootmans, Corneel, *Paas- en koudemarkten te Bergen op Zoom, 1365-1565*, Bijdragen tot de geschiedenis van het Zuiden van Nederland, 64-66, 3 vols (Tilburg: Stichting Zuidelijk historisch contact, 1985).

Smail, Daniel Lord, *Imaginary Cartographies: Possession and Identity in Late Medieval Marseille* (Ithaca NY: Cornell University Press, 1999).

Soens, Tim, *De spade in de dijk? Waterbeheer en rurale samenleving in de Vlaamse kustvlakte (1280-1580)* (Ghent: Academia Press, 2009).

Soens, Tim, Stabel, Peter, and Van de Walle, Tineke, 'An Urbanised Countryside? A Regional Perspective on Rural Textile Production in the Flemish West-Quarter', in *Economies, Public Finances, and the Impact of Institutional Changes in Interregional Perspective: The Low Countries and Neighbouring German Territories (14th-17th Centuries)*, Studies in European Urban History 36, ed. by Remi van Schaïk, (Turnhout: Brepols, 2015), pp. 35-60.

Soens, Tim, Van Onacker, Eline and Dombrecht, Kristof, 'Metropolis and Hinterland? A Comment on the Role of Rural Economy and Society in the Urban Heart of the Medieval Low Countries', *BMGN – Low Countries Historical Review*, 127 (2012), 82-88.

Hugo Soly, 'De brouwerijenonderneming van Gilbert van Schoonbeke (1552-1562)', *Belgisch Tijdschrift voor Filologie en Geschiedenis*, 40 (1968), 339-92, 1166-1204.

Soly, Hugo and Thijs, Alfons, 'Nijverheid in de Zuidelijke Nederlanden, 1490-1580', in *Algemene Geschiedenis der Nederlanden*, 15 vols, ed. by J. A. Van Houtte, J. F. Niermeyer, J. Presser (Haarlem: Fibula-Van Dishoeck, 1977-1983), VI (1979), pp. 38-41

Sortor, Marci, 'Saint-Omer and its Textile Trades in the Late Middle Ages: A Contribution to the Proto-Industrialisation Debate', *The American Historical Review*, 99 (1993), 1475-99.

Sreenivasan, Govind, *The Peasants of Ottobeuren, 1487-1726: A Rural Society in Early Modern Europe* (Cambridge: Cambridge University Press, 2004).

Stabel, Peter, 'Bevolking en sociale gelaagdheid: Eeklo en Kaprijke gedurende de late middeleeuwen', *Appeltjes van het Meetjesland*, 38 (1987), 161-84.

Stabel, Peter, 'Demography and Hierarchy: The Small Towns and the Urban Network in Sixteenth-Century Flanders', in *Small Towns in Early Modern Europe*, ed. by Peter Clark (Cambridge: Cambridge University Press, 1995), pp. 206-28.

Stabel, Peter, '"Dmeeste, oirboirlixste en proffitelixste let ende neringhe": een kwantitatieve benadering van de lakenproductie in het laatmiddeleeuwse en vroegmoderne Vlaanderen', *Handelingen van de Maatschappij voor Geschiedenis en Oudheidkunde te Gent*, 51 (1997), 113-53.

Stabel, Peter, *Dwarfs among Giants: The Flemish Urban Network in the Late Middle Ages* (Leuven: Garant, 1997).

Stabel, Peter, 'Entre commerce international et économie locale: le monde financier de Wouter Ameyde (Bruges fin XVe-début XVIe siècle)', in *Finances publiques et finances privés*, ed. by Marc Boone and Walter Prevenier (Leuven & Apeldoorn: Garant, 1996), pp. 75-100.

Stabel, Peter, 'Guilds in Late Medieval Flanders: Myths and Realities of Guild Life in an Export-Oriented Environment', *Journal of Medieval History*, 30 (2004), 187-212.

Stabel, Peter, 'Labour Time, Guild time? Working Hours in the Cloth Industry of Medieval Flanders and Artois (Thirteenth-Fourteenth Centuries)', *TSEG – The Low Countries Journal of Social and Economic History*, 11 (2014), 27-54.

Stabel, Peter, 'Marketing Cloth in the Low Countries: Manufacturers, Brokers and Merchants (14th-16th Centuries)', in *International Trade in the Low Countries (14th-16th Centuries): Merchants, Organization, Infrastructure. Proceedings of the International Conference Ghent-Antwerp, 12th-13th January 1997*, ed. by Peter Stabel, Bruno Blondé and Anke Greve (Leuven: Garant, 2000), pp. 15-36.

Stabel, Peter, 'Markets and Retail in the Cities of the Late Medieval Low Countries: Economic Networks and Socio-Cultural Display', in *Fiere e mercati nella integrazione delle economie europee, secc. xiii-xviii*, ed. by Simonetta Cavaciocchi (Florence: Le Monnier, 2001), pp. 797-817.

Stabel, Peter, 'The Move to Quality Cloth: Luxury Textiles, Labour Markets and Middle Class Identity in a Medieval Textile City: Mechelen in the Late Thirteenth and Early Fourteenth Centuries', in *Europe's Rich Fabric: The Consumption, Commercialisation, and Production of Luxury Textiles in Italy, the Low Countries and Neighbouring Territories (Fourteenth-Sixteenth Centuries)*, ed. by Bart Lambert and Katherine Anne Wilson (Farnham: Ashgate, 2016), 159-80.

Stabel, Peter, 'Patronen van verstedelijkingin het laatmiddeleeuwse en vroegmoderne Vlaanderen: demografische ontwikkelingen en economische functies van de kleine en secundaire steden in het Gentse kwartier (14-16de eeuw)' (unpublished doctoral thesis, Ghent University, 1995).

Stabel, Peter, 'Public or Private, Collective or Individual? The Spaces of Late Medieval Trade in the Low Countries', in *Il mercante patrizio: palazzi e botteghe nell'Europa del Rinascimento*, ed. by Donatella Calabi and Silvia Beltramo (Milan: B. Mondadori, 2008), pp. 37-54.

Stabel, Peter, 'Town and Countryside in Medieval Europe: Beyond the Divide', in *Town and Country in Medieval North Western Europe: Dynamic Interactions*, The Medieval Countryside 11, ed. by Alexis Wilkin, John Naylor, Derek Keene, and A.J.A. Bijsterveld (Brepols: Turnhout, 2015), pp. 313-23.

Stabel, Peter, 'Urbanization and its Consequences: Spatial Developments in Late Medieval Flanders', in *Raumerfassung und Raumbewußtsein im späteren Mittelalter*, Vorträge und Forschungen, 49, ed. by Peter Moraw (Stuttgart: Jan Thorbecke Verlag, 2002), pp. 179-202.

Stabel, Peter, 'Working Alone? Single Women in the Urban Economy of Late Medieval Flanders (Thirteenth-Early Fifteenth Centuries)', in *Single Life and the City, 1200-1900*, ed. by Julie De Groot, Isabelle Devos and Ariadne Schmidt (Houndmills: Palgrave, 2015), pp. 27-49.

Stabel, Peter and De Meyer, Anke, 'Craft guilds as Vectors of Middle-Class Values', in *Inequality and the city in the Low Countries (1200-2020)*, Studies in European Urban History (1100-1800), 50, ed. by Bruno Blondé and others (Turnhout: Brepols, 2020), pp. 271-87.

Stein, Robert, Boele, Anita and Blockmans, Wim, 'Whose Community? The Origin and Development of the Concept of *Bonum Commune* in Flanders, Brabant and Holland (12th-15th Century', in *De Bono Communi: The Discourse and Practice of the Common Good in the European City (13th-16th Century)*, Studies in European Urban History (1100-1800), 22, ed. by Élodie Lecuppre-Desjardin and Anne-Laure van Bruaene (Turnhout: Brepols, 2010), pp. 149-70.

Strubbe, Egied, 'Het houden van de doorgaande waarheid in het Vrije van Brugge', *Annales de la Société d'Émulation de Bruges: revue trimestrielle pour l'étude de l'histoire et des antiquités de la Flandre*, 66 (1923), 249-53.

Sturge Moore, Thomas, *Albert Dürer* (London & New York: Duckworth and company, 1911).

Sturtewagen, Isis, 'All Together Respectably Dressed: Fashion and Clothing in Bruges during the Fifteenth and Sixteenth Centuries' (unpublished doctoral thesis, University of Antwerp, 2016).

Thijs, Alfons, 'Les textiles au marché anversois au XVIe siècle', in *Textiles of the Low Countries in European Economic History: Proceedings of the Tenth International Economic History Congress, Leuven August 1990*, Studies in Social and Economic History, ed. by Erik Aerts and John Munro (Leuven: Leuven University Press, 1990), pp. 76-86.

Thijs, Alfons, 'Van "werkwinkel" tot "fabriek". De textielnijverheid te Antwerpen van het einde der vijftiende tot het begin der negentiende eeuw' (unpublished doctoral thesis, University of Ghent, 1978-79).

Thirsk, Joan, 'Industries in the Countryside', in *Essays in the Economic and Social History of Tudor and Stuart England: In Honour of R.H. Tawney*, ed. by F.J. Fisher (Cambridge: Cambridge University Press, 1961), pp. 70-88.

Thoen, Erik, 'A "Commercial Survival Economy" in Evolution: The Flemish Countryside and the Transition to Capitalism (Middle Ages – 19th century)', in *Peasants into Farmers: The Transformation of Rural Economy and Society in the Low Countries (Middle Ages – 19th century) in light of the Brenner Debate*, ed. by Peter Hoppenbrouwers and Jan Luiten van Zanden (Turnhout: Brepols, 2001), pp. 102-57.

Thoen, Erik, *Landbouwekonomie en bevolking in Vlaanderen gedurende de late Middeleeuwen en het begin van de Moderne Tijden. Testregio: de kasselrijen en van Oudenaarde en Aalst (eind 13de – eerste helft 16de eeuw)* (Leuven: Belgisch centrum voor landelijke geschiedenis, 1988).

Thoen, Erik, 'Rechten en plichten van plattelanders als instrumenten van machtspolitieke strijd tussen adel, stedelijke burgerij en grafelijk gezag in het laat-middeleeuwse Vlaanderen: buitenpoorterij en mortemain-rechten ten persoonlijken titel in de kasselrijen van Aalst en Oudenaarde vooral toegepast op de periode rond 1400', *Machtsstructuren in de plattelandsgemeenschappen in België en aangrenzende gebieden: Handelingen van het 13de Internationaal Colloquium Spa, 3-5 sept. 1986*, Gemeentekrediet, Historische Reeks in-8°, 77 (Brussels: Gemeentekrediet van België, 1986) pp. 469-90.

Thoen, Erik, '"Social Agrosystems" as an Economic Concept to Explain Regional Differences: An Essay Taking the Former County of Flanders as an Example (Middle Ages – 19th Century)', in *Landholding and Land Transfer in the North Sea Area (Late Middle Ages – 19th century)*, ed. by Bas van Bavel and Peter Hoppenbrouwers (Turnhout: Brepols, 2004), pp. 47-66.

Thoen, Erik and Soens, Tim, 'The Family or the Farm: A Sophie's Choice? The Late Medieval Crisis in Flanders', in *Crisis in the Later Middle Ages: Beyond the Postan-Duby Paradigm*, ed. by John Drendel (Turnhout: Brepols, 2015), pp. 195-224.

Tilly, Charles, *Coercion, Capital, and European States, AD 990-1990* (Cambridge MA & Oxford: Basil Blackwell, 1990).

Tilly, Louise and Tilly, Charles, *Class Conflict and Collective Action* (Beverly Hills & London: Sage, 1981).

To Figueras, Lluís, 'Wedding Trousseaus and Cloth Consumption in Catalonia around 1300', *The Economic History Review*, 69 (2016), 522-47.

Trompetter, Cor, 'On Entrepreneurship and Capitalism: Joseph Schumpeter and Max Weber on the Role of the Entrepreneur in Capitalist Development', *Economisch- en Sociaal-Historisch Jaarboek*, 52 (1989), 270-87.

Tys, Dries, 'Domeinvorming in de "wildernis" en de ontwikkeling van vorstelijke macht: het voorbeeld van het bezit van de graven van Vlaanderen in het IJzerestuarium tussen 900 en 1200', *Jaarboek voor Middeleeuwse Geschiedenis*, 7 (2004), 31-83.

Unger, Richard, *Beer in the Middle Ages and the Renaissaince* (Philadelphia, 2004).

Valenze, Deborah, *The Social Life of Money in the English Past* (Cambridge: Cambridge University Press, 2006).

van Bavel, Bas, 'Early Proto-Industrialization in the Low Countries? The Importance and Nature of Market-Oriented Non-Agricultural Activities on the Countryside in Flanders and Holland, *c.* 1250-1570', *Revue belge de philologie et d'histoire*, 81 (2003), 1109-65.

van Bavel, Bas, 'History as a Laboratory to Better Understand the Formation of Institutions', *Journal of Institutional Economics*, 11 (2015), 69-91.

van Bavel, Bas, *The Invisible Hand? How Market Economies Have Emerged and Declined since AD 500* (Oxford: Oxford University Press, 2016).

van Bavel, Bas, *Manors and Markets: Economy and Society in the Low Countries AD 500-1600* (Oxford: Oxford University Press, 2010).

van Bavel, Bas, 'The Medieval Origins of Capitalism in the Low Countries', *BMGN – Low Countries Historical Review*, 125 (2010), 45-79.

van Bavel, Bas, 'Rural Wage Labour in the Sixteenth-Century Low Countries: An Assessment of the Importance and Nature of Wage Labour in the Countryside of Holland, Guelders and Flanders', *Continuity and Change*, 21 (2006), 37-72.

Van Bruaene, Anne-Laure, *Om beters wille: rederijkerskamers en de stedelijke cultuur in de Zuidelijke Nederlanden (1400-1650)* (Amsterdam: Amsterdam University Press, 2008).

Van Bruaene, Anne-Laure, '"A Wonderfull Tryumfe, for the Wynnyng of a Pryse": Guilds, Ritual, Theater, and the Urban Network in the Southern Low Countries, *ca.* 1450-1650', *Renaissance Quarterly*, 59 (2006), 374-405.

Vandamme, Ludo, 'Calvinisme, textielindustrie en drapeniers te Nieuwkerke in de 16e eeuw', in: *Westhoek – Jaarboek*, 1 (Ypres: Westhoek, 1984), 114-30.

Vandenbroeke, Chris, 'Sociale en konjunkturele facetten van de linnennijverheid in Vlaanderen (late 14e – midden 19e eeuw)', *Handelingen der Maatschappij voor Geschiedenis en Oudheidkunde*, 33 (1979), 117-74.

Van de Putte, Ferdinand, 'Notes et analectes devant servir à une histoire complète de Neuve-Église', *Annales de la société d'émulation pour l'étude de l'histoire et des antiquités de la Flandre*, 8 (1850), 254-90.

van der Meulen, Jim, 'Corporate Collective Action and the Market Cycle in Nieuwkerke, Flanders, 1300-1600', *Social History*, 43 (2018), pp. 375-99.

van der Meulen, Jim, 'Get Rich and Try Dyeing: Cloth Production and Social Inequality in Town and Countryside (Sixteenth Century)', in *Inequality and the city in the Low Countries (1200-2020)*, Studies in European Urban History (1100-1800), 50, ed. by Bruno Blondé and others (Turnhout: Brepols, 2020), 45-62.

Vander Straeten, Edmond, *Le théâtre villageois en Flandre*, 2 vols (Brussels: Claassen/Tillot, 1874/1880).

Van der Wee, Herman, *The Growth of the Antwerp Market and the European Economy*, 3 vols (The Hague: Nijhoff, 1963).

Van der Wee, Herman, 'Industrial Dynamics and the Process of Urbanization and De-urbanization in the Low Countries from the Late Middle Ages to the Eighteenth Century: A Synthesis', in *The Rise and Decline of Urban Industries in Italy and the Low Countries (Late Middle Ages – Early Modern Times)*, ed. by Herman Van der Wee (Leuven: Leuven University Press, 1988).

Van der Wee, Herman, 'Structural Changes and Specialization in the Industry of the Southern Netherlands, 1100-1600', *The Economic History Review*, 28 (1975), 203-21.

Van Dijck, Maarten, 'Het verenigingsleven op het Hagelandse platteland: sociale polarisatie en middenveldparticipatie in de 17e en 18e eeuw', *TSEG – The Low Countries Journal of Social and Economic History*, 2 (2005), 81-108.

Van Onacker, Eline, *Village Elites and Social Structures in the Fifteenth- and Sixteenth-Century Campine Region* (Turnhout: Brepols, 2015).

Van Uytven, Raymond, 'The Fulling Mill: Dynamic of the Revolution in Industrial Attitudes', *Acta Historiae Neerlandicae*, 5 (1971), 1-14.

Van Uytven, Raymond, 'Vorst, adel en steden: een driehoeksverhouding in Brabant van de twaalfde tot de zestiende eeuw', *Bijdragen Geschiedenis Hertogdom Brabant*, 59 (1976), 93-122.

Van Werveke, Hans, 'De koopman-ondernemer en de ondernemer in de Vlaamsche lakennijverheid van de middeleeuwen', *Mededeelingen van de Koninklijke Vlaamsche Academie voor Wetenschappen, Letteren en Schoone Kunsten van België*, 8 (1946), 5-26.

van Zanden, Jan Luiten, 'Do We Need a Theory of Merchant Capitalism?', *Review (Fernand Braudel Center)*, 20 (1997), 255-67.

van Zanden, Jan Luiten, 'Early Modern Economic Growth: A Survey of the European Economy, 1500-1800', in *Early Modern Capitalism: Economic and Social Change in Europe, 1400-1800*, ed. by Maarten Prak (London: Routledge, 2001), pp. 67-84.

van Zanden, Jan Luiten, *The Rise and Decline of Holland's Economy: Merchant Capitalism and the Labour Market* (Manchester: Manchester University Press, 1993).

van Zanden, Jan Luiten, 'A Third Road to Capitalism? Proto-Industrialisation and the Moderate Nature of the Late Medieval Crisis in Flanders and Holland, 1350-1550', in *Peasants into Farmers? The Transformation of Rural Economy and Society in the Low Countries (Middle Ages – 19th century) in light of the Brenner Debate*, ed. by Peter Hoppenbrouwes and Jan Luiten van Zanden (Turnhout: Brepols, 2001), pp. 85-101.

Veal, Anthony J., 'A Brief History of Work and its Relationship to Leisure', in *Work and Leasure*, ed. by John T. Haworth and Anthony J. Veal (London and New York: Routledge, 2004), pp. 15-33.

Verbeemen, Jan, 'De buitenpoorterij in de Nederlanden', *Bijdragen voor de Geschiedenis van de Nederlanden*, 12 (1957), 81-97

Verbist, Botho, 'Traditie of innovatie? Wouter Ameyde, een makelaar in het laatmiddeleeuwse Brugge, 1498-1507' (unpublished doctoral thesis, University of Antwerp, 2014).

Verhelst, W., *West-Nieuwkerke. Beschrijving en geschiedenis* (Bruges, 1877).

Verhulst, Adriaan, *The Rise of Cities in North-West Europe* (Cambridge: Cambridge University Press, 1999).

Verriest, Léo, 'Une institution judiciaire en action: les "franches vérités" du bailliage de Flobecq Lessines en la seconde moitié du XIVe siècle', *Revue du Nord*, 40 (1958), 411-21.

Verlinden, Charles, 'Brabantsch en Vlaamsch laken te Krakau op het einde der XIVe eeuw', *Medeelingen van de Koninklijke Vlaamsche Academie voor Wetenschappen, Letteren en Schoone Kunsten*, 5 (1943), 16-33.

Verlinden, Charles, 'Draps des Pays-Bas et du Nord-Ouest de l'Europe au Portugal au XVe siècle', *Annuario de Estudios Medievales*, 2 (1966), 235-61.

Verlinden, Charles, 'Markets and Fairs', in *The Cambridge Economic History of Europe*, ed. by Michael Postan and others, 8 vols (Cambridge: Cambridge University Press, 1966-1989), III, *Economic Organisation and Policies in the Middle Ages*, 119-53.

Vermaut, Jos, 'De textielnijverheid in Brugge en op het platteland, Westelijk Vlaanderen voor 1800: konjunktuurverloop, organisatie en sociale verhoudingen' (unpublished doctoral thesis, Ghent University, 1977).

Vermeir, Maarten, 'Chancellor Jean le Sauvage/Ioannes Sylvagius: Erasmus' *Princeps Christianus* and a Prince of Utopia for Thomas More', *Moreana*, 53 (2017), 269-82.

Vermeulen, Frank, 'The Basic Roman Road Network in the *Civitas Menapiorum*', in *Ancient Lines in the Landscape: A Geo-Archeological Study of Protohistoric and Roman*

Roads and Field Systems in Northwestern Gaul, ed. by Frank Vermeulen and Marc Antrop (Leuven: Peeters, 2001), pp. 77-81.

Volckart, Olivier, 'Die Dorfgemeinde als Kartell: Kooperationsprobleme und ihre Lösungen im Mittelalter und in der frühen Neuzeit', *Jahrbuch für Wirtschaftsgeschichte / Economic History Yearbook*, 45 (2004), 189-204.

Vries, Peer, *Escaping Poverty: The Origins of Modern Economic Growth* (Vienna: Vienna University Press, 2013).

Vries, Peer, 'Inevitable Decline? A Review of Bas van Bavel, *The Invisible Hand? How Market Economies Have Emerged and Declined since AD 500* (Oxford: Oxford University Press, 2016)', *International Review of Social History*, 62 (2017), 131-47.

Wallerstein, Immanuel, 'Merchant, Dutch, or Historical Capitalism?', *Review (Fernand Braudel Center)*, 20 (1997), 243-54.

Weber, Max, *The Protestant Ethic and the Spirit of Capitalism*, trans. by Talcott Parsons (1930; London & New York: Routledge, repr. 2005).

Weber, Max, *The Theory of Social and Economic Organization* (New York: Oxford University Press, 1964).

Welch, Evelyn, *Shopping in the Renaissance: Consumer Cultures in Italy, 1400-1600* (New Haven & London: Yale University Press, 2005).

West, Patrick, *Conspicuous Compassion: Why Sometimes it Really Is Cruel to Be Kind* (London: Coronet Books, 2004).

Whittle, Jane, *The Development of Agrarian Capitalism: Land and Labour in Norfolk, 1440-1580* (Oxford: Oxford University Press 2000).

Wilson, Katherine Anne, 'Commerce and Consumers: The Ubiquitous Chest of the Late Middle Ages', *Journal of Interdisciplinary History*, 51 (2021), 377-404.

Wyffels, Carlos, *De oorsprong der ambachten in Vlaanderen en Brabant* (Brussels: Koninklijke Vlaamse academie voor wetenschappen letteren en schone kunsten van België, 1951).

Zell, Michael, *Industry in the Countryside: Wealden Society in the Sixteenth Century* (Cambridge: Cambridge University Press, 2004).

Ziegler, Uwe, *Die Hanse: Aufstieg, Blütezeit und Niedergang der ersten Europäischen Wirtschaftsgemeinschaft: Eine Kulturgeschichte von Handel und Wandel zwischen 13. und 17. Jahrhundert* (Bern: Scherz Verlag, 1994).

Index